SEA STORIES

Reminiscences of a Navy Radioman
1952-1977

by

Larry Bucher

authorHOUSE®

AuthorHouse™
1663 Liberty Drive, Suite 200
Bloomington, IN 47403
www.authorhouse.com
Phone: 1-800-839-8640

First published by AuthorHouse 10/23/2007

ISBN: 978-1-4343-3049-9 (sc)

Printed in the United States of America
Bloomington, Indiana

This book is printed on acid-free paper.

To all the people who worked with me, who worked for me, and for whom I worked — with the exception of only a very few assholes — this book is dedicated. Thanks for the memories, guys.

Table of Contents

PREFACE

The army calls them war stories. The navy calls them sea stories. One term is undoubtedly adapted from and patterned upon the other, but which came first and gave rise to which may never be known. Etymologists pay relatively little attention to military language (although a few do investigate it), while military people — especially the enlisted ranks wherein many of the more colorful terms and iconoclastic views are nurtured — tend to be on the average less literate than most professions and the written record is correspondingly more barren.

War stories or sea, the terms tend to imply a narrative *probably* grounded in fact, but perhaps less than fully factual in the recitation. "Sounds like a sea story to me" implies that the speaker is skeptical of what he has just heard, but not necessarily to the point of believing its narrator a convicted liar – yet.

The sea stories herein are the residue of 23 years of active service -- 1952-1956 and 1958-1977. They are the sort which are told over a beer at the club, on the fantail at sunset, when work is caught up on the midwatch, or whenever/wherever two or more sailors embark on prolonged conversation about their past experiences. The stories are loosely embedded in a text which is part autobiography, part reminiscence, part opinion, and with a bit of travelogue. Sometimes, too, I mount my soapbox and rant about things which displeased me. The stories are as truthful as memory can make them – with one deliberate exception, in the *USS Iowa* chapter, which I think will be readily apparent to the reader. I will be critical of the navy in places, highly critical in others, praiseful in a few.

If you can't annoy someone, there's little point in writing. (attributed to Sir Kingsley Amis)

The navy is a totalitarian institution, only slightly and occasionally inconvenienced by being answerable to a democratic government. (The same is true of the other services, of course.) As such, it is highly allergic to criticism and especially to criticism from within its own ranks. Its first line of defense has long been to ignore the critic, as unworthy of reply. It is predictable that my work will be reviled and denounced (privately) by any senior officers, both active and retired, who may happen to read it. The condemnation by less senior career officers and by career enlisteds will be only somewhat less universal. Whatever praise I may garner will come, mostly, from those who have served less than ten years.

You'll get over it, Willie. I was gonna write a book exposin' the army once meself. (caption on a Bill Mauldin World War II Willie and Joe cartoon)

Memory is fallible, and mine perhaps more so than most – especially 30-50 years later. Most conversations are approximate. Rather than qualify each one, I have used a device to indicate those few that are, to the best of my belief, *exactly* word-for-word accurate: an asterisk at the beginning of the quoted words, like "*this".

I have used 24-hour time (1300 = 1 p.m.) and day-month-year dates. Both are standard practice in the military (and much of Europe) and have long been my habit; I feel that both are more logical and sensible.

All errors, omissions, inaccuracies, and any other lapses herein are the work of my unwelcome but inescapable collaborator, Dr Alois Alzheimer.

I - BONNIE'S MISTAKES

Bonnie, her husband Maury, and Maury's parents lived on a farm just outside Virden, Illinois. Although not technically my relatives, they functioned as aunt/uncle and grandparents in my childhood. I spent long chunks of summers on that farm.

Bonnie worked in nearby Springfield early in their marriage. The details are vague in memory, but she typed addresses on some sort of machine, in connection with periodical subscriptions. Her output emerged on a card of a sort: a rectangular rim of stiff, buff cardboard about 5x2" surrounding an interior rectangle of translucent tissue paper on which the inked addresses appeared. Her machine was unforgiving; when she made a typing error there was no backspacing, no erasing; she had to start over on a new card. One day she brought her accumulated mistakes, maybe 40-50 of them, home, thinking that I might somehow "play" with them. She was right.

Her "mistakes" became ships. Among the old books in the farmhouse was *The Century Book of Facts*, a sort of an almanac which I had recently been perusing. It listed the ships of the U.S. Navy — as of 1900! I had no inkling that all of those ships were long since scrapped (or, in a few cases, converted to insignificant auxiliaries). I thought (without really thinking about it) that steel warships, unless sunk, lasted more or less forever. On the cardboard rims of Bonnie's mistakes I pencilled ships' names and the various data available from the book: displacement, armament, speed, dimensions . . .

This was the summer of 1941, when I was going on eight. My obsession progressed from that beginning. It was not so much the navy that enthused me, but ships — specifically warships, and still more specifically modern steel warships. I was less interested in merchant ships and passenger liners, and completely indifferent to sailing ships. I pestered Bonnie for more "mistakes" and she obliged from time to time, but eventually cut me off citing company policy — customer addresses might get into the wrong hands or be somehow misused. So I had to make do with a stock of somewhere between 100-200 cards. I read everything I could find in the newspapers and magazines about warships, and was also fueled by occasional gifts: a small boys' book with pictures/data on a sampling of modern U.S. warships; a couple sets of small metal generic warships. I can still count the latter: two battleships per set, one aircraft carrier, two or three cruisers, four destroyers, one submarine — the battleships nearly 2" long, the sub barely 3/4". The cardboard rims of Bonnie's mistakes were repeatedly erased and re-erased as my knowledge increased or my interests shifted. (I had to use the rims because the central tissue paper was not hospitable to either pencil or ink.) I didn't really "do" much of anything else with the cards — I suppose I lined them up in "battle formations", but I lacked any precedent or guidance for devising anything resembling war games with them.

It was also about this time that I began to take some interest in international developments. I had known, somewhat vaguely, that wars were in progress overseas and that Germany and Japan were the bad guys, but I was completely unaware, for example, of the chase and sinking of the *Bismarck* (spring 1941). Beginning with Pearl Harbor, I became an avid war-news (and particularly naval-news) buff.

Back in Bradford (my little home town, a hundred-some miles north), my harping on the navy and on ships became a continual annoyance to my schoolmates. We were all superpatriots. What was already programmed in school, at home, and from each other, was heavily reinforced by radio (Captain Midnight, Jack Armstrong the All-American Boy), by movies, by newspaper comics, and by comic books. (I have long felt that the effect of those comic books, especially,

2

on my pre-television generation is quite overlooked and understudied by scholars, and would be worth several PhD theses.) Every boy would have enlisted immediately if allowed. Each boy had his favorite branch of service but these preferences basically reduced to two: the air corps (flying was glamorous, daredevil, still relatively new) and the marine corps (partly because it had achieved much of its John-Wayne image well before John Wayne achieved his, and partly because of a widely-believed capsulization: "the army fights on land, the navy fights on the sea, the air corps fights in the air, the marines do all three"). Only one boy — me — preached the virtues of the navy, while the army had no partisans at all (but no critics, either).

I, and because of me the navy, drew much juvenile criticism. In fourth grade the teacher had the class produce a weekly mimeographed "newspaper". I was elected editor. Down in Virden the Sunday newspaper regularly carried a small box, *Fighting Ships of the World's Navies*, with a picture, vital statistics, and brief history of a selected ship. I very much wanted to copy this concept (minus the picture, obviously) for the class newspaper. But I knew I would encounter staff revolt: "Oh, Bucher and his ships, *again* . . ." So I devised what I thought was a clever scheme. I would begin with *Fighting Planes of the World's Air Forces*, sure to defuse opposition. Once I had run through all the airplanes, nobody would have grounds for complaint if I continued with ships! Fair is fair. My genius had failed to allow for one small complication. At most there could have been only about 30 issues/weeks available in the school year. (I believe the paper was discontinued after four or five "issues" anyhow.) In the best case I could not have exhausted the eligible warplanes before I moved to the upper grades. Moral (I guess): to a fourth-grader in September, the school year stretches to infinity.

The authorities — the media and the government — exhorted the population in general and children, in particular, to write to servicemen to keep up their morale at mail call. It was presented as virtually a patriotic duty. And I had no one. I envied other children who had brother, uncle, whomever, to whom to write. I did have a cousin in the marines but that family lived in far-off Denver and I had never met them. Moreover said cousin was taken prisoner early in the war and died

3

by accident in a Philippine prison camp. Down in Virden, however, the son of the farm family just to the west of us was in the military — in the navy yet — and had seen combat on the *USS Enterprise (CV-6)*. When he came home on leave, I could not have been in much more awe if it had been the President.

The *Enterprise* had recently been in the battle of Santa Cruz, where she had been ably defended by the superb antiaircraft fire of a new battleship, which the navy would identify only as "Battleship X". Perhaps there was some good reason for this disguise but, from what I have since come to know of overdone military secrecy, I doubt that one casualty would have been caused, or the war lengthened by one day, if the ship had been identified by name. At any rate, I was curious but hesitant to ask Homer directly. I didn't need to. When I gingerly mentioned Santa Cruz and Battleship X, he at once said, "That was the *South Dakota." (BB-57)*

I was elated. *I* knew a *military secret*! My claim of inside knowledge failed to impress my Bradford schoolmates though, few if any of them followed the war in enough detail to have heard even the mention of Battleship X.

On a shopping trip with the functional grandparents in the summer of 1943, rambling around downtown Springfield, I wandered into a bookstore. There I discovered *Jane's Fighting Ships*, the 1942 edition. I was dazzled — the pictures, the data . . . Never before (and perhaps never since!) had I desired quite so much to possess something. But if I was dazzled by the book, I was dazed by the price, burned into memory that summer, never forgotten, nineteen dollars and (2% tax) thirty-eight cents {$232}. Far beyond my means . . . my immediate means, but I thought I saw a way to acquire it. Shortly before leaving Bradford for the farm I had acquired a job of sorts. The proprietress of the restaurant right across the corner from our house had engaged me to haul cases of soft drinks upstairs from the basement for replenishment, and haul cases of emptied bottles to the basement, at the princely sum of 30¢ {$3.59} a day — $2.10 {$25} a week! My allowance at the time was 25¢ {$3} a week, this was an unbelievable financial windfall. I calculated

4

that I could repay the purchase price over a reasonable term, relocated the "grandparents", begged, and pleaded. I was refused immediate gratification (although consultation with the aunt/uncle in Bradford, who reared me, was promised and future purchase was not ruled out). I went into an all-the-way-home sulk.

(Everyone knows that there has been inflation over the years, but the cumulative impact is often astonishing. In order to give the contemporary reader a better feel for old-year dollar amounts, I have made use of a very handy web site, www.westegg.com/inflation/, to determine 2006 equivalents. These appear within braces: {$0.00} and I have usually rounded them to the nearest dollar.)

The consultation took place, the results were favorable, and I got my desire. It was accompanied by one rule: I could look at the book for only one hour a day. The reasoning, well founded, was that otherwise I would spend far too many hours engrossed in it when I should be outdoors in the sunshine, developing my youthful muscles, etc. I was already accustomed to being under heavy adult fire for being a bookworm to the neglect of physical activity; I did not protest (but I did sneak extra, surreptitious peeks at *Jane's* when unobserved opportunity arose). Having absorbed occasional misinformation from newspapers and elsewhere, I thought there were some inaccuracies in *Jane's* — with functional-grandparental approval I wrote to Jane's editor about them. (I was wrong about every one.) I was slightly surprised to get a brief, courteous reply, which somehow survived the years:

HODDESDON 2464

From	MANDEVILLE,
The EDITOR of	HODDESDON,
"JANE'S FIGHTING SHIPS"	HERTS
Published by	
Sampson Low, Marston & Co. Ltd.	

6 August, 1944.

Mr. Larry Bucher
214, W. Loud Street,
        Virden, Illinois.

Dear Sir,

Your letter of July 10 has been
forwarded on to me here.

A new edition of "Fighting Ships" is
now in the press.   It will be published in
this country next month and in New York soon
afterwards.

Its contents will include a plan of the
IOWA, which has two funnels, not one as you
state.   The main armament comprises nine
16-inch guns, not 12.   Dates of launching
of the ALASKA, GUAM, SHANGRI-LA and many
other ships are given.   BATAAN is ex-
Buffalo, one of the nine aircraft carriers
of the Independence class.

TIRPITZ is the full name of the German
battleship of 45,000 tons now in Altenfjord.
The only German warship which included the
word "von" in its name was the tender VON
DER GROBEN, of 525 tons, which has been lost.

                    Yours faithfully

                    /s/ Francis McMurtrie
                    (very ornate signature!)

(Among my incorrect assertions — derived from news articles and/ or comic books — was that the full name of *Tirpitz* was *Admiral von Tirpitz*. In the back of my mind I had harbored some hope that a somehow cheaper supplement or update to my 1942 edition might be available; I saw no hope of ever buying the next edition itself.)

I returned to Bradford and disaster. In my absence the restaurant lady had hired an older boy to do her bottle-toting; she felt (correctly) that the cases were somewhat heavy for me anyhow . . . I reported the sad news at home. The debt was posted on the kitchen doorframe: "Larry owes:", and over a year or two, with some help from Christmas and birthday "presents", it was liquidated.

At some point I learned of the naval academy and formed a vague ambition to attend it. In the town library I found and read *Navy Blue and Gold*, a novel about football players at the academy, and absorbed it. I became a fan of the Navy football team, another idiosyncrasy that estranged me from my peers, who were solidly for Illinois (if Protestant) or Notre Dame (if Catholic). But my future went a-crashing in the spring of my freshman high-school year. Taken along to a baseball game at Sportsman's Park, St. Louis (the Brooklyn Dodgers' Ralph Branca outdueled Howie Pollett and the Cardinals, 1-0), I could not make out the numbers on the scoreboard across the field. Eye examination. Glasses. The academy required 20-20 vision uncorrected. End of that ambition.

My interest in warships was slowly dwindling, but by no means disappearing. The unachievable naval academy had little to do with the dwindle, it was rather caused by general maturation plus the ending of the war and consequent diminishment of naval news. As a senior, required to submit a term paper, I chose "Warships" and needed to do very little research for it.

(As an adult, many decades later, after retirement from the navy, I began to purchase and accumulate a shelfful of warship reference and photo books — and among them rests my 1942 *Jane's Fighting Ships*.)

II - SKINHEAD

I had been the class "brain" in my little high school, but in college my grades deteriorated and I was put on scholastic probation after the first semester of my sophomore year. This was largely due to immaturity and mental laziness, but I also felt that I was pursuing a mischosen major (geology). With the draft facing me anyhow, now or later, I thought that I would benefit from taking a time-out to consider alternative studies; I also would earn G.I. bill money for the remainder of college. I made a tentative decision to enlist at the end of the school year and, although my grades did improve enough to get me off probation, I did so.

The navy was my natural choice because of my juvenile fascination? Not at all. That was another time, another me. Childhood enthusiasms were forgotten. The army was out – why, after all, did I see many of my contemporaries opting for four-year navy or air force hitches in order to escape two in the army? I had no desire to become a mud-slogging rifleman. The marines were out, partly because of the same infantry hazard, partly because I perceived them, then and still, as the most chickenshit of the services. The year was 1952. Stalin still lived; Korea had degenerated into stalemate but not yet a truce. I felt World War III to be a quite plausible scenario during the next four years. The Soviets had a huge army and a formidable air force, but their navy was much smaller, largely obsolete, and promised to remain so indefinitely. I judged the navy to be much the safest place in the event of hot war, and chose it over the air force solely for the entirely selfish reason of personal safety.

And if I could go back in time and remake that decision, knowing what I know now . . . ? I would choose the air force, partly because I had no appreciation then of just how cramped, privacy-lacking, and unpleasant shipboard life would prove to be, and also because I soon came to perceive (and still perceive) the air force to be the *least* chickenshit of the services. (Which is not to be construed as praise, but rather as recognition of a lesser evil.)

And so, on 12 June 1952, I was sworn in, in some facility in downtown Chicago. The process is mostly lost to memory; I do recall standing in line in front of the desk of one "David Glennon, MMC", who was energetically stamping our papers without making eye contact with the chain of young men passing through his chokepoint. I had no idea what the nameplate initials (Machinist's Mate, Chief) signified. (The trivial things that somehow lodge in long-term memory are even more mystifying than the consequential things that evaporate.) At some point we were herded onto a northbound train to U.S. Naval Training Center, Great Lakes, Illinois.

We encountered a sort of harassment as soon as we detrained, from recruits observing us from inside the fence. Their comments were not exactly sympathetic. I attracted one particular observation: I had worn a quite short crew-cut for some time; I was told, "You look like you've been here before."

Our haircuts were indeed soon to follow. My barber did find a little hair to whack off, but I think he did so more from conscientiousness than from necessity. The haircuts gave us our new designation. No one called another recruit *boot*, the appellation of choice was *skinhead*. (One fellow-skinhead, derided as such while marching, rebutted his roadside critic with, "*How'd you know I was circumcised?")

We were herded into a barracks — and here I'll describe the typical navy barracks of the time. Imagine a letter H with an abnormally long crossbar. The main entrance is at the center of that long crossbar; the crossbar also contains the heads, staircases, and a few small rooms usable as offices, storage, closets, etc. The sidebars of the H contained the sleeping spaces, thus one two-story barracks had four such spaces, each accommodating a recruit company of 60-70 sailors in upper-and-lower beds. We never called the beds *beds*, they were *racks* or *sacks*, narrow, thin-mattressed. The springs, if one can call them that, were not the coiled metal the word usually brings to mind, but wire interlaced in small rectangles — length and width, but no depth. I was to find that this was the typical enlisted-man's bed throughout the navy, but I slept well enough.

At taps — lights out — the barracks became pandemonium. Every comedian asserted himself, loudly and continually. The night was memorable for one repeated call in a high falsetto: "Chessster — oh Chessster!" After perhaps 20 minutes of this the lights flashed on and we were subjected to brief but ominous and credible threat of what would befall us if there were any more noise. There was no more noise.

We had not yet received uniforms. Someone came around to toss us watch caps — our first uniform item, a sort of blue knit stocking cap. Probably that someone said something about us being required to wear them, but I was far from the center of the barracks and did not hear it if it was said. I was unimpressed with the caps. Big deal. When it became time to go to chow, everyone was putting their caps on. Ever a nonconformist, I did not. Someone told me, "You better wear your cap!" I ignored the advice.

As we proceeded toward the chow hall, our disorganized column was halted by a chief for reasons I forget. After chewing out the leaders for whatever, his eye fell on me near the end of the column — "Where's that man's hat?" The front of the column tossed the question back to me: "Where's your hat?" The truthful answer would have been that I didn't want to wear it, but I had just enough sense — barely — not to say that, and enough presence of mind to lie:
"I forgot it."
Front of column to chief: "He forgot it."
"Well, he'd better not forget it again."
"Yessir." In my direction: "You better not forget it again."
I didn't. I was learning.

We received the rest of our uniforms quite soon. We were divested of our civilian clothing and ordered to put it in boxes to mail home. Among prohibited items which I had to so treat was my electric shaver — the navy apparently considered them newfangled, or untraditional, or unmanly, perhaps a bit of all three.

Let me see how much of the seabag's contents I can remember . . . (*Seabag* is used not only to denote the large duffel bag which serves as a sailor's suitcase, and as his closet when necessary, but also as a collective noun for the complete issue of uniform items.) Six skivvy shorts, six skivvy shirts. Six pair of black socks, the same number of white ones. Four white jumpers, four white trousers. Three blue trousers, three jumpers — two undress, one dress, the latter with white piping and stars on the collar. Four white hats. One *flat hat*, dark blue, beret-like, with *U.S. NAVY* on the headband. (It has been obsolete for some time now, but was then worn with the winter uniform. A naval expression of reassurance or conviction, *I hope to shit in your flat hat*, parallels a similar army phrase targeting *mess kit*.) A raincoat. A pea coat (a short, dark-blue jacket of winter-coat thickness). Three sets of dungaree shirts and trousers. One black belt, one white belt. One neckerchief. Swimming trunks. Two pair of black dress shoes, one pair of high-top work shoes (to be worn with dungarees). A pair of rubbers and a pair of sneakers. Two mattress covers (*fart sacks*). Two brown blankets. A ditty bag — a white bag about a foot deep, with drawstring, used to hold razor, toothpaste, toilet articles in general. A number of clothes stops, lengths of thick twine, about 8", used to tie washed items on the clothesline and also to tie around rolled-up uniform items for more compact storage. A *Bluejacket's Manual* — which struck me as a grown-up, navy version of the Boy Scout Manual. (It included illustrations of, and instructions on how to tie, many of the same knots.)

Those items were our personal possessions. In addition we were issued several items to be retained only through boot camp then returned. The most obnoxious of these were the leggings: stiff, brown canvas wraps for the lower leg, ankle to mid-calf, with maybe ten holes to be laced up. They were a time-consuming botheration to put on or take off; we had to wear them much of the time. We were also issued guard belts (a three-inch wide tan belt worn over the uniform — often worn to signify petty authority, for instance by a sentry), ponchos for rainy days, and ancient rifles which had to be carried on most marches.

I was fortunate (*I* thought) in getting the newer zipper-fly blue trousers instead of the traditional 13-button. The latter had inadequate pocket space and were a time-wasting nuisance in the bathroom. But my opinion was a minority one; most sailors thought the old style made them "look better" — and they eventually prevailed, the zipper-flys were phased out in the early 1960s. I preferred convenience over vanity.

The uniforms fit well, there was no occasion for that old army phrase of "two sizes: too large and too small". Every uniform item had to be stenciled in prescribed places. Surprisingly, this was done for us, initially. (Possibly they did not trust us to do it right.) I was issued two thin-but-stiff, brown cardboards bearing my cut-out name and service number; they were to be placed on a uniform item and marked through the holes with "stencil pencils", toothpaste-like tubes containing white or black ink.

Our stripes were also sewn on for us. We rated one small, diagonal stripe, as Seaman Recruits, but wore the two stripes of Seaman Apprentices because graduation in three months would automatically confer the latter status.

Our service numbers – seven digits in three groups, e.g. 123 45 67 – had been assigned to us early on, and we had been cautioned – *strongly* cautioned – never to forget them. It is a rare serviceman from that period who cannot still recall today his service number. They were superseded by social security numbers in the 1970s. We were also required to know, and to be able to recite, our chain of command and their ranks and names – from our company commander up through assorted intermediaries, battalion commander, regimental commander, etc., up to the rear admiral commanding the Ninth Naval District.

The navy enlisted ranks had always confused me, even in childhood, so I will try an explanatory rundown here. First, understand that enlisted men do not have *rank* — that is for officers. Enlisted men have *rates* and *ratings*. Rate is the enlisted equivalent of rank, but it doesn't begin until a sailor becomes a third-class petty officer, those below are *non-rated*. Rating is a man's occupational specialty: Boatswain's Mate, Gunner's Mate, Yeoman, etc., some 60 others (at that time). The term *pay grade* is also used: E-1 is the lowest level, E-9 the highest. The distinction between *rate* and *rating* even confused sailors, many of whom used the terms more or less interchangeably without ridicule or reproach. Context always made one's intended meaning clear.

In my entire career I saw only one sailor actually wearing the one stripe of a Seaman Recruit. He was a burly, downcast man of about 30, obviously the recipient of a court-martial sentence (one ingredient of which can be reduction to the lowest pay grade, often accompanied by a less-than-honorable discharge). Six months after becoming a Seaman Apprentice a sailor was, provided he completed a written seaman examination successfully, advanced to the three white or blue stripes of a Seaman, or E-3. (Some segments of the navy, however, had different designations and different-colored stripes for their non-rated men: e.g. Fireman/Fireman Apprentice; red stripes. Similarly: Airman, green; Constructionman, light blue.) Then come the petty officer rates: E-4, E-5, E-6; Third Class, Second Class, and First Class Petty Officer; wearing an eagle (never called such, but always a *crow*) with one, two, or three inverted chevrons below it. Between the crow and the top chevron was a symbol of one's rating, for example the crossed anchors of a Boatswain's Mate, the crossed cannons of a Gunner's Mate, the crossed quills of a Yeoman (helping to affix to the last-named the pejorative of *feather merchant*).

(Yeoman is just one of several ratings with more-or-less impolite nicknames: Boatswain's Mates: anchor clankers. Signalmen: skivvy wavers. Hospital Corpsmen: pecker checkers or chancre mechanics. Aerographers: weather guessers. Postal Clerks: stamp lickers. Commissarymen [cooks]: belly robbers. Electronics Technicians and other technical ratings: twidgets. Engineering and hull ratings as a group, and their non-rated Firemen, are *Snipes* [probably from the British navy, which characterized its early engine-room spaces, steamy and puddled, as "snipe marshes"]. Aviation ratings are *Airedales*. Non-rated men in the deck rating group: deck apes. In a more polite vein, Corpsmen and Dental techs were often addressed as *Doc*, Signalmen as *Flags*, Radiomen as *Sparks* [from the four sparks of their rating insignia], Boatswain's Mates as *Boats*, and Gunner's Mates as *Guns*.)

The rating insignia was also worn by many seamen and seaman apprentices, just above their three or two stripes. This was required if the sailor was attending or had completed a service school, or had passed a test for third class but had not been promoted because of quota limitations. So worn, they were derisively termed a *racket mark* by those non-rateds who were ineligible to wear them. The sailor wearing one was officially a *striker*, striving to become rated in the rating which he displayed. This term came in for considerable satirical use. If, say, one Fields was a notorious alcoholic, a sailor who came back to ship drunk a time or two might be labeled a "Fields-striker". And admirals and senior officers who were perceived as excessively chickenshit or imperious toward subordinates might be described as Patton-strikers – from the World War II army general.

Above first-class comes the Chief Petty Officer (E-7) with a very different set of uniforms, more officer-like. I was initially unaware of the special status of chief petty officers but rapidly came to appreciate it. The chief's insignia adds a curve over the top chevron of a first class, rating insignia between the curve and the chevrons. When I enlisted, that was the top. But in 1958 Congress legislated two additional enlisted ranks. There was some debate over what they would be named. The cynical suggestion of "super chief" was not taken seriously. (The humor here may not be fully apparent to younger generations. "Super chief" was then the well-known title of a high-status railroad train.) E-8 became Senior Chief Petty Officer with one star above the crow, E-9 became Master Chief Petty Officer with two stars above.

If you realize that an E-7 Yeoman can be described either as a Chief Yeoman (YNC) or as a Chief Petty Officer (CPO) with equal accuracy and acceptability, you now understand the navy enlisted rate-and-rating system better than I did before boot camp.

The story (surely mythical) is told of a sailor who happened to be temporarily at an army base on his way from wherever to wherever. The WAC who was logging him in asked for his rank. "Boatswain's Mate Second Class."

"What? I never heard of that. I can't put that down. What would you be if you were in the army?"

"Oh . . . probably at least a lieutenant colonel."

In the confused first week, various navy people told us to go here, go there, do this, do that. One face became more familiar than the others and slowly I began to comprehend that he would be in charge of us throughout boot training, that he was called a company commander, and that we were Recruit Company 261.

If Hollywood had been casting for a recruit company commander, for a navy equivalent of Jack Webb in *The D.I.*, they could not possibly have improved upon Harley R. Frank, BTC (Chief Boiler Technician). Ramrod military posture, impeccable dress khaki uniform, permanent scowl. On the rare occasions when he could not stifle a smile, he turned his face away to attempt to hide it. He spoke in a low, slow, direful voice and said little more than was necessary. Imagine Burt Reynolds in his mid-30s, very slightly balding, delete his mustache, give him a 1950s haircut, replace his smile with an implacable glower, and you won't be far off.

In our conversation, he was *The Chief.* If speaking of any other chief, that chief had to be further identified; *The Chief* did not. But we never called him Chief, or Chief Frank. We said Sir, or Mister Frank. We were required to address all chiefs, and any first-class petty officer whom we knew to be a company commander, as if they were officers, and to salute them whenever appropriate. The purpose was to accustom us to the proper way to address and salute officers after we left boot camp, and since we recruits seldom came in contact with actual officers the requirement was more sensible than many.

Our company contained primarily midwesterners, Michigan and Illinois origins predominated. A scattered few came from more distant parts: West Virginia, North Dakota, Texas, western New York. We were overwhelmingly white; one American Indian joined us early on, one Black came in midway through. And we were Anglo-Saxon almost as overwhelmingly — four men's surnames proclaimed Italian descent, one Polish.

The Chief queried us to identify those with prior military experience. I had had two years of involuntary army ROTC at college, but I was "outranked" by a couple others with superior qualifications. The Chief laid his hand on one and announced sternly, "*This man is an acting chief petty officer." The term itself made little impression on me, but I did gather that he was put in charge in some way. This was standard practice, each recruit company had its ACPO — at no extra pay, but with considerable prestige and responsibility, and exemption from most "shit details". Our first was John W. Giesberg, known to all as "Tex". Early on, during a noisy taps, he walked the darkened barracks cautioning, "Now y'all better quiet down . . ." There was a brief drop in the noise level then one giggling recruit was unable to repress himself: "*Where y'all from, Tex?" Collective yankee merriment — but soon, quiet.

There was a brief fad of awakening those who had already gone to sleep. Sometimes it was accompanied by a query, "You awake?" and a follow-up to whatever mumbled answer of "Good." More often it was explained as, "Piss call — the world's on fire, everybody gotta help put it out." Less often heard but more imaginative was, "Piss call — there's a seaplane coming in, everybody gotta go piss on the runway."

Two early evolutions were shots and dental examinations. During the former, pranksters sought to unnerve the gullible by warning of the worst shot of all: the one given with a square needle in the left testicle. We heard by recruit grapevine that the word "railroad", if spoken during the dental exam, signified that a tooth would be pulled. This rumor was true; such a tooth was marked over with two parallel lines — the "railroad" — on our dental charts. I heard the dread word right away: "Railroad one." I had a wisdom tooth growing at a slight angle and with the rear side just barely through the gum. A wiser dental officer decided against extraction when he saw it (and it is still in fine shape), but there was ample other dental work that I did need. Still, I came away better than some others — two or three of our company were in such bad shape that all of their teeth were pulled and they were issued false teeth. In at least one of my subsequent appointments I was worked upon by two overbearing dentists who were obviously fresh out of dental school. They were having a great time enjoying their officer status and lording it over the boots. A couple years later two upper incisors which they had "filled" required root canals, and one was eventually lost. But with that one boot-camp exception, all of my navy dental treatment was first-class insofar as I can judge. And I received a plenty of it; for many years I jested that if I had one more filling put in I was going to switch from Colgate to Brasso. Porcelain crowns have diminished the utility of that wisecrack, but at age 74 I have all but two of my teeth – the roots of them, at least – and am optimistic that I'll never need dentures.

We were given a few dollars of our first navy pay, an advance of sorts, and right at the end of the pay line we were required to spend much of it on a few requisite items: soap, toothpaste, and the like. They were things I would certainly have bought anyhow, but I was quite indignant (silently!) at being told how I *would* spend my own money. The pay for a Seaman Recruit, per a 1950 reference, was $75 {$613} per month, increasing to $82.50 {$674} for Seaman Apprentice and $95.55 {$781} for Seaman. It was probably the same for me in 1952.

Another early event was testing. We were cautioned that the tests were very important and could have much influence on our future and our likelihood of getting a navy school, and that no one should "goof off" on them — and also warned that no matter how badly someone might do, it would not result in a discharge! There were four tests: the GCT (General Classification Test, an IQ sort of thing, the most important); the ARI (Arithmetic); the CLER (clerical ability); and the MECH (mechanical aptitude). My GCT score was 76 — 77 was perfect; they said I had erased and changed one right answer to a wrong one. My ARI was perfect, at 73. My CLER was, at 70, short of perfect but very high. My MECH was an unimpressive 57, above average but not by much.

None of this came as a surprise to me. I knew I was intelligent, I knew I was good at taking tests, and I certainly knew that I was no mechanic. (Before using either hammer or screwdriver, I first consult the operator's manual.) What did come as a surprise . . . I had enlisted with an overconfident, naive expectation that as soon as the navy saw how smart I was, I would be put right into officer training. I had asked the recruiter about such a prospect; he responded with a vague, "Oh, I think they give you a chance for that after you get in." (This was not to be the last time a recruiter would mislead me by telling me less than he could have. But full, accurate information would not have altered my plans to enlist; no harm was done.) The hard facts: 20/20 vision uncorrected for either the naval academy or naval ROTC (and with two years of college already completed I would not really have wanted to start over anyhow). Officer Candidate School required a bachelor's degree *already attained* no matter how smart you might be. And LDO (Limited Duty Officer — "mustang") programs required at least six years in the enlisted ranks before application. But I had kept my expectations to myself (fortunately); I now kept my disillusionment to myself.

Later (a day? a week?) we were given a slide-show, a rundown describing the various ratings, and were advised that we would be able to express some choices — which of course would not necessarily be honored. We might or might not be assigned to a navy school right after boot camp; those who failed to get a school would be sent to ship or duty station as ordinary seaman apprentices. Our test scores would carry considerable weight in this process. Still later (another day? another week?) we underwent an interview process. The Personnelman who conducted my interview was willing to spend extra time with me because of my test scores, the highest he'd seen. I didn't really know what to choose. I had come out of the slide show without any overriding I-want-*that* preference; my mind mulled over several options: Yeoman (widely regarded as a cushy job, typing and office work). Electronics

Technician (a very long school right there at Great Lakes — and recruit rumor, utterly false, claimed that it was such a booming field that one might make chief in as little as two years). Journalist (I'd worked for the home town weekly a couple of summers, and year-round as an unpaid sportswriter). Surveyor (I'd just finished a geological mapping course wherein I used surveyor-type instruments, and enjoyed it).

The Personnelman flatly refused to let me choose such a mixture. Those four choices were in three different groups. The ratings were divided into a dozen different *groups*. Deck (Boatswain's Mates, Quartermasters, a couple others). Administrative and clerical (Yeoman, Journalist, Radioman, Teleman, and others). Engineering (the guys deep in the hull who run the machinery). Aviation. Seabee (Surveyor and others). Ordnance (Gunner's Mates, Torpedoman's Mates and others). Miscellaneous (Printer, Musician, three others). And four "groups" with only one lone rating each: the Stewards (officers' servants), Hospital Corpsmen, Dental Techs — and Electronics Technicians. The Personnelman's sense of order was offended by my scattershot choices and he insisted that I choose three in the same group or somehow related. In some way the Teleman rating came up for discussion. It was primarily teletype communications, said to be "the coming thing"; Telemen also ran the navy's post offices. It somehow became my first choice. One reason for my receptiveness to it was a mention in the slide-show that Telemen sometimes worked with cryptography. I liked to work crossword puzzles, and had had some success with the "cryptoquotes" that sometimes accompanied the puzzles, I thought the cryptography might be interesting.

To jump ahead of the story, I received my first choice. But it was near the end of my *second* enlistment, when I was no longer a Teleman, before I ever did any crypto work — and it bore no relationship whatever to those cryptoquotes!

Now for another "what if" — what if I could remake that choice? I would choose Yeoman for two reasons. First, it would have enhanced my chance for eventual embassy duty (working under a naval attache somewhere). I didn't know it then, but that was just about the plum of all assignments. And second, Yeomen are everywhere. I would have been more likely to get a small ship or command. (In general — not without exceptions — the smaller the ship/command the less chickenshit. The farther removed the martinet is from his subordinates, the more layers between, the less his conscience bothers him about their dissatisfactions — in fact, the less he is even aware of them.) As for Teleman, I found the hard way that it entailed a lot of round-the-clock watchstanding and consequent all-night watches, but otherwise it was fairly decent. Journalist remains attractive, but they tend to be found in the larger ships/places. Surveyor also is still enticing, Seabees get few shipboard assignments. But I'm not so confident that their shore locations are all that desirable. Electronics Technician: I'm thankful I was talked out of that one; I'm no more a technician than I am a mechanic.

I mentioned above that one reason I was attracted to the Electronics Technician rating was because it entailed a long school at Great Lakes. Some background is called for here, which will explain that as well as some future oddities. If the Guinness Book of Records had an entry for acuteness of late-onset puppy love, I would surely hold it. I succumbed about five months before I enlisted. The co-ed's home was Racine, not far north of Great Lakes. That long electronics school would have kept me in her vicinity for a good many more months. Fortunately she had a good deal more sense than I had. (The wisdom of hindsight: marriage would have been disastrous.) When it became obvious to her that my absence (in San Diego) was not diminishing my ardor in the slightest, she had the decency to end it in person when I was back on campus on leave.

As the preliminary evolutions began to diminish, our days began to become more structured. The day was broken up into periods of about an hour each. Some of them were devoted to classroom instruction, some to practical hands-on training. Swimming, fire fighting, shooting range, gas masks, were some of the latter. Whenever we did not have anything scheduled in a period, we spent it marching and drilling. (And we marched to/from everywhere we went.) The Chief began us on the basics, standing at attention, keeping in step, etc., and patiently progressed us to the more advanced commands. Three or four of the most inept marchers were banished to a semi-separate formation a few paces behind the rest of the company, and were dubbed "the goon platoon". Simultaneously we learned the manual of arms with our rifles, and the semaphore alphabet. We performed the latter by shouting out the phonetic names — Able! Baker! Charlie! Dog! — while making the appropriate semaphore sign with our arms, and ended by spelling out U.S. Naval Training Center Great Lakes Illinois. Much later in our training The Chief taught us more advanced evolutions: the Queen Anne Salute, performed kneeling with our rifles, and "Left by the Right Flank Double to the Rear with a Slight Hesitation — March!".

We marched on the street from class to class. When we had a period with no class, we marched on a "grinder" — one of the open spaces covered with black asphalt. If it was raining, we marched inside one of the drill halls — vast structures of quonset-hut shape, with more than enough room for several companies. The "Hut, two, three, four", famous from Hollywood depictions of army marching, was never heard. The navy version, as best as I can reproduce it in print, was a sing-song something like: Hiiip hop hip-hop yo lep hoddio lep hop hip, and variations thereon. The high-top work shoes — which were rarely seen after boot camp, most sailors discarded them — received the name of "hip-hops" from this chant. There were also various chants, mostly obscene, which we proclaimed while marching. Those I remember:
I got a gal in Kansas City, she's got a mole on her left titty.
I got a gal lives on a hill, she won't fuck but her sister will.
I don't know but I've been told, Eskimo pussy is mighty cold.
more days and we'll be home, drinkin' beer with lots of foam.

Our marching prowess won us just two battalion drill flags. There was a weekly competition in which all companies were graded. Higher honors were the regimental drill flag and the brigade drill flag. There were other flags to be won. There was the C flag ("tangible attributes of good citizenship" — I have no memory of what factors contributed to the winning of it). The star flag was awarded for cleanliness of our barracks, our persons, and our seabags, as determined by weekly inspections. The A flag was for athletics, the I (intelligence) flag was won by the company with the highest scores on a weekly multiple-choice test. Finally there was the "rooster flag", awarded to the company with the best overall performance in all the above fields. Companies which won flags carried them in the van of their column while marching, throughout the following week.

To Yossarian, the idea of pennants as prizes was absurd. No money went with them, no class privileges. Like Olympic medals and tennis trophies, all they signified was that the owner had done something of no benefit to anyone more capably than everyone else. (Joseph Heller, *Catch-22*)

In addition to our two lowest-level drill flags, we won only one other flag, an A flag. We had a very good middleweight boxer in the company, appropriately nicknamed "Jabber", which fit his J.A.B. initials and his volubility as well as his boxing. (Unfortunately there was another middleweight in another company who was just a little bit better than Jabber.) We lost one star flag in part because the inspecting party discovered a spoon in the head; this led to some pointed remonstrations to the head cleaners: "How come you guys can't learn to put your silverware away when you're done eating?" (The head cleaners rated the derisive titles of *Captain of the Head* and/or *Colonel of the Urinal*.)

We saw, and envied, other companies marching with three, four, and more, flags in their forefront. We had heard that The Chief's previous companies had been prolific flag-winners. We wanted badly to win flags for him, our failures rankled us the more because we knew we were The Chief's last company before he was transferred. We felt we were letting him down. We didn't lack desire but we lacked . . . I never have been able to complete that sentence.

Tex became a casualty of our failings. After three or four weeks The Chief replaced him as ACPO with E.C. Donald. I had liked Tex, but Donald was indeed more of a "leader". We called him, simply, Donald. That was the prescribed way to address any enlisted man below chief, by the last name. Only a few were addressed otherwise: Tex, Jabber, Chester (from his role in the first-night noisemaking), and an overweight member of the goon platoon often heard "Jellybelly". The

Indian was of course "Chief", it had not yet become politically incorrect to address an Indian thus and no one intended anything derogatory or racist by it.

Our failure to win an I flag reflected directly upon me. In our first week The Chief had halted us one day and announced that he wanted a volunteer with a master's degree in education. Unsurprisingly no one responded. He lowered his standard by stages until he was seeking simply someone with a college degree, for the position of Educational Petty Officer. No luck, and he adjourned the search for the time. Later I told Tex of my two college years and my interest in the position. I got it. The duties consisted chiefly of holding a cramming session just before the weekly test.

When the cramming sessions had failed to yield an I flag over several weeks, I thought up an involved scheme for cheating. The multiple-choice test questions were on slides and were projected on a screen in front of us, one at a time. The tests were regularly held in the same room; we marched to the building then marched by column into the building and took seats in a prescribed order. By reconfiguring positions in our marching formation, I was able to produce a seating that would scatter our better brains in locations where they would be visible to a maximum of others, and also provide "relay men" with a good view of the brains. Everyone, and the brains in particular, would signal the right answer, after they marked it, by resting their pencil northwest for A, northeast for B, southwest for C, southeast for D. A pencil poised straight up meant "I don't know, you're on your own." Donald explained the plan to The Chief who, although skeptical, allowed us to try it. His response may have included one of his frequent cautions: "Don't get caught!"

The strategic seating worked out as planned, the cheating went undetected, but the signaling was only partially successful. A few dunces did make surprisingly high scores but others did not (I could only conclude that some were just too dense to understand the signaling system), and the overall improvement was not enough to produce an I flag. We never tried it again, partly because the testing building and room were changed.

In addition to ACPO and Educational PO, there were a number of other recruit positions in the company. Running (very) roughly from highest prestige to lowest, they were Master-at-Arms, Boatswain's Mate of the Watch, Gunner's Mate, Athletic PO, two Platoon Leaders, Clerk, Mail Clerk, six Squad Leaders, and two Guides. All involved petty responsibilities of some sort.

My Educational PO position yielded shamefaced embarrassment for me one day. The company was seated in a quonset-hut classroom, the day was hot and muggy, I may have had a night watch and been short of sleep . . . I was suddenly nudged awake and faced the just displeasure of the instructor, a chief. I had ample company, about five others had similarly succumbed. The instructor reiterated the rule: you can stand up if you are in danger of dozing off, but you *cannot* sleep in your chair. Then he said that he wanted all the culprits to have a post-class session with the Educational PO to fill them in on what they'd missed and, "Who's the Educational PO?"

The word "sheepish" was coined for just such moments. I raised my reluctant hand.

He called me up to his lectern to inspect my class notes. Fortunately I had dozed off only seconds before the mass awakening. My notes were in good order. He directed one minor addition to them and bade me return to my seat. After the class, Donald felt obliged to inform The Chief of what had occurred — it may have been my imagination, but when The Chief learned that I was one of the offenders, I thought I detected a grin beneath his scowl.

We began to be assigned watches very early. The navy has a compulsion for watch bills and duty lists. Everyone except the commanding officer and executive officer — and sometimes the most senior chief petty officer in a command — is expected to be on a watch bill or a rotating duty list of some sort. If no necessary watches and duties exist, something is amiss, higher-ups are uneasy, and you can count on the invention of a newly "necessary" watch or duty to be shared. I recall being assigned a "fire watch" before we had even received uniforms. Another recruit and I were to walk a barracks area keeping our eyes open for fires! We strolled along the assigned sidewalks, casually conversing, and were called into an office by two chiefs and chewed out for doing exactly that — strolling! We were to walk our post *in a military manner*! Later a watch was established for our barracks wing; a man was posted round the clock except during the class day.

Our barracks life was made inconvenient in a number of ways. No lockers were provided, we had to live out of our seabags which were hung on central rails. We rapidly learned to park our blues and items not needed for the present at the bottom, but the frequent uniform changes from whites to dungarees or vice-versa yielded aggravation enough. No laundry service, no laundry machines, we had to wash our clothing on a sort of table-trough combination equipped with running water outside and to the rear of the barracks, then affix them to adjacent clotheslines with the aforementioned clothes stops. (What a recruit would have done in mid-winter I am thankful never to have learned.)

Saturdays usually entailed an intensive cleanup of the barracks in the morning ("field day"), and an inspection thereof, the afternoons might or might not be free. On Sundays we were pretty much left alone, except for the requirement to march to and from the chow hall for meals. We were told that we had to attend religious services unless we had declared ourselves as an Atheist when enlisting — spoken with intonation and body language that indicated the speaking chief had never heard of, nor ever expected to hear of, such a thing. But it was apparent that attendance was not being enforced, no names taken, and after the first Sunday or two only the incorrigibly devout continued to attend. Many of us used Sundays to catch up on sleep. We were *not* allowed to sleep late; we underwent the same early-morning reveille, marched to breakfast, and performed minimal barracks cleanup chores before having most of the day to ourselves. Letter-writing, relaxation, and horseplay (sailors' term: grab-ass; official term: skylarking) were the main Sunday activities. It was said that immersing a sleeper's hand in a pail of warm water would cause him to wet the bed — this was tried several times; I do not recall whether it ever succeeded or was an unfounded superstition. One unlucky sailor had his hands and feet tied to his bedposts with clothes stops while asleep, the malefactors then used stencil pencils to decorate his penis with black and white stripes.

I was victimized (although not on a Sunday) by a couple of recruits who entered the barracks in simulated agitation saying, "Short-arm inspection! Everybody stand by your bunks and drop your skivvies!" At least a dozen of us did exactly that, until the grins of the tricksters gave them away. *Short arm* is military slang for the penis. And short-arm inspections were, although rare, no myth. I recall on board ship being told to "skin it back and strip it down". The purpose was to detect anyone who might be concealing gonorrhea; a sufferer might do so in order to avoid being restricted to the ship, which was automatic until his affliction was cured.

There were other diversions on the evenings and weekends for those who had the time and energy. There was a recreation center with various activities, I visited it once but I was disgusted to learn that I could *not* remove my jumper in order to play ping-pong unencumbered. A group of us once went to watch Jabber box, and during the preliminary bouts we were chewed out by a couple front-row chiefs for just sitting and watching – they ordered us to applaud, make some noise, show some enthusiasm. Another time we went to an evening outdoor movie, free I believe, first-run out of Hollywood, with a haunting theme song – *High Noon*.

I encountered my first "screamer" in swimming class. Screamers, although rare – I was fortunate to observe only two over my career – are yet common enough to have received their specific name. Actually "shouter", "yeller", or "roarer" would be more accurate. The term describes a person who takes pleasure in belaboring a subordinate at the absolute top of his voice; psychologists would probably have some insight into their makeup and motivations.

I hated to get my head underwater as a child, and was consequently stuck at second-class boy scout from failure to learn to swim. But swimming was the *first* requirement in freshman physical education class, and an elderly, patient college instructor, who encountered others just like me every year, knew exactly what to do about it: he towed me, and a couple other aquatically-retardeds, across the shallow end of the pool with a rope, underwater. We soon swam well enough to pass the college requirements. The navy course had some 10-15 "stations" of progressive difficulty. I did all right until I got to the fifth one, where I was supposed to dog paddle. In college I had learned only the breast stroke, side stroke, and back stroke. And naturally the fifth station was the domain of the screamer. I had to endure his high-volume wrath, but only for a short time – he soon tired of my efforts and waved me to the next station, with the comment that I'd never make it anyhow. He was wrong. I was apprehensive about the final station, where I had to jump from an eight-foot platform wearing a life jacket. But I survived it, and was now, according to the navy, a swimmer. But if I had ever had to swim 100 yards for my life in even slightly choppy water, it is unlikely that I would be alive to write this. Nor did I ever learn how to dog paddle.

About half way through training, our section of the camp was being closed down and we had to move to another barracks. Hot, sweaty, tired, and in dungarees, we completed the move in the late afternoon, with not much time left until the chow hall would close. Donald sent a runner to the chow hall to explain our situation and request permission for the company to eat in dungarees. The runner returned. Permission denied. Groans and profanity throughout the barracks. We were so outraged by the injustice of it that we made a collective decision: to hell with it, we'd skip chow. I don't believe there was a single dissenter. Then, at about 2100, the barracks fell suddenly silent. There stood The Chief, scowling, arms akimbo. *You people have missed a military formation.* He had been called in from home. He was not happy. We held an unscheduled and unnecessary field day until around midnight. We were not happy.

One day we, along with several other companies, were marched into one of the huge drill halls and seated to hear an address by a naval officer – a commander I think, possibly a captain. I do not remember anything at all from that speech, but I well remember the instructions given from the podium by a chief, prior to the great man's arrival. We were to rise when called to attention for his entrance, take seats when so ordered, and sit at attention. And . . . *you do not applaud a military address!* I sat stupefied. My thoughts ran: they can't very well order you to applaud, that could come out faint or half-hearted. So, by forbidding applause, they prevent *any possible way* of showing disapproval of what you have heard! How *clever!* How *ingenious!* The bastards have thought of everything! My paranoia about naval Authority was already well-begun, and was to increase in the future, but I don't think any one factor contributed more to it than did that episode. However, never once after boot camp did I again hear of, or read of, any such applause prohibition. I sat through my share of "military addresses", and they were without exception applauded.

In one of our classes on naval customs, traditions, courtesy, etc., the instructor was telling us how to observe the morning (0800) and evening (sunset) colors ceremonies. You stopped, faced the flag or in the direction of the music and saluted. Several of the sailors began to mine the possibilities for what-if loopholes. What if you were in a rundown between second base and third? You stopped and saluted. What if your hat had blown off? You stood at attention without saluting and retrieved your hat later. What if you were driving? You stopped the car, got out and saluted. What if you were in civvies (stand at attention), or on a street just outside the base (same as if you were on the base). Finally one sailor inquired, "*What if you're swimming?"

The chief started to say something, cut himself short, shook a finger, and erupted: "*Salute! *By all means*, salute!" After the laughter faded, he continued with some choice reproaches along the lines of using common sense and not getting ridiculous.

In another class we went through a gas-mask drill. We were to remove our masks just before we exited, to be educated by just a whiff of the tear gas – but they hustled us out so rapidly that I never got that whiff. In yet other classes we learned to tie knots, row, hoist, and lower boats, and box. After basic boxing-for-beginners we donned gloves and were lined up in two facing rows and told to apply what we had learned to the sailor opposite. It was my misfortune to be paired with the biggest man in the company. But he was a gentle giant, we merely pawed at each other until the exercise was halted. And we learned how to sight anti-aircraft guns and handle their ammunition, learned basic first aid, fire fighting.

We sat through several sessions on the UCMJ – Uniform Code of Military Justice – which was then quite new. There was a distinct undertone to these lessons, conveyed mostly by intonation and body language, that no matter what Congress had enacted you still didn't have a chance if you displeased Authority. We were also indoctrinated – overindoctrinated – on the infallibility and omniscience of officers and the need for obeisance and servility on our humble part.

We absorbed naval terminology, both the official and the unofficial (i.e. obscene) – not so much from the classroom but from The Chief and from the everyday conversations we heard around us. Head, deck, bulkhead, ladder, overhead, aft, forward, port, starboard, abaft, topside, below . . . all, or nearly all, were already known to us, just not yet part of our customary usage. We learned that the remedy for crabs was whiskey and sand. The central area of our barracks wing, nearest the exit, was designated as the "quarterdeck". I was somewhat bemused by one usage: I overheard The Chief, standing on quite solid ground, ask another chief if the latter was "going ashore" tonight – i.e. off the base. I heard a voice of dissent from another chief some years later: "As far as I'm concerned the only decks are the steel decks on a ship and the only bulkheads are on ships. I think all these people that come ashore and call floors decks and stairs ladders are just trying to show off how salty they are." (Salty, in naval slang, implies having considerable time aboard ship, at sea. It is more often used in sarcasm or ridicule than in its basic sense.)

About halfway through training, we were given one liberty on a Sunday. It expired at midnight ("Cinderella liberty"). I headed north to Racine and the girlfriend. Driving around town with some of her friends, the driver did not place as much importance as I did on the time my return train would leave. I missed it by a matter of minutes – and as a result I was three hours late returning. I was in trouble. I had to go to mast (non-judicial punishment) in front of an officer. The Chief had to go with me. He spoke well of me and I was let off with a warning. Most of the company had headed for downtown Chicago; some returned with tattoos and many returned drunk. But no one else was late.

We came to a week that we dreaded: Service Week. It came in the seventh or eighth week of our eleven-week training. Classes were suspended and we took our turn at performing various jobs, almost entirely food service. (There was also some lawn mowing and other miscellaneous chores, dependent on base needs at the time.) As we had been told to expect, The Chief had considerable say about who got assigned to what. The deadheads, non-performers, those who had displeased him the most, got the worst, dirtiest jobs – the grease pit, cleaning pots and pans, etc. There was no one who had pleased him, only some who had displeased him less than others. I was among the latter and got a quite soft job in a chow hall storeroom: some lifting and carrying, and some sitting around, but more of my time was spent adding up columns of numbers for an arithmetically-challenged senior petty officer who lacked an adding machine. Except for having to rise at some despicably early hour with the rest of the company, Service Week for me was a snap.

Recruit training ended with a graduation ceremony at a stadium-sized field. Relatives were invited and the family from Bradford came. We stood in ranks, with other graduating companies, across from the grandstand, were speeched at and then marched around the oval and past the grandstand while a navy band played march music. After this, in our barracks packing our seabags to leave, we were in high spirits. I had been one of the few non-smokers in the company. Someone

offered me a puff on his cigaret; I took my first-ever puff to laughter
and applause.

III - TELEMAN

We were allowed fifteen days annual leave after graduation and were then to report back to Great Lakes for further transportation. This was more leave than we had "on the books" — leave was earned at 30 days a year; in our eleven weeks of boot camp we had only earned about seven days. The navy's rationale (I presume) was that (a) seven days was pretty short, and (b) better for both the sailor and the navy if he takes leave between assignments rather than becoming a functioning member of a ship or command and then seeking time off. I, however, had grown up with a somewhat spartan attitude toward spending what I did not yet have — primarily with regard to money, but that mindset also applied to leave that I had not yet earned. (That childhood *Jane's Fighting Ships* fiasco may have had something to do with this!) I took only seven days of leave and returned to Great Lakes. I have no recollection of how I spent that leave, probably a few days at the girlfriend's and a few days at home in Bradford.

At one point I was in Chicago's Union Station, in uniform. In boot camp we had had it drilled into us that you *always* wore your hat outdoors and *always* removed it indoors. Union Station, though high-ceilinged and enormous, was clearly indoors. I sat on a bench with my hat in my lap. Army MPs came by and ordered me to put it on! I felt that they were clearly in the wrong, but by this time I had become wise enough to comply without debate. I was later to find that the definitions of *outdoors* and *indoors* can be whatever Authority chooses to make them – in the navy as well as the army.

My early return was unusual but not unprecedented. It didn't speed my transfer to San Diego in the slightest. Recruits were outprocessed by company, so I had to wait a week for the rest of my company to return. During that time I was assigned to take care of an office coffee mess: making coffee as needed and keeping it cleaned up, not an unpleasant task at all. When the rest of Company 261 had returned, we were put through various evolutions, some necessary, many unnecessary time-fillers. (Yet *another* seabag inspection.) I was excused from all but the truly essential ones in order to continue my stewardship of the coffee mess. The chiefs were happy with my work; I was even happier at escaping the unnecessaries. My transportation to San Diego was available early; I was one of the first to leave. I recommended a friend to take over the coffee chores and headed for nearby Naval Air Station Glenview.

It was the second time I had ever flown. (In 1940, give or take a year, I had been treated to a birthday flight in a barnstorming old Ford trimotor.) As we neared our destination I saw the ocean for the first time. A bus took us from the Naval Air Station to the Naval Training Center and no sooner did I debus than I encountered an embarrassing problem. My destination lay on the far corner of a huge asphalt grinder. Other sailors shouldered their seabags and strode off to wherever. I shouldered mine, staggered a few steps, and had to de-shoulder it. I was narrow-shouldered and not particularly muscular, and the seabag may have been a hair heavier than some — I had not discarded my high-top work shoes; I may have had a few books inside . . . I tried again. And again and again. I heard nothing, saw no grins, but had the certain impression that anyone who chanced to be watching from a distance would be wearing a grin and commenting to his fellows. I tried the seabag on my back with a strap over a shoulder and still could get no farther than a few steps. Finally I abandoned all dignity and, red-faced, *dragged* the damn thing to where I had been told to go. The drag wore a small hole in the bottom of the seabag and a larger hole in my disposition.

The barracks in San Diego were almost identical to those of Great Lakes in layout, but they looked a lot better. Instead of the weathered white clapboard of Illinois they were southern-California adobe, and the floors were tile vice wood. We had lockers and I no longer had to use my seabag as a closet, but the racks were the same, upper and lower.

An early disappointment was learning that the next class at Teleman school was filled, and that it would be several weeks before I could begin the school. Along with others so situated I was assigned to a Master-at-Arms force for various work details and odd jobs. Painting prevailed.

Painting inside a barracks along with three or four future classmates, we indulged in considerable conversation and occasional horseplay while working. Much of the talk was of the aggressive, macho sort, common to young men thrown together. Someone asked me some impertinent "Why . . ." question and I responded with a standard high-school formula: "*Why don't you go take a flying fuck at a rolling doughnut?" Although the phrase was even then of considerable antiquity, grins and half-smothered chuckles from my co-painters testified that none of them had encountered it before.

Later that day the target of the moment – a short, chubby youth – sought to rebut a tormentor with the phrase, imperfectly remembered: "*Awrr, go fuck at a rolling doughnut."

His critic said, "*Start rolling."

One of my painting companions was a jovial, rotund Greek from Detroit. We were amused by his impression of a big-city gangster: "*Nobody fucks wit' Big Nick. Dat is . . . nobody but Big Nick's goilfriend."

Many sailors would, when not under the direct eye of Authority, wear their white hats perched far on the back of their heads. "Square your hat!" – i.e. wear it with the brim approximately horizontal, an inch or less above the eyebrows – was a phrase often heard from the Shore Patrol or Master-at-Arms force. Shortly after arriving in San Diego I reasoned to myself roughly: I'm out of boot camp and things ought to be a little less chickenshit. I don't care for that show-off hat on the back of the head anyhow, but I'd like to wear it the way I used to wear civilian caps – slightly tilted back, the brim even with the front hairline.

I tried. I got a block and a half before a car full of officers pulled up beside me and I was directed to square my hat. End of that experiment. Another uptick in paranoia.

An unauthorized modification that many sailors performed on their hat was to fold creases into it, halfway up each side, putting "wings" on the hat. Oddly, the wings did not seem to disturb Authority nearly as much as did a hat even slightly tilted backwards. One would not wear a hat with wings to a personnel inspection, but otherwise they were rarely reproved.

The Service School Command, a sub-component of Naval Training Center (NTC) San Diego, while not nearly as chickenshit as boot camp, was quite chickenshit enough. Authority's mindset seemed to be: we have all these kids just out of boot camp; we don't want to let them throw off all restraints. We could not keep civilian clothes in the barracks, but we now addressed chiefs as "Chief", and no longer saluted them. And I was reunited with, and used, my electric shaver.

One command directive stated: whenever three or more sailors are proceeding from one place to another, they will be organized into a group by the senior man and *marched*. (I believe the italics were in the original!) Impossible to be more comprehensive, but also impossible to enforce. Once my classes began, we did have to march from the barracks to the school in the morning, march from the school to the noon meal, again from the barracks to the school, and from school to barracks at the end of classes. At meals, each school's formation stopped on the huge grinder near the chow hall; Authority then directed traffic, calling schools to break ranks and enter the several chow lines in the order of arrival. We did not have to march to breakfast; Authority no doubt realized that too many sailors would skip breakfast rather than bother. We did, at first, have to march from the barracks to the chow hall for the evening meal, but this was easily avoided. If one did not mind eating a few minutes later, stragglers could walk over individually, form up in a "straggler formation" and be called to eat after all the marchers from the various schools had been called. The marching formations got rather thin (they were also depleted by sailors who chose to eat at the snack bar or off the base on liberty), the straggler formation got quite large. Authority did not like that. One evening a chief came through the stragglers with a clipboard, noting to which particular school each straggler belonged. The purpose, no doubt, was to generate statistics with which to berate the officers in charge of those schools with the most offenders. (Surely the honors would have been about even.) Then, to my surprise, not long afterwards the requirement to march to the evening meal was rescinded! A rare instance in which Authority chose to back down in the face of common sense and human nature.

I learned quite soon to try to delay falling in to march as long as I could, hoping to get at the very rear of the formation. Many sailors at the school had not come directly from boot camp but had been sent to the school from their ship, to which they would return; indeed some of these had already been promoted to third-class Teleman. The term for them was "fleet sailors". Too many of them had forgotten how to march. If I fell in anywhere but the end, I was at hazard of having my heels stepped upon and my shoeshine scuffed by the man behind me.

The Naval Training Center was located at the tip of a peninsula enclosing San Diego Bay, and it was a common sight to see destroyers passing by rather closely. I gazed on them with some awe, these ships that I had known only from books. They were the first surface warships I had ever seen. At age 10 or 11, crossing the Illinois river bridge at Peoria, I had stared open-mouthed at a submarine – one of 30 that were built on Lake Michigan during the war – on her way down river to New Orleans and the Gulf.

Eating a bowl of oyster stew in the chow hall one weekend, I crunched down painfully on a hard object. While mentally abusing the fucking cooks for not taking the fucking shells off the fucking oysters (my fluency in naval terminology was steadily progressing), I located and removed the object – it was a tiny pearl! Finding a pearl in one's oyster soup had been a staple for comedians and cartoonists in the 1940s. I was amazed that it could occur in real life, and had. The pearl was smaller than a BB, had little or no luster, and I probably couldn't have gotten a nickel for it from a jeweler. I still have it in my souvenirs.

Ah, navy chow . . . It's not nearly as bad as sailors swear it is, and not nearly as good as the navy tries to claim it is. Over the course of my career, I'd give it about a B-minus. There were several things that particularly rankled me over the years:

– The ground meat dishes. I denigrated them as gristleburgers, gristle loaf, gristleballs . . . They were no doubt nutritious, and they were flavorful, but far too often they were so full of gristle (and the occasional bone fragment) that I spent much of a meal picking out of my mouth and discarding the unwanted, and culinary enjoyment was destroyed. Had a civilian eating place served such preparations, they would have had no repeat customers.

– Frankfurters. They had an unpleasant, undefinable taste which I never encountered outside the navy. Perhaps a preservative of some sort caused it.

– The desserts (sometimes). I grew up in a middle-of-the-middle-class household, and *never* did my aunt serve dry cake or cookies *alone*. They came as an accompaniment to canned fruit, pudding, Jello, ice cream, custard, whatever. Not in the navy.

– Ethnic food. In my first years, spaghetti, corned beef/cabbage, chili, and chop suey were about the only ones. In later years pizza, soul food, and Mexican food occasionally appeared. The chili was not bad, but the others were all pretty sorry facsimiles of the real thing and the navy would have done better not to bother.

– "Orange" juice adulterated with grapefruit juice to the point that I could taste only the latter and not the advertised flavor.

The food most generally and universally hated was one that I rather liked. The official title was *cold cuts* – bologna, salami, and other such sliced meats. It was known contemptuously as horse cock, with occasional variants of pony peter, pinto pecker, donkey dong, mule tool, mustang whang, and bronco boner. It spurred many a cursing sailor to turn away from the chow hall and head for the gedunk (snack bar). But I found that, if given at least some of the right accompaniments – catsup, cheese, pickles, tomatoes, onion and the like – I could construct a quite enjoyable sandwich. Too often, though, those condiments would either not be provided or already be depleted. And too often the bread would be less than fresh. But I still grin to think of those who detoured to the gedunk and then paid for a submarine sandwich.

Lars Hansen (next chapter) used to say that when he was discharged, he would easily be able to cleanse his naval language and revert to acceptable civilian standards, with one exception. He said that surely, eventually, he was going to say at the table, "Mom, please pass the horse cock."

Most of the other slang, mostly obscene, names for food were common to all the services and well-known to civilians also: shit on a shingle (ground beef on toast), creamed foreskins (creamed beef) on toast, baby shit (mustard), bug juice (Kool-Aid type drinks), rat turds and dog turds (beans and franks). One, though, was unique to the navy: red lead – catsup, derived from the red paint used on hull bottoms.

Time passed, slowly, and finally I began classes. They began with navy mail – how to operate a navy post office. This occupied about half the time, the other half was typing; we alternated between an hour of one and an hour of the other. The navy assumed that no one knew how to type; those of us who did spent many wearisome hours just practicing our typing. We used communications typewriters, which had no lower case, had a numeral "1" key, and had the other numerals offset one key to the right from their positions on a "standard mill". Someone told me that the teletypes to which we would progress had the numbers similarly offset, so I put considerable effort into reprogramming my typing into the strange configuration. But that someone lied. (Not deliberately, I'm sure, but from having himself been misinformed.) I would have to reprogram myself again. And after *two* reprogrammings, it took many years before my numeral typing regained the degree of confidence and speed that it had once had.

The class contained about 66 people (16 of them Waves), and was divided into two sections for classroom purposes. As with boot camp, it was heavily Caucasian (two Blacks – one of them a Wave, the other so light-skinned he could have "passed") and heavily Anglo-Saxon. Two had Italian surnames (one of them a Wave), and there was the aforementioned Greek. Looking at old class photos and reviewing memories, eight of the Waves were quite fetching, five were clock-stoppers, and three fell in the "wouldn't kick her out of bed" gray area. I would not be surprised if navy-wide proportions ran just about the same. Somewhere around half the male students were fleet sailors. I identified more, and hung out more, with those who, like myself, had come to the school directly from boot camp.

The Waves came in for a good deal of semi-hostile criticism from male sailors – not the individual Waves in the class, but the Waves as an institution. Much of this, I am sure, was simple male chauvinism, and it was seldom voiced within a Wave's earshot. But there were some specific criticisms, some of which had at least a grain of validity. Waves were exempt from some of the dirtier, less desirable jobs such as mess cooking (the navy-wide equivalent of the boot camp service week). Waves held down shore billets and thus deprived sailors of shore duty. (This was particularly silly, *ships* had to be manned and male sailors had to do it.) Waves were perceived as less likely to be punished, whether by formal action or a simple chewing out. (But they probably committed fewer actions deserving punishment.) And they were perceived as sexually "easy" and were the butt of cynical jokes. (What's the difference between a Wave and a submarine? I don't know, I've never been in a submarine. And: if all the Waves in San Diego were laid end to end, it wouldn't surprise anybody a damn bit.)

I spent occasional weekend days in San Diego, when I had liberty. We were on four-section liberty – 25% of the evenings and weekend days I "had duty", could not leave the base, and was vulnerable to barracks cleanup duties and any projects for which Authority might need bodies, but the latter was rather seldom. I developed a highly favorable opinion of southern California, both San Diego and Los Angeles – clean, generally friendly and helpful people, great climate. That was then, before the population exploded. You could not tempt me to live there today.

Many sailors spent an occasional liberty sampling the sexual pleasures of nearby Tijuana. Shackled by the delusion that I had found my one true love, I abstained. I have never yet been in Mexico.

One duty Saturday they wanted volunteers for a college football game. They parked us at various spots around the stadium walkways where we stood at parade rest. I don't remember that we had any responsibilities or purpose except to show a navy presence to the public, but I got to see the game free.

San Diego had an excellent zoo, but otherwise I didn't find a great deal to do except to walk the streets and explore. One day I walked into a Mexican restaurant a couple blocks off the main street, ordered a meal and a beer. (I didn't expect to get the latter; California's drinking age was 21.) The thirtyish waitress asked if I was 21; I confessed that I was not. She apparently sized me up as truthful and unlikely to be any trouble, and served me the beer. I made that kind restaurant a regular stop on future liberties.

I would occasionally take in a downtown movie, but was more likely to go on the base, where it was cheaper. The base movie entailed a humiliation, which however was brief and endurable. At the end of the movie, Authority directed traffic in accordance with the caste system. Officers were the first to leave, then chiefs, then lower enlisted *with dependents*, and I do not need to explain who was last and lowest. The seating was similarly segregated.

Some of the sailors had radios in the barracks, and the most popular station was one on Santa Catalina island. I well remember two theme songs it used to play: the familiar *Avalon*, and another that I have never heard elsewhere, *Santa Catalina, Island of the Sun*. Andy Griffith's *What It Was, Was Football* was often heard, as was some parody of a rustic religious service . . . something about grandma's lye soap.

Sunday reveille in the barracks was usually pretty perfunctory and mostly ignored. But one Sunday morning a sadistic chief or duty officer put on a particularly rousing version of the reveille bugle call and played it at a maximum, thunderous volume at 0600. This was not welcome to the sailors, few of whom had had eight hours sleep and a number of whom were sleeping off hangovers. When it did not cease after a couple minutes, one of the fleet sailors, cursing, climbed up on a top rack and wrenched the speaker completely off the wall, severing the cables and restoring silence. Those who wished resumed slumber. We could still hear the bugling, faintly, from neighboring barracks; it continued for a full ten or fifteen minutes. If there was any subsequent investigation into the vandalism, I never heard of it.

That Sunday-morning atrocity emanated from some central watch office in the Service School Command. In our barracks there was a duty instructor, who had a room on the lower deck and could speak over the barracks loudspeakers from there. Many announcements were met with profane rejoinders in the barracks wings. One day Del, a first-class who was one of the most popular instructors, had the lunch-hour duty. He made the standard announcement for all hands to fall in out in the street to march back to school. He surely knew full well the typical reactions to such announcements and he may have been inspired thereby, but more likely he overheard a particularly loud cry of defiance all the way down in his office. Whichever, his timing was perfect. He keyed his mike again and said softly, "*Fuck you, too."

School progressed and we graduated from the typewriters to teletypes and began to learn their operation. The sitting-and-listening half of the classes shifted from navy mail to communications procedures.

I visited the Los Angeles area several times. Reed Hay, my closest friend from second grade through junior year in high school, had eloped not long before, and he and his bride were living in Pasadena. I found Euclid Avenue, but the house number was nonexistent and I gave up, puzzled. It turned out that what I had been trying to find was his former street address in Princeton, Illinois! I went back later, armed with more accurate information, and found them.

On another trip I looked up relatives of the Virden family in suburban LaVerne. There I was briefly introduced to the Rev. Bob Richards, who was something of a sports celebrity at the time due to his pole-vaulting at the Olympic Games. On Sunday morning I was not asked whether I wanted to go to church – it was one of those families where it was taken for granted that anyone able to walk, went to church. It was the last church service that I ever attended.

During the Christmas/New Year break, anyone who desired a two-week leave could take it. Most did, I did not. Not only was I saving my leave days for use after the school ended, but also I would have had to pay for my own transportation if I had gone back to the midwest. Regular classes were suspended, but those of us who stayed had to report to the school building as usual, practicing on the teletypes, studying, etc. And we had a pain-in-the-ass temporary move to another barracks – Authority cared not at all about the inconvenience to us, but seized the opportunity to save on electricity and heating by closing down many barracks completely and consolidating the stay-behinds in others that remained open. During one of those moves I found an abandoned pipe in a locker into which I moved. A bit later I bought a can of Prince Albert and began to experiment with pipe smoking.

Wisconsin made the Rose Bowl that year. And the coed came out with a group of Wisconsin students. And every day that she was there I took a bus to Los Angeles right after school hours and a bus back to return me in time for school hours. I could not sleep on the busses. On New Years Eve, she and I went to an all-night party. We went to the game (Wisconsin lost 6-0 to Southern California) without sleep. By prearrangement we then went to Reed Hay's house and crashed. I think we may have slept twelve hours. It was the sleepiest I have ever been. I did the figures at the time but have forgotten the exact number: something like 80-90 hours with only one hour of real sleep.

Classes resumed to a little more variety. We practiced on voice radio procedures, got a small dose of very basic electronics, Ohm's law, etc., and learned how to read teletype tapes from the pattern of punched holes.

I wish I did not have to write this paragraph, but conscience (or something) insists. Near the end of school several of us from the duty section were drafted for a Saturday painting detail. As we were finishing and preparing to put paint cans and brushes away, I got into some sort of dispute with one of the two shortest men in the class. He was scarcely over five feet. I don't remember exactly how it started, some silly thing, paint nearly spilled on someone's shoes . . . All of a sudden we were both standing there with fists raised. I did not yet have the maturity to decline to fight in such a situation. I landed a couple blows, it was too obviously a mismatch, I called a halt.

*Never pick on **nobody** **under** yo' own size, Mr. Mouse. . . if you **wins** you is a **bully** an' if you **loses** you is a **bum!** Fight **bigger** fellas ... win or lose, you is a **hero**.* (Miz Beaver, in the *Pogo* daily comic strip, 18 September 1953)

I ran into Sully on a snowy London street three years later. (He had gotten attache duty there.) We shook hands, conversed about five minutes about where we'd been since school . . . but the warmth and camaraderie that I wished could have been there, could not be. I believe that "fight" was the last time I ever struck another American in anger – with a drunken semi-exception which I'll recount in the next chapter.

I passed the seaman examination and now became a TESN – Teleman Seaman. A prerequisite was completion of a seaman course by correspondence. It was quite easy. I still recall one Q/A with amusement. End of the chapter question: How do you know if you have an anchor watch? Back of the book answer: Look on the anchor watch list.   (An anchor watch is a reduced watch, stood while the ship is in port.)

Walking on a downtown San Diego street, I was startled by an unexpected newsstand headline: **Stalin Dead**. From FDR's kindly Uncle Joe to the ogre of the cold war, he had been a fixture on the world horizon; I wondered who would replace him and what might lie ahead.

Toward the end of school I was locked in a close race with one of the Waves for the highest grade in the class. She edged me out at the end, 98.18 to 97.98. Some of my friends thought her triumph undeserved, somehow, and offered me a good deal of sympathy. I've forgotten whatever factors caused their perceptions, but I never agreed with them. Maybe I "should" have won academically, but there was another factor here: typing tests, on both teletypes and typewriters. I was pretty good at both, but she was a whiz. On the final teletype test, she had "one of those days" and I outscored her. Whatever bad breaks, if any, I might have had on written tests were more than compensated for by that teletype test outcome. She won fair and square and deservedly.

The high finish conferred a much-desired prerogative. Future assignments were determined by Washington and a list passed down to the school; the school then determined who got which one. The top three students got to make their own choices from what was available. The Waves were assigned separately (and the fleet sailors already knew they would return to their ships) so I effectively had first choice. U.S. shore duty was rare, but nearly every time in the past there had been at least one or two overseas shore duty assignments. Navy wisdom holds that, "the worst shore duty is better than the best sea duty," words that I already believed and have never had reason to question.   (There is a gung-ho phrase of counter-wisdom, "sailors belong on ships and ships belong at sea", to which I never subscribed.)

But *this* time there were no shore assignments. Every choice open to me began with USS (with one exception, but it also floated). I received quite a bit of sympathy from the instructors. They seemed to think the exception might be a little bit better – only a little – and I went along with their judgment and chose it. It was COMBATDIV TWO – Commander Battleship Division Two – a rear admiral's staff *on a ship.*

And then. Larry Rinne, a classmate, had requested duty with his brother on the *USS Iowa (BB-61),* one of the other choices. COMBATDIV TWO was aboard the *Iowa.* BUPERS (the Bureau of Naval Personnel, in Washington) mixed up our orders. I got the *Iowa.* Rinne got the staff.

I will be mentioning Rinne frequently in the next chapter. We became closer friends on the ship. He was from the San Francisco bay area, of Finnish descent; the name was pronounced Renny. We addressed each other by last name as was customary among enlisteds.

APPENDIX A - NAVAL COMMUNICATIONS

An appendix *between* chapters? Well, why not? It may be unusual but it is not illegal, and if a reader is going to tackle it this is the logical point at which to do it. Many of the details of naval communications would be of lesser interest except to other communicators, so I have chosen to label them as an appendix. Much of what I treat here applies to the other services as well, and to many other government agencies. Should a non-communicator tackle this portion, I recommend skimming or speed-reading, slowing whenever you hit something that looks interesting. Or, skip past the part dealing with "format lines"; what follows is a bit more interesting (less uninteresting?). A lot changed over time, and has surely changed some more since I left the field. (Much of what I have written in the present tense probably belongs in the past tense.) I start with a hypothetical naval teletype message:

1	ABC123
2	RR BEPC BFRC BFLC
3	DE BMPC #1234 01/1234Z
4	BFRC T USS NEVERMORE
5	R 011244Z
6	FM COMDESRON EIGHT
7	TO BEPC/CNO
	AIG 64
	ALNAV
8	INFO BFRC/MSTSO NAPLES

```
         BFLC/DESRON EIGHT
         ZEN/USS VARIANT
     9   XMT USS BORDERLINE
    10   NAVY GRNC
    11   BT
    12   PLENTY OF TEXT
    13   BT
    14   C WA COMMENCE - OPERATIONS
    15   01/1335Z
    16   (2 carriage returns, 8 line feeds, 4 N's, 12 "letters" functions)
```

The numbers in the left column are the numbers of the "format lines" (F/Ls). They would *not* appear as part of a message; they are for illustration and reference only. Taking them in order:

F/L one is transmission identification, or channel number. A message may pass through intermediate relay points, sometimes many of them, from its origin to its destination(s) and would acquire an added channel number at each such point. The three letters identify a particular circuit from one station to another; the numbers are consecutive and begin again each day. A missing number indicates a missing message, retransmission would then have to be requested by service message. (I will comment more on service messages later.) The channel number is followed by two letters functions, five spaces, two carriage returns, and a line feed. (The end of every line was followed by *two* CRs, one LF – the two were to make sure that the electronic impulses didn't outpace the mechanical apparatus and that the type box got all the way back to the left margin before it started to print characters.)

F/L two is the routing line. First the RR indicates the precedence; that is, the relative urgency of the message and consequently the order in which it should be handled. From lowest to highest: M - deferred; R - routine; P - priority; O - operational immediate; Y - emergency; Z - flash. In a 1960s simplification, deferred and emergency were eliminated, reducing the six to four. Operational immediate was relabeled as simply immediate, but the old O was retained. Unlike the evasions and tinkerings which followed the reduction of classification levels (treated below) this one largely stood. Precedence inflation, and the overload of flashes in combat or crisis situations, did cause the much-later introduction of CRITIC, which strictly speaking was not a precedence but was generally understood to be hotter-than-flash.

Following the doubled precedence come the routing indicator(s). BEPC was the old navy Washington DC unclassified communications center – B = navy, E = east coast, P = primary relay station, C = the comm center associated with that primary relay. BEPCR would indicate the cryptographic section of that comm center, BEPCS the service message section. A bare BEP was the primary relay itself. There were some other suffixes in (rarer) use.

There were also major relay stations, minor relay stations, and tributary stations. The navy primaries and majors included Washington, Port Lyautey (French Morocco), London, Naples, San Francisco, Honolulu, Yokosuka, Guam, the Philippines, and various others which I've forgotten. These changed from time to time due to world politics or simply to realignments. Rota, Spain became a major after we signed a bases-treaty with Franco and were not quite as welcome as we had formerly been in independent Morocco. Asmara (Eritrea) also became a major for a while.

There were not many minor relays. They were just what their name implies, they were usually connected to only one major with two or more tributaries subordinate to them. The tributaries – BEPC was one – had no relay responsibilities; they were where messages reached their destinations or were originated.

The format of the designations also changed over time. An R was added at the front: BEPC became RBEPC (this was done to differentiate the main communications network from temporary theater stations which were prefixed with a U). Then the B of the now-second position, together with the air force J, all became U's (service unification – the army was already using U). So old BEPC was now RUEPC. NATO stations used X in the second position; our various allies used various other letters there to brand their communications turf.

49

F/L three probably had a more formal name, but it was called simply "the DE line". DE here signifies "from" and is followed by the routing indicator of the station that originated the message, then a serial number (starting at 0001 each new day) and a time of file. The time of file was, in theory, the date and time the message was delivered to the originating communication center. In practice, no one paid much attention to it. Some comm centers routinely made it ten minutes before or after the date-time group. The format was a two-digit date, slant sign, four-digit hour-minute time. The Z signified Zebra time (= Greenwich mean time), soon to become Zulu time when the phonetic alphabet was changed in 1956. This whole format changed in (?)the mid-1960s; a Julian date replaced the date of the month, the slant and the Z were dropped as unnecessary or self-evident, and the time of file became simply seven digits. The "Julian dates" numbered each day of the year from 001 to 365 (or 366). Thus the 01/1234Z of my sample message would become (assuming the month is February) 0321234.

Communications operated, in general, on Zulu time and the 24-hour clock. Each of the planet's 24 time zones had its own identifying letter; these could be used in message texts when necessary to clarify the time zone applicable. A "radio day" began and ended at midnight Zulu.

F/L four was sort of a catchall for Tare (later, Tango) instructions, operating signals (three-letter Q and Z signals; I'll discuss them later), etc. In my sample message, I have only one Tare instruction: BFRC is told to deliver (**T**ransmit) the message to a specific ship. In later years this line was used to accommodate computers; ZNR UUUUU for an unclassified message, ZNY CCCCC (or SSSSS or TTTTT) for a confidential (secret or top secret) message.

F/L five was the date-time group line. It began with the precedence (not doubled as in the routing line). It could show two precedences: O P would indicate that the precedence was immediate for the action addressees, priority for the information addressees. Then came the date-time group (DTG) itself: six digits, two for the date and four for the

Zulu time. This was usually pretty close to the time the message was delivered to the originating comm center. But this was not mandatory. I used to argue that nothing in the regulations forbade assignment of a DTG that was days earlier or later! Or months or years even. If there was such a requirement I never discovered it, and I believe that only custom and usage governed. Then, too, if some office delivered a stack of ten, or fifty, messages to the comm center at the same time, they would each have to have a different DTG (but could, indeed should, all have the same time of file). Naval messages were filed and referenced by this DTG, which therefore had to be unique for that originator/that message. In the (?)1960s it became required to follow the DTG with three-letter month and two-digit year: 011234Z FEB 65; this was helpful in many ways. The DTG also could be followed by operating Z signals in some instances.

F/L six is easy: the from – FM – line, indicating the originating ship or activity.

F/Ls seven and eight contained the action and information addressees, prefixed where/if appropriate by the routing indicator of the station responsible for delivery to that addressee. ZEN/ indicates an addressee who has received the message by other means. There were a couple of wrinkles here; my example contains an address indicating group (AIG 64) and two collectives (ALNAV and DESRON EIGHT). An AIG might contain anywhere from half a dozen to a hundred or more addressees. It was useful in saving typing, both at the originating office and at the comm center; it was typically used when recurring information – e.g. a daily intelligence report – was regularly sent to the same recipients. There was a thick publication containing the breakdowns of hundreds of AIGs; the problem here was that AIGs were frequently added but rarely pruned and deleted. Some were the result of a bright idea that turned out to be not so bright and were almost never used. Others lost their reason for being over the years. Each ship, or comm center, had to know in which AIGs they were contained.

Collectives were somewhat similar, but self-evident without the need for a special AIG. Here, ALNAV was all navy – the whole damn works. It's a poor choice for inclusion in my example because only the Secretary of the Navy was authorized to use it. It is one of a number of "general messages" which were numbered serially and had to be retained in separate general message files until cancelled. Others: NAVOP, ALMAR (marines), ALCOM (communications matters). There were about a dozen such. The other collective, DESRON EIGHT, indicates the eight or so ships of Destroyer Squadron Eight.

Instead of plain language, call signs and address groups were often used for the addressees. Call signs were groups beginning with N – three letters for shore-based radio stations, four letters for ships. NSS - the radio station at Washington DC. NEPM - *USS Iowa*. Address groups were used for all other commands and activities, and could begin with any other letter. Only two have survived in my memory: SQNF - COMIDEASTFOR (Commander Middle East Force); XYKD - COMSIXTHFLT. Thick publications were devoted to encode and decode sections for all these disguises; each AIG and collective also had its address group. The short groups saved some typing and transmission time, and also served to make it harder for eavesdroppers to figure out who was who. I'm sure the Soviets had little problem doing so, but casual ham operators did. As more and more circuits became "covered" (totally encrypted), these signs/groups slowly lost their reason for existence.

F/L nine was the exempt, or XMT line. If a particular ship or organization within an AIG or a collective did *not* need this particular message, it could be indicated here and would save the exempted from processing and distributing the message. But for this to work, the drafting officer would (a) have to be familiar with and understand the procedure, (b) realize that certain entities did not need the message, and (c) give a damn. The line was seldom seen.

F/L ten, when used, could contain an accounting symbol – here NAVY – to indicate who paid if the message passed through commercial circuits, or a group count, or both. Here, GRNC indicates "groups not counted". Encrypted messages usually contained a numerical count, e.g. GR138.

F/Ls eleven and thirteen: BT. These simply indicated the beginning and end of the text. In voice communications, they were spoken as "break". They had a special symbol in Morse code: — • • — or B plus T, but sent as if one character, without any pause between the B and the T.

F/L twelve was the text. But let me dispose of lines 14-16 first. Line fourteen could be used to correct an error. It was used mostly in CW (Morse code) communications, or in the rare event that a teletype operator was connected directly to the circuit and transmitting "live" as he typed. Nearly all teletype messages were first prepared as a tape (more on this later), then proofread and corrected if necessary before the tape was transmitted; F/L 14 faded its way into obsolescence.

(Remember that CW abbreviation; I will use it hereinafter. Communicators rarely spoke of "Morse code" but rather CW. It stood for Continuous Wave.)

F/L fifteen was just a repetition of the F/L three time of file. It was rather superfluous and also faded away at some forgotten point.

F/L sixteen contained the ending functions. At first these were two carriage returns, eight line feeds, sixteen letters. The letters functions were easily recognizable on tapes and made a convenient place to tear message tapes apart. Four N's were introduced later, for some computer purpose or other; the functions became 2 CR 8 LF 4 N's 12 letters.

And now the text. In my earliest days it was simple. The drafter said what he needed to say as briefly as he could, and that was it. The only exception was that a classified message bore its classification at the start of the text – spaced out, i.e. S E C R E T. Any message lacking such classification was automatically assumed to be unclassified. No bureaucracy can tolerate such simplicity.

There were four levels of classification: RESTRICTED, CONFIDENTIAL, SECRET, and TOP SECRET. UNCLAS began to be required as the first word of an unclassified message. In the 1950s RESTRICTED was eliminated in the name of simplification.

Ha.

Unlike the reduction from six to four precedences, reduction from four to three classifications only produced increased chaos and ambiguity. The navy now came up with UNCLAS E F T O (encrypt for transmission only). The State Department produced LIMITED OFFICIAL USE, which was on the one hand unclassified, but on the other hand treated *as if* it were confidential. I've no doubt the other services and government agencies generated equivalent evasions, but I've lost whatever knowledge I might once have had. Quite a number of restrictive tag-along attachments to classifications were invented: NOFORN (no foreigners), NAVY EYES ONLY, RELEASABLE TO NATO, etc. FOUO – For Official Use Only – had already been around for some time. I never understood what purpose it served; the instructors in Teleman school had taught that *any* naval message was for official use only!

Over the years, complexity inexorably elbowed out simplicity. I won't even try to recall the decade/year or the sequence each change was cranked in, but . . .

A Standard Subject Identification Code was required right after the classification, i.e. UNCLAS//N12345//. For the computers of course; it facilitated computerized distribution of messages. A publication was printed listing several hundred codes.

A subject line was required – and had to be followed by an abbreviated classification: (U), (C), (S), or (TS) pertaining to the subject line alone. This did have some minimal utility; it allowed, say, a message-center watch to telephone the duty officer and read an unclassified subject line, helping the latter to determine whether he needed to view a classified message right away or not.

As a result of the *USS Pueblo* fiasco, which was due in part to messages being delayed because operators in an army or air force relay station were unfamiliar with the locations of some of the navy addressees, *every* addressee not only had to be followed by a geographical location, that location also had to be spelled out in full. Ships and afloat commands obviously had to be excepted, but they were the only ones. Because of this bureaucratic "corrective action" overkill, you could no longer send a message to CNO, nor even to CNO WASHDC, you now had to send it to CNO WASHINGTON DC.

References were required to be lettered A, B, etc., and appear below the subject line. Each paragraph had to be numbered and marked with its own one- or two-letter classification; each subparagraph had to be indented and lettered and done similarly. And finally the message, if classified, had to end with instructions on when it could be declassified (i.e. ADS 15 SEP 76); the rules for determining this were quite complex. Much of this was brought about by outside criticism (well-justified) of military secrecy and overclassification.

Communications publications contained an elegant sentence which I have long admired: "Brevity must not be attained at the cost of accuracy; rather, brevity will be achieved through the proper choice of words and good writing technique." Brevity was indeed important in my earlier days, it had been preached since even earlier times, when radio communication was in its infancy. The very best CW operators could barely achieve speeds of 40 wpm, and they were the elite – most operators were competent only in the 20-30 wpm range. Because of this long messages were discouraged and nearly all messages were in "telegraphese" – with a, and, the, this, that, and many other short words, obvious from context, omitted from texts. Another factor contributing to brevity and telegraphese was carryover from the civilian world, where telegrams were charged by the word. A story is told of a reporter on distant assignment replying to an unreasonable demand from his editor with UPSTICK ASSWARDS – thus conveying a normally five-word sentiment for the price of two.

Early on, there was much emphasis on abbreviations – and the navy had a publication listing hundreds of them. If you typed ADDEE (for addressee) rather than the authorized one-d ADEE, you could be gigged for a mistake. Some drafting officers were quite proficient at telegraphese, others were not. I preached and practiced telegraphese and brevity to the maximum (and sometimes had minor clashes with superiors as a result of my efforts). Any little thing that would shorten a message, however trivial, was a concomitant reduction of my workload and I deplored each change that came along that required any extra wordage.

As the 60-wpm teletype circuit speeds of my earliest days increased to 100-wpm, then 200-wpm, then up and up and up, the need for brevity decreased accordingly, and by the time I retired it had almost vanished. The machinery was no longer overloaded, but now the operators often were! That publication listing authorized abbreviations became defunct before the 1970s. Also, with the increased capacity of communications, many matters formerly handled by correspondence began to be handled by message.

Brevity was given its final death notice in the 1970s. When an already-long message approached three pages in length, it had to *begin* with a brief summary paragraph.

"Service messages" were sent from one communications activity to another for various purposes. They were usually short, a line or two, and seldom contained from and to lines – the routing and DE lines sufficed. Probably the commonest were requests for a repetition of a missing channel number or broadcast number, or for a portion of a message that had been received garbled. Also common was correction of an error that had been detected in a message after it had been transmitted. Services had to be for official purposes only, no unofficial chit-chat, and I never saw this violated in the navy. They had to minimize plain language and make maximum use of the "operating signals" – three-letter groups beginning with Q or Z, sometimes suffixed with a numeral.

The Q signals were worldwide, also used by ham operators and other civilians. The Z signals were military and governmental, but unclassified. They could be preceded by INT -- interrogative, which was the functional equivalent of a question mark. Some of the most used: ZDK - repetition. INT ZDK - repeat. QRT - stop sending. QSL - acknowledge receipt. A few passed into spoken jargon among communicators. ZUJ - stand by. QRU - officially, I have nothing for you; spoken, I'm QRU = I'm all caught up. The ultimate communicator-to-communicator insult was ZBM2 - place on watch a competent operator. I discovered another possibility for snide sarcasm, and regret that I never found opportunity to use it – a situation never quite arose where the guy on the other end was dense, uncomprehending, or stubborn enough to deserve it. It was intended for use with facsimile transmissions. ZAN2 - I am unable to transmit pictures.

ZZZ, which was blank in the publication with no assigned meaning, was said to mean, "You have bird shit on your antenna." QFA, although it did have an assigned meaning (relating to meteorology), was sometimes used to convey, "Quit fucking around."

The "tracer message" was a specialized variety of service message, and higher-ups usually got involved with them. A non-delivery – a message that fails to get everyplace that it was supposed to go – is the ultimate sin in communications. The reasons are obvious – a great many messages are inconsequential and would never be missed, but if a really important one fails to get through, the aftermath can be grim. The tracer starts from the station that originated the lost message, which tells the first station down the line essentially "we sent it to you at whenever under channel number whatever, what did you do with it?" That station researches its logs and sends the same sort of query to the next relay point, and so on, until one station discovers its guilt and "accepts responsibility". The admission typically contains a boilerplate phrase: "corrective action taken". Tracers are also used, less often, to determine the cause of delay when an urgent message does not reach its destination as quickly as it should have.

Naval communications doctrine states three fundamental requirements of communications: reliability, security, and speed. It goes on to explain that situations can arise where speed is more important than security and the latter can be sacrificed, and vice-versa. But reliability is always paramount and can never be sacrificed. A good doctrine in concept, but that part about reliability *never* being sacrificed breaks down into absurdity when closely examined. Imagine a message center with four eight-man watch sections and one day-working traffic checker. One man on each watch also checks the traffic handled by his watch to ensure that nothing has been done wrong. Now take one man from each watch and add him to the day-working traffic check. Next have two men vice one on each watch check the traffic, only five left to do the work. Each of these changes increases reliability by a fraction. Carry such changes as far as you can and ultimately you have one man working and 32 checking on his work. The last changes increase reliability by only .000(a hell of a lot of zeros)001, but they do increase it to its maximum. Anything less sacrifices reliability by however microscopic a fraction. Not much work will get done. (And some idiot will still find a way to lose a message.)

The haze-gray teletype machines to which I was introduced in Teleman school remained unchanged for decades, at least in outward appearance and basic configuration, whatever improvements may have been made to their innards over time. (In my second career, I decommissioned the teletypes in favor of computer terminals at embassies or consulates in 1983, 1985, and 1989.) The keyboard had only three rows of keys, and the teletypes printed only upper-case. There were special keys for figures, letters, carriage returns, line feeds, etc. To type numerals, one had first to hit the figures key – the numerals were the "upper case" of the QWERTYUIOP row. Various punctuation symbols were upper-case on the other two rows. When done typing numerals, one then hit the letters key to return to the alphabet.

Above and behind the keyboard was space for a bulky roll of teletype paper. Usually buff-yellow, it could be single-ply or two- or three-ply (carbon between the plies of the latter two). In front of the roll was a ribbon (identical to typewriter ribbons except for the reels on which it was wound), a type box which moved back and forth on heavy guide wires, and a fast-moving little gadget which aligned with the type box to strike the proper characters in the proper sequence. Manuals and civilians called this gadget a print hammer. Sailors called it a peckerhead.

To the left of all this was the machinery that produced tapes. The teletype tape was also a buff-yellow color, about 3/4-inch wide, whereon five hole-positions would be either perforated or left unperforated. The particular combination of perforated/unperforated was different for each character. Between the second and third hole positions was a sixth set of holes – much smaller, and used only for a sprocket to advance the tape. A completed tape was fed thereby through a TD – transmitter-distributor – where sensing pins read the holes and, depending on the purpose, either sent the message over a circuit, or printed it out locally, or produced a duplicate tape. There were chad tapes (punched completely) and chadless tapes (the chad pushed up and left partially attached). We communicators knew well the term "chad", decades before the days of Florida miselections. The hoppers below chad punchers filled up with material that made good New Year's Eve confetti.

I probably could make only 45 wpm on a teletype at the conclusion of teletype school, but over the years I got up to 60 and may have exceeded 70 at times. On the rare occasions when an officer had occasion to type on a teletype, he was likely to be slow and hesitant. Sometimes an alert comedian would pick up a fire extinguisher and stand to such typist's side, in silent satire, until noticed.

Teletype test tapes often contained line after line of RYRYRYRY and SGSGSGSG; the character R had holes in the second and fourth positions, Y in the first, third, and fifth. S and G were similarly complementary. THE QUICK BROWN FOX also did a good deal of jumping. The "letters" (all five holes punched) and "figures" (only the third hole unpunched) functions were readily recognizable, as was the "blank" (no holes punched). The latter was useful in feeding a tape into a TD and in separating one message from another.

Most tapes also bore the printed message but, especially in earlier days, some did not. In Teleman school I was required to learn to read unprinted tapes from the pattern of holes, and I never regretted the skill so gained. It was useful in a variety of ways; one of the more notable (and equally usable with printed tapes) was that with a very sharp lead pencil a non-hole could be converted to a hole, and this could sometimes save running a long tape through a TD in order to correct one garble. It was a delicate operation, had to be done *just* so, and didn't always work – I'd guess I was no more than 80% successful when I tried to do it.

In front of the tape apparatus was a three-position switch: K, K-T, T. In K, keyboard, no tape was produced, only paper hard copy. In T, only a tape was produced. This was known as "cutting in the blind" and was seldom done. By far the most typing was in the K-T position, yielding both outputs. Most tapes, when completed, had to wait their turn to go wherever they were going. So if longer than a couple feet, a tape would be grasped between the middle and index fingers and wound up figure-eight fashion around the thumb and little finger, then stapled to its associated hard copy until needed.

Another interesting bit of gadgetry was the "tape factory". I encountered it only at relay stations, where a tape might come in that needed to be relayed over (say) six circuits. The operator performed appropriate actions, ran the tape through, and six tape copies of it whizzed out and were placed for transmission at the appropriate positions.

Early on, ships sent most of their outgoing messages to shore stations by CW, and received by "fleet broadcasts" which were both teletype and CW. The broadcasts emanated from the major shore radio stations and were prefixed by a letter or two: W NR123 was the CW broadcast from Washington; WR was its teletype counterpart. The R signified RATT – RAdio TeleType. A given message might be for only one ship copying that broadcast, it might be for the whole fleet, or anything in between. Any missing numbers had to be serviced for retransmission. The CW broadcasts were not hand-sent by an operator but were automated and ran at a constant speed, 22 wpm I believe. (Memory is unreliable, it might have been as high as 30.) As a ship transited ocean areas it would shift to another broadcast at an announced time, customarily at midnight Zulu. I remember K/KR from Port Lyautey, J/JR from Asmara, E/ER from Londonderry.

As communications progressed, the CW broadcasts diminished and the RATT correspondingly flourished, and entire broadcasts as well as station-to-station circuits became covered (encrypted). Ships could send their outgoings on an as-needed covered teletype connection, and some (larger ones especially) could "terminate" – hook up around the clock with a shore station and, in effect, become a tributary station, both sending and receiving over that termination. But they still had to copy those RATT broadcasts, which themselves became multi-channel (as many as eight).

The early cryptographic machines were cumbersome things that required hand-typed input. This was almost always done by junior officers, or sometimes the most senior enlisted. The mushrooming of covered circuits greatly reduced the need for them, but they hung around. One continued use was for sensitive personnel matters that Authority didn't want exposed to enlisted-man gossip.

A ship might also send messages to other ships in company and to harbor activities by flashing light, flag hoist, semaphore, and voice radio. This was a relatively minor component of the communications workload, and the first three were done by the Signalmen on the bridge, communications tasked only with filing and distribution.

IV - PIG-IRON BITCH

I had planned to take two weeks of leave on the way to Norfolk, the first half in Illinois and the rest in Wisconsin. The navy paid for most of the ticket; I had to cover the extra for deviation from a direct San Diego-Norfolk route. It was my first time on a commercial flight. Somewhere over the southwest the rear side door of the passenger compartment slammed open. It was impossible to close in flight, so the crew just stayed away from it. This was a propeller aircraft, flying at a much lower altitude than later-year jets, no pressurized cabin, no problem as long as no one fell out the open door. The plane made a stop in Albuquerque, and after we got on the ground we heard that it had landed in a strong crosswind requiring all the pilot's skill to counter. There was indeed a stiff wind at the air strip when we deplaned briefly.

In Wisconsin the girlfriend broke off with me, with as much regret and understanding as she could manage. I didn't want to hang around under the circumstances and arrived in Norfolk several days earlier than planned.

On the bus taking me through the Norfolk Naval Shipyard (which is not in Norfolk, but across a river in Portsmouth) I saw the impressive tower mast of a battleship. It was not the *Iowa* however, but the mothballed *USS Massachusetts (BB-59)*. The *Iowa*, even more impressive, was not far away. She was in drydock, and as I crossed the gangway the floor of that drydock looked a long way down. I presented my orders to the JOOD (Junior Officer of the Deck – the OOD himself was stationed at the forward [officers'] gangway). CR division (Communications - Radio) was notified of my arrival and a seaman sent to fetch me.

My first impressions were of the smell, sound, and sight of welding torches and other tools, and of hoses and cables of various sizes and purposes snaking over decks and through passageways. A ship in a shipyard is not at its most presentable. The civilian shipyard workers were busy at numerous repairs, modifications, and improvements. I soon learned that the applicable derogatory term – for civilian employees of the navy in a wider sense, but especially for shipyard workers – was *sand crabs.*

The *Iowa* and her three sisters – *USS New Jersey (BB-62), USS Missouri (BB-63),* and *USS Wisconsin (BB-64)* – were the last U.S. battleships to be completed. *Iowa* was commissioned in 1943. She had nine 16-inch guns in three triple turrets, two forward and one aft, plus 20 five-inch and a large number of 40-millimeter scattered around the superstructure. She was 887 feet long. Her displacement (weight), *officially* stated as 45,000 tons because of a treaty limitation, was probably more like 48-49,000.

The *Iowas* are generally regarded as the acme of battleship construction, the finest ever built, partly because of their high speed. But even while building they were being relegated to obsolescence by the aircraft carrier. In early 1944 *Iowa* and *New Jersey* encountered and fired upon light Japanese units near Truk, a half-size light cruiser and two destroyers (one destroyer escaped; the others were sunk). Save for that one mismatch, none of the *Iowas* ever fired their guns at an enemy surface warship. They served for shore bombardment and as antiaircraft platforms protecting the fast carriers and they were superb in both roles.

If my nine-year-old self could have known that ten years later it would be aboard any battleship, let alone *this* battleship, it would have been ecstatic. My nineteen-year-old self was not ecstatic.

The CR berthing compartment was on the second deck, one deck below the main deck, toward the starboard side of the ship and not far aft of the barbette below the second 16-inch turret. I was shown an empty rack and locker, and moved into them. The rack was second from the top in a tier of four, about chest height. On one side was a much-traveled passageway, on the other was the rack of another sailor just inches away. At one end was a less-traveled passageway and at the other end the rack of still another sailor. I was dismayed but had no choice.

Within two or three weeks, though, a sailor was departing. He had a rack I coveted. I asked him if anyone was taking it, and surprisingly the answer was no. I quickly and happily took possession. It was a bottom rack in a tier of three, bulkheads to one side and at one end, an open space where sailors accessed their lockers at the other side. Best of all, a locker on the open side obscured my head, at least, from public view. The rack afforded about as much privacy as was obtainable and I kept it until I left the ship. Most sailors were indifferent to their fishbowl living conditions, but I was not. Just forward of our compartment was a smaller space containing a pea coat locker, where we could store our bulky pea coats and raincoats on hangers, and also stash our AWOL bags. The latter were small satchels, nearly always blue, used to carry toilet articles, a change of underwear, etc., when going on overnight liberty.

Our principal working spaces were slightly forward of the berthing compartment and down a ladder to the third deck. A passageway encircled the second barbette; in the aftermost point of its circle an entrance door opened aft into Radio One, also called Main Radio. It contained the enlisted watch supervisor's desk, several CW (Morse code) operator positions, and a great deal of equipment, mostly receivers and patch panels. To starboard was the teletype room, to port was Main Comm, where I would do most of my work. The latter contained the Communication Watch Officer (CWO) desk, four desks with typewriter wells – writeup positions – and a mimeograph machine. A door in Main Comm led aft to the small crypto space. The encrypted messages were handled entirely by the officers; we seldom entered, and only when all crypto gear was stowed away. A pass-slot from Main Comm connected to the Radio Annex, a small, little-used space which could be entered only from the circular passageway.

Main Comm also contained, above the CWO desk, an array of some 6-10 pneumatic tubes leading to various other locales. Some of them were probably dead ends, no longer functional; the only one that got significant use was that to the signal bridge. Messages were rolled up and placed in cylindrical metal containers of about 2" diameter, known as *bunnies*, which were placed in a tube and given a blast of compressed air. Since an incomplete puff could fail to get the bunny to its destination, the routine over the intercom was, "Signal, Main Comm – bunny on the way." "Roger rabbit."

Aft of these spaces a long, center-line passageway, "Broadway", led all the way back to the base of the aft 16-inch barbette. Its designed purpose was to enable transfer of 16-inch ammunition from the after turret to the forward ones or vice-versa if combat situations demanded. A heavy overhead rail ran its length for this purpose; I never saw it used. About halfway aft and to starboard was Radio Two, chiefly a transmitter space. Near the aft end of Broadway and to port was Radio Three, used largely for storage and hanging out. There were still more "Radio" spaces, at various places up in the superstructure, ranging all the way up to Radio Seventeen. Many of the intervening numbers, however, had been converted to other uses over time and were no longer "owned" by us.

The ship had been mothballed after World War II and reactivated for the Korean War. The reactivation was done on the west coast and much of the new crew had come from the west and southwest via San Diego's boot camp and training schools; when I was the new guy they were the veterans. *Iowa* had gone from reactivation directly to Korea, and thence to her new home port, Norfolk, arriving not long before I joined the ship.

Lieutenant Samuel L. Gravely, Jr., the division officer, was one of the first black officers in the navy, went on to become its first black admiral, and retired a vice admiral. He was large and jolly and popular, thoroughly respected by the enlisted men – only a handful of hard-core bigots found it necessary, once in a rare while, to reinforce their prejudices out loud. I was told that some time earlier LT Gravely had convinced a gullible young seaman that the ship carried some carrier pigeons, clinching his case by pointing out a line in a publication that listed "trained animals" as one of the methods of communication, and conned the seaman into submitting a written request to be assigned duty taking care of the pigeons! LT Gravely was transferred only two or three months after I arrived, and replaced by Lieutenant (junior grade) John R. Bianchi, who was equally well-liked. Even-tempered and congenial, the John Paul Jones-derived phrase "an officer and a gentleman" – so often inapplicable – fit him as well as any officer I ever encountered. He stayed in the naval reserve after his active duty and retired a captain. Two more LT(jg)s, Mahlon "Hugo" Hewitt, a ruddy Iowa farmer, and William Spooner, an aspiring dentist, rounded out the junior officers for whom I initially worked.

There were about 50 enlisted men in CR division. Some that I remember better than others:

Richard C. "Lars" Hansen, RM2, a fiery-tempered redhead from Montana. If he didn't like someone, he let them know it and made absolutely no pretense otherwise. Fortunately I passed whatever his subconscious tests were and got along fine with him. I still have his cribbage board; he willed it to me as a parting gift when he left for discharge. The primary target of his dislike was . . .

Don Austin, also RM2. He kept trying to smooth things over with Lars; Lars would have none of it. I don't know how the rift between them started, perhaps it went back to Radioman school or even boot camp. I found nothing to dislike about Austin.

Tester, a TE3 who came aboard after I did, was Lars' other pet hate. I found nothing to dislike about him either, but he was not too popular. He had the bad luck to be made division PPO (Police Petty Officer) which was a contributory factor, but others held that post without arousing the same antagonism.

Mike Madrid, an argumentative, outspoken, good-natured New Mexico Hispanic. He had the shape of a sumo wrestler, somewhat reduced and all muscle. I heard that after the navy he played football for the U. of New Mexico, as did . . .

Gus Benakis, a big Greek from Albuquerque, my first supervisor.

The Harwell brothers, Emmer and Skosh, from Georgia. Emmer came from M.R. initials. They were both short, Skosh a hair the shorter, his nickname came from the Japanese word for that quality.

Oley Lundquist, constantly broke, constantly in trouble. At change-of-command inspection, when they got to Oley, the old captain turned to the new and said, "*This is one of our bad boys . . ." Oley grinned.

Pete Germani, my frequent companion on liberty (especially after the flag, and Rinne, moved to another ship). We shared allegiance to the St. Louis Cardinals – Pete because Allentown PA, his home town, harbored a Cardinal farm team.

Perry Prewett, from Missouri, the division's third Cardinal fan and a player on the ship's baseball team.

Sam Fowler, Alabama farmer, all-around good guy. He once took a surplus playing card from a deck, wrote my name on it and posted it on the Radio One entrance door as commentary. The card was *Extra Joker*.

Carl Soares, New England Portuguese, Red Sox fan, cribbage opponent.

Gedunk. He'd have been a nerd if the word had existed then. He lived for electronics and chocolate, the latter germinating his nickname. Pale and horn-rimmed, he spent his time in Radio Two with the transmitters. Many volts lurked in those transmitters, and Lars said that some day Gedunk would stick his screwdriver in the wrong place and nothing would be left but a little pool of melted chocolate on the deck. There was speculation on whether Gedunk would go topside to look for his shadow on Groundhog Day.

Pat Ryon, a TE1 who ran the post office. I didn't get to know him that well on the ship, but our paths were destined to cross several times over the years. Fifty-plus years later we still exchange Christmas cards. He'd been in on the tail end of World War II, joined the reserves, was called up for Korea, and stayed on active duty.

Spider, a lanky Kentuckian. He stayed in the navy and made warrant officer.

Bill Gorham, one of the division's four enlisted Blacks. He also stayed in, and made Lieutenant Commander.

I was put on a communications watch section and given not quite the lowliest of jobs: writeup man. I retyped both incoming and outgoing messages onto a "ditto mat", which had a waxy white front page backed by a page of dark blue inky substance. The two were separated by a flimsy which was removed before typing began – or was *supposed to be* removed. On rare occasions there would be a burst of profanity in Main Comm when I, or another, discovered that we had typed an entire page but had overlooked that removal step. I added peripheral data such as the time of receipt and the distribution to various offices. My work was then reviewed and initialed by the CWO and was ready for runoff. The back page was discarded, the front page secured in a slot on the drum of the "ditto machine", and the requisite number of copies cranked out. Depending on whether we were at sea or in port (with fewer people on watch) there might or might not be another sailor assigned as runoff man. And there might be still another assigned as messenger; a function performed by the ship's marines some, but not all, of the time. The messenger delivered the message copies to their destinations. I sometimes performed the latter two functions, but worked mostly at writeup. There was a second writeup man, a flag man. Four flag communicators, including Rinne, rotated on this job, supervised by a flag RM1.

I was vulnerable to a possible three-month assignment to mess-cooking. The ship's various divisions had to provide bodies for this dreaded duty, to do the dirty work in the galley under the supervision of the cooks, starting very early in the morning. It was typically given to the most junior and/or most newly arrived non-rateds, sometimes modified by an award to someone who had gotten himself on the shit list. CR division was tasked to provide only one, and happily I escaped. Another such duty (not nearly so bad as mess-cooking) that I evaded was compartment-cleaner, cleaning CR's berthing space.

I made a new-guy mistake that did not enhance initial impressions of me. The division PPO was looking for players for an inter-divisional softball game. Sure. I got back late in the afternoon, showered, changed into whites, went to chow and, intending to go on liberty, went down to Main Radio to obtain my liberty card.

"*You got the watch, Buddy." I certainly did. I had misread/ misunderstood the format of the watch list and gazed at it again, still puzzled. The supervisor had refused to release the offgoing writeup man until I showed up, and the latter had missed supper. (The supervisor's refusal was uncharacteristic. Chickenshit at division level was rare in CR division.)

I managed to avoid asking one dumb question that, if asked, would have raised eyebrows and raised further doubts about me. Long before enlisting I had read civilian magazine descriptions of the large warships as "floating cities" with libraries, barber shops, soda fountains, laundries, medical and dental facilities, etc. I had earned many of my college expenses by setting pins in the campus bowling alley. I thought it just possible that a "floating city" might have a small, two-lane alley, and I even mentioned to my campus friends that if it did, I might supplement my navy pay by setting pins. Fortunately I realized the implausibility of my imaginary alley very early, and never inquired.

Communication watches run on a different schedule than standard four-hour shipboard watches. On ship or shore, communications nearly always runs on three eight-hour watches, approximately 23-0700 (midwatch), 07-1500 (day watch), and 15-2300 (evening watch), modified as necessary to take meal times and any other local factors into account. After a midwatch we were authorized to sleep during the day – but only until 1300, and even that was not allowed if the ship went to general quarters or if there was a personnel inspection or if . . . There were a lot of sleepy communicators.

The midwatch received "midrats" which had to be picked up from the galley. At their worst, they might consist of a sandwich with a slice of bologna, and nothing more. Once in a rare while, the cooks might have some leftovers that were more toothsome than usual, or a more conscientious cook might be on duty, and we got something enjoyable.

But on the whole, the average tended toward the low end of the scale. I think most cooks viewed the preparation of midrats as an imposition to be disposed of with as little effort as possible.

At about 0500 on one of my earlier midwatches, caught up and trying to remain awake, I wandered into the adjacent comm spaces and discovered that I was the *only* one awake. Even the supervisor had succumbed. I mused. If something important happened (World War III?), it would be up to *me* to react, if only by wakening others. Very unlikely, but *if*. . . Being the only person awake in a battleship's communications spaces made me feel somehow important.

Rinne had arrived a few days before me, and helped me to get oriented. He graciously offered to swap with me to undo the damage of our orders-switching at BUPERS. I was severely dejected by unrequited romance, as well as moderately dejected at not getting shore duty; I didn't much give a damn. And it was already apparent to me that any advantages gained by being on the staff were trivial or less. I thanked him for the offer but said never mind. I never regretted my decision.

On my first trip through the chow line, it looked pretty good. Two attractive meat entrees. I took the first one, held out my tray for the other. The serving mess cook started to give it to me and abruptly jerked it back. No conversation or eye contact was possible, a metal partition blocked the upper bodies of the mess cooks from the view of the chow line and vice versa. I eventually figured out that when there were two entrees, you got one but not both. The mess cook had viewed me as some smart-ass trying to get away with something.

There were two chow lines, port and starboard, supervised by the Master-at-Arms force. The lines were long. During good weather, they ran up a ladder and were on the main deck, thus requiring the wearing of a hat. In inclement weather they ran back through berthing compartments and I could leave my hat in my locker.

In order to eat the evening meal, and for weekend meals, I had to change into the uniform of the day – whites or undress blues depending on the season. There were "dungaree passes" available to men who had reason to be in dungarees – but it had better be a damn good reason, and going on or coming off watch did not qualify. They were issued very grudgingly. We saw, and envied, dungaree chow lines on less chickenshit ships, chiefly destroyers. On the *Iowa* one had to be in the uniform of the day even to appear on a weather deck outside working hours. If the uniform of the day was whites, we also had to change our socks to white. It was tempting for sailors to omit this step, and Masters-at-Arms patrolled the weather decks: "Get below and get white socks on."

The shipboard butter was broken out of freezers and served in hard, unspreadable pats. I often just dropped it in my soup or on other warm food rather than trying to chop it up and somehow distribute it over a slice of bread. The serving mess cook used two forks, with one tine on each bent perpendicular. He would spear a pat on a bent tine, then knock it free with the other fork (usually, but not always, with accurate aim) onto the tray of a sailor. Rumors are rife on ships, often scoffed as something heard on the mess deck. An improbable rumor would be dismissed as coming from a mess *cook*. And the unimpeachable source for the most unlikely rumors of all would be cited as, "the guy that bends the tine on the fork for the butter server on the starboard mess line".

Other divisions were likely to attribute a rumor as something heard from a Radioman. When interesting information arrived by unclassified message, communications was indeed the first to know of it. RM was sometimes said to stand for Rumor Monger.

The *Iowa* was scheduled to make a midshipman cruise in early summer, embarking middies from the naval academy and from various university ROTC units, for their summer training. She was then to take part in a NATO exercise in the fall, and to go to the far east for another stint off Korea early the following year (1954). The *Missouri* had been the only battleship not decommissioned after World War II (Missourian Harry Truman had something to do with that). When the Korean War broke out, *Missouri* was sent thence and the other

72

three *Iowas* were demothballed, refurbished, and took their turns one by one bombarding railroads and other targets on the Korean coast. The *Missouri* had run aground not far from Norfolk in early 1950 and had been stuck on a sandbar for two weeks to the navy's considerable embarrassment; sailors with orders to *Missouri* were subject to the jibe, "Oh, going to the amphibs, huh?" It was said, I think inaccurately, that the *Missouri* was a dirty ship except for the plaque topside where Japan's surrender had been signed, which was kept immaculate and highly polished.

The CR-division sailors referred to the *Iowa* as "this pig-iron bitch", and felt that her proper disposition was to be melted down for razor blades. "Seagoing boot camp" was also heard on occasion. (I've smiled to hear, decades later at *Iowa* veterans' reunions, that she has now become "our beloved ship".) Sailor opinions of Norfolk were even more scathing. Norfolk was known throughout the navy, deservedly, as *Shit City*. It was also sometimes spoken as *Nofuck – Nofuck, Vagina*. I heard claims that this was the way the natives pronounced it, but to me their rendition sounded more like NAW-f'k.

Norfolk's vile repute was in large measure due to sexual imbalance. It was overrun with sailors, underrun with approachable females. Aside from sex, there were far too many sailors for local hospitality (if there had ever been any) to accommodate. Also contributing was the infamous East Main Street area – a dismal string of bars interrupted here and there by a barber shop, a newsstand, a souvenir shop, an eating place, a tattoo parlor, a shoeshine stand. The barmaids were generally slovenly, gaptoothed, straggle-haired, unattractive for one reason or another. (I remember just two that were cute enough to escape the generalization – out of dozens.) And yet each of those slatterns could have had her pick from fifty or a hundred suitors had she so desired. Only beer was served; Virginia allowed sale of hard liquor only in package stores. Hillbilly prevailed on the juke boxes. ("Country" and "Country & Western" had not yet become general usage. Aboard ship the term was *shitkicking music*.)

73

It was said that during the World War II years there had been signs at places in Norfolk: No Dogs or Sailors. There is no truth to it. Www. snopes.com has conclusively debunked it. But sailors were more than ready to believe it.

I began my drinking in Portsmouth, where there was a string of bars along the street outside the shipyard gate. They were identical to those of East Main Street. I was playing the role of the spurned lover drowning his sorrows, and drank all too heavily. I learned that my maximum capacity was nine bottles of beer, and that anything in excess of three would produce a hangover. (And be they four-beer or nine-beer, my hangovers were not just a next-morning inconvenience, but lasted all day and into the following evening.)

Rinne was a frequent companion on my drinking excursions. If we decided to go to Norfolk instead of Portsmouth, we had to cross a river on a ferry. Cars were accommodated on the broad middle, pedestrians sat on benches in two side compartments – one side for whites, one for coloreds. One day the ferry functionaries got their wires crossed with their traffic-directing barriers, and we found ourselves and a few other whites misloaded onto the colored side. Didn't bother us, we sat down. But the ferry didn't leave, and a grandfatherly ferry official came to shoo us over to the white side. I believe he said something along the lines of, they don't like you to be over here any more than you'd like them to be over there. Somehow I doubted that. I looked at Rinne. He looked at me. We obeyed. The shipyard at that time also had water fountains labeled white and colored.

As Rinne and I got to know each other better than we had at school, we discovered quite a few mutual likes and dislikes. We both enthused over Walt Kelly's *Pogo* comic strip, and *Mad* magazine (then in its infancy), and were both taken by the work of Dave Morrah – a humorist who frequently appeared on the *Saturday Evening Post's* Postscripts page, turning out brief pseudo-Pennsylvania Dutch pieces, e.g. *Der Wizard in Ozzenland, Fraulein Bo-Peepen, Der Smallisch Johann Horner.* And we were both repelled by Bill Stern – a sportswriter/commentator of the time who never let facts interfere with a good story (Rinne dubbed him Fool Stern) – and by the starlet Piper Laurie. I don't know why we were turned off by Ms Laurie and I may not have known then. Perhaps we felt her undeniable charm was too put on, too artificial. Or it may have been simply her name – too hokey, too Hollywood, too obviously changed from something more prosaic.

Zone inspections were held periodically, mostly for cleanliness but also for any other things the inspecting officer might find amiss. An inspecting officer was assigned to cover a certain "zone" of the ship. Part of our cleanups entailed "shining" the bare-metal steel deck in Main Comm with sheets of very coarse emery paper; we put one foot on a sheet and shined while standing. One Saturday morning, nursing one of my hangovers and with a zone inspection scheduled, I was doing my best to be unfindable and escape the preparatory cleanings. But Tester found me walking on the main deck and told me to go assist in one of our spaces. I mumbled a dreary OK and never obeyed. Quizzed later, I could offer only a lame and obviously false, "I forgot." I and two others who had sinned, similarly or otherwise, were sentenced to an evening of chipping paint off the deck in the Radio Annex. Performing that chore was no problem when hangover-free.

It was presented to me as an option. I had done (or rather not done) something that was grounds for being placed on report and going to captain's mast. But, if I didn't object, the deck-chipping punishment would be substituted. Of course I made no objection. I had done wrong, and I knew it. When done in this fashion, this is a fair and common-sense way to handle minor disciplinary matters at a lower level (although I understand that even so there is some doubt about its legality under military law). However it is not always done in this fashion. Too often the offender is *not* given any option, but is ordered to perform his punishment, perhaps under the guise of "extra military instruction" or some such euphemism, and a man who feels the punishment is unfair or that he is innocent has no recourse. I was to run crashingly afoul of the latter method in a distant future year.

The captain of the *Iowa* when I came aboard was Joshua Cooper. He was relieved four months later by Wayne R. Loud. Both would later be promoted to rear admiral. They were two of a kind, distant, seldom-seen, neither liked nor particularly disliked by the crew (which did think highly of a Captain Smedberg who had captained *Iowa* during her Korean cruise). The sailors' rancor focused much more on Earl Gardner, the executive officer (exec, or XO - number two on a ship, or at a shore command). It took several more years and duty stations before I understood the psychology of it. Using the exec as the lightning rod is unwritten, but common, navy practice. The captain says to the exec, "Do this. Do that." Naval leadership doctrine holds that, when passing orders downward to subordinates you do *not* say, "The captain wants . . ." or "The captain says . . ." Rather, you repeat the orders as if they were your own. When it works, and it usually does, the exec is cast as the bad guy, unpopular orders are perceived as his idea, and the captain retains his image as a detached, more-or-less benevolent father-figure – with the crew only occasionally wondering why he never does anything to rein in his chickenshit exec.

Humanity's capacity to divide itself into us vs. them groups is infinite. There are the racial and religious divisions of the larger society, obviously, and the large-scale navy vs. marines vs. army vs. air force divisions, and there were many such divisions within the navy: Atlantic Fleet vs. Pacific Fleet, 20-year men vs. first-hitch sailors, regulars vs. reserves, ship's company vs. any transients (the flag staff, middies, etc.), day workers (aka day wreckers or day shirkers) vs. watchstanders, rebels vs. yankees, single men vs. "brownbaggers", surface navy vs. submariners vs. airdales, and surely others that don't pop to mind. Here I want to mention Radiomen vs. Telemen. On the *Iowa* I came to understand how each rating fit into the communications picture. CR division was about evenly split between the two. Four or five Telemen operated the ship's post office and had no communications duties. Radiomen sent and received Morse code, Telemen did not. (Morse code was never spoken of, the term for it was CW – Continuous Wave – which I will use hereinafter.) Radiomen were more technically oriented and, often assisted by Electronics Technicians from another division, did most of the repair and maintenance work on transmitters, receivers, antennas, and other equipment. Telemen were utilized more on clerical tasks and paperwork. But there was plenty of overlap; most of the various jobs of CR division could be, and were, performed by either rating. A standing navy joke held that the Teleman rating originated when a Radioman fucked a Yeoman. (The Teleman rating had been established only in 1948, Radioman dated to 1921.) A Teleman might disparage a Radioman as *dit-happy*, from the dits and dahs of the code coming through his earphones. And even within the Teleman rating, communicators belittled "post-office Telemen".

The term *lifer* didn't replace *20-year man* until the later 50s or early 60s, but when it did it drove the latter virtually out of existence. *Lifer* later gave birth to *lifer juice* as a synonym for coffee. Still later, some unknown but inventive low-ranker – more than likely in the army – contributed the riddle: Why are lifers like flies? They eat shit and bother people. The many phrases that hammered the obvious in response to a question (Has a cat got an ass? Does a bear shit in the woods?) were supplemented by Is the Admiral a Lifer? The 20-year men wore diagonal stripes on the lower arm, one stripe for each four years of service completed. The formal name for them was service stripes, the informal one was hash marks. Rinne and I called them stupidity marks. The 20-year men maligned first-hitch sailors as draft dodgers – often with a good bit of truth, and certainly so in my case.

Time passed, the shipyard stay ended, the sand crabs vanished, the drydock was flooded, and we moved to the Norfolk naval base. We usually tied up alongside a pier there, but sometimes the pier capable of berthing *Iowa* was full and we would have to anchor out in the harbor. In the latter case we faced a lengthy ride in a whaleboat to fleet landing if we went ashore. I believe we anchored out in every other port we visited with one exception: New York City. Even the short trip Portsmouth-Norfolk was enough to produce a sour smell of vomit below decks, as new sailors got their first experience of the sea. The *Iowa* was so large and heavy that she didn't buck and pitch, just rolled gently from side to side – with one exception: when returning to the coast from the open ocean, she would occasionally rise up forward and drop with a whump as she encountered the groundswell when entering the waters of the continental shelf. I was luckier than some, the *Iowa's* motions bothered me not a bit.

We made several trips to Guantánamo Bay in Cuba, one during the middie cruise, and perhaps a trip earlier and a trip later. Those visits mingle in memory and there is no hope of separating them, so I will chronicle my Gitmo memories all in one place without any attempt to be chronological.

It was rarely spoken in full, nearly always as *Gitmo*. The official communications abbreviation GTMO perhaps contributed to this, but the polysyllabic foreign word would no doubt have acquired an unofficial shortening in any case.

On the voyage south, I noted the floating seaweed in the Sargasso Sea and recalled childhood comic books that pictured that sea as virtually a floating jungle, with ancient derelicts still entrapped therein by the horrible seaweed. The reality: water a-plenty between plentiful, but rather small, brown seaweed clumps which barely broke the surface. I was surprised to see all the flying fish; I had thought that they were a rather rare creature.

One weekend day at sea, when Rinne and I were both off watch, we decided to do some sightseeing and donned the required whites. We went to the extreme bow of the ship, gazed at the sea and at the ship itself from that vantage point, then decided to go to the oh-eleven (011) level – the very top of the tower mast. We took in the view from there for ten minutes or so and went back down. On the way down we noticed a couple of Masters-at-Arms ascending. It might have been coincidence but I think we had been noticed by the bridge and that the MAAs had been sent to investigate our presence there and shoo us away.

Two of the MAAs were more familiar to us than most. One was a meek-appearing and mild-voiced BM3 (Boatswain's Mate) with two or three stupidity marks; he was derided ship-wide as "Fearless Fosdick". He was frequently seen in the company of a larger CS3 (Commissaryman) who was more outspoken and domineering. We thought that the CS3 should also merit a nickname. Rinne produced it: Prick Tracy.

I managed to avoid victimization by a couple of hoaxes sometimes played on unsuspecting boots. One is the mail buoy watch, a nautical snipe hunt. The victim is told that the ship's incoming mail is left attached to a mail buoy, told that he has the watch to sight it, and left there indefinitely. The other is the sea bat, one of which has allegedly been captured on a weather deck. The curious one finds an upended box, several salts gathered innocently around it, and is told that he must get his head down on the deck for a quick peek when the box is briefly lifted. When he does, he gets a "sea bat" all right, from a broom or wooden paddle. I heard tales of junior ensigns being thus taken in and quite indignant about it.

And no one tried to send me on searches for such items as a left-handed monkey wrench, a bottle of propwash, a can of relative bearing grease, and the like. I know of only one such item that is unique to communications: a box of line feeds. They are the electromechanical function that causes a teletype to advance its printing to the next line. But I know of one seaman returning successfully from such a search – the person he had approached had sat down at a teletype and produced a long teletype tape containing repeated line feed functions. The acme of success at such endeavors is achieved when some innocent approaches a Wave officer in quest of a fallopian tube.

It got hot. And there was no air conditioning in the berthing compartments. Ventilation, yes, but the ventilators merely brought down the warm, humid air from outside. The weather decks were breezy and cooler than the compartments and many sailors hauled their mattresses topside to sleep on the deck. The first night that I attempted this ploy, I was a little too late. The decks were full, except forward of the superstructure. I took a space there – but I and a few other encroachers were rousted up by the Master-at-Arms force and ordered to move farther aft.

Officers' Country. No officers were standing there or strolling there, much less sleeping there. Dog in the manger, with gold braid. I stared up at invisible Authority on the bridge and "if looks could kill" I would have produced shrieks of anguish there. I searched again for unoccupied footage farther aft, found nothing, returned below, and slept in sweat and anger. On future southern nights, I made sure to get a spot in Radio Two or Radio Three before they were all taken. These spaces were air conditioned. The navy then would spend money to keep expensive electronic equipment from overheating, but not for the comfort of sailors.

There were shipboard movies in the evenings, on the fantail (that part of the weather deck aft of the after 16-inch turret). Officers sat on chairs, sailors sat on their blankets. We had to be in the uniform of the day (a major disincentive to attendance) and had to come to "attention on deck" if the captain's arrival was announced. Standing on the fantail with Rinne one evening, the chaplain came on the 1MC for the evening prayer. Masters-at-Arms yelled at us, "Take off your hats! Take off your hats!" I looked at Rinne. He looked at me. We took off our hats.

Gitmo was a large naval base, its bay a spacious harbor. We noticed a harbor dredge there, indistinguishable from one we often saw around Norfolk. Rinne claimed that it was the same one, that it followed *Iowa* in order to dredge the chickenshit.

There were a number of commands/activities at Gitmo; the one with which we were most involved was FLETRAGRU – Fleet Training Group. On weekdays most of the ships present would go out to sea in the morning, returning in the late afternoon. At sea, gunnery practice and various training drills were conducted, communications played little part in them. The ship was always at general quarters when the guns were fired – everyone at a prescribed station (mine, in Main Comm, became somewhat crowded) and all doors and hatches sealed shut. Typically we went to general quarters soon after breakfast, remained there until 1100, returned to GQ at 1300. *Playing war,* we sometimes called it, and looked at one another rather foolishly as we performed the ritual of rolling down our sleeves and rolling our trousers around our ankles and tucking them into our socks. Apparently the reason was to lessen the danger from burns or radiation that might occur in real combat.

When the big guns fired, we knew it. They were typically fired one three-gun turret at a time, but the last salvo of the day was usually a full nine-gun broadside and these would dislodge a sprinkle of small flakes of paint and rust from our overhead. Rumor claimed that the full broadside caused the ship to move a foot sideways in the water. This was totally false. The recoil was completely absorbed by the guns themselves; the ship did not even roll. Not even the smaller guns were fired unless the ship was at GQ. Austin once said he would swap GQ stations with me so that I could, from his upper-level radio-space GQ station, see the guns fire, but the opportunity never came before I was transferred. Sailors sometimes said that a more appropriate target for the gunnery practice would be downtown Norfolk.

Usually we engaged in a high-speed run at least once per visit, the ship shuddering for a half hour or so while the engines put forth maximum effort. The results must have been classified, we neither saw nor heard any figures. Varying claims for the top speed of the *Iowas* can be found, but it almost certainly lay between 32-35 knots.

The most interesting part of all this training was, I think, the anti-submarine exercises. *Iowa* carried an extensive paint locker, from which a mixture could be produced which would exactly match the color of the water, be it deep blue, muddied brown, clouded-over gray, whatever. When a submarine was detected, certain instruments and tables were consulted, paint was mixed into the appropriate shade, and spread over a wide area of water. The ship(s) would retreat just outside this painted area and the Sonarmen would emit noises that simulated gradually-diminishing and eventually-ceasing propeller sounds. After a while the submarine would come up to take a peek and see if things were indeed safe. When her periscope breached the surface, it would acquire a coat of paint, the same shade as the water. She could not tell that she was at the surface and would keep rising. They would wait until she got up a few hundred feet and shoot her down with the anti-aircraft guns.

(I do not think that I need to insert this paragraph, but just in case: as mentioned in the preface, the story in the preceding paragraph is the one that is *not* true.)

During the drills conducted by the FLETRAGRU a lot of "simulation" was done. Simulate this, simulate that. And one sailor, relaxing with his feet on a desk, announced that he was simulating "turn to".

Turn to was part of one of the standard announcements made over the ship's public address loudspeakers (the "1MC"). It was made at 0800 on weekdays; the full announcement was, "Now, turn to. Commence ship's work." Other such often-heard announcements:

"Knock off ship's work." At 1600. (In satirizing *Iowa* chickenshit, Rinne claimed that someone had been put on report for *not* knocking off ship's work when the word was passed.)

"Now sweepers, man your brooms. Clean sweepdown fore and aft. Sweep down all decks, ladders, and passageways. Empty all trash cans over the fantail (or: on the pier)."

"Taps. Taps. Lights out. All hands turn in to your * racks and maintain silence about the decks. The smoking lamp is out in all berthing spaces." (The grin-word *own* was sometimes inserted at the asterisk. Apparently it didn't bother Authority. The implication was that gay sailors might be in someone else's rack.)

(The *smoking lamp* is a bit of tradition, preserved in phraseology, reaching back before lighters, before matches, to days when a literal *lamp* was maintained from which sailors could light their pipes. If it is lit, smoking is permitted. It was out "throughout the ship" when fueling, taking on ammunition, or at general quarters. Lars once said, "The smoking lamp's never out in Main Comm", and we did indeed disregard it there.)

A 1MC announcement was featured in a cartoon that tickled me. I think it was in *Navy Times* in the 1960s. A little flying saucer spiraling up out of a commode, little aliens faintly visible through a glass dome.

The caption: "Now, the navigator! Lay up to the bridge! ON THE DOUBLE!!!"

Naval mythology (it always happened on some other ship, some years ago) held that a Boatswain's Mate had once announced over a 1MC, "Now all hands are advised to watch their language. There's cunt aboard." It could have been based on reality – somewhere, some time. Rinne heard and repeated to me a parody announcement: "Now hear this. All hands aft, lay forward. All hands forward, lay aft. All hands amidships, stand by to direct traffic."

During the middie cruise the 1MC was busy with announcements pertaining to the midshipmen from various colleges. I overheard one Boatswain's Mate's droning announcement directed to, "all midshipmen from . . . the University of This, the University of That, the University of Here, the University of There, the University of . . ." (puzzled pause of about ten seconds during which guidance must have been sought, then confident resumption) "the University of U-C-L-A, the University of . . ."

The question that preoccupied everyone on Gitmo visits was: will we get Gitmo city liberty? Authority did not like to grant it. Gitmo city's chief attraction was prostitutes, available at quite reasonable prices. Authority knew that Gitmo city liberty would produce a number of VD cases and also a number of disciplinary actions necessitated by other antics of drunken sailors. Authority was schizophrenic on the subject of sailors on liberty. In the more realistic portion of its mind, it knew quite well that sex and alcohol were the main objectives of most sailors, it knew quite well what complications would ensue therefrom, and it was often humorously tolerant thereof as long as no trouble developed. In another mind-compartment, it had to pretend that nearly all sailors were sober, celibate, intent on sightseeing, friendship, international goodwill, and "wholesome" recreation, and that sex-seeking boozers were an insignificant few. This was the image that it had to present to the public, especially the U.S. public, and to which it had to adhere in official documents. Authority would rather not have allowed Gitmo city liberty at all, but sailors had to get foreign liberties at least once in a while, if only not to invalidate the "join the navy and see the world" recruiting enticement.

Thus it turned out that only twice, a week apart, did we get Gitmo city liberty. Prior to boarding a ramshackle train for a 15-20 mile ride to the city, a couple of chiefs lectured us on behavior and warned of the high VD rate and the necessity of condom usage. Authority never described VD rates in liberty ports as anything less than "high", and never mentioned percentages. I would guess that the rates in most such places were well under ten percent, and most sailors would cheerfully take those odds even when sober. Sailors sometimes defined the VD rate in a specified port as "about ## dollars". I walked the city streets for a while, reflecting that for the first time in my life I was on foreign soil. I soon found my way to a bar/whorehouse where I spent the rest of that liberty, and all of the next one, in the embraces of Eloisa, a curvaceous mulatta who I'd guess was 16-17. I enjoyed Hatuey, the Cuban beer named for a bygone Indian chief who had resisted the Spanish conquest. Despite the expectorative sound of the name it was surprisingly good. In the course of my later travels I would form the opinion (there will be dissenters) that U.S.A. beer is the world's second-worst – the booby prize in that category easily going to the British isles.

Some weeks later I detected an itchiness in my groin and, after scratching, my fingers bore a smell that reminded me of the box-elder bugs of my Illinois childhood. The corpsmen said it was the worst infestation of crabs they had ever seen, and were relieved to hear that I slept in a bottom rack, thus negating the possibility of migrants installing on sailors below me. They gave me a big, brown bottle of anti-crab soap which I had to tote to each shower. I was embarrassed and didn't speak of my woe in the division, but it was impossible to conceal the bottle while in the shower and I saw knowing smirks at times, presumably from former sufferers. Two others in CR division were similarly inconvenienced and less reticent about it. Only one owned to a case of gonorrhea. If I could have done it over, I would not have let Eloisa get on top.

On the more numerous times when we did *not* get Gitmo city liberty, we were not amused by the officer who assured us that the VD rate on the base was very low.

On those base liberties, there were the usual recreational things to do. We had at least one division picnic with softball-and-beer game. I had stripped to the waist as if I were in Illinois, and the southern sun gave me blisters the size of tennis balls (or close to it – memory may be exaggerating, but not by much). Rinne talked me into going for a swim at a beach where there was surf, and tried to teach me how to dive into the oncoming wave. I wasn't much good at it and didn't enjoy it much. At one point, as I was struggling to get back to the beach, he saw the look of distress on my face, put a hand in my armpit and assisted me. I'd probably have made it anyhow – but it's just possible that you could say he saved my life.

It may have been that day or another, and I don't remember whether Rinne challenged me or I him, but we described the event as: who could drink whom under the table. The Gitmo EM club served drinks for a ridiculously short time, Authority knowing full well what grief longer opportunity would produce. Uncertain memory says it was for only two hours. Our drinks were (in Cuba, what else?) rum and coke. At fifteen minutes to closing we were tied at 15-15. At closing we were still tied, at 20-20.

Neither of us remembered all of the subsequent events. During the next day's hung-over post-mortem we stitched together a more-or-less complete chronicle partly from Rinne's memories and partly from my own. It was pretty drunk out. Headed for the fleet landing to catch a boat back to the *Iowa*, we got lost and were rounded up by the Shore Patrol in an officers' housing area. For the Shore Patrol, this was an everyday occurrence, they were not out to incarcerate peaceful drunks, merely to set them on the right course. They shepherded us to the fleet landing.

We got into a crowded, noisy *Iowa* liberty whaleboat and soon after it left the pier Rinne was misinspired. He said, "What's the matter with the spirit on this boat? I heard there was a fight on here last night!"

A first-class replied, "Yeah, and there's gonna be one tonight too." He emphasized his point by knocking Rinne down.

I said, "*Why, you dirty so-and-so!" (Rinne swore that those were my exact words. I obviously had more work to do in acquiring command of seamanlike language, my criticism of San Diego cooks and oysters notwithstanding.) I was now the next target; the dirty so-and-so had to step onto and over a low bench-seat to get at me and was consequently looming somewhat above me. I cocked my arm to deliver an upward punch at his jaw, started to punch, lost focus, drew back, recocked, punched . . . I didn't recall feeling contact, and it must have been much more of a push than a punch, but the so-and-so fell backwards over the bench. Perhaps I hit his chest with enough force to topple him, perhaps he simply lost balance without any assistance from me. Or perhaps I did strike the jaw I intended. Whatever, he got right back up, tore into the closest innocent bystanders, and a general melee ensued. I helped Rinne up and we retreated to the gunwale and stayed out of it. Rinne was drunkenly grateful for the revenge I had exacted – if indeed I deserved any credit for such.

Just prior to the middie cruise there was a lot of compartment-shuffling to make room for them, and CR was one of the unlucky divisions that had to move. This inconvenience did not exactly endear the middies to us. Their status was rather strange. They ranked below warrant officers and above chiefs, but for practical purposes they were the lowest on the ship. Both sailors and middies recognized the contradiction and there was minimal friction. We had our share of middies in communications, observing and learning what we did. They wore enlisted working uniforms with one distinctive difference: the upper half of the band on their white hats was a solid blue. After their departure a sailor-to-sailor insult was, "Hey, when did you bleach your hatband?"

At sea, during good weather, "air bedding" was performed. A 1MC announcement designated a number of divisions to air bedding that day, and when it was our turn we carried our mattresses, pillows, and blankets topside, hung them over lifelines and secured them with straps, then retrieved them in the evening. I've never known whether this practice conferred any actual health or sanitation benefit or was just another idiosyncrasy/tradition of Authority. The bedding didn't seem at all musty before we began, and the humidity of the sea air seemed hardly conducive to improving it. I don't recall this being done on future ships, but that could be due to faulty memory.

Another evolution that affected CR division (and perhaps some others) was burn runs. In every comm center, ship or shore, *all* paper waste, classified or not, was placed in burn bags – brown grocery-store-type bags, maybe a yard tall and sized to fit in a wastebasket. When full, they were stapled shut and stored in comm spaces. When enough had accumulated, a burn run was scheduled and the division PPO rounded up enough off-watch sailors to haul them up to the ship's incinerator. It was an easy job and didn't take too long.

The laundry was another minor chore. Dirty clothes were placed in mattress covers and the compartment cleaners hauled them to the laundry weekly and hauled them back when done; the clean items were then identified by the names stenciled thereon and tossed on the racks of their owners. After my boot-camp-stenciled items had faded or worn out, I never stenciled my name where it was supposed to be, above the dungaree shirt pocket or above the trousers rear pocket. I didn't like to be that readily identifiable to Masters-at-Arms or 20-year men, and put my name on an invisible shirttail or the inside of the trousers. It must not have bothered Authority; I was never reproved for it. All of an individual's socks were tied together with a clothes stop, to make the sorting easier. I had a pair of non-regulation silk black socks which I had received as a present. I liked them and wore them on liberty. One day I found that my bundle had been untied, that pair removed by a thief, and the clothes stop thoughtfully retied.

Occasional annoyances were "quarters for entering (or leaving) port" and its close relative, "manning the rail". The former required us to stand in ranks at our prescribed quarters location for about half an hour as the ship neared land. Oddly, we secured from it *before* we actually tied up or dropped anchor. I never understood this, but I never complained about the early release. Manning the rail was somewhat more ceremonial, for special occasions, and spaced sailors were at the lifelines all around the main deck and various upper decks.

Holystoning was a shipboard chore that I often witnessed and was grateful that it did not affect CR division. It was performed by deck-division seamen, usually barefoot and with pants legs rolled up. The brick-like holystones (sandstone?) are said to have received their name from being about the size and shape of a bible. A wooden handle fitted into a socket on the stone, water and soap were liberally lathered on the deck, and a row of seamen worked their stones from side to side, scrubbing the teak planking to a clean white.

Water hours were often a nuisance at sea. A few days after leaving port, the exec would speak on the 1MC, say that fresh water was getting low, usage was too high, the ship's capacity could not keep up, and that water hours would have to be imposed if the crew did not reduce its water usage. Usually he would repeat the same message over the next two or three days, his warnings a bit more dire each time and, usually, water hours would follow. Drinking and washing water would then be available only in the mornings and evenings and noon hour. There was no shortage of sailors insisting that they could make all the water they wanted, it just cost money they didn't want to spend. A "guy in the engineering department" was often cited as the source for this revelation. I never learned the truth of the matter. On the one hand I would not at all put it past Authority to dissemble about it. On the other hand contrary rumors would be inevitable even if all of the 1MC exhortations were impeccably factual.

Our first port of call on the middie cruise was Edinburgh, Scotland. We anchored near the famous Firth of Forth railroad bridge, an impressive structure far higher than the ship, familiar to me from childhood reading. It was pea coat weather in July. The pea coats served an unintended purpose and received a supplemental name: makeout mattresses. Downtown Edinburgh was centered around the Princes Street Gardens, a long park which contained a Sir Walter Scott Monument climbable for a small fee. A piece of paper still in my possession certifies that I climbed the 287 steps to the top of the 200-foot monument on 29 July 1953. The Gardens also contained girls. Many girls. Friendly girls. Girls quite amenable to forming friendships with American sailors and strolling in the park for that very purpose. In the evenings action shifted to the Palais Ballroom. Its feminine contents were identical.

The thing to buy was a 400-day clock, German made, in a glass bell jar. A vendor had a concession to come on the ship and proffered them, boxed up and ready to mail home. Many of us bought them and did so. When the Illinois family died off in the 1990s I reacquired mine and it sits in my living room today.

Always interested in sampling new foods, I wanted to try Scotland's haggis. Surprisingly, it was hard to find, but I finally found a restaurant that had it on the menu. It was disappointing and rather tasteless. Scottish cooking is no improvement over English cooking. We had "Cinderella liberty" – back by midnight – here and on all overseas liberties. On the busses going out to the distant fleet landing were not only sailors but also a goodly number of girls, some accompanying their lover of the day, some who lived out that way. They sang on the busses; I remember those girl-voices on the traditional Scot oldies: *Loch Lomond* and *Roaming in the Gloaming.*

One evening Rinne and I wandered away from usual sailor pathways and found ourselves in a pub. The patrons, most of them at least, were friendly, bought us drinks, and sang Scottish songs for us. On a head break, a couple of younger Scots accosted us and told us (politely enough, I must admit) that it was a neighborhood place and that contrary to appearances we were not *really* all that welcome therein. We thanked them for the advice and eased out. Afterward we wondered if perhaps they were anti-Yank with an agenda of their own.

Back on the ship, one of the comic lines heard was, "I thought that being in Scotland, I should use the head for *Laddies*. Came to find out they spell it with *two* d's." And the division gay reported embarrassment from using the phrase, "Let's face it, she's an idiot." He said *let's face it* was an invitation to 69 in local slang. (He presented this as having occurred in a heterosexual context. Though obviously gay, he dared not venture *too* far out of the closet.)

Our next stop was Oslo, Norway. After having left one of the world's outstanding liberty ports, we eagerly anticipated more of the same in Oslo. On the way up Oslofjord, it was rumored that the signal bridge was spotting topless bathers on the beaches through binoculars. But then, what a letdown! The Norwegians weren't exactly *un*friendly, but they certainly were not very friendly. The girls were unimpressed by American sailors. And a few of the swankiest places in town – restaurants, night clubs, hotels – did not admit enlisted men in uniform. (Some months later in Norfolk, Rinne and I met a couple of Norwegian sailors in a bar and drank with them a while. We voiced our displeasure at having been barred from such places. The Norwegians didn't exactly apologize; their response was that yes, they knew, and it pissed them off too.) On the positive side I remember an excellent meal – rump steak – and I went on a tour that took in a sculpture garden and a museum where Thor Heyerdahl's *Kon-Tiki* raft was on display. We headed back across the Atlantic cursing all things Norwegian.

I spent much time in Main Comm, even when off watch. The ship had a small library, and a tiny crew's lounge, but there was not really anything to do there but sit. Basically we could spend our free time on the weather decks (when weather permitted), in our racks, or in our working spaces. I worked on some correspondence courses. (Radio Three was the best place for study.) A course on the Teleman rating was required before I could take the examination for third-class Teleman. It was simple, multiple-choice, and I already knew over 90% of it from school; the requirement accomplished little except to provide employment for sand crabs back in the U.S. who graded my papers. With that out of the way, I completed a USAFI (U.S. Armed

Forces Institute) course on second-semester Spanish and began courses on Basic Psychology and Analytic Geometry. These were college-level courses administered by and graded at, I was pleased to learn, the University of Wisconsin.

Main Comm gatherings often took the form of bull sessions. I remember when one of the division's farm boys was being taunted with charges of on-the-farm bestiality and was testifying in his own defense: ". . . you lying bastards! I never fucked a sheep in my life!" Someone said, "*How about a cow?" The accused started to say something, couldn't get it out. He hung his head and turned as bright a red as I have ever seen.

At another session a 20-year man was present. I've no idea how the discussion led up to it, but somehow the Adriatic Sea arose. The 20-year man declared authoritatively that it was up north between Iceland and Greenland. Rinne and I exchanged silent grins at the confirmation of our opinions about the intelligence of 20-year men. Rinne later drew a 20-year man's world map, using the mislocated Adriatic as its starting point. I can't remember any of its other details; I wish it had survived. It would almost have been worthy of *Mad* magazine.

This was the time when Herman Wouk's *The Caine Mutiny* appeared in paperback. I think that every enlisted sailor who read books at all absorbed it with delight. I am sure nearly every officer read it, some perhaps with less delight. LT Thomas Keefer's words

The Navy is a master plan designed by geniuses for execution by idiots. If you're not an idiot, but find yourself in the Navy, you can only operate well by pretending to be one.

were greeted with amens, quoted, requoted, often misquoted. When the movie was made, and the navy forced the modification of the phrase to ***This ship*** *was designed by geniuses to be run by idiots* as the price of its cooperation, we chortled and snorted over Authority's sensitivity to criticism and concern for its image. However I was squelched one day at my next duty station when I invoked "designed by geniuses to be run by idiots" anent some new work procedure that I deemed pointless. My supervisor said, "Yeah, and *you're* running it – get busy!"

Captain Queeg's penchant for rolling steel balls in his hand at times of stress also drew comment. Anyone exercising authority was vulnerable to allusions to steel balls, to his face when we were merely joking, out of his hearing when we were not or when he outranked us. I have to admit that when I first read the book I was so entranced by the anti-authority, navy-bashing portions that I completely missed deeper themes. I thought LT Keefer a hero and thought it rather strange that Barney Greenwald would throw a drink in his face. After seeing the movie and a re-reading or two I finally got the point.

Authority's attitude toward beards was then quite different from what it would become in the 1960s, and sailors' attitudes were also different. Anyone could grow a beard, provided he first submitted a "special request chit", which would – at that time – routinely be approved. The theoretical reason for the chits was so that a delinquent shaver could not escape censure by falsely claiming to have just begun a beard. A few sailors experimented with beards, but beards were not yet "in"; none kept them for long. I was nevertheless offended by the idea that Authority could grant, or withhold, permission for such a personal choice. I filled out a chit, not because I had any intention of growing a beard, but because I wanted the chit for a souvenir of a sort – to remind me of Authority's ways in case I ever had any thought of reenlisting. I saw wording on other sailors' chits: "Request permission to grow a beard. I will keep it neatly trimmed." I wasn't going to be obsequious about it; I omitted the second sentence.

At some point some of the veterans got together and wanted me to run a slush fund. I didn't know that they were illegal, and the division's chief Teleman was one of those who approached me, so I readily agreed. The slush fund worked like this: anyone who wished could become a member by buying shares in it, at $5 {$37} a share, to a maximum of five shares. Then any member who wished could borrow from the fund, to a maximum of $25 {$183}. Repayment was on payday at very high interest. It may have been 50% or 100%, I forget. There were enough who were chronically broke enough soon enough to provide a brisk business. I kept the books and kept the money, had bought a full five shares, and never borrowed. After a few months the fund was liquidated by general agreement. A couple sailors had transferred owing the full $25 and there may have been a few owing lesser amounts, but I and others who had shares turned a handsome profit even so. (Better than doubled my money, I believe.) I think our officers knew about the fund and winked at it. In any case there was never any trouble over it.

There was a pizzeria on East Main Street which, despite its location and its rather drab and dingy decor, served pizzas which are still near the top of my all-time favorite list. My choice was *pizza alla marinara* which featured, more than any other ingredient, garlic. And, unlike any other garlic I have encountered, it stayed on the breath all night and well into the following day. The smell pervaded any compartment where I remained for long, and many a time CR division awoke at reveille to groans, oh-shits, and not-agains. Spider once threatened to piss in my mouth the next time I did it. Critics compared the smell to burnt rubber.

Looking for reading matter in an East Main Street newsstand, I noticed a magazine I'd never seen before. The cover claimed that it contained Marilyn Monroe's nude calendar picture. Skeptical, I opened it up and yes – nipples! Wow! The first time I had seen such exposure openly available for purchase on a newsstand! It was the first issue of *Playboy*. I bought it, kept my eyes peeled in the future, bought the second and third issues and then took a three-year subscription when they opened to "charter subscribers". After about a year, though, the nipples disappeared. Their absence was because *Playboy* was seeking second-class mailing privileges and was having a hard time getting them from the puritanical Post Office. They couldn't explain this openly and I had no way to know; I concluded "fool me once, shame on you" and let my subscription expire. There was about a seven-year gap before I again bought a *Playboy*.

In early September COMBATDIV TWO shifted his flag to another battleship in order to allow COMSECONDFLT to board the *Iowa*.

COMSECONDFLT would be the big honcho for the forthcoming NATO exercise in the North Atlantic. This flag was a bigger one, with more flag communicators invading our space and much more message traffic. We soon regretted the change. With a variety of accompanying U.S. ships, we joined the warships of other NATO countries, of which I remember only *HMS Vanguard*, Britain's only remaining battleship. The exercise took us north between Iceland and Greenland, and above the arctic circle. It was cold. I did not venture onto a weather deck during the exercise, and never set eyes on another ship. Our compartment was colder than customary, but not intolerably so, and I was comfortable enough under my navy blankets. It was also rough, and the ship rolled more than we had yet experienced. We heard a rumor that our maximum roll during one nasty spell had been 26 degrees. This was one of the rare times that a rumor was spot on; I read confirmation of that figure in reference books decades later. *Vanguard* had fared better, rolling only 15 degrees in the same seas. The rolling caused some heavy spare equipment to slide off shelving in Radio Three. Had anyone been sleeping on the deck below, as we did in the Caribbean, they would have been killed or seriously injured.

The exercise completed, we headed for Portsmouth, England. We had already heard that it was "England's Norfolk", so our expectations were not high. The description was accurate, still, it was not nearly as bad as America's Norfolk. On the street with a CR-division group, an Englishman walked rapidly past me and said to himself (but plainly intending to be overheard), "I'm glad I'm a commie." Girls on the streets were amused but uncooperative when we told them we were looking for Girl Guides (an English organization similar to Girl Scouts). By evening we repaired to a large dance hall and laughed about a prominent sign which hung over the corridor to the rest rooms: *Beware of Pickpockets.* Ha-ha, look at that sign, never see anything like that in the States! Late in the evening, despairing of making any feminine connections, I was at the bar drinking straight gin. Spider had preceded me at that pursuit and was well ahead of me. When it became time to return to the ship I was still functional, but Spider was a-stagger. We took careful charge of him, took his wallet to avoid loss, and shepherded him back to the liberty boat and to the ship. We presented his ID and liberty cards to the JOOD for him.

Guess who just then found he did *not* have a wallet, nor ID and liberty cards to present? Funny sign, indeed! Since that incident I have never again carried my wallet in a rear pocket, but in a side pocket. I developed a further security measure: a habit of flicking a wallet-corner with my thumb as my arms swung while walking.

We sailed next to Copenhagen, Denmark. I remember little there. Drinking in a bar with half a dozen other CR-division sailors and a couple of girls, quite attractive. They claimed to be models, asked for and got U.S. dollar bills "for souvenirs", left promising to return, and didn't. I sampled Denmark's over-ballyhooed cherry heering, a syrupy concoction more akin to cough medicine than to a beverage. It may have been here or earlier that I first observed "mandatory quotas". Well-intentioned local functionaries would devise tours or other entertainments for the visiting crew. Authority knew that most sailors would have other priorities, and imposed quotas on each division in order not to appear ungrateful and disappoint the tour-arrangers with low turnout. You would think that anything *mandatory* would be levied on the duty section rather than the liberty section. You would be wrong. CR division was only hit for one or two, but the individuals affected were not at all happy about it.

From Copenhagen we went to Lisbon, Portugal. I remember even less of Lisbon; a third-rate brothel with indifferent damsels. I must have wandered the wrong portions of that city; other sailors were more praiseful. After leaving, the rumor circulated: that "some guy" in (whatever) division was being treated in sick bay for a chancre on his lip.

The equivalent post-Copenhagen rumor had been that another "some guy" had taken a Danish girl to a hotel room, placed his hand between "her" legs, and discovered anatomy that he was not expecting.

I had learned fairly early that sick bay was worthless unless you were sicker than sick. It was preached everywhere that the best thing for colds and flus was bed rest. The navy did not agree. When a sailor went to sick bay with cold or flu, he might get a light-duty or no-duty chit – if he was sick *enough*. My colds/flus made me miserable and desirous of recumbency, but they did not raise my temperature enough to rate such consideration. What lesser sufferers got was APCs (All-Purpose Capsules – containing aspirin, phenacetin, and caffeine) and normal duty – after a prolonged wait standing in sick-call line. Authority feared malingering and set the standards of proof far too high.

After COMSECONDFLT debarked, we hosted no more flags for the rest of my stay on *Iowa*. In August I had taken the navy-wide examination for TE3, and was promoted to third-class Teleman in November. At some point I was moved away from the writeup job and spent some time in the teletype room tuning in the fleet broadcasts and copying them. The broadcasts came over high-frequency (HF) short wave, which was subject to static, fading in and out, and consequent garbling, even though the broadcast came simultaneously over a dozen or more different frequencies. Reception problems were imperfectly countered by a three-tier piece of equipment called a converter-comparator. One receiver was patched into the top converter which showed a flickering, green display, supplementing earphone sound with a visual tool to judge the quality of the signal. Another receiver, on a different frequency, was patched into an identical bottom converter. The comparator, in the center tier, then took the best-behaving frequency of the two at a given instant and passed it along to the printer. If I had enough spare equipment I could copy two more frequencies on another printer, further reducing the chance for indecipherable garbles. Sometimes things would go smoothly and the broadcast would come in perfectly for hours on end, but sooner or later one frequency, or both, would begin to fade or take static hits. I would have to search for other frequencies to which to switch, and sometimes messages would be missed completely or be garbled beyond reconstruction, and we would have to service for a repetition.

Although Rinne was no longer on the *Iowa*, we often got together on Norfolk liberties. Rinne's resentment of the officer-enlisted caste system took drunken but concrete form after some of our drinking sessions. As he reported it to me, he went back to whatever battleship the flag was then on and snuck into officer's country – their stateroom area. In the passageways there he unscrewed every light bulb, including even the red light within a Coca-Cola machine, and disposed of them, leaving the passageway in total darkness. He did this at least twice, and told me that as a result he had observed a night sentry posted in the area of his depredations.

I think the phenomenon known as *the phantom shitter* has similar motivations. I only heard stories, was never on a ship where one was operative, but I believe such stories are mostly true. The phantom leaves his deposits in places most apt to displease Authority, e.g. outside the door of the captain's cabin, or a door to the wardroom. I never heard of a phantom being caught.

I thought Rinne's forays were foolishly reckless. I didn't have that much bravado drunk or sober. But I empathized. On my one brief visit to *Iowa's* wardroom as a messenger I had noticed displays of athletic trophies – trophies surely won by predominantly *enlisted* athletes but viewable only by officers. I think the wardroom contained other items of interest from the ship's history. Civilian guests could examine these things when the ship was open to visitors. Enlisted men never could.

We went aboard the *USS Des Moines (CA-134)*, a heavy cruiser, looking for a Teleman school classmate, good old Harry, a skinny, likeable, red-haired Oklahoman. We found that Harry had gotten a discharge already. This didn't mean anything to us, it could have been medical or whatever. There, or by some other means, we learned that he was living in suburban Washington DC and working for the government. Washington was reputed a good liberty town. Harry would surely be able to connect us to something in skirts. The next time Rinne and I both had weekend liberty we Greyhounded thence.

Harry was sharing an apartment with another young man, Ray. They had a well-supplied liquor locker. Our objective was not being met, and we inquired again. Harry waved a dismissive hand, ". . . oh, yes, we know lots of girls." By bedtime all four of us were pretty drunk. It was arranged that I was to sleep in a double bed with Harry, Rinne with Ray. No physical contact took place in the beds. The next day we were all nursing hangovers. A couple of male visitors showed up but the conversation seemed tentative and guarded. We met the apartment landlady, a spunky woman who expressed misgivings about the visitors but seemed to have no qualms about Harry and Ray. We took our hangovers back to Norfolk.

The next time I saw Rinne, a week or two later, we compared notes. I had received a warm, friendly, innocuous letter from Harry inviting us to come again. Rinne had received a similar letter from Ray. I looked at Rinne. Rinne looked at me. We had finally figured it out.

In late October I took a couple weeks leave to Illinois/Wisconsin and was gratified when Wisconsin defeated Illinois soundly. (It was Alan Ameche's heyday.) I cut my connections a little too closely and didn't nurse my money quite carefully enough, and when I returned to Norfolk I found that I lacked enough money to pay full cab fare to the naval base. The cab driver was sympathetic but not *that* sympathetic, he cruised until he found another fare heading to the same place. *Iowa* was anchored out. I got to fleet landing at 2345 (my leave expired at midnight), just in time to see *Iowa's* liberty boat about a hundred feet away on its return to the ship. It didn't make another run for two or three hours and thus I was absent over leave.

I had to go to executive officer's mast for this crime. This was a preliminary to captain's mast; the exec screened offenders, dismissed some, referred others to the captain. It was said to help if a superior from your division went along and praised you. Austin offered to go with me. Without going into a lot of detail I explained how I came to be late, Austin said some good words about me, and the exec dismissed me with a warning.

I had brought a few civilian clothes back to Norfolk with me, and I rented a locker in a locker club. These establishments were found wherever ships homeported. Single sailors would keep civvies there and go to change into them when they went on liberty. Norfolk being Norfolk, it didn't really accomplish a great deal, but I felt a bit less subhuman in the civvies.

The Korean War had ended in a truce in late July. In late 1953 or early 1954 we learned that *Iowa's* far east deployment was cancelled. The battleships were no longer needed there. Reaction to the news was mixed. Some had looked forward to the cruise, others would just as soon skip it. My own feelings were mixed. I wouldn't mourn the long times at sea, but I had entertained visions of far-east liberty. A Teleman-school classmate had written me from an aircraft carrier in the far east, rubbing it in about Norfolk and extolling the pleasures of the Orient. As proof he had taped a swatch of black hair to the bottom of his letter and labeled it "hair off a Japanese pussy".

But what now? I looked forward to a dismal vista of Norfolk and Gitmo, only relieved by occasional middie cruises and the like. Not even Med (Mediterranean) cruises. Battleships were banned from the Med by international treaty, so CR-division wisdom held. (But there was no such treaty, it was only navy policy and priorities at the time that kept them out of the Med. *Iowa* did make a Med cruise in 1955.)

Things got worse on the *Iowa*. Weekend after weekend, a personnel inspection was scheduled for Saturday. Then a half-hour or less before inspection time, the 1MC would announce that the inspection was cancelled. This would provoke roars of rage below decks. Although we were glad to avoid going up on deck to stand and stand until the critical eye of the inspecting officer reached us, we were convinced that the aborted inspections were a ruse used because "the exec doesn't want to give 72s". (The time from 1600 Friday until 0800 Monday, really only 64 hours, is always called a "72".) One who did not have the duty on the three weekend days could be gone for that length of time – *unless* there was a personnel inspection, in which case he had to be present for it.

And one Ensign Slenker arrived in CR division. Worse, he was made the division officer. It is odd that I can recall hardly any specific incidents to justify my dislike of Slenker, which arose the first time he appeared in the comm spaces. But I was not alone, no one else liked him either. He was a regular Doctor Fell.

Note to junior officers: if you want to know how you stand with enlisted men, try to eavesdrop some time when no officers are present and you are under discussion. If they respect you, they will refer to you as "*Mr* Bianchi" even in your absence. If they do not, they will omit the Mr and use your last name only, with a greater or lesser touch of contempt according to the depth of their dislike. (Both the use of Mr and its omission occur subconsciously.) I have adhered to that practice in this book. Exception: if you have acquired a nickname, whether uncomplimentary or favorable, it will be used.

A second note to junior officers: when you have complaints about your living conditions or your treatment by superiors, and you *will* have them, do not voice them within earshot of enlisted. Their living conditions, and often their treatment, are so much worse than yours that they will have no sympathy and will regard you as a whiner. Slenker had a five-o'clock-shadow problem and I remember hearing him gripe to a sailor about how the exec had castigated him for not shaving.

I had been acquiring some collateral duties, and when their number got up to three I was taken off watches to devote full time to them. On paper I was also assigned as "day writeup man" but I ignored this and pretty much went wherever I pleased whenever I pleased. The collaterals were (1) files – filing the new messages, keeping the files in order, disposing of older ones when the time came; (2) Class Easy clerk – keeping tabs on the money and paperwork when a sailor sent a telegram back home, and (3) division supply petty officer – ordering, picking up, stowing, etc.

We pulled a New York City visit at some point. It may have been for Veterans Day (then still Armistice Day). We tied up at a West Side pier. I caught shore patrol duty and two of us patrolled a street from the pier up to a main thoroughfare, without incident. I remember rats and garbage on the street, and a police station with stereotypical Irish cops, where we took coffee breaks and got out of the cold.

On Thanksgiving, Soares and another CR-division sailor went to the mess decks to eat an early Thanksgiving dinner. Soares had just arisen, had a major hangover, and was in a foul humor. He didn't even notice the presence of enlisted wives and families who were aboard for the meal. He glared across the table at the other sailor and observed, "You're an ugly fuck."
"What's that, Soares, I didn't hear you?"
"I said you're an ugly fuck."
"What's that, I still can't quite hear you?"
"I SAID YOU'RE AN UGLY FUCK!!!"
That part of the mess deck got quiet for a little while.

Mr Hewitt was assigned to conduct a zone inspection and asked if I'd like to accompany him as his "yeoman". Each inspector needed a clipboard-carrier to accompany him in order to record any discrepancies or notes the inspector wished to record. It was interesting, part of his assigned zone was down in the ship's vast machinery spaces where I had never penetrated.

I heard a story about a zone inspection. A story that probably isn't true, but a story so good that, if it isn't true, it ought to be. This is how it goes . . . A pompous, chickenshit, and thoroughly unpopular junior officer was assigned as inspector. Knowing who was coming, the sailors in a certain head prepared for him. They gave their head the cleaning of cleanings, got it shiny and spotless beyond criticism. From the galley they obtained a gob of peanut butter, which they affixed partway up the immaculate metal inside of one commode. Calculating the inspector's probable course, they chose a commode that was likely to be near the end of his circuit. The plan worked to perfection. By the time the inspector neared the end, he was getting a bit frustrated at finding nothing to gig. He spotted the doctored commode and demanded, "**What** is this!!!"

The man in charge of the space leaned to look. "Why . . . it looks like shit, sir." He dipped a finger and brought it near his nose. "Smells like shit." He put the finger in his mouth and rolled his tongue judiciously. "Tastes like shit too. I believe it's shit, sir."

I forget whatever description I heard of the officer's reaction. You will have to imagine your own.

Oley got in trouble again and was given brig time again, on bread and water ("piss and punk"). The marines ran the brig. A marine escorted Oley on a head visit, to wash up, brush teeth, shave, etc. Somehow Oley disappeared when the marine's back was turned. Somehow, he got rid of his prisoner clothing, somehow he got off the ship before the alarm was raised, and somehow he got completely off the base. It was quite a feat. We never saw Oley again, but we heard that he was apprehended by civilian police somewhere to the south (Georgia?) and returned to naval custody. Time in a naval prison followed by a less-than-honorable discharge is a reasonable assumption.

With the far east cruise cancelled, I speculated with Rinne about getting transferred to the flag with him. The flag RM1 knew I was a good worker and he would be favorably inclined. I don't know in what way I thought I'd have been better off, I suppose I was just restless and suffering from an "anything's better than this" feeling. But the personnel office of COMBATCRULANT (Commander, Battleships and Cruisers, Atlantic) took a hand in my future before we took any steps toward this.

The *Iowa* had been puffed up to nearly full complement in preparation for deployment. But now she wasn't going anywhere, and other ships were. COMBATCRULANT commanded us to transfer an assortment of ratings, including five or ten Radiomen and Telemen, to other ships. Volunteers were supposed to get first pick of the destinations available. I did not volunteer at first. But Austin came to me asking me to volunteer in order to save a TE3 from the post office from being designated. The latter had fallen in love in Scotland and was fighting the red-tape battle to get permission to marry a foreigner. Transfer would have caused him a major setback in this endeavor. I already knew this and had been thinking about possibly volunteering, to rescue him; Austin's approach wiped away my indecision.

I was now a volunteer, I ought to get to choose a ship in Boston vice Norfolk, or so I thought. But Slenker, possibly miffed by my last-minute decision to decamp, thought otherwise. I found myself slated for the *USS Macon (CA-132)*, homeported Norfolk. The morning that I learned of this, I went to appeal to the new operations officer, a commander. The matter was complex and I was not in the best condition to argue my case; I was hung over and reeking of garlic. The ops officer heard me out and chewed me out (correctly, and not as severely as he should have) for not following the chain of command, i.e. not informing Slenker that I would come to see ops. He promised to look into it, but he advised me that the ship, and not myself, would decide where I went. I was not at all surprised when Slenker was upheld and I remained pointed at *Macon*.

I did get one small, trivial bit of satisfaction from my effort. The guys told me that when Slenker was phoned to go see ops about my transfer, he exited Main Comm saying, "God damn that fucking Bucher!"

At this writing the ex-*Iowa* rests in Suisun Bay, an arm off northern San Francisco Bay, in a "reserve fleet" with other hulks awaiting disposition. It is not exactly a ship graveyard, more like a ship mortuary. It appears probable, but not yet certain, that *Iowa* will become a museum ship berthed at nearby Vallejo. Her three sisters are already museum ships at Pearl Harbor, Norfolk, and Camden, New Jersey.

V - TWO TRANSFERS

From the *Iowa* it was a short walk down two or three piers to the *Macon*. She was a late-war heavy cruiser, commissioned a couple weeks after the Japanese surrender, nine eight-inch guns. She was preparing for a midshipman cruise that coming summer. I had been aboard her only two weeks when I learned that I would be transferred again in two more weeks – as a result of my own request.

Any enlisted man could request overseas shore duty, the only limitation was that he had to have been on board his current ship at least six months before so requesting. Six months, *to the day*, after reporting aboard *Iowa* I had submitted my request. I had just about forsaken hope of anything developing from it, because one had to have two years remaining in order to accept overseas orders. (There was the option of signing an agreement to extend or reenlist, if the two years were lacking, but I would never have done that.) That two-year point was fast approaching. Three choices were allowed; I had chosen London (widely, and correctly, regarded as enlisted men's heaven), LaPallice (a very small activity in southwest France, near Bordeaux), and my third choice was Anywhere Overseas.

I got my third choice. And, indeed, it might well have been number three on my list if more than three choices had been permitted. It was Naples, Italy, and it was far preferable to many of the places that might have materialized from "anywhere". Sailors sometimes pronounced it as *Nipples*.

Shortly after learning of the assignment, I happened to reflect that by coincidence I had not yet heard or read the name of the *Macon's* commanding officer. I resolved, secretly, to avoid remedying that ignorance, if I could. This was partly a trivial anti-authority gesture – it is a grievous naval sin not to know the name of one's captain! – but mostly it was to provide fuel for future bull sessions: "I was on one ship where I never even knew who the captain was!" I succeeded, and I do not know today who commanded the *Macon* during my short stay.

In preparation for the arrival of the middies, some of *Macon's* enlisted, including CR division, were subjected to the same compartment-shuffling that had happened on *Iowa*. We had to vacate ours and move elsewhere just two days before I was due to leave the ship. In view of my imminent departure, I requested permission to stay where I was for those two days. I received the permission. I had made a mistake.

I intended to take a couple weeks leave before heading overseas, to say goodbyes in Illinois and Wisconsin. On the day of my departure, for some forgotten reason, I returned to the compartment during noon hour and for some equally-forgotten reason I took out my wallet and left it in my locker. I only half-noticed two or three sailors taking siesta on the now-empty racks – deck division sailors assigned to clean up in preparation for the middies. I returned to the compartment in the late afternoon and right away, oh-shit, I saw that my locker did not appear to be fully closed. It had been crowbarred open and my wallet emptied of slightly over $200 {$1456} – my going-on-leave money. I went to the radio shack and reported the crime; one of the junior officers loaned me $10 {$73}, enough to get to Western Union and beg Illinois for help. As my plane took off from Norfolk, I silently voiced my sentiments: "Goodbye, Shit City, and may we never meet again."

The thief was caught; the case was cracked fairly easily. The deck-division men working in the space were known; it took only a few questions about who might have been broke but had suddenly become prosperous enough to head off on weekend liberty. About $100 {$728} was recovered and sent to me in Naples. At his court-martial the supposedly-contrite thief promised to repay the remainder but no one followed up to make sure that he did, so of course it never happened. He was given some brig time and an undesirable discharge. I learned about all this later, in Naples.

Following leave, I reported to the Naval Receiving Station in Brooklyn, adjacent to the Brooklyn Navy Yard. It was an eight-story, red-brick building with barracks spaces on the top two or three floors. On one of the lower floors was a large waiting area with rows of benches, enclosed on three sides with the service counters or glassed-off cubicles of assorted offices. I spent much of my time therein, just reading and hoping for news of my onward transportation to appear on one of the many bulletin boards. The intermediate floors (decks, of course) contained chow hall, sick bay, and the similar necessary functions.

Never needing to go outside the building, unless to go on liberty, I could leave my hat parked in my locker all day? And would never need to salute? No. Authority had thought of that. Wearing the hat was required in all passageways (corridors) and on all ladders (staircases). I remembered those Union Station MPs. Another disconnect with the more usual definitions of *indoors* and *outdoors*.

While marking time at the RecSta I took in at least one baseball game at the Brooklyn Dodgers' old Ebbets Field. My Cardinals got men on first and second, and I overheard a man in front of me remark to his teen-age son, "A hit means a run."

The boy corrected him: "It means two runs – Musial's up next." (Stan Musial was known for hitting even better against the Dodgers, and in Ebbets Field, than he did against other teams and in other parks.)

It was at the RecSta that, for the second and last time, I observed a "screamer". He was a balding, portly Lieutenant Commander who inhabited one of the glassed-off offices adjacent to the waiting area. Fortunately, I had no occasion to enter his sanctum. Once or twice a day his roars at some unfortunate who had dared to approach him resounded throughout the waiting area from his open door. I remember in particular a chief, visible at rigid attention, enduring a tirade. The sight was disgusting.

After a week or two . . . or three? . . . I was listed for, and embarked on, a troop transport. The accommodations were even more austere than on the *Iowa* or the *Macon* – canvas racks, five high, no lockers. This was understandable – the ship's original purpose was to short-haul invasion troops, rarely for more than a month, rather than to serve as a semi-permanent home for them. But being understandable didn't make it any more pleasant. Air force and, especially, army enlisted far outnumbered the few transient sailors. By and large we had "nowhere to go and nothing to do". Officers, and enlisted men accompanied by their families, rated staterooms and fared far better. I have no idea what facilities and amenities they enjoyed; a rigid segregation kept them out of our eyesight and vice-versa.

During the 10-14 day Atlantic crossing I spent much of my time speeding through a book equivalent to first- and second-semester Italian, working out all the exercises. On the day I arrived in Naples, I probably spoke and read Italian better than at any subsequent point, from a grammatical standpoint at least. (Working with and living with other Americans was not conducive to further improvement, but my vocabulary and comprehension no doubt increased somewhat.) I did most of my studying on those portions of the weather decks that were not forbidden to us.

Our first landfall was Casablanca, in what was then still French Morocco. We were permitted a few hours ashore on a tour of sorts. An Arab peddler showed me a rather large, impressive-looking watch, with dial showing many fancy extras, phases of the moon etc. He began at $25 {$182}; I bought it for $10 {$73}; sailors to whom I showed it in Naples said it was worth about $2 {$15}. It tarnished rapidly, and I could never get it to do anything but keep time. That was probably all that it could do – and in any event the peddler had neglected to include an instruction manual. However it did keep the time well enough for a couple of years; I replaced it more because I wanted something that looked better rather than a need for something that worked better.

We transited the strait of Gibraltar during the night, thus depriving the ship's crew of the opportunity of playing the common hoax over the loudspeaker: "Now the ship is passing the Rock of Gibraltar. All hands who have not made the passage before are invited to lay topside and view the Prudential sign."

Our next stop was Livorno (Leghorn) in northern Italy. Again we were allowed a few hours ashore for a tour, which took us to the famed Leaning Tower in nearby Pisa. Concerns about its stability had not yet arisen, and we were permitted to climb the interior circular stairway to the top. That climb was a strange experience. The tower was windowless, without anything to orient oneself except the interior – which *to the eye* appeared plumb vertical. Thus, because of the lean, the sensation was that gravity alternated from light-as-a-feather to exceptionally heavy. I floated up for a dozen steps then trudged up the next dozen with much greater effort.

One more day. Naples was next.

VI - IN NAPOLI . . .

Naples is a lovely city when seen from the sea. Or from any other distant vantage point, for that matter. It's not so bad close up either, although it certainly is *different*, especially to someone with no more experience of foreign lands than the port visits I related in the last two chapters. Vesuvius, in the hazy distance off to the right, is the first thing one notices. Closer up, medieval forts and castles on the waterfront and on hilltops stand out. *Vedi Napoli e poi mori* – see Naples and then die – is an oft-quoted remark about the city, although no one seems to know just where or when it originated. The important word is *poi* (then); the message is that Naples is the one place everyone should see in their lifetime and, once you have seen it, anything else you might have missed is of lesser import – you can die knowing that you have viewed the one most essential place of all. While if you haven't seen Naples yet, you should arrange to postpone death until you do.

On my first day in Naples I was disappointed to learn that the barracks was full, and that until a place opened I would live on a ship. The ship was *USS Benewah (APB-35)*, a barracks ship tied up near the shoreward end of a long pier, the *Molo Angioino* (= Anjouan Mole, from when Naples was under the suzerainty of the kingdom of Anjou). She rarely went to sea and served as a sort of receiving station, accommodating sailors who were in transit to ships or places around the Med, and was also the flagship for COMFAIRMED (COMmander Fleet AIR MEDiterranean). *Benewah* was named for a county in Idaho – which raises the question whence did the county acquire its name? Answer: a Coeur d'Alene Indian chief.

At liberty call I headed out the dock-area gate and was taken in tow by a self-appointed, money-hustling guide. (I seldom have any truck with that sort; this was an exception.) He steered me to bars, a restaurant, and before long a whorehouse. I bought the services of an enthusiastic young redhead who provided unimpeachable confirmation of an opinion I already held: I was going to enjoy this place.

Common in the navy then was a double-hook gadget which could have one hook affixed to a belt loop, and keys or any miscellaneous items dangling from the other hook. They were popular because of the pocket-space shortage in many enlisted uniforms, notably so in the whites I wore that day. I had keys and a pocket knife attached to mine, easily visible. House policy: I was required to leave the knife at the front desk before taking the girl upstairs! She was amused by this and repeatedly called me a "Siciliano".

On the next day I was delighted to learn that a place in the barracks was already open, and I moved thence. The barracks was an unusual one. The navy leased several floors of a second- or third-rate hotel, the *Albergo Grilli*. (Albergo = hotel. Grilli: the owner's name.) It was about a mile and a half east from the dock area (where I would work) and from the main navy offices. It was near the main railroad station, in a rather lower-class and small-industrial part of town. My new home was a single cot (for the first time in the navy no one slept *above* me) in an eight-man dormitory room on the (?)fifth of the hotel's (?)eight floors. A galley was a deck or two below; it also served as an evening movie theater. A small-capacity elevator (human operators) was near the lobby. Down the street, at the hotel's far corner, was a spiral ramp allowing cars to drive up to rooftop parking. Near the bottom of the ramp was a small sidewalk bar serving cold Peroni beer.

Communications was on the second floor of a two-story structure known as the Guggenheim Building, inside the *Stazione Marittima* – the restricted, fenced-off dock area. Most of the other navy offices were in the "CINCNELM Building", outside the dock area and three or four blocks away. CINCNELM was the short title for Commander

IN Chief NorthEast atLantic and Mediterranean – but he was located in London. My new command in Naples was COMSUBCOMNELM/COMHEDSUPPACT – and that was the "short" title! The full version was COMmander SUBordinate COMmand NorthEast atLantic and Mediterranean/COMmander HEaDquarters SUPPort ACTivity. The "short" title was sometimes further shortened, unofficially, to CSCN/CHSA. The commanding officer, a captain, "wore two hats", one as CINCNELM's deputy in the Med and one as a support facility for the Sixth Fleet.

What did you do on your ship? Writeup man. So I was put on a watch as writeup man, typing messages on ditto mats identical to those on the *Iowa*. Two men I knew from Teleman school were already there and I was put on the same watch with one of them. In the message center there were usually about five RMs and/or TEs to a watch, plus a seaman messenger *and* a Seabee driver. (Those were the days – when both government and private industry usually hired enough people to do the job, and sometimes with a small surplus to make sure that it got done right. I suppose that having *both* messenger and driver make the deliveries around town provided some extra security cushion in case of auto accident or whatever – the messenger did carry classified messages, well sealed from his view, at times – but it struck me as rather a waste of manpower.) We also had a crypto center harboring the CWO and two other junior watch officers.

Next door to the message center was a major relay station where about the same number of people jockeyed incoming teletype tapes and sent them on to their destinations. The relay also eavesdropped on the teletype transmissions of AP, UPI, and others, and we often walked over to read the latest news.

The message center jobs were supervisor, incoming and outgoing circuit operators (the latter also typed most of the teletype tapes for outgoing messages), writeup, and distribution/runoff. The supervisor routed the messages, indicating what office was action, what offices got a copy for info, and what activities, if any, received "distribution". This latter term was for independent activities such as MSTS (Military Sea Transportation Service Office), the U.S. Consulate, etc.

On one of my earlier watches the supervisor called to me, "Hey, you got us a non-delivery." I had indeed, he had indicated distribution to MSTS and I had missed it when I typed. (He had missed it too, when he checked the traffic later, but . . .) I didn't yet appreciate the gravity of a non-delivery in the communications world; I just shrugged. It may be that this caused him to sour on me and try to get rid of me, or it may have been just coincidental personnel-shuffling that would have happened in any event, but I was placed on a different watch section about a month after arrival. I stayed on my new section the rest of my time in Naples.

Our watches ran 3-3-3-72. That's shorthand for three evening watches, 24 hours off, three midwatches, 24 hours off, three day watches, then 72 hours off. That was pretty standard for shore communications then; a more popular rotation was invented in later years. Unlike on ship, I could sleep as long as I pleased, but I seldom got a full eight hours after midwatches – mostly because of disrupted circadian rhythm, partly because of the normal daytime noises in the hotel.

Our hotel floor was cleaned by a couple of diminutive, middle-aged Neapolitans, Franco and Angelo. They supplemented their salaries by black-marketing cigarets from the PX. We had ration books entitling us to a fixed number of cartons every month; non-smokers could sell their ration to the cleaners for a modest profit. It was illegal, but a common practice. Franco and Angelo were somewhat furtive about it, with over-the-shoulder glances during transactions. It seemed to me that the traffic was only technically illegal, given the lack of enforcement, and I became one of the sellers.

The hotel had bedbugs; the only place I've ever encountered them. They were tiny, red, pinhead-sized. For some reason a damp towel struck them as an ideal lurking spot, but it also made them very visible against the white, and I often picked a few off my towel which hung on the end of my rack. Their bites were too trivial even to notice – unfelt, leaving minuscule welts if any; even their crawling was undetectable. The floor was fumigated a time or two with no noticeable effect on the bugs.

The room had one large window, barred but unscreened, which overlooked an area of one- and two-story workshops, apartments, etc. It was left open most of the time during warmer months. At times the sounds of neighborhood music festivals penetrated, disturbing some, enjoyed by others. One day the shouts and clangs of some metal-workers below were annoying a sailor, who said, "Hey, Franco, tell those guys to shut up."

Franco put a knee on the low window sill and complied: "Hey, son-a-ma-beesh, shudda op – I'm-a sleep!" It had no effect; the noisemakers were too far off to hear.

Smells also came through the window – Neapolitan cooking, garlic, tomato paste, olive oil, industrial odors, all perhaps underlaid by the salt sea of the bay. All in all, it was not unpleasant. I wish I could get a momentary whiff of it again, in order to satisfy nostalgia and to refresh memory of what I am inadequately and incompletely trying to inventory and describe. Few or no insects invaded the unscreened window, the attractions at street level far outweighed anything at higher altitude.

There were no other communicators in my room. We had a mixed bag: a Boatswain's Mate, three or four Seabees, a Storekeeper, a Yeoman. A corpsman arrived not long after me; his last duty station had been in Turkey and he became The Terrible Turk to us. Mostly, though, we just called him Doc.

Charlie, one of the Seabees, sometimes dominated the conversation in the room. He was one of those rare fortunates who enjoy an ideal, flat-stomached, well-muscled physique without doing anything at all to maintain it. He had been under mental treatment in Germany in the recent past and made no secret of it. I first heard from him a couple of phrases that were in vogue in the command, an expression of emphatic

115

indifference ("I don't give a fuck if it rains straight up!") and one of flamboyant agreement or affirmation ("*Sì*, by God!").

Charlie had some prejudices and often vented them. He had outspoken contempt for President Eisenhower, Rocky Marciano, and Marilyn Monroe ("If she had as many dicks sticking out of her as she's had stuck into her, she'd look like a porcupine."). By contrast he held Doris Day in high esteem.

Charlie once returned to the room in mid-day, thoroughly drunk. He collapsed on his rack, immobile but fully articulate. I had been about to leave, but I had been saving up some harassment for the right opportunity. I went over to him and announced my departure and ". . . before I go I want you to know that Eisenhower's the greatest president we ever had, Rocky Marciano could whip Dempsey, Tunney, and Louis in the same ring at the same time – and Doris Day couldn't wear Marilyn Monroe's *skivvies*."

Charlie was rendered speechless; his reaction was a series of, "Whaa – whaa – whaa . . ."; his look one of uncomprehending disbelief.

"Harass" was not a term used by the sailors. They said *hard-ass*, which could be either verb or noun. Someone who hard-assed another sailor was himself a hard-ass.

On another occasion Whitey, the Yeoman, was the foil of the moment, and was being hard-assed by a Seabee who included "four-eyed" in his denunciations. I was on my rack, peacefully reading; the Seabee included me in his indictment of the bespectacled. The Seabee was quite corpulent. I said in self-defense, "*I'd rather have four eyes than four chins."

I exaggerated a trifle; he only had three. I was now a certified hard-ass.

I was struck by terminology in the room during post-movie critiques. The movies were often westerns. Male actors therein were spoken of

116

by name (be it screen name or real name), but heroines were routinely referenced as *the cunt*. This is not unheard of in man-talk, but I have nowhere seen it observed as consistently and matter-of-factly as in that room.

Most of the movies shown were Hollywood product, but all too often British films were our fare. They seemed unappealing to Americans and were indeed pretty dismal. It reached the point where the J. Arthur Rank studio logo alone (a man striking a big gong) was enough to shoot a number of cursing sailors out of their seats bound for other pursuits, without waiting for title or further information.

A common remark upon sighting a Neapolitan funeral procession was, "There goes a *good* Guinea." In sailor talk *wop* was almost never heard, *guinea* was universal. A popular Teresa Brewer song of the time contained fast-paced lyrics, "Skinny Minnie, skinny Minnie, fishtail." Sailors altered them to "Skinny guinea, skinny guinea, wop-wop."

Alone in the room one weekday, Roscoe walked in and I made his acquaintance. I was told he had been born on the hotel's spiral ramp. He identified with the navy, collectively, and favored no one individual. Of medium size and uncertain lineage, he had adapted to the navy with above-average canine ingenuity – or I might say he had adapted the navy to him. He knew the navy bus routes and the bus stops as well as any sailor and he used them; he knew the other navy vehicles as well and would hitch a ride with whatever was handy. He sometimes spent the midwatch with us in communications, asleep on the floor. He was so well fed by so many sailors that he more often than not turned up his nose at the midrats we offered him. More affection was offered him than his capacity for it would abide, and he was more tolerant than grateful when petted or praised. I heard it said that he would sometimes accompany sailors to a whorehouse and they would pay one of the girls full price to give Roscoe a hand job. I'm not sure that is true, but I don't totally dismiss it.

On midwatches, and on weekend watches, we sometimes played hearts. And we often played 20 questions, at which I excelled. Al

Seebohm, the supervisor, was incensed one night when I nailed his obscure subject (King Zog of Albania) on the 16th question. Arguments sometimes arose over answers and definitions. I once chose Arthur MacArthur (the general's young son). Asked if he was famous, I said that he was. Several people contended that the general was famous, the son was not. I argued that they all knew of the son; therefore he must be famous by definition. It went unsettled. Another time I read the press in relay just before a game and noted that Soviet diplomat Andrei Vishinsky had just died. Perfect. The others would have had no trouble pinning down a *live* Vishinsky, but I had answered that my subject was dead. The kibitzing messenger spoiled my dirty trick; he, too, had read the press and he updated the others. The CWO, LT(jg) Joe Fontaine, gave me a look of disappointment and words of reproach. I said that if I had answered that my subject was living, it would have been a lie. He was not mollified.

Al was an energetic, skinny, almost skeletal, redhead. He was a first-class Radioman and rated a private room in the barracks. He was single but I think there was a deserted wife somewhere in his past. I got along fine with him but oddly we almost never drank together. Al favored the bar in the *Londres* (London) *Hotel*, which I didn't care for because of bright lights and hard, uncomfortable, backless bar stools. My favorite place (when I intended drinking only, and not sex) was the Swiss Bar, a little hole in the wall which would have been crowded if it ever had 20 patrons at once. Both places were in the general area of the CINCNELM building and the docks.

The Swiss Bar served Kindlbrau, an obscure Bavarian beer which came only in double-sized (at least) bottles, and which I still rank as number one among the beers I have encountered. The place had atmosphere; dimmer lights, wooden benches and tables, mottos on the walls. (I remember only *In Vino Veritas*.) An occasional streetwalker wandered in hoping for business. They were none too attractive, but at least didn't try to cadge drinks. Tina, the manager, looked far better. She would flirt with customers, but flirt only. I was told that she had committed the sin of sins in the Naples of that time – she was an unwed mother, with a teenage son and an Italian boyfriend. Hans, the white-haired owner, sometimes came by. Roving musicians occasionally came in and played a few songs on their mandolin (or whatever instrument). *Johnny Guitar*, from the movie, was one of the most often heard, along with *Granada*, two or three favorites from the current Neapolitan hit parade, and the old standbys *O Sole Mio, Santa Lucia,* and *Come Back to Sorrento.* I learned to play a game which my tutor said was *Sette Bello* (beautiful seven), although its actual name was *Scopa* (scoop). It used the Italian 40-card deck which resembled tarot cards more than U.S. cards – the suits were clubs, swords, cups, and coins.

Along with Al, I remember Harvey best. I'll use Al's word for him: Harvey was a *jewel.* He was around 30 (thus ancient from my first-hitch perspective), an RM3 with two or three hash marks. He was the distribution/runoff man on our watch. He had a history of trouble and had been busted back to seaman a time or two, and there was an army hitch in his past. (He liked to brag of his good-conduct ribbon, earned in the army at a time when eligibility required only six months of not-getting-caught vice the navy's three years.) He was happy-go-lucky and took life as it came. He liked to say, "I'm too lazy to work and too scared to steal; the navy's the only place for me." He was intelligent, but uneducated (I doubt that he got past eighth grade), didn't care, and did little to increase his knowledge. He spent his pay on liquor and women. When he reenlisted, he collected his bonus, unused leave, regular pay, etc., entirely in Italian lire. His $1600+ {$11,648} came to slightly over a million lire and, he said, he would ever after be able to say that he had once been a millionaire. He turned it over to his current favorite among the night-club girls, who took careful charge of it for him and ensured that he didn't spend it too fast or too foolishly.

Al and Harvey were both Atheists. Ski, our Seabee driver, was a chaplain's joy – celibate, teetotal, regular mass-goer. Al was an outspoken ex-Catholic. It made for some interesting dialogues. Shortly after Harvey reenlisted, I was sleeping after a midwatch when he shook me awake at about 0900. "Hey, what's that you said I was if I wasn't an Atheist?" I had recently explained the term *agnostic* to Harvey; he had been unfamiliar with it. The whole story was that Harvey had listed *Atheist* in the space for religion on his reenlistment papers, and some meddler in the personnel office had brought it to the chaplain's attention. The chaplain, secure in his officer status and having the power to order enlisted men around, had summoned a resentful Harvey for spiritual reclamation. Neither converted the other.

I remember one particular Al/Ski interaction. It didn't relate directly to religion but rather to Ski's holier-than-everyone distaste for profanity. Getting ready to go from the hotel to the midwatch, Roscoe jumped into the van to ride with us. Al greeted him: "Hello, Roscoe, you little bastard . . ."

Ski: "Aww, Al – a dumb animal . . ."

Al: "Ski, if you can show me his father and mother's marriage certificate, I'll take it back."

On watch, the driver would sometimes take orders for pizzas then go out and obtain same. Neapolitan pizza was so different from the American version that the two really should be treated as two different foods and not compared. I'll compare them anyhow: the Neapolitan version was thicker, doughier, oilier, chewier, and had rather little in the way of toppings. It was quite good in its way, but I preferred the American.

My crash course in Italian on the troop transport enabled me to decipher the local graffiti in a couple of instances. Just about any wall, public or private, seemed to be fair game for the posting of various notices by various entities. The death of Alcide De Gasperi, the postwar prime minister, was announced by many such posters. To the bottom of one, someone had penned *finalmente* (= finally). And I was able to translate the following on a rest room wall:

Piangete, donne,	Cry, women,
e lacrimate forte.	and weep strongly.
Il re dei cozzi	The king of the cocks
è condannato a morte.	is condemned to death.

As early as boot camp I had formed two goals for my navy hitch: to get an honorable discharge as soon as possible, and to attain the highest rate achievable within that time. I found that the second goal was now in jeopardy. I approached the Chief Teleman in charge of the message center about taking the second-class exam in August. He informed me that no one got recommended for the exam until they had taken *his* "training course", which he taught in the evenings. (The evening schedule, at least, was to his credit. Elsewhere, such training almost invariably occurred during the working hours of the trainer – and the free time of the watchstander.)

Just before I left the *Iowa*, Slenker had told CR division at morning quarters that all those being transferred would have a recommendation for the next rate exam placed in their record. I decided to check with the Naples personnel office to see if such recommendation perhaps overrode the chief's policy. There was no such recommendation in my record. I don't know if its absence was due to malice or incompetence on the part of Slenker; either is plausible and I'd call it 50-50. So I could not take the August exam and would have to wait for February. If I encountered no more delays, I could still make first-class before my hitch was up, but just barely.

I still had no specific plans for future studies upon return to college. Browsing in the navy library one day, I picked up a book on the Russian language. It seemed somewhat interesting and the strange alphabet did not seem all that difficult. My thoughts ran: I've had very high grades in two semesters of Spanish; I must have some language aptitude. Russian speakers are in demand by the government now. And if the Soviets ever declare peace on us, the demand by private industry ought to become significant. It wasn't an instantaneous decision, but over a few weeks I decided to drop Analytic Geometry and begin correspondence-course Russian. USAFI was not happy with me and remonstrated; I was about halfway through the geometry with near-perfect marks (but I'd come to an impasse at one exercise that I somehow could *not* quite figure out). I explained my reasoning; USAFI would allow enrollment in not more than two courses at a time, and I wanted to get busy on Russian in hopes of completing two semesters of it in my remaining navy time. They honored my wishes.

There were no typewriters in the barracks. I went to communications on my time off in order to type up my assignments. One evening a CWO recalled that some directive forbade us to be in the building in civilian clothes, and had me ousted. No major problem; I just timed my typing for when *other* sections were on watch thereafter. The navy supposedly encouraged self-improvement; correspondence study, etc. – not at the expense of chickenshit, though. That particular CWO stayed in the navy and retired a commander.

I put that typewriter to another use. There was a suggestion box in the barracks. I produced a three-page screed criticizing several things that annoyed me. My main wrath was directed at a chow hall policy that allowed us to eat in civvies only on weekends; I argued that this was unfair to watchstanders who got their 72s on weekdays as often as not. I also criticized the locker space, and room assignment policies. I was not diplomatic. I was not surprised when there were no changes – except for a trivial one. As a chow-hall afterthought, I had said that they ought either to observe the "take all you want, eat all you take" slogan or else take their lying signs down. They did remove the signs. As a measure of my continuing paranoia about Authority: I carefully handled my typed sheets by the corners – no fingerprints! – and waited for an opportunity to slip them in the box when no one was watching.

The suggestion box was near the elevator on our floor; the Masters-at-Arms stood a 24-hour watch there. The area overlooked an open space within the hotel which was too small to be called a court and too large to be called an air shaft. It afforded an excellent view of windows in lower-floor rooms and the MAAs watched with close attention when something interesting was on exhibition. Bargain vacationers, notably English schoolteachers, sometimes stayed there; one such schoolmarm was famed for devoting her vacation (almost) entirely to sex with sailors. John Woram called the MAAs, when so engaged, the Audible Boy Bird Watchers – a term borrowed from the *Pogo* comic strip.

John was an RM3 and one of the most intellectual among the enlisted. He was an aspiring archaeologist and took me along on one of his jaunts through the ruins of Pompeii. He also convinced me to

122

attend an opera, *Boris Godunov*, with him. It being opening night, suit and tie would not do – tuxedos for civilians, dress blue uniform for us.

The single, small elevator in the hotel was less than adequate. Waits were variable and sometimes prolonged; sailors would often, especially when downward bound, use the adjacent staircase. There was considerable discontent and friction during one period when the fringe Monarchist Party held its convention in the hotel, its delegates wearing *Viva il Re* pins. The owner of the hotel was a party bigwig and had ordered the elevator operators to service the politicians on the lower floors, never mind the sailors. The poor operators (all young men) were caught between the abuse of irate sailors and the potential displeasure of the owner.

Prostitution was still legal in Italy at the time. The houses of excellent repute had no signs, no advertising, and were known by a number rather than a name; you had to know where to go. The Number Two featured one Sonia, who was said to give the best blow jobs in the Mediterranean. I never patronized them after my first night, preferring the night clubs and all-night dalliances. The price for the latter was a pretty standard 7000 lire, about $11.20 {$82} U.S. Sailors insisted that Italian patrons got a lower price. Tourists were likely to hear 10,000 quoted. The girls sang a parody of an American love song, *[I Love You] For Sentimental Reasons*, their version went: *I'm-a love you, for dieci mille [ten thousand] lire. Two thousand for the room. One thousand for the taxi. Five hundred for a tip.*

My favorite club at first was the *Moulin Rouge*. Along with a number of others, it was located in the general area of the navy offices/ dock gate. *The Black Cat* was said to be owned by exiled American gangster Lucky Luciano, and it was said that he could sometimes be seen taking the sun on its front patio. Here and there a girl would brag of having been patronized by this or that vacationing American movie star; I don't remember any specific names. Sailors claimed that they had encountered, and drunk with, actress Tuesday Weld in one of the clubs. I was in a club one evening when the girls were a-twitter over

123

visiting bigwigs from Milan, apparently talent scouts for the night clubs in that more prosperous city.

The gesturing endemic to Italians drew burlesques from sailors. I was riding in a navy car with two others when the driver goofed slightly and had to make an abrupt, bouncy stop at an intersection. Two Italians in a car across the intersection saw this, and one of them made the ubiquitous and classic gesture: palm up, fingers raised to a meeting point, hand bobbing up and down. (For that particular gesture, I've never been able to think of a more accurate translation than *What the hell?*) The other two sailors immediately started to run through every gesture they knew; the Italians knew they were being satirized and laughed appreciatively.

The two-finger gesture known to Americans as either *bull shit* or *hook 'em 'horns* depending on geography had a completely different meaning in Italy: *cornuto* (= horned, the horns of the cuckold). It was a potent insult. In one of the many curio/souvenir shops I purchased a little two-inch cameo (ivory?) hand making this sign; alas it later disappeared to a covetous thief from my campus apartment. Its designed purpose was to accompany an ashtray as a cigarette tamper-outer. A gesture – not exactly a gesture, but I don't know what else to call it – used in the night clubs was a rapid flicking of the tongue against a corner of the mouth, with an audible clicking sound. It advertised a desire to perform cunnilingus.

The place to eat, for barracks sailors who decided to skip the chow hall fare, was Mike's *(Trattoria da Michele)*, just a few steps away from the hotel and across the street. There were several other *trattorias* on the same street but I never tried another nor did I hear of anyone else doing so. There was no need. Mike's food was fabulous. The standard order was bean soup, salad, steak and eggs, and a half-liter of red wine. On one 72, I had decided to make a night of it. I was going to start out at Mike's then walk downtown to the *Moulin Rouge* and, I planned, spend the night with Nelly. But, in an expansive mood, I ordered a full liter of wine. I did not remember exiting Mike's, nor anything thereafter, until I awoke in Nelly's room the next morning. She had removed her usual fee from my wallet, and reproved me: "*God*, you drunk!" My hangover detracted from, but did not cancel, the already-purchased pleasures of the morning. How there could be such a vast discrepancy between the effects of a half-liter of wine (which did not even give me a hangover) and those of a full liter (just described) remains a mystery unsolved.

In *Tropic of Cancer* Henry Miller wrote about an ignorant customer who shat in a whore's bidet. On my first night with Nelly, I had very nearly done just that. The room was near-dark; I didn't know. There must have been others equally uninformed, because when Nelly saw me sit she immediately cautioned me and explained that the commode was down the hall. She was just in time.

Was there anyone who did *not* contract diarrhea? The naval hospital was at the far end of Naples, an hour or half-hour bus ride. It was too long and the diarrhea too urgent, and I soiled myself – but only slightly; and I was producing not much but clear liquid anyhow.

In the winter I took two weeks of leave, hitch-hiked on a navy flight to London, and took the Royal Scotsman – the train to Edinburgh. After re-sampling that place, I spent some time in London. Pat Ryon, ex-*Iowa*, was working in communications there. I mentioned more in jest than anything that if he knew anyone there who would like to swap, I would be glad to do so. Pat said that he knew one guy who might, but I never expected anything to come of it.

I taught Harvey how to play cribbage. We were playing in the barracks on one rainy winter night when I turned over a five – and I was staring at a 29-hand! Harvey, a neophyte, had no conception of the rarity of the occasion. It was amateur night – a cynical term for payday. I took my 29-hand and looked in other rooms for *someone* with whom to share the moment. The barracks was near-deserted; I found only one sailor and he didn't play cribbage.

In my post-navy years, I was to hold 29-hands twice more. They both came against my wife, while playing at home, alone. She was no more knowledgeable than was Harvey. *Three* 29-hands, and never anyone present sufficiently savvy to whom to exhibit and gloat! The odds of a 29-hand on a given deal are one in 216,580 (fact). If there are nine deals to the average game (guess), and if someone played one game *every* day, and if my math is sound (a risky assumption), a 29-hand would be expected about once in 66 years. I am way over my lifetime quota.

I am looking forward to my next one.

(Payday is known as "amateur night" because the amateurs, who have been broke for days, take their pay and race downtown. Those wiser, more patient, and better disciplined save their excursions for less-crowded times with less competition. For the same reasons I always stayed in the barracks when major elements of the Sixth Fleet were making a port visit.)

There was a weekly high-level meeting of the command bigwigs. Usually the communications officer, a commander, attended. But one week the comm officer and his next-in-lines were all out of town and Mr Fontaine was called upon to represent communications. We had some minor gripes – I don't remember just what they were, but I do remember that they were (a) trivial, and (b) easily remediable. Mr Fontaine promised to take them up at the meeting. When he returned, we were eager to hear the results. In a downcast tone he said, "I was told by a captain and seven commanders that enlisted men always bitch, not to worry about it."

There was an epidemic of "mammy talk" on our watch section – insulting one another's mothers during verbal give-and-take. Somehow *mother* became transmuted to *mammy*, which bore an unfortunate touch of racism, but I report it as it was. Mr Fontaine discouraged it and, hoping to hold me up as an example to the others; he asked me if I used such terminology in the verbal jousts. I responded with a mock-innocent (and lying), "*No, sir," which generated hoots and contradictions from the rest of the section. Frequently heard was, "*Your mammy's a red-headed Guinea," an indirect critique of Al's red hair. Harvey produced one of the most potent and admired: "*Your mammy's a Wave in the Limey navy."

British and French warships also patrolled the Mediterranean and I heard tales of international frictions. It was said that more than one Anglo-American brawl had been precipitated by a drunken Yank climbing on a chair, raising his drink, and proclaiming, "God fuck the Queen!" The French sailors wore a beret with a red top-knot, and some American sailors saw these as dandy souvenirs. They would sneak up behind a victim, seize his hat, and run. The victimized took understandable exception to larceny, and mayhem could result if the thief was not as speedy as he thought he was.

We had an aging mustang lieutenant in communications who was not all that disagreeable, but was quite useless. He had been given an unnecessary fifth-wheel job as "day CWO", supplementing the junior officers on each watch, just to give him something harmless to do. We ridiculed him behind his back as *Steppin' Sam* and *Yangtze Sam*. (He rated and wore the campaign ribbon for the pre-war Yangtze River Patrol.)

It was in message center discussions that I first heard the brownbagger vs. single men controversies argued out. As singles saw it, the brownbagger received extra pay, a quarters allowance for housing, and commuted rations, unrelated to his value to the navy. Commuted rations (comrats), though smaller in dollars, were a particularly sore point – the brownbagger who received them was still able to eat at the chow hall whenever he wished, by paying a set price for that particular meal. (If he ate *every* meal at the chow hall, his expense would exactly equal the sum he received as comrats.) Menus were published in advance, and when steak was the entree many brownbaggers lunched at the chow hall. When less-desirable foods were served, they brought their meal from home – typically in a brown paper sack, and therefore the term "brownbagger". The single man who forwent his free chow-hall meal to eat at Mike's didn't receive a dime in compensation. Worsening the pay gap, the allowances were not taxed and thus, thanks to exemptions for his dependents, the brownbagger paid *less* income tax on *more* money.

Single men also complained that, living in the barracks, they were readily available to Authority whenever some unforeseen after-hours task arose. As for the brownbagger, it would be too much trouble to locate him and get him in to participate. The brownbagger arriving at a new ship or station was generally given a week or more to locate housing and get his family settled; the single man threw his seabag into his locker and was ready. There was a perception that the brownbagger who ran afoul of military justice was more likely to be given a warning only, or at least a lighter sentence. A fine, or a bust to a lower pay grade, would hurt his family as well as him, restriction to ship or base would produce family separation. Brownbaggers' ration cards allowed them to buy liquor at the PX. Singles could not, on the rationale that, living in the barracks, they had no place legally to keep it.

The brownbaggers' rebuttals were rather weak. They claimed that as a group they were more stable, mature, reliable, less likely to get into trouble, and a steadying influence. *As a group*, that was probably true – but with many exceptions on each side of the divide. Many of them would agree that single men were shafted but, "what can you do about it?"

From these seminars, Harvey conceived a scheme to beat the system. He would strike a bargain with a Neapolitan maid. They would marry, but Harvey would himself pocket the extra money. Her reward would be immigration to the Land of the Big PX when Harvey's tour was finished, and the marriage would then end. (Harvey would sometimes add, with a leer, that he might sample the wares a time or two.) His first problem was to find a receptive candidate.

Neapolitan society at that time recognized only three categories of women: virgins, wives, and whores. No gray areas, no overlap. The whores would never pass the marital red-tape background check; the wives were out for obvious reasons. Harvey set out to find an interested virgin. I don't know how he found one, but find one he did, somehow. He began the paperwork gauntlet. Sailor opinions were mixed. Some viewed Harvey's plan as immoral and unethical; others saw it as a reasonable, clever, and justified riposte to military inequities. I tended toward the latter view.

At one point I overheard Mr Fontaine declare that Harvey's plan would never succeed; he said that if it ever came close to fruition he would put a stop to it. I asked why.
"*Why . . . why . . . it's sacrilege!"
"*But Harvey's an Atheist," I said. "*He can't commit sacrilege."

I can remember maybe two or three times in my life when I have said something that was so outlandish to the listener, so totally foreign to his or her thought-processes, that I evoked only an utterly blank stare and no spoken response. This was one of those times.

But actually Mr Fontaine may have been on firmer ground than I was. I'm not sure whether civil marriage was even possible in Italy then – the Catholic church quite possibly had the monopoly – and if so Harvey could not have finalized the marriage without going through religious monkeyshines and, in a sense anyhow, committing sacrilege.

When I left Naples, Harvey was still ensnarled in paperwork and I never did receive trustworthy word about subsequent developments. However some 5-10-15 years later, while comparing past duty stations and possible mutual acquaintances during a bull session with someone, my interlocutor "thought" he remembered Harvey. If – and it is a very big *if* – his identification was correct and his information accurate, then Harvey did succeed in accomplishing his marriage and had brought his bride to Norfolk. But his plan had miscarried in one respect: the marriage had endured. And Harvey had made first-class.

John Woram and Ski occupied a smaller three-man room in the barracks. Their roommate was leaving, they were looking for a congenial occupant, and invited me. It was arranged and I moved. A few months later, John's tour was up. He and I conspired to get Harvey into the room – Harvey + Ski! But Ski was an easygoing sort and kept his disapproval of Harvey's lifestyle largely to himself. When I left Naples, Harvey was working on a scheme to seduce Lucia, a maid

129

who sometimes assisted Franco and Angelo, and to time it so that Ski would walk in to catch them in the act. I doubt that it would ever have succeeded. Lucia was friendly and moderately good-looking, but if she ever engaged in sex-with-sailors she was quite discreet about it; I heard no such tales.

Al wandered by the room once when Harvey was engaged in his marriage maneuvers. Harvey was napping on his rack. Al asked me something about Harvey's immediate schedule and my answer ended with, ". . . then he's got to go see his sweetie." Al snickered and Harvey, not fully unconscious, growled and called both of us names.

The *Iowa* dropped anchor in Naples for a port visit. I put on my uniform, caught a liberty boat, and renewed old acquaintances. The guys were supposed to meet me on the beach that evening, but my directions for finding the Swiss Bar must have baffled them; they never showed.

To my considerable surprise, Pat Ryon *did* find his man willing to swap with me. We began the paperwork at each end; the swap was approved and scheduled for June 1955. I passed the second-class exam in February and was to be promoted in May.

An "Italian-American Club" had been formed by Naples university students. American college graduates or students were welcomed, and I joined. I went on several activities with them, including a trip to Sorrento. Once when I was visiting the university at the invitation of some Italians there was a parade of students in the street. The occasion for the demonstration was Trieste, which was still up for postwar grabs between Italy and Yugoslavia. But the signs being carried demanded not only Trieste but Fiume, Nice, Tunisia, Corsica, the Dodecanese Islands; virtually every piece of ground that Mussolini had owned or even had his eye on!

At another function I met a girl who was quite attractive, had a sparkling personality, and seemed very friendly. My interest was all too obvious. A boy (her fiancé?) semi-tactfully steered me away and introduced me to another, much plainer, girl, Imma. Well, one takes what one can get. I invited Imma to . . . something or other, which was out of the question. But she counter-invited me to her home on a Sunday evening. It turned out that there were regular Sunday-evening gatherings of young people there, and there was a ping-pong table. I went often, whenever my work schedule permitted.

One weekend the Club had scheduled a trip to . . . ? Somewhere or other. I went to the designated meeting place and only one other person showed up – the trip had been cancelled and we were the only two who did not know that. The other person was a friendly Canadian college student who was taking a year off to work as a governess for a wealthy Italian family; I had not met her before. Finding ourselves both there for nothing, it was only natural to spend the rest of the day together, and I began to date her as often as my schedule and her duties would permit.

We went to places that I probably would not have seen otherwise. Luna Park, a waterfront amusement park was one. The little ferris wheel there revolved *backwards* from American wheels, and we formed the dogma that, if the Italians couldn't find a way to do something backwards, they did it half an hour late. We went to the Isle of Capri by ferry, where we intended to see the famous Blue Grotto. But the grotto was small, the boats waiting to go in were many, and we faced such a long wait that we gave it up and returned to the island. We went to the summit of Vesuvius by cable car, and she introduced me to Caserta. I had not known about Caserta. It is some 20 miles inland to the north of Naples, an 18th-century royal palace surrounded by well-kept parklands, waterways, and fountains, altogether a scenic and beautiful place. We rented bicycles there to ride through the park. It was my first experience with a bicycle with the brake on the handlebars, and I was fascinated by the ability to "pedal" backwards. While bicycling I inflicted on her the story of "antisubmarine operations" (*USS Iowa* chapter). She said, "*But how could they . . . OHHHH!" She took off at maximum speed and I had a time of it to catch her. She didn't appreciate being fooled in that manner.

131

Another sailor spotted us sitting at a sidewalk café, and when he next saw me he asked, "Who's your guinea girlfriend?" I took her to the Swiss Bar, where she sniffed in disapproval of "the scarlet woman" when a streetwalker entered. I also took her to Imma's; she said they no doubt thought it scandalous that she came with me unchaperoned.

A new night club, *La Conchiglia* (= the seashell), had opened and had become *the* place to go for sailors, who pronounced it as "The Lock and Key". Some girls from the older clubs had migrated thence. They had a fabulous four-piece band – Marino Marini was the leader/pianist; his recordings were soon to become available internationally. One of their most-often-heard numbers went something like: . . . *Is the number 65? That is not the number.* Working up to 68 in the same manner, then: *I don't know the number – naughty, naughty number.* Then beginning again at about 73 and working downward until, after 70: *Is the number (loud, long roll of drums for finale).* I don't know whether it had a title and they probably never recorded it. When a sailor left the club with a girl, they were likely to be serenaded from the tables: *We know where you're going! We know where you're going!*

The London sailor with whom I had swapped arrived in early June. I crossed paths with him about eight years later; he said the swap was the worst mistake he'd ever made. I was sufficiently enamored with the Canadian that I delayed my departure until the very end of June, causing London to send a message to Naples asking when the hell I was coming.

In that last month a new guy arrived on our watch section. He said that he didn't want to patronize the whores, but that he would like to meet "nice" Italian girls. How, he wondered, would one strike up an acquaintance? How, for example, would you say, "Good evening, miss"? Harvey and I taught him: *voglio mangiare tua figa* (= I want to eat your pussy). I hate to tell about this because I hate to leave it unfinished, but I must. I never did learn whether our educational efforts accomplished their intended goal.

VII - BLOKES

What did you do in Naples? Writeup man. So I was put on a watch section for more of the same. Pat Ryon was a watch supervisor; it was natural that I be put on his section. The London message center was very much like Naples – a relay next door, a crypto center with junior officers and – in London – Waves. All had about the same number of people doing the same jobs. But London was busier.

There was no retyping here of entire messages onto ditto mats. The teletypes were furnished with ditto *rolls*; all I had to do was add distribution and peripheral information and correct garbles, if any. The correction process worked like this: say half a line had garbled into upper case. With a razor blade I scraped the garble ink away from the back side of the top ditto sheet. Then I backed it with a virginal portion of a bottom sheet, and typed the proper version on top of the garbled stretch.

Si, a TE1, was number two on the section and Bob Dulin, a TE2, was number three. Jim O'Donnell, an RMSN, handled the runoff/distribution. Some of the communicators were attached directly to CINCNELM's staff; others, including myself, belonged to COMNAVACTS UK (Commander Naval Activities United Kingdom).

The watch rotation was 6-6-6 – six days of evening watches, six days of mids, six days of days. There were 48s and 72s mingled in between the strings of six. I rather liked it. I encountered one hazard not present in Naples. It became my habit, after a midwatch, to retire to bed with a bottle of Tuborg (Danish beer) and the morning paper. I had no bedside table. One time I woke up very shortly after I had fallen asleep, in a puddle of beer. I only did that once.

There was no barracks and no chow hall. I enjoyed nearly all the privileges of a brownbagger, except that my housing and cost-of-living allowances were somewhat lower than they would have been with dependents. For the first 90 days I received a substantial additional sum as a "temporary lodging allowance", which theoretically expired earlier than 90 days *if* I found permanent quarters before that time. The navy was chintzy about one allowance though, and it was withheld from both married and single: a civilian clothing allowance. The navy did not want all those U.S. uniforms all that visible all the time in a high-class London area. On the other hand, it did not want to pay the money. So, ingenuity: they decreed that the uniform of the day was either (a) civilian clothing with tie and jacket, or (b) dress blues. Both of Authority's objectives were thereby accomplished.

A navy housing office assisted newcomers to find accommodations, and they steered me to my first place – the third floor of a middle-class home which the family rented out. It was a rather tiny ex-attic with a combined bedroom/living room and a little kitchenette. The landlord apparently had had past experience with American sailors, he hinted that it was a family home with a young daughter and that seamanlike conduct would be frowned upon. I abided by the restrictions but chafed under them and sought other premises before long. (I was also concerned about that 90-day temporary allowance. Although it didn't seem to be monitored and enforced, I didn't want to risk the chance of being hit for a refund.) The family invited me to a meal one Sunday and I had to pretend that the cooking was not atrocious. My apartment had an electric heater – a *fire* in England English. As the weather cooled I used it, and began to leave it on at times so that the room would be toasty when I returned. (My room was metered separately and I paid for electricity; the heater took quite some time to dissipate the chill.) The landlord came to my room for some reason while I was out, left me a note about whatever, and added to the end, "*I found your fire on!"

He had turned it off. I never did figure out whether leaving it on in my absence was some kind of safety hazard, or simply an extravagance unthinkable to the English.

American expatriate communities, military or civilian, nearly always adopt a shorthand word for the locals. Sometimes it is offensive, sometimes neutral, but it always carries an us vs. them flavor. In Iraq today it is *hajis*, in my part of Vietnam it was *zips* or *zipperheads*, in Pakistan simply *Paks*. An ex-Reykjavik sailor referred to the Icelanders as *mojacks* – an intriguing and probably offensive term, probably from the Icelandic language; internet search fails to enlighten. In Italy it was *guineas*. And in London it was *blokes*. As in: you had a bloke girlfriend, or you bought something on the bloke market.

I recalled something I'd read years before on Anglo-American counter-perceptions. An American sees an Englishman as someone who carries an umbrella when the sun is shining, can't make decent coffee, drives on the wrong side of the street, and talks funny. An Englishman views an American as someone who gets caught in the rain without an umbrella, can't make decent tea, drives on the wrong side of the street, and talks funny. I had also read of the World War II taunt, "The trouble with you Yanks is that you're overpaid, oversexed, and over here." To which the rebuttal was, "And you Limeys are underpaid, undersexed, and under Eisenhower." The London streetwalkers were known by a term which I suspect dates back at least to World War I: *The Piccadilly Light Infantry*.

I finally figured out a couple of English terms that puzzled me for a while. Most newspaper front pages, in a little box with basic weather data, carried *Lighting Up Time*. At first I thought it somehow connected to smoking, but how? It turned out to be the time that vehicle lights must by law be turned on, half an hour after sunset (and until half an hour before sunrise). It seemed to be somehow of major importance to know and observe the exact hour and minute. And I saw many a sign reading *Players Please*. This was often seen outside a pub, and I took it to be a recruiting pitch for darts games – until I learned that it was simply an advertising slogan for Players-brand cigarets.

A difference in English driving law which I enthusiastically approved was that headlights were not used – only parking lights – on well-lighted urban streets, which in London was virtually everywhere. Night driving in traffic was much more pleasant without the glare of oncoming lights. I think I only used my headlights once during the whole tour, when returning to London from a trip. Another law difference which I relished – at the time; I would not support it today – was that smoking was permitted in movie theaters. I enjoyed many a movie while contentedly puffing my pipe.

Communications, and most of the navy offices, were in a building on North Audley Street, at the northwest corner of Grosvenor Square (pronounced grove-ner). The huge American embassy that dominates the square today had not yet been built; the embassy of that day was across the square to the south. Prominent in the parklike square itself was a statue of Franklin D. Roosevelt. Around our corner and a short walk east off the square was Claridges, one of the most prestigious London hotels, and a few doors beyond it was the Douglas House – a club operated by the U.S. air force, shortened in conversation to *the dog house*. It had better food than any English eating place and I ate there often. I was vexed by one restriction: if I wanted to bring in a guest, I had to make a reservation for her by name a day in advance. Brownbaggers, of course, met no such obstacle when they brought their wives. I was told that, before the rule had been made, English girls used to hang out at the club entrance hoping to be picked up and taken in by a Yank. This would not have bothered me at all – quite the contrary! – but it must have bothered wives, chaplains, and other bluenoses.

I heard that one of our more senior Waves – thirtyish, stern-faced, with a reputation (deserved or not) for affinities to sex and alcohol – was drinking in the dog house with several sailors. She announced her intention to make a rest-room trip. One of the sailors made a comment, one more frequently made male-to-male: "Well, what do you want me to do about it – go along and hold your hand?" She said yes. He did. He was barred from the club for a period.

During my search for new quarters, Si steered me to apartment buildings where he and some other married sailors lived. A furnished one was open at the right time, and I took it. I packed my things in a fair-sized wooden crate that had been used to send them from Naples. I had intended to call a taxi and rely upon the driver to assist me in getting it down to the cab, but Pat asked me if I needed any help moving and I gladly accepted. That crate was heavier than it looked, and it was just barely within our capacity to wrestle it down the stairs. Then partway down the stairs the crate came partially apart and many of my possessions were strewn on the staircase. We eventually got everything into Pat's car (large, American) and completed the move. Pat got more than he had bargained for and I was surely grateful for his offer and his presence that day. If it had happened with the theoretical taxi driver, I think he would have disowned me in disgust and I don't know what I would have done.

My new apartment was about two miles north of Grosvenor Square. It had a two-cot bedroom at one end and a living room at the other. A hallway connected the two and opened on the two intervening spaces: narrow bathroom and narrow kitchen. The hallway also held the entrance door from the outer hall. Someone told me of a cleaning lady; I contacted her and had her come in once a week. There were a couple of mysteries about the apartment: from the time I moved in until the time I left, about eight months, I got regular delivery of the daily and Sunday *Telegraph*. I had never ordered it nor did I ever pay for it. And the garbage pickup: there was a pass-through in the wall for that, and pickup was covered as part of the rental. When I put garbage there (typically a case of empty Tuborg bottles), it wasn't picked up. But when I put a case there and another case just outside, on the floor in the hall, then the case outside (only) *was* picked up. No one ever contacted me at any time about garbage neither in criticism of my actions nor otherwise.

I continued to pursue my correspondence Russian. At some point I had learned of the State Department's Foreign Service, and also of an "International Relations" major at Wisconsin. My ambitions began to take more concrete form. I considered applying for attache duty in Moscow. I would have had to extend my enlistment for two years to get it, which I was loath to do. But it was not on a ship. I wrote the head of the Russian department in Madison setting forth pros and cons (two-year delay in resuming college, etc.) and asking for his advice. He strongly recommended that I try to experience Moscow if possible, so I applied. The application was turned down because there were no billets for Telemen in Moscow.

In late 1955 there were some news items about the USSR opening up to tourists. Jim O'Donnell was also interested in a trip thence, so he and I visited the Soviet embassy to check out the possibilities. The officials there seemed somewhat surprised by our inquiries, one questioned, "You want to go to Russia?"

We were both quick to respond, "As tourists!" "As tourists!" I forget just what the obstacles were, but nothing ever came of it.

I learned of an institution called *The Linguists' Club*, checked it out, and joined. They had a number of conversational classes, mostly in the Romance languages, but also a weekly Russian class. It was led by a pleasant, elderly lady who I believe was minor tsarist nobility. I spent a lot of time at this club for other reasons and made a lot of friends there. In addition to the classes, it served as a meeting place and hangout for a wide variety of foreign students studying in London. France, Italy, East Germany, Pakistan, Ghana (then still the Gold Coast colony), Iran, Greece, Hong Kong, India, Hungary – and those are just the ones I knew and can remember. I occasionally ate a meal in the cafeteria, although the food was English unspeakable, but most of my time was spent in the table-tennis room. It was a popular place, but there was only one table. You signed up on a long clipboard waiting list, and when your turn (finally) came up, you could invite anyone you wished to be your opponent.

(I have slammed English cooking at least twice by now, and I don't retract a word of it. Even the Italian restaurant across the street from our navy offices was, for Italian food, very substandard. My *least-favorite* English foodstuff was orange marmalade. Rarely was any other spread provided for toast or bread. The stuff had thin strips of orange *peel* in it, and it tasted like those peelings; the memory is still repellent. But in fairness I have to balance by reporting on a three-week stay in London in 1994. The food during that stay was nothing but superb. Partly this was because my wife found a Thai restaurant near our hotel and we took every evening meal there – immigration from many nations since 1956 has certainly contributed to London's improvement. But the hotel breakfasts were also praiseworthy, and even the hospital cuisine was enjoyable and incomparably superior to American hospital fare. Sidewalk produce stands sold lichees, from Madagascar but as good as any from southeast Asia if not better. We would buy a pound by weight for a pound in money, go back to the hotel and gorge.)

The most interesting man I met at the Linguists' Club was Bonito Olympio, one of the better table-tennis players. He was bilingual in French and English, carried a Brazilian passport, but spoke not a word of Portuguese. He had finished his education and subsided on an allowance from his father, who was involved in international politicking and had some connection with the multinational Lever Bros. firm. More than once we collaborated on parties, for which I furnished the liquor and Bonito furnished the women. He had more girlfriends than any one man I've known. He told me the story of his one visit to the U.S., when he had passed through JFK (which was then Idlewild) as a transient. He had several hours between flights and strolled out of the airport. Immigration, security, etc., were far looser then than today. He stopped at a shoeshine stand and sat down for a shine. The white shiner looked at him with less-than-friendly surprise, finally asked, "You from the airport?" Bonito said that he was, and received his shine. He seemed much more amused than offended by the racism.

I never met Bonito again, nor corresponded with him, after London. In 1961 his father, Sylvanus Olympio, became the first president of the newly-independent little African nation of Togo, but was killed in a one-death coup d'etat in 1963. For many years Bonito and his more prominent younger brother tried unsuccessfully to topple the military dictator who had killed their father. Bonito died in Accra, Ghana, where he owned a bakery, in 1994.

The most memorable woman I met at the club was Parvine. She was from a Muslim country, had finished college in France, and was spending a year in London to improve her English; she hoped to work at the United Nations eventually. Her father was a high-level VIP in his country and was an ambassador at this time. She came to the first party I held at my new apartment, but proceeded to flirt with an Italian man, playing him and me against each other. I have near-zero tolerance for such female games; I decided the hell with it and got drunk. Nevertheless I invited her to Pat Ryon's New Year's Eve party. She wanted to attend festivities at the club. We argued about it. The upshot was that she would go solo to the club, later take a taxi to Pat's and meet me. She never showed up (taxis unfindable on the busy holiday night) and I remained a disappointed stag. She "lost my face" as I saw it, and it was a few months before I again invited her anywhere.

Another memory of that first party: two Italian girls locked themselves in my bathroom and required rescue. They weren't really locked in, it was just that the key was *very* hard to turn. There was some language difficulty, but I finally managed to convey that they should put the key on the newspaper that I slipped under the door so that I could pull it through and open the door from the outside. It worked.

One did not really need a car in the London of that time. The tube (subway) and the busses afforded excellent transportation. Lower enlisted would have had trouble affording a car. Many higher-rankers – perhaps out of habit – chose to have a car; some did not. A number of the drivers owned small European cars. These dominated the London traffic, English Fords, Morris Minors, a surprisingly large number of Volkswagens, an occasional Fiat or Peugeot. The Volkswagen then had its turn signals located on the upper sides just aft of the doors: foot-long sticks, hinged at the top, which stuck out horizontally and flashed when the driver signaled a turn. Americans had named these gadgets *idiot sticks*.

Quite a few sailors had acquired foreign cars which they intended to ship back to the U.S. at the end of their tour. (There were not yet any "U.S. specs" to worry about.) I had come into an inheritance of about $2000 {$14,487} from my late grandmother on my 21st birthday. My thoughts began to turn carward. The Ford Anglia, a popular choice among other sailors, was the most economical and could be had for about $1200 {$8692}. But there was an obstacle: I had never learned to drive. Si was one of those who were carless by choice. I approached him with a proposition: if he would teach me to drive, I would furnish the transportation to and from work for both of us. He agreed. In December I took title to the car.

It came with a square, plastic, affixable white magnetic placard with a large red letter L (for "learner") about a foot high. English law required that this be displayed on the rear whenever a non-licensed driver was at the wheel, and of course a licensed driver had to be in the other front seat. Some sailors found it humorous to attach a placard to the car of a perfectly competent driver without his knowledge.

One day, driving to our offices in mid-morning, I had to make a right turn from a small side street onto one-way North Audley. I waited until Si told me to go ahead, turned, and was immediately passed on my left by a massive, horn-blaring Rolls-Royce. It was driven by an elegant, middle-aged lady who radiated wealth and quality. She had to stop at a stop light, where she turned almost fully around and bestowed a furious glare of reproach and indignation on me. Perhaps she was looking for some sign of contrition. She prolonged her glare.

Si gave her the finger.

I have never seen, nor will I ever see, a faster eyes-front. I was still much too much of a neophyte driver to pronounce judgment on my actions, but Si said that I had not done wrong and that, even if I had, the lady should have had more tolerance because of my L placard. I expect she had a tale to tell her friends about the rude barbarians she had encountered in traffic. She may also have had a sore neck.

The English road test to obtain a license was extraordinarily tough. I failed on my first try and was somewhat apprehensive – what if I couldn't pass it before I went back to the U.S.? But Si somehow learned of a special licensing procedure for tourists, foreigners, etc. We tried that avenue and, although I thought I drove worse than on the first test, they passed me.

Early one morning, about 0600, I was driving to work through one of the notorious London fogs. My route took me past one side of Regent's Park, a very large park, where the fog was at its densest. I was going slowly and navigating by my distance from the park's tall, black, iron fence visible on my left; there was a sidewalk between the fence and the street. Suddenly a black lamp post loomed ahead, alarmingly close to my left fender. I veered to the right and felt both my left wheels bounce down off the low curb. Somewhere behind me there had been a curbless driveway, my left wheels had come smoothly up on the sidewalk, and I had been driving I know not how far with two wheels in the street and two on the sidewalk! I rolled down my window and stuck my head halfway out to get a better view of the curb, the fog lessened after I passed the park, and I reached work without further mishap.

In those pre-Volkswagen-invasion days, the cheapest, most basic Detroit product couldn't be had for anything under $2000 {$14,487}. People in *my* income bracket were expected to make do with third- or fourth-hand junkers and somehow keep them running. U.S. manufacturers (when they couldn't avoid the subject altogether) were peddling the lie that the failure of the late-1940s Crosley proved that there was no market for small, cheap cars in America. I vowed never to own an American-brand car, and I never have. I took my Anglia back to the U.S. and drove it, sometimes with a smug smile, until 1962. I had to endure some wisecracks: "Where do you wind it?" but I got off my own share of remarks about ". . . fish-tailed, gas-eating, *Dee*troit monstrosities." And if I had a passenger when I noticed that the tank was low, I would complain, "Damn, I just put gas in it *last* month."

Newspapers published in Germany and aimed at U.S. servicemen often carried ads for contact lenses. I was tempted. All of the eye doctors so advertising were in Germany. I took a week or so of leave and took the train to Frankfurt. It was a scenic ride through Belgium and then up the Rhine with views of many old castles. At a stop in Cologne I saw the famous cathedral there, amid much war damage still unrepaired. The lenses were a major disappointment. They were much thicker than the lenses of later years. The doctor said you had to practice a few minutes every day, to get used to them, but I never could. I soon gave up.

Three times in my life I have been totally entranced on first hearing a piece of music. The first time was at the London Palladium, Louis Armstrong live, *Mack the Knife*. I had read recent mention of that song in the *Stars and Stripes* and by the third verse I had figured out what song I was hearing. But I hadn't figured out many of the lyrics! The next day I obtained the record and began to wear it out, and only then did I decipher Louis' gravelly rendition. At the Palladium I had thought it started out, "Oh the shop lights . . . on the streets, dear . . ."! (The other two times? The radio on while I was doing something else in each instance. Duke Ellington's Newport Jazz Festival *Diminuendo and Crescendo in Blue*, and Hank Williams' *Miller's Cave*.)

Pat Ryon was moved to a day-working job about halfway through my London time, and Frank Farrell, equally copacetic, replaced him as section supervisor. At one point a few non-deliveries perturbed Authority. One of the day-working chiefs recommended a system that he had used, and allegedly had worked well, at one of his former locations. It involved assignment of an in-house serial number to each message as it arrived, logs for same, and a checkoff by the traffic checker when they reached him – thus theoretically ensuring that no message could completely disappear.

It was implemented. I deplored it from its start. I felt that heavy workload was a cause of mistakes, and that adding another step, making the work more complex, only added to the burden. I felt that it was a perfect example of "designed by geniuses to be run by idiots", and I began referring to "idiot numbers" and "idiot logs". My terminology was popular; it took root immediately and was used on all sections by all concerned.

We continued to criticize the system, particularly by complaining to Pat Ryon, who was sympathetic. After a couple of months Pat prevailed and idiot numbers and idiot logs were trashed. We were on midwatches when the discontinuance occurred and we made a medal for Pat. We took a round piece of cardboard and covered it with the pseudo-gold foil with which English milk bottles were sealed. We attached red teletype tape to form a couple of notched ribbons hanging from the bottom, and taped a paper clip to the reverse so that it could be worn on a pocket. Inspired by the *Grin and Bear It* cartoons of Lichty (George Lichtenstein) who often caricatured Soviet dignitaries wearing "hero" medals, we cut out red H-E-R-O letters and glued them to the front. When Pat arrived for work we put the medal on him. He was pleased and amused but started to take the medal off – we insisted he leave it on. I saw him at a party that night. Someone asked him how the day had gone. He chuckled, "Two chiefs wouldn't speak to me all day long!"

Another of our day-working chiefs was from Mississippi and the hardest-core bigot I've ever seen. At least twice when race came up during bull sessions I heard him recite his bitter dogma, "*A nigger's a nigger and that's all he'll ever be, is just a nigger." This chief claimed he would never salute, nor say "sir", to a black officer. Jim O'Donnell and I joined in wishing that he would have to work under Sam Gravely at his next duty station. Sad to say, black officers were still so uncommon then that the chief probably reached retirement without encountering one.

Jim had a prejudice of his own – against the English. He had Irish roots, of course, and he had gone to Ireland on leave before I arrived in London. There he had fallen into the hands of the IRA and had been thoroughly indoctrinated by that organization. He was bitterly hostile toward the *Sassenachs* – a contemptuous word that the Irish use for the English – and denounced them in many a message center bull session. The rest of us regarded his fixation with some amusement and baited

144

him at times. Once I referred to the ISSRA which, when asked, I defined as the Irish Soviet Socialist Republican Army and endured Jim's heartfelt dissent thereto. We harassed him by surreptitiously taping to his back such sentiments as *God Save the Queen* and *There Will Always Be an England.*

Bloody, in England, was then a word just about as powerful and shock-producing as *fucking.* So naturally sailors made a great deal of use of it. Jim had said that he felt he ought not to say it within the hearing of American women, even though . . . One day he was sitting on a counter and vigorously expounding on the sins of the English: ". . . shooting the bloody people in the bloody streets!"

Doris, our Wave chief, in crypto, was peering through the pass slot behind him, and listening. I pointed her out and said, "*What kind of streets, Jim? What kind?"

"*Streets!!!"

English girls, having somehow learned our phone number, sometimes called the message center to flirt, hoping to be asked out. I fielded one such call and wound up making a movie date. She was allegedly a nurse. I was to meet her at a subway stop, nearly the last one out to the east. She was rather plain, slightly fat, and, I would guess, about 16. I took her to the movie, groped her a time or two (more from habit than desire) without objection, then put her back on a train home. I had no wish to see more of her. I got a pleading, sorrowful letter from her which I ignored, then she called the message center, tearfully insisting to speak to me. I refused to come to the phone. I was sorry for the poor girl but I didn't know anything I could say – and certainly nothing that I could do – to ease her off her infatuation.

London being London, many of the brownbaggers had something going on the side. We singles had a pretty good idea of who did and who did not. We often commented on how it seemed that in general the guilty had unsuspecting, trustful wives, while the innocent were under perpetual suspicion and demands for accountability. We sometimes sabotaged the latter when a wifely telephone call came. Without covering the phone mouthpiece: "Hey, it's your wife. Are you here?"

I got a flier in the U.S. mail from some lonely-hearts organization. Some prankster had sent a request purporting to come from me. I was sure Si had done it. I said nothing, but during the next few weeks Si received advertisements for clothing for big men, a course to improve his English, and another that I forget. But my masterpiece was when he received, addressed to "Georgia M. Simons" rather than George M., material touting a new, miraculous, whirling-spray douche bag.

Spring 1956 was enlivened by the paper-clip wars. They began when someone discovered that, when holding a lead pencil by the eraser end, a paper clip could be slipped over the point, tensioned, and propelled with surprising velocity, to the discomfiture and anguish of an unsuspecting target. This monkey business became a fad for several weeks when things were relatively caught up, toward the end of a midwatch or on weekends. We began, I believe, with target practice: shooting from several feet away at a matchbox perched atop a teletype. But the pastime rapidly escalated to anti-personnel actions, with paper clips flying all over the message center and every man for himself. An hour or so before our watch ended we observed a cease-fire, and spent the remaining time picking up the spent ammunition from floors and surfaces. We were fortunate that no one was ever hit in an eye.

Then, late one April Sunday morning, unseasonably warm and sunny, two sailors hit upon a variant. From our third-floor window, they opened fire on the occasional pedestrians on the far side of the nearly-deserted street. They had scant luck for some time. A few paper clips struck clothing without reaction, and quite a few rebounded from shop windows, sometimes puzzling the targets by their *clink*. Presently a tall, briskly-striding, thirtyish Englishman approached, decked in his Sunday finest, bowler hat, umbrella in the crook of an arm. Obviously a man of distinction. He was glancing at his Sunday newspaper as he walked and, when he was nearly opposite our window, he must have encountered an item of absorbing interest. He made the mistake of stopping, the better to peruse it.

A barrage of paper clips rained around him, off his trousers, off his newspaper, off the shop windows behind him, and I believe at least one struck his hat and came to rest on the brim. Nothing disrupted his concentration on his newspaper. Finally one smote him on the side of his neck, just above the collar.

When narrating this incident I have sometimes used the cliché, "He jumped a foot!" In truth he didn't reach quite that altitude, but he did most definitely *jump*. His hand shot to his stricken neck. Open-mouthed, he stared at our building, glanced down at the paper-clip-bestrewn sidewalk, glared again at the building and our open window. The snipers had ducked out of view as soon as they saw their success, but computation of two plus two was instantaneous. With an air that said "I know *just* what to do about *this*", the victim carefully folded his paper, tucked it under an arm, and marched across the street to our entrance where he made due complaint of injury first to the marine guard and then to the duty officer. The latter pacified him with apologies and assurances of justice, and contacted the CWO. The CWO was not unaware of the paper-clip wars and surely must have known that the culprits were within his purview. He went through the motions of "investigating" (no one seemed to know anything about it) and reported his failure to the duty officer. The CWO was one of our better junior officers. The guilty went undetected and unpunished.

I witnessed the fun from an adjacent window which was closed and, moreover, separated from the sniper window by a quite long internal wall, ruling me out as a suspect if my description had been given, but it apparently was not. The victim's interaction with the ground-floor authorities is of course my assumption.

Another bit of message center tomfoolery that I recall: one day Si and I were both sitting at desks and he was attempting to harass me by flicking lighted matches in my direction. With one index finger he would hold a wooden match perpendicular to his matchbox, the head touching the striking surface, then snap it toward me with his other index finger; thus igniting it on the fly. He could not achieve much accuracy with this method, but I kept a wary eye on his activities, ready to dodge if necessary. After several near misses, he achieved a direct hit – not on me, but on the burn bag in the wastebasket beside me. The match went straight down the mouth of the burn bag, smoke curled back upward. As an innocent and aggrieved party, I was not inclined to assist Si's fire-fighting efforts. His attempt to stomp it out failed and very shortly he was quick-timing out of the message center toward the head, carrying wastebasket and all, pursued by my righteously-delighted guffaws. For a few days I called him "Smokey Stover" after the old time comic-strip fireman.

I don't know how sailors acquired firecrackers in London but some did, and they found use for them. One stunt was to throw a lighted firecracker into an occupied elevator just as the door was closing, closeting the occupant(s) to bear the blast. Another was to enter an empty elevator, push the button for the ground floor, then jump back out and deposit a firecracker within. This was best done at about 0300-0400, when it would disrupt the slumber (or at least the tranquility) of the marine guard and any other ground-floor people who chanced to be awake or sleeping lightly.

I sought a roommate to share my apartment and pay half the rent. I couldn't interest Jim, but found a taker from another watch section. Dick was a heavy-drinking RMSN with a steady English girlfriend. It didn't work out very well. We didn't have any open arguments or friction, but he decided to move out again after a month. During his stay he came home late one evening when I was almost, but not quite, asleep. A girl – and not his regular girlfriend – was with him. Amatory sounds from the other bed, and the lady's unavailing requests for an encore, kept me awake for a little while. The next morning I was up, had had breakfast, and was about to go out when a haggard Dick stumbled out of the bedroom and asked me, "*Hey . . . hey . . . who the fuck is *she*?"

I explained that he was more likely to have that information than was I.

Nikita Khrushchev and Nikolai Bulganin, supposedly co-equals in power at that time, came to London in April. They had arrived in Portsmouth on the Soviet cruiser *Ordzhonikidze*. The ship was open for visiting and several of us drove down to see it – but our information was defective; we arrived after visiting hours had closed and got only a distant view. B&K, as the press dubbed the visitors, stayed in Claridges and the heavy security there somewhat impeded our access to the dog house. Held up in halted traffic one day as their motorcade went by, I glimpsed Bulganin's white-goateed face peering from the curtains of their limousine.

At loose ends one spring day, and with no female interests currently on my docket, I called Parvine and invited her to a movie. She accepted instantly. I began seeing her regularly, taking her to movies, the dog house, and on a drive to Dover to see the white cliffs with Bonito and one of his girlfriends. Then at one movie she became quite cranky and hard to please. I didn't contact her again. She phoned a week or two later and asked me to come see her at her rooming house. She said, "*Larry . . . you should get for me . . . a doctor."

Abortions were still illegal in the UK at that time. It was not easy to find an abortionist, but Pat Ryon knew of someone who had had an abortion. He made some inquiries and put me on the right track, including the pub where the man could usually be found at certain times. We found him and the abortion was scheduled for the last few days before I would be leaving London.

I had passed the test for first-class Teleman in February, and was promoted to TE1 in May. The term for me was now *slick-arm first*. Slick, because of the lack of hash marks on my sleeve – unusual for a first-class. (There was also a derisive, and often envious, term for someone who gets promoted rapidly: *rate-grabber*.) The promotion gave me some pride, and the satisfaction of reaching a goal, but otherwise it held little value for me – only a month of somewhat higher pay.

In those last days, the old phonetic alphabet – Able, Baker, Charlie, Dog – was replaced by a new one: Alpha, Bravo, Charlie, Delta. The change was to provide an alphabet for all of NATO, and terms more recognizable in a wider variety of languages were substituted for most of the old ones. I gloated about being so short that I didn't need to bother to learn the new ones.

At that time, too, a new designation for my service status was introduced. The simple USN on my ID card became USN U-1, which had something to do with my reserve status after discharge. I was obligated for an additional four years in the reserves but, barring national mobilization, it was merely a paper obligation entailing no meetings, drills, etc. Nearly every first-hitch sailor was similarly affected and, in a silly bureaucratic exercise, we all had to get new ID cards. I did get some wise-guy mileage out of my new card though, I would display it to other sailors and say, "*I'm U-1 – are you U-1 too?"

I was entitled to ship hold baggage, and the packers came to my apartment to handle it. I had quite an accumulation of PX liquor, acquired without a great deal of thought or consideration of how long I had left and how much I (and guests) was likely to drink. Brownbaggers could ship four bottles, which was also the maximum allowed by U.S. customs. Single men could *not*. (The technicality here was that marrieds were allowed a *household effects* shipment but singles were not. The four bottles were legal in these shipments. Both marrieds and singles were entitled to ship *hold baggage*, but liquor was banned from hold baggage.) I respected the customs laws; I did not respect the naval discrimination. I sold most of my liquor (illegally) to the cleaning lady, but included four bottles with my things to be packed. The packers said, well, they weren't supposed to pack it, but never mind, they would. When the bottles were packed near the *top* of the barrels they used, I thought nothing of it at the time.

Parvine came to my apartment for her abortion and stayed with me for about a week. I had to leave her alone for a day while I drove my car to one of the ports for shipment and took a train back. During that week we became closer than ever before. Parting was not easy, harder on her than on me I believe. I mentally contrasted the Canadian's upturned nose at the "scarlet woman" with Parvine's comment when she saw London streetwalkers on a cold night: "*Oh, the poor girls . . ."

During the search for an abortionist, when I was not yet having any luck and Parvine was discouraged and tearful, I had asked if she would marry me. She thanked me for the offer but said only if we could not arrange the abortion, only if her father approved. It was for the best that it did not happen. At home she was used to an upper-class life with servants (she told me once that she could not cook, "not at all"). It would be hard to imagine her as the wife of a college student working part-time, in a small apartment – and with a new baby yet. Somewhere I've read the applicable wisdom: those who marry for love without money have happy nights and sorry days.

And yet. Fifty-plus years later she is still the Woman of All Women.

After returning to the U.S. I received one letter from her; after that I heard nothing from, or of, her.

Enough.

I went back to the U.S. on a troop transport identical to the one that had carried me from Brooklyn to Naples.

VIII - REENLISTMENT BLUES

I spent a few days in the Brooklyn receiving station again for discharge processing. I had daydreamed of a scenario in which I would be urged one last time to reenlist. Had it happened, I was going to make a counter-offer. I would relate how I had been set back six months on promotions because of the Naples chief's policy and say, "Remedy that, pay me the difference in pay that I would have received if I'd made both second-class and first-class six months earlier, and *then* I'll talk about reenlisting." I knew that they would never do that – but then I'd never have reenlisted either. Anyhow the last-time pitch was so short and low-key that I had no opportunity. I met one other exiting slick-arm first at Brooklyn, a Machinist's Mate I believe. He didn't change his mind either.

I became a civilian eight days early, on 4 June 1956. I picked up my car at the Bayonne MSTS terminal, drove no more than 10 or 15 yards on the wrong side of the street before I corrected myself, and headed for the midwest.

My hold baggage from London arrived at my campus apartment. I found that three of my four bottles of liquor had vanished, obviously stolen by the cooperative packers. I suspected that they had left the fourth untouched in order to further "incriminate" me, as a deterrent to possible complaint. I did complain though, both to the packing company and to the navy supply office in London. To the former, I pointed out that the majority of their navy clients were career people who would be in no position to report the theft of an illegally-packed item. They responded with a whitewash stating that they had interviewed their packers, who claimed innocence. (The packers sought to cause me trouble by telling of my sale of my excess to the cleaning lady.) I sent another letter in rebuttal but heard nothing more. What happened to the surviving bottle, a French champagne, will be told in a future chapter.

A few months later I received a bill from the British telephone office, sent to the navy and forwarded to me, billing me for service not only for part of the time I was there, but also for several months after I had departed. (I hadn't even thought about discontinuing service when I moved out.) When I left London I was owed three debts of about $50 {$364} each – deposit on the apartment, some sort of rebate from car purchase, and a third that I can't recall. Britain's financial situation at the time was so shaky that payments outside Britain were forbidden. I think all three debts were deliberately delayed and that the moneys probably wound up in the pockets of middle managers. I replied to the telephone bill by pointing out the unfairness of the one-way law that allowed creditors to receive money from me, while making it impossible for me to collect just debts. I declined to pay, but detailed the three debts owed me, and gave the telephone office my blessing to seek collection from the entities involved. I heard no more.

There were many other veterans on campus and I heard many stories. Two of them deserve to be told here.

During World War II about a dozen servicemen were stationed together at an isolated outpost of some sort – weather observers, perhaps, or a radar station. They took meals together, and a custom developed. Whenever someone requested or referred to an item at the table, it had to be prefaced by *fucking*, e.g., pass the fucking salt. Omission of the keyword earned the forgetful one a rap on the wrist from his neighbor's silverware.

They had agreed to keep in touch after the war and have a reunion some day. Several years after the war they did that, now with wives and children in tow. It was an outdoor cookout in a park. Beer flowed freely; it became just like old times. Seated at a park table, one man broke his conversation to say, "Hey, gimme the fuh . . . uh . . . uh . . . the catsup, please."

Eyes met, grins were grinned, and the catsup-seeker said, "Hah! Thought I'd fuck up, didn't ya?"

That story came to me second-hand, if not more remotely, and may or may not be true. The next came from one who was present and I have every confidence in its truth – although "five minutes" may be a bit of an exaggeration.

The narrator and several of his friends were at a medium-sized overseas army movie theater. This was postwar and an ample number of dependents were present. He didn't remember the name of the movie, he remembered only that Shelley Winters was in it and that they were up in an airplane.

At a tense and dramatic moment in the film, the audience hushed and expectant, one of the narrator's friends exploded a thunderclap fart, heard throughout the theater. Before there was time for any reaction, up on the screen, with perfect timing, Shelley Winters said something like, "What was that strange noise?" He said it was five minutes before the soundtrack could again be heard over the laughter.

Note: some time after writing the above, I think I pinned down the movie – *Phone Call From a Stranger*. I watched it on satellite TV, hoping to verify Ms Winters' exact words. She did not say them, nor anything reasonably close. But everything else fits – it was a 1952 movie, she was indeed in the passenger section of an airplane for a substantial portion of the first half of the movie, and the character she played was a first-time flyer, nervous and jumpy. Television too often cuts portions of films, to fit their time slots or for other reasons, and I think that is the explanation.

Not to omit mention of my own flatulary talents: I worked at the desk in the student union bowling alleys, a rather small, enclosed cubbyhole from which I served customers over the counter. I smoked an aromatic pipe tobacco. My then-girlfriend was chatting with me over the counter when I emitted a silent-but-deadly (uncharacteristic; I am usually more renowned for melody than for fragrance). Presently she paused, sniffed – "Is that a different tobacco you're smoking today?"

I went to the Veterans Administration hospital in Milwaukee for a few days for removal of nasal polyps. Some weeks later I heard from the VA that I was adjudged 10% disabled and received $17 {$124} a month from them for a year or more, until I was required to be reevaluated and it was revoked. I thought it was ridiculous but I cashed the checks. A side benefit: when subjected to physical horseplay by friends, I could upbraid them for their callous treatment of a disabled veteran.

Thanks to correspondence courses and two summer schools, I had more than enough credits to graduate early, in February 1958. The low C of my first two years improved to a low A for the last two. I now faced an unforeseen problem: employment.

I had three irons in the fire: the State Department, the CIA, and a civilian job with ONI – the Office of Naval Investigations. One by one they petered out.

In hindsight, it was probably a good thing that I lost out on those jobs. I would not have made a good diplomat. I probably would not have cut it with the CIA either, and they have done some things over the years with which I would not have been proud to be associated. ONI – I'd have done better at that, and I'd have been delighted to be in on such efforts as the roundup of the Walker family spy ring, but I fear too much of the job would have entailed chasing gays and pot smokers, efforts with which I would have had steadily less sympathy over time.

I had a year or more of GI bill money left. I considered pursuing a master's degree in geography but was discouraged by the experience of a preliminary course I audited. Instead I fell back on six months of GI bill unemployment pay. I began to read the newspaper employment ads regularly, and mailed off an occasional application. The 1958 recession was in full swing. A few applications were rejected by an obvious form letter, most were simply ignored. Employers treated applicants like shit then, and I suspect that is even truer today. It is fitting that I recognize and praise one honorable exception, the one corporation that sent me a reasoned and sympathetic *non-form-letter* response, even though it did not offer a job. Thank you, Brunswick Bowling.

Anyone who is willing to work and is serious about it will certainly find a job. Only you must not go to the man who tells you this, for he has no job to offer and doesn't know anyone who knows of a vacancy. This is exactly the reason why he gives you such generous advice, out of brotherly love, and to demonstrate how little he knows the world. (B. Traven, *The Treasure of the Sierra Madre*)

Looking for a job is the worst job in the world. For some reason I don't understand, the people in charge of hiring, who certainly must have looked for a job themselves at some point in their past, seem to forget it and proceed to humiliate applicants. (Andy Rooney, column of 9 January 1998)

And I would add to Rooney's observation that they also seem to forget that most applicants will, in time, find employment and become prospective customers for their firm's product or services.

As time went by and I became more and more apprehensive, I began to think the unthinkable. I went to the navy recruiting office and spoke with the recruiter about becoming an officer. It sounded good in a way. I would have gone to Officer Candidate School (the "90-day-wonder" factory, also known as "charm school") in Newport and would have received the pay of my first-class rate while attending. Application cost nothing and committed me to nothing, so I applied. There were two obstacles, both physical. Unaided eyesight of no worse than 20/100 was required – but a waiver, of up to 20/200, was possible. One of my eyes was 20/200. Similarly, my nose/sinus was in question after the VA polypectomy, but this was also within waiverable limits. One or the other, or the combination, caused me to be rejected. I say again, it was the 1958 recession. The navy wasn't scraping the bottom for bodies.

But, as with the unattained civilian options, I think it is a good thing that I was rejected – for me, and for the navy. I can imagine scenarios in which I might have had a successful career as an officer, but it would have hinged on what sort of assignments I was given, where, and most of all for whom I worked. Everything would have had to go just right for me at duty station after duty station. I can imagine many *more* scenarios in which I would rapidly have gotten on Authority's shit list, my fitness reports would have looked like used kitty litter, and I would either have been selected out or resigned to avoid same.

More time passed, and I spiraled down to the even more unthinkable. Any sailor who was discharged, and eligible to reenlist, could do so within 90 days after getting out and retain his rate as of discharge. But *critical* ratings – those ratings in which the navy was severely undermanned, and for which it had the most difficulty in retaining people – had a full two-year window in which to do this. Teleman had been a critical rating since forever; in the worst case I could go back in as a first-class up until June. I spoke again to the recruiter.

He told me that the Teleman rating was being disestablished. Existing Telemen were to convert to Radiomen or Yeomen, and Yeomen were to take over the post offices. The recruiter had to query Washington for specific authority whenever a Teleman sought to reenlist. No problem, I was sure. Having worked entirely in communications I was sure to be destined for Radioman, and Radioman had also been critical since forever. But when Washington replied, they authorized my reenlistment only as *second-class*.

I was disgusted at what I perceived as unfairness. But worse was to come. I had not yet given up completely on the ONI job, and procrastinated. The time window Washington allowed had expired. The recruiter sought an extension. Washington's impatient reply was yes – as *third-class*.

158

I talked to the air force recruiter. They would offer me the same E-4 paygrade that the navy was now offering. I posed the question, suppose I do very, very well in the air force – what's the minimum time in which I could make E-6? Three years, he said, and he was very pessimistic that it could be done that quickly. I could do it in two in the navy. I was more interested in rapid promotion than I was in escaping shipboard duty. I also spoke to the local naval reserve center to see if there was some way I could be sent to active duty, while remaining a reserve, and retain first-class. There was not.

For the second time, a recruiter misled me by not telling me all that he could have. This time harm *was* done. The navy had raised the time requirement between second-class and first-class from one year to two. It was not surprising that they had done it; the sight of slick-arm firsts opting for discharge must have played hell with the morale of second- and third-classes with multiple hash marks. Now there would be no more slick-arm firsts. From E-4 I could not get back to E-6 in less than three years. I had discussed my promotion and timing concerns vis-à-vis the air force with the navy recruiter. *He* certainly knew about the change. I did not. He said nothing. Had I known of the change, I would surely have gone air force. I did not learn of it until after he had me safely reenlisted.

When my last hope (the ONI job) finally evaporated, I decided to reenlist in early September. In a last-gasp effort to find work and avoid it, I drove to New York City – reasoning that there, if anywhere, there would be overseas jobs, or international-relations-connected jobs. I spent a week there, had no luck, and returned. I understood – too late – that private U.S. business does not hire Americans for overseas jobs if they can possibly avoid it. The locals are cheaper (and that was much more true back in the 1950s) and incur no transportation costs to get them there. Finally, if a firm *must* have an American in a certain position, say in Italy, they don't look to hire someone who speaks Italian. They look for an *attorney* who speaks Italian, or a *secretary* who speaks Italian, or an *accountant* who speaks Italian. Decades later I was amused by a friend who wrote in his magazine of his "history major, aka terminal unemployment". I knew whereof he spoke.

On 10 September 1958 I reenlisted in Chicago as a TE(RM)3 and drove my Anglia to the receiving station in the Anacostia section of Washington DC, where I would await the navy's decision on what next to do with me. On my first night there, back in an upper rack in a moderately-noisy barracks, all too familiar and unwelcome, I had a brief *Oh, no, what have I done?* moment. It was the only one; from then on I made the best of things.

IX - RADIOMAN

Walking from the barracks to the chow hall, I was surprised to see a face from campus – so surprised that I didn't hail him, couldn't believe my eyes. But later that day or the next we passed again and this time I made contact. Bob was familiar from bridge games at the student union. He had, while an enlisted man, been accepted for the naval ROTC program at Wisconsin, but he had dropped out of it and the navy had shanghaied him to serve the remainder of his four-year enlisted hitch as a consequence. He was now again an ETSN – Electronics Technician Seaman. We couldn't locate any other bridge players in the barracks, so we played a lot of cribbage. We experimented with reverse cribbage – where you try *not* to get points and whoever goes out first loses. Kibitzers did not know this and we didn't tell them; some of the comments on our play were most amusing.

The navy could not find my boot camp test scores – odd, because they show up on old documents turned over to me when I finally retired. I had to retake the tests. Conventional naval wisdom holds that it is useless to retake the tests, that everyone that does so does worse. (Sailors who missed eligibility for something or other by only a few points would sometimes seek to do so. Permission was not often granted.) I had mixed results: GCT down from 76 to 71, ARI up from 73 to 77, MECH down from 57 to 54, CLER up from 70 to 74. (How could my ARI rise when it was perfect the first time? Different test versions with different maximums.)

I was not eligible for a reenlistment bonus, but I did receive a uniform allowance – enough to buy a whole seabag. I had preserved my old uniforms and had to spend very little, the rest was found money.

I was used in a variety of ways while waiting, none particularly onerous, and stood duties and watches. One day they were looking for typists – I was sent across the Anacostia river to a naval intelligence building where I typed roughs of background investigations into smooths alongside an attractive corps of secretaries for about a week. Their supervisor praised my output, and I was quite disappointed when her superiors decreed that, their backlog having been reduced, outside assistance was no longer required. I should have typed slower.

After about four weeks I was transferred to the Naval Training Center at Bainbridge, Maryland, for Radioman A School. Bainbridge was almost at the Pennsylvania border, maybe a dozen miles north of the northern tip of Chesapeake Bay. It had a variety of other schools, and a Wave boot camp. It has been closed since 1976.

(One sailor told me that, passing within earshot of the Wave grounds, he had overheard a Wave chief, company commander, exhorting her charges: ". . . and when I call ya to attention from parade rest, I wanna hear them pussies *snap!*")

Bainbridge, though smaller, was the east coast's version of San Diego, and equally chickenshit – for seamen out of boot camp. Being a petty officer, I escaped the worst of it. I didn't have to do any marching, and slept in a barracks bay with other "convertees" (the seamen were "trainees") in a single rack (no upper). The navy was encouraging petty officers in overcrowded ratings, provided they were qualified by test scores and otherwise eligible, to convert to critical ratings. There were probably more Telemen in the barracks than any other rating, but we also had Boatswain's Mates, Stewards, Storekeepers, etc., who were attempting to convert. Four other convertees, all Telemen, were in my school class and we stuck together a lot.

At the start of school I sat – again – pounding on a typewriter. We also had basic electronics classes – much more of it, and in more depth, than there had been in Teleman school. But the primary activity was Morse code.

I attacked the code with gung-ho determination. I wanted to be the *best* at it, as I had been with teletypes everywhere I'd worked. It was not to be. I did get way out ahead at first. I zipped rapidly up to copying 10 words a minute when nearly all the class was only at 4 or 6. I then progressed more slowly and, at about 14-16 wpm I hit the granddaddy of all learning plateaus. I was stuck in that range for a very long time and by the end of school I was barely making the 22 wpm required for graduation. By that time many of the class had gone up higher, some as high as 30.

(I have long attributed my efficiency, in particular with typing and teletyping and also with clerical tasks in general, to laziness. I didn't want to work. I'd rather read, play cards, talk, whatever. When the work was caught up, I could do other things with a clear conscience. And so I bent every effort to get the work out of the way as fast as possible – and as accurately as possible so that more work, in correcting mistakes, would not result. If a shortcut could be found, I would find it. Perhaps I can coin a phrase: *Laziness breeds efficiency.* Or maybe it would be better as: *Laziness is the mother of efficiency.* I also like a term I heard from a State Department political officer: *constructive laziness.*)

That infamous learning plateau, known to all educators, was not my only problem. My curiosity was another. I did better with the five-letter coded groups of encrypted messages, because they were a meaningless jumble. But when copying plain language, my brain *insisted* that I read what I was copying. A good operator cannot do that; he cannot copy and read at the same time. He cannot even copy and *think* at the same time; his brain must be disengaged. Indeed – and I have never read whatever psychological or neurological explanations may exist for this – the better copiers lag at least several characters behind the earphone sound, and the very best may lag behind for a full printed line or more. I could not come remotely close to such feats.

Receiving was only half of the code. I also had to learn to send it. This was relatively easier, but I never got really good at it. The class began to work on sending only later in the school schedule. Before Radiomen could be recommended for advancement exams, they had to pass performance tests on the code. For second-class it was relatively low, maybe 14-16 wpm. I hoped to take the February exam but the performance test was a month or two earlier and I had not yet even begun sending. I tried the test anyhow but the tester, with sympathetic sorrow, broke off my hapless "sending" before the test was even finished – my untutored effort had not even come close.

There were some people who just could not learn the code at all. The seamen may have been given some sort of auditory aptitude test before being designated for the school, but converting Telemen had not. One of the other convertees in my class was unable to make much progress and after several weeks he was transferred to the Yeoman school on the same base.

I think it was during this time that I spent a weekend in Baltimore or Philadelphia and took in a burlesque show. The theaters typically have a stable of locally-based strippers and a ballyhooed visiting star who performs for a week and moves on. This night there were two visiting stars. Star #2 boasted enormous, almost freakish, breasts. She did her act, then Star #1 came out for hers. When she reached the point where she bared *her* breasts, a critic near the stage observed loudly, "*I've seen bigger." The house collapsed in laughter and, far from being offended, Star #1 was equally in stitches.

As school progressed we went on from basic electronics to classes on more specific equipment, receivers, transmitters, etc. We also covered (re-covered, in my case) many of the same things I'd learned in Teleman school: teletypes, communications procedures, message format, circuit procedures. But the classes remained heavy on electronics, and the code practice never ceased.

The week before Easter one of the instructors was telling the class what schedule modifications would be made for Good Friday. He summed up by saying something about, ". . . all you Catholics and prostitutes . . ." He immediately corrected himself; it was a genuine slip of the tongue (and brain) and he was most embarrassed. As soon as the seamen had gone off to some evolution, leaving only us convertees and the two Waves, he apologized profusely to the Waves. They were quite forgiving, it was so obviously an unintended blunder.

At an earlier point one of the seamen thought he was being funny by sneaking a condom into a Wave's purse. She found it and made an indignant fuss about it. The guilty man confessed and apologized; she was satisfied and disciplinary action was averted.

These Waves were not a scholastic threat. I finished first in the class of 78. Unlike Teleman school, there was no assignment-choice benefit accruing to a high finish – and even if there had been, I was the only third-class in our class and would have been in competition with no one but myself. My orders arrived: COMSIX AFLOAT. Of COMSIX I knew. Afloat puzzled me.

The Commandant of the Sixth Naval District was located in Charleston, South Carolina. The "Afloat" tag-on covered a variety of small ships under his jurisdiction, minesweepers, tugs, etc., located at various places all over the southeastern states, some on rivers, mostly connected with naval reserve activities. The precise destination for me would be determined by COMSIX.

It would have been a small ship, without much navy around, which was good. It was not overseas and would not be going overseas, which was bad. I could have done worse. Three or four convertees intended to drive to BUPERS in Washington to see what prospects they had for receiving assignments or for changing assignments already made, and asked if I wanted to go along. I did. The warrant-officer detailer with whom I spoke was somewhat grumpy. I had orders to good duty, he said. I said that yes, it would be great indeed for a married sailor – but that I was not married, and I preferred overseas, or a ship that would go overseas. Presently he offered me Asmara.

Most sailors regarded Asmara as the boondocks and would have wanted no part of it. That is, most of those who *knew* about it – very few had even heard of it. It was near the Red Sea coast of Ethiopia, and the command was NAVCOMMU THREE (Naval Communication Unit). I had known (very slightly) a couple Ethiopian students on campus; they were slender, fine-boned, handsome young men; I anticipated (correctly) that the females of the race would be equally well-favored. Required to do a term paper for a course on the United Nations, it happened that I had chosen to write on the U.N. Commission in Eritrea, so I was at least minimally informed about the place if only in book-learning fashion. And the very obscurity of a corner of the world where few Americans ever penetrated appealed to me. Yes, I'd have preferred London or Naples again – but I did not hesitate to accept the detailer's offer.

With graduation I lost the clumsy TE(RM)3 identification and became officially an RM3. I left Bainbridge on 17 April for another stay at the Anacostia RecSta where my transportation would be arranged. My duties there were often as a "chaser" – escorting prisoners from the brig to various work details. Other Asmara-bound sailors were also there marking time. Asmara was being beefed up, it seemed. We had to obtain passports in order to enter Ethiopia. One RM2 had a prisoner escape while on prisoner-chasing duty; the fugitive climbed the base fence and was sped away in a waiting car. The RM2 had to go to mast about it, as a matter of policy, but received no significant punishment. We tormented him with jokes about "boosting the guy over the fence".

In Bainbridge I had heard a surprised "Hey, Larry!" hail one day. It came from Bob Dulin, ex-London. He informed me that Si was also nearby, working in the big naval communication site at the Washington suburb of Cheltenham, Maryland. (This was the NSS and RBEPC mentioned in Appendix A.) While at the RecSta I learned where Si lived and knocked on his door unannounced. He called me an ugly son of a bitch and invited me in. I went along with him to one of his

Cheltenham midwatches just to see and experience the place. One evening I was at Si's and we were playing cribbage, half-listening to a baseball game on the radio. As the game reached the late innings we listened more carefully and soon gave it our undivided attention. Harvey Haddix was pitching his 12 perfect innings. Si's wife, who was English, returned and we tried to explain to her the historic nature of what we were hearing. She was unimpressed.

Eventually my transportation was scheduled and I headed to Charleston AFB in South Carolina to catch an air force flight. On my first morning in Charleston I ordered a fried-egg breakfast and it came with a strange, grainy, whitish substance which I had not ordered. I guessed, correctly, that it was grits. I sampled it, didn't much like it, but I ate it all – damned if I would let rebels think I *couldn't* eat it. In later years I developed a taste for the stuff and now always have it with breakfast when I'm in the south.

In the waiting room for my flight were a couple of other Asmara-bound sailors. One came over to me and introduced himself: Bill Mote. He was from Delaware, had been a ham radio hobbyist, had made RM3 in the reserves and volunteered for active duty. He was only 19, distinctly chubby with a rather high-pitched voice. We became the best of friends and made many excursions together, both in Asmara city and to the countryside.

Our flight was a marathon. I think it took two days, perhaps more. Passenger jets were still in the future, but the propeller flight beat a troopship. Our first stop was at Lajes AFB in the Azores, pretty and green. The next one was at Wheelus AFB, Tripoli, in pre-Qadhaffi Libya – nighttime, hot desert air, not much to see. The flight ended at Dhahran AFB near the Persian Gulf coast of Saudi Arabia. We were met by Byron Graham, a chief that I knew from London. He saw my third-class crow and said, "Jesus Christ, didn't you make second-class *yet?*" (I had been second-class, and briefly first-class, all that tour in London, but his memory wasn't that precise.)

167

We had to wait a day or two for a Dhahran-Asmara flight. I left Dhahran with two memories. One was of a local Arab employee who had an expensive-looking piece of elaborate ivory(?) sculpture that he was trying to peddle for $20 {$135} – a four-poster canopied bed with a couple thereon in a quite explicit missionary position. (This in the supposedly super-puritanical Muslim kingdom!) The other memory was the sand. Sandy sand. Fine-grained sand, far finer than anything I had ever seen on a beach, more dust-size than sand-size, the least breeze stirred it up, it adhered to everything. I gained a new appreciation of what a *sandy* desert is really like.

The 1 June 1959 Dhahran to Asmara flight was a short hop southwest over the Arabian desert, the Red Sea, a very little bit more of desert and then, with no loss of altitude, suddenly the ground was *much* closer than it had just been. We had come over the edge of the Ethiopian plateau and minutes later we were on the ground at Yohannes IV International Airport. Our passports were immediately confiscated by U.S. Authority, which did not trust us to retain them. (We might lose them? We might misuse them to go AWOL? Both? I never knew.) On the bus ride to the base I saw a small stone building, a sign proclaiming that it was a bar, and a doorway covered in half-inch-wide plastic strips of various colors hanging from the top nearly to the floor. These strips substitute for a screen door and do nearly as good a job, they can easily be brushed aside to enter. I knew them well from Naples, and the sight convinced me: this place might not be Naples or London, but I was going to like it.

APPENDIX B - A QUICK SKETCH OF ERITREA

Unlike Appendix A, I do recommend the reading of this appendix, and the next one, as useful backdrop to my (mis)adventures in Asmara.

The Amhara people of central Ethiopia and the Tigree people of central Eritrea and northern Ethiopia have many things in common. Although the two countries fought a bloody border war in 1998-2000 and are still at loggerheads, the two peoples share the same religion and culture. They see themselves as one people vis-à-vis others, and the collective name for both languages and peoples is Habesha. An Ethiopian or Eritrean will not tell you that he speaks Tigrinya, or Amharinya (Amharic), unless there is a specific need to differentiate – he speaks *Habesha*. Habesha possibly derives from Arabic and may mean "mixed", although scholars are not unanimous on either point. Ethiopia's older name *Abyssinia* is thought to derive from Habesha. Eritrea/Ethiopia are where Semitic peoples of Arabia crossed the Red Sea and mixed with indigenous Africans to produce the populations of today. Migrations of the past produced a patchwork of languages, cultures, complexions, religions, tribes, and sub-tribes.

The Tigree people of Eritrea occupy the high plateau. The seacoast, the north, and the western desert are home to a variety of smaller peoples, nearly all Muslim, many nomadic. The Christian-Muslim split in Eritrea is approximately 50-50. Tigree also dominate Ethiopia's northernmost province, Tigrai. In Ethiopia itself the Tigree and Amhara, even added together, do not quite make a majority of the population – Somali, Galla (or Oromo, the politically-correct term today), and others collectively outnumber them.

Asmara sits right on the brink of the Great Rift Valley where continents are slowly inching apart. That geological feature reaches from north of the Dead Sea down the Gulf of Aqaba and the African Red Sea coast. Not far south of Asmara it breaks inland, bisects Ethiopia, and extends south through the African great lakes Tanganyika and Nyasa. Asmara's altitude is roughly 7700 feet. From sea level at the port of Massawa it is 40 air miles to Asmara – but 72 miles by the road, which snakes up the escarpment on a multitude of hairpin curves.

Archaeological knowledge of the area is well outweighed by archaeological mystery. The ruins of the ancient city of Aksum in Tigrai province contain the tallest standing obelisks from the ancient world; an even taller and more massive one lies fallen and broken. The religion then was moon-worship, imported from south Arabia. The Aksumite emperors converted to Christianity in about 330 CE.

Ethiopian Christianity is an offshoot of the eastern orthodox branch, with a special mythology of its own. Their religiously-correct version is that the Queen of Sheba visited King Solomon, returned to Ethiopia pregnant, bore a son (Menelik I) who visited his father in Israel and absconded with the Ark of the Covenant. The Ark, with the original copy of the ten commandments therein, resides in Aksum today and is so holy that only one guardian priest, designated for lifetime, may ever enter its sanctuary – which he never leaves.

The Queen of Sheba (properly called Saba), if she existed outside of biblical myth, would have ruled a part of present-day Yemen, across the Red Sea. Since a great deal of culture was transmitted to Ethiopia from that area, there is at least a tenuous connection to the myth. Aksumites today point to one ruin as "the Queen of Sheba's palace", and identify the ancient reservoir, football-field size, as "the Queen of Sheba's bath". Archaeologists do not agree.

At its peak Aksum controlled stretches, inexactly known but substantial, of Ethiopia, the Sudan, the lands now inhabited by Somalis, and south Arabia. It declined and fell, the fall perhaps accelerated by the rise of Islam. Political power shifted south; Aksum, and Eritrea, became a loosely-held fringe area owing allegiance to the Amhara emperors more in theory than in practice. Today's Eritrea became known as *Mareb Mellash* (beyond the Mareb [river]) or *Bahrmeder* (Sealand) and its local ruler as the *Bahr Negus* (King of the Sea). There were lesser kings here and there in Ethiopia – the title rendered in English as Emperor is, literally, King of Kings in Habesha.

Subsequent centuries were a mix of semi-stable periods and anarchy. The emperors often had no fixed capital, moving around with their tents and retinue. Local warlords controlled their own areas for practical purposes. A period of exceptionally feckless emperors ended in 1855 when Tewodros (Theodore), a former bandit, attained power.

(Every emperor had to have, or to forge, descent from the line of Menelik and Solomon. Some of the claims, notably that of Tewodros, were pretty strained. It should not really have mattered – by the 19th century and well before, every living Tigree and Amhara were descendants of the Aksumite emperors simply by the laws of probability over the generations. Still, usurpers had to claim a more recent, and plausible, link.)

Tewodros apparently fell victim to imperial hubris. Historians question his sanity in his later years. Angered by Great Britain having ignored a letter he had dispatched to Queen Victoria, he took several Europeans as hostages. The British sent an army from India, landed it a few miles south of Massawa, marched halfway down Ethiopia and besieged Tewodros in his mountaintop fort in 1868. Tewodros shot himself.

A Tigrai-province chief, Ras Kassa (Ras, derived from the word for "head", is the highest-ranking title in Ethiopian nobility), took the throne, probably aided by weaponry that the departing British left behind in appreciation for his cooperation. He took the throne name of Yohannes IV – hence the name of the Asmara airport. He was killed in battle with the Dervishes, who were attempting to expand from the Sudan, in 1889.

Meanwhile Egyptians, who were themselves subordinate to the Ottoman Empire of the Turks, had taken over much of the Red Sea coast and were edging into the fringes of the highlands. They had fought two battles with Yohannes' forces in Eritrea in 1875 and 1876, but the menace of the Dervishes drove the Egyptians to pull back from these coasts. And Italy entered the picture.

Italy became a united country in 1870. In 1869 the Suez Canal had opened, and in that same year an Italian entrepreneur had bought the port of Assab, in far southeast Eritrea, from its local sultan. Italy was a latecomer to the "Scramble for Africa" of the 1880s and not much was left. Britain encouraged Italy's colonial ambitions, preferring that Italy rather than France should obtain what Britain didn't want or couldn't absorb. In 1885 Italy moved into the vacuum in Massawa. Expansion therefrom was sporadic and interrupted by military setbacks. In 1889 the Italians arranged a treaty with the new emperor, Menelik II of Shoa – the Amhara region surrounding Addis Abeba – giving them title to approximately the present extent of Eritrea.

In 1890 the colony of Eritrea was formally established, with Massawa as capital. (The capital was moved to Asmara in 1897.) The name came from the Erythrean Sea, the ancient Greek name for the Red Sea. (And – no surprise – Erythrean = red.)

Having assured the approval or the indifference of other European powers, the Italians began a slow-motion advance south, using both Italian soldiers and Eritrea-recruited askaris, and got about 250 miles into what they considered their new protectorate. There were occasional clashes, the Italians felt they might be somewhat overextended, and retreated northward. Things came to a head in a battle near Adwa (40 miles south of Eritrea) on 1 March 1896. The Italians, on the short end of 4-1 odds, were soundly defeated by Menelik's army. Half their force was killed, captured, or missing. They pulled back into Eritrea and stayed there for nearly 40 years.

Addis Abeba ("New Flower") is not an ancient city; it was founded only in 1885. Menelik reigned therefrom until his 1913 death. Several years of power struggle followed – liberals vs. conservatives. Menelik's grandson and heir, Yasu (ultraliberal), fled and remained a fugitive in the deserts until 1921, a prisoner thereafter. The upshot was rule by a triumvirate: an aging war minister (arch-conservative), Menelik's granddaughter (conservative, designated empress), and young Ras Tafari Makonnen (liberal), a distant cousin of Menelik. Ras Tafari was designated regent and heir to the throne.

(The Rastafarian cult of the Caribbean, believing that Ethiopia was heaven and Ras Tafari was God, took their name from him. Ethiopians were rather bemused by this phenomenon; they didn't repudiate it but largely ignored it.)

The old war minister died off, so did the empress, and Ras Tafari was crowned emperor in 1930, taking the throne name Haile Selassie I. Haile Selassie = Power of Trinity. It is a common name in Ethiopia but most so named treat it as one word: Haileselassie. By inserting the space, Haile Selassie bequeathed a useful, if unintended, touchstone for exposing writers posing as experts on the country. Truncating the name to Selassie, as if it were a family name, is on an exact par with referring to the King of Spain (Juan Carlos) as Carlos, or to the late pope (John Paul) as Paul. Whenever I see Selassie standing alone – wire services and news magazines were often guilty – I dismiss the writer as a dabbler who has done a superficial study to bone up on his subject.

Meanwhile the Italians had slowly developed and modernized Eritrea. The buildup, and Italian immigration, accelerated in the 1930s as Mussolini prepared to "avenge the shame of Adwa" and claim Italy's "rightful" empire. An incident was provoked well inside Ethiopia's southern border (adjoining Italian Somaliland). Ultimatum followed and, in 1935, invasion.

It was a short campaign. Addis Abeba fell in May 1936, Haile Selassie escaping by train to French Somaliland and thence Britain, and remaining a diplomatic, at least, irritant during his years of exile. But for a short time it came close to turning out otherwise. A force led by Ras Imru turned the Italian right flank and came within sight of their supply depot in Eritrea. It was then that the Italians resorted to mustard gas, dropped from airplanes. It may or may not be true that only the gas warfare saved the Italians from a major disaster. (Ras Imru was to have another brief moment in history in 1960.)

Eritrea, Ethiopia, and Italian Somaliland were combined to form the new colony of Italian East Africa. Eritrea, with boundaries expanded to take in most of the former Tigrai province, became one of the provinces of the colony.

When Italy entered World War II in 1940 her east African armies advanced a few miles to seize border towns in Kenya and the Sudan. Then they stopped. Britain had many other worries and higher priorities in the Mediterranean and Middle East, but by early 1941 she had scraped up enough troops – Sudanese, Indian, South African, a few Free French, and British regulars – to go on the offensive. The major goal was to take Massawa and thereby remove the threat to Red Sea shipping. The advance from the Sudan was halted for nearly two months at the fortified defensive position outside Keren, a town 80 miles northwest of Asmara. Once that position was forced, the rest of the story was British advance, Italian retreat. The last Italian remnants in central Ethiopia and Assab surrendered in June 1941 and Haile Selassie was restored to his throne.

The U.S. military made its first appearance in Eritrea in 1941, at Gura, an ex-Italian air base some 25 miles southeast of Asmara which became an Anglo-American aircraft repair facility. Not long thereafter Radio Marina – the Italian navy's radio station in Asmara city – began to be used for U.S. communications purposes.

After the war the victorious Allies had a problem: what to do with Eritrea? Haile Selassie naturally wanted it. Italy, having switched sides during the war, would have liked to have it back as a reward, if only as a ten-year trusteeship. The USSR was arguing for one or more of the Italian ex-colonies to be put under its trusteeship. Some Eritrean groups wanted independence, but it was given little consideration due to Eritrea's small size, poverty, and backwardness. There was a suggestion for partition: the western lowlands, west of Keren, to the Sudan, the rest to Ethiopia. It made considerable sense ethnically and religiously, and Britain – then still overlord of the Sudan – thought it a rather good idea.

There was a lot of unrest and banditry during the postwar years, some of it politically motivated and encouraged, some pure opportunism. The four foreign ministers of the big powers could not reach agreement, and turned the problem over to the United Nations. The U.N. sent a commission to Eritrea in 1949, and finally reached a – I shouldn't say a *solution* in view of what was to develop in future years, but at least an arrangement.

Eritrea was to be "federated" with Ethiopia. It was to be co-equal, to have its own flag, its own constitution, its own legislative assembly, all under the sovereignty of the Ethiopian crown, Ethiopia responsible for defense, foreign relations, and currency. This was implemented in 1952 and the 11-year British occupation finally ended. Haile Selassie got what he wanted as far as the map showed, but he didn't get the power and control he wanted. Ethiopia chiseled away at Eritrean prerogatives. The separate flag went. Amharinya replaced Tigrinya and Arabic as the official language.

And that was where things stood when I arrived for my 1959-61 tour. I sensed no signs then of any Eritrean discontent, at least not among the Christian Tigree. Every business and indeed every private home displayed at least one prominent picture of the emperor, often with the empress as well. When Haile Selassie visited Asmara the people lined the streets, cheering as he passed.

In 1960 Eritrean exiles in Egypt formed the first of what were to be a bewildering variety of liberation organizations. These groups feuded, fought each other over turf and doctrine, and merged and splintered repeatedly. They were largely Muslim at first, but Christian presence and influence grew over the years to reach and perhaps exceed the 50-50 split of the population. In 1962 Haile Selassie strong-armed the Eritrean legislature to vote itself out of existence, the federation was dissolved, and Eritrea became simply a province of Ethiopia.

The fortunes of these liberation movements waxed and waned over the next three decades. Haile Selassie was deposed in a military coup led by junior officers in 1974 and died in 1975 at age 84 – they smothered him with a pillow, it is said. In 1977 Somalia invaded Ethiopia, the Eritrean rebels came very near to victory, and there was a massive geopolitical reshuffling. Ethiopia was saved from two-front disaster only by Soviet and Cuban help; she became a USSR satellite, which caused former USSR-satellite Somalia to turn to the west in response.

The U.S. army turned over all its facilities to the navy and evacuated in 1974, the navy civilianized much of its operations and then evacuated completely in 1977. The pullout was partly because of the deteriorating political situation and partly because satellites had made Asmara increasingly less necessary. The U.S. consulate in Asmara was also closed in 1977.

As the USSR headed toward breakdown in the late 1980s, its assistance to Ethiopia evaporated. The Eritrean rebels occupied Asmara in 1991 and, almost simultaneously, Ethiopian rebels (led by the Tigree of Tigrai province) routed the military dictatorship and took power in Addis Abeba.

Eritrean independence was proclaimed on 24 May 1993 and the former U.S. consulate in Asmara re-opened as an embassy. (And that September I began my third tour in Asmara – as the first State Department communicator in that embassy.)

Hopes were high in those days. Asmara was bustling and the people were busy, happy, and optimistic. Isaias Afewerki, the guerilla leader and now the president, was enormously popular; he walked

Asmara's streets without a bodyguard. Eritrea and Ethiopia were the best of friends. There was talk of tourist resorts on the Red Sea coast, of Asmara becoming a major airline hub which would enable flights to bypass troubled areas in the Middle East . . . Alas, it was all too good to last. Isaias metamorphosed into "just another African dictator", and the 1998-2000 war between the two countries was a senseless tragedy. I'm certainly no qualified political analyst, but I see it as a conflict between two stiff-necked dictators, former revolutionary colleagues, each determined not to take any shit off the other. Worse, their leadership(?) has imbued their respective nations with the same antagonistic attitudes. And what the future may hold . . .

Should anyone have interest in further reading, *I Didn't Do It For You*, by Michela Wrong, 2005, is the best book yet written on 20th century Eritrea.

APPENDIX C - LANGUAGE IN ASMARA (POLITE AND IMPOLITE)

Tigrinya was far and away the most widely-spoken language on the plateau, but many Eritreans knew two languages – if not more. Amharinya was the official government language, taught in the schools, and Italian was spoken not only by the Italians who still remained (some 20,000 in an Asmara population of 150,000 – wild guesses, both) but also by many Eritreans. Arabic had a significant presence, especially in the lowlands, where a variety of other limited-population tongues were also spoken. Finally there was English – not only because of the American presence, and the earlier British occupation, but also because of English's growing position as *the* international language.

Tigrinya and Amharinya are both descended from Geez – the liturgical language of the Ethiopian church, otherwise no longer spoken today. A comparison often made is: Geez is to Tigrinya and Amharic as Latin is to Italian and French. Professional linguists might nitpick the parallels, but I cannot. Tigrinya descended from Geez like Italian did from Latin, and did so in the ancestral area. Amharinya, like French, developed in a neighboring area and departed farther from its ancestor linguistically. Geez and its descendants are Semitic languages related to Arabic, Hebrew, etc.

Eritreans say that it is much easier for them to learn Amharinya than it is for the Amhara to learn Tigrinya. (If I asked Amharas, I might get an opposite opinion – ?)

The same written characters are used for Geez, Amharinya, and Tigrinya (for the three of which I'll use the collective term *Ethiopic*). They came by way of south Arabia, and ultimately trace back to the Phoenician writing from which our own alphabet and so many others evolved.

I used to annoy people with the trick question: how many letters in the Ethiopic alphabet? The nitpickingly correct answer is zero – it is not an alphabet but a *syllabary* – with each character standing for a syllable; a consonant *plus* a following vowel sound. To restate the question more fairly: how many characters in the Ethiopic syllabary?

I don't know. I don't think anyone knows. I have read at least four different counts and I could probably find more if I looked harder. There are obsolete characters, there are new characters (devised for sounds in foreign words), there are punctuation and numeral symbols, and some consonants are not always recognized with all seven vowel endings . . . It all depends on the counter and on what he thinks ought to count. On one thing all agree: the total is somewhere up in the high two-hundreds – and just possibly over three, if all gray areas are resolved in favor of countability.

That is a daunting number, but things are not as bad as they might seem. Let me illustrate with the letter "T", which in Ethiopic is basically the same as the lower-case hand-printed t in English. The plain, unadorned t is the basic Ethiopic letter: *te* (as in Ted). Halfway down from the crossbar, place a short, horizontal line (or a small square, used in typeset print) on the right and you have *too*. Next, to the basic form add that line or square all the way down at the bottom right instead: *tee*. Bend the bottom half of the basic form far to the left and it is *tah* (as in Tom). Putting a small circle on the bottom right of the basic form gives *tay* (as in table). A line or square on the top left of the character produces *t* — either no vowel sound at all (as at the end of a word) or a minimal sound (as in tin). Finally a circle at the very top yields *toh* (as in toe, tow).

So instead of 200+ separate and distinct characters, the system can be viewed as some 40 or so, each with seven variations. And the variations follow a pattern of sorts: a line/square at the bottom right of a letter is generally going to indicate an "ee" sound. (Unfortunately the variations are not completely consistent, there are quite a few variances from the variations . . .)

All in all I found the alphabet, oops, *syllabary*, a good deal easier to fool around with than either Arabic or Thai, both of which have far fewer characters but have plenty of other oddities to sabotage an English-reader. At my best (long since rusted away) I had probably 95% recognition of the syllabary — any comprehension of what I was reading was quite another matter though.

I liked to toy with my knowledge in the downtown bars. I would claim to be able to read Tigrinya. This would be scoffed, so I would find the appropriate bottle and slowly and hesitantly sound out "Ko-ka-ko-la" and gloat. (That ploy will work in many another country.) When I was hooted down I would locate a bottle of the local beer and repeat my performance with "birra", "Melotti", and "Asmara". I would still be considered a fraud and eventually someone would find a newspaper or other written material with which to challenge me. I would feign embarrassment with an "Oh, oh, the game is up, I've been exposed" manner, and try to evade the test, but at some point I would take the paper, pretend puzzlement, then slowly, running my finger along a line, start to rattle off the characters in a low, mumbling voice. My accent must have been horrible and my mispronunciations many, and I understood only about one percent of what I was "reading", but in the wake of the phony buildup my performance was usually sufficient to provoke a fair degree of astonishment.

Much of the rest of this appendix is a listing of the various "bad" words I learned – insults, profanity, etc. – and a few other interesting words. I have had several problems in preparing it. I have presented the terms in a spelling that seems, to me, to be the best way for an English-speaker to grasp their pronunciation. I have boldfaced the accented syllables, and I have used the "schwa", the upside-down "e" symbol used in phonetics to represent that indefinite almost-no-vowel-at-all sound. Verbs, nouns, and possessives all vary according to the sex of the *person addressed*, and I have indicated the female version in parentheses. The "way I heard it" may not always be fully accurate, and my translations may also be suspect. The latter are what I was told when I asked, and their accuracy may be affected both by prudery on the part of whom I asked, and by the respondent's lack of full fluency in English. In short, my effort should in no way be confused with scholarly research.

President Eisenhower's "people-to-people program", intended to promote good relations between America and foreign populations, was in place at this time. One of its requirements was that overseas military installations provide instruction materials in the local language and encourage servicemen to learn it. So I had plenty of resources and help in studying Tigrinya? None at all. Amharinya then? Not even. In Asmara, Authority weaseled around the requirement by providing materials in *Italian* – the language of the recent colonial masters! – on the rationalization that it was widely spoken and understood as a commercial language. All of my Tigrinya-learning had to be done with the help of Eritreans, and the very scanty material I turned up in local book stores – first-grade primers, and one thin book on Amharic which helped with the writing. By no stretch did I ever become fluent, far from it, but I'm sure I surpassed 99% of other Americans.

The caveats and disclaimers out of the way, forthwith to the words:

torəwa(waee) - the basic: fuck you.

adeeha(hee)təwa - fuck your mother. One of two insults that were learned by all Americans, even those who never learned to say yes and no. Adee = mother, **ha(hee)** = your; I am unsure whether torəwa shortens grammatically, or whether it is simply pronounced so rapidly that syllables seem lost.

jigəjig - sexual intercourse. The word might have been Arabic, I think it's widely used around the Middle East.

*shar**moo**ta* - whore. Also used as an exclamation of anger or disgust at a refractory inanimate object, just as Hispanics and Italians use *puta*. I've wondered whether this is from Italian influence, or if shar**moo**ta was used in this manner even before the Italians came.

*kontrr**moo**ro* - street prostitute. When I first heard this I was sure it was picturesque Italian: *contro* (against) + *muro* (wall). Eritreans insisted not so, that it was pure Tigrinya. I still wonder.

wədy _____ - son (of) _____. Wədy shar**moo**ta. Wədy **kal**bee: son of a dog. Wədy ts**vey**ty: son of a woman (I am unsure whether this implied bastardry or effeminacy). Wədy lə**ma**ne: son of a beggar. And I was once called *wədy Eisenhower* on the street – the girl who was with me laughed and said, "Sure, why not?"

gwal _____ - daughter (of) _____. Feminine parallel of the foregoing.

shəwate - seven. This was the second insult unfailingly learned by all Americans. The understood full phrase is shə**wa**te ə ma**kwor**ka (-kee) – seven (times) up your ass.

*ə ma**kwor**ka too*yo (*-kee **too**yee)* - shove it up your ass.

. . . and this is a good spot to mention the difficulties of a sailor named McQuitty. The sound was quite close to Tigrinya's *my ass*. His name often produced slightly startled expressions and hesitant grins.

zoobra - cock. Another sailor, one Zuber, had problems of his own with this one.

əndelka (-kee) - literally, I don't know you. Conveys roughly "don't speak to me" and/or "none of your business".

ɔndeladeeha(-hee) - I don't know your mother. Same thing, stronger and more impolite.

nɔaldeenik - an all-purpose racial, religious, and cultural insult. An Ethiopian can use it to a foreigner, an Amhara to a Tigree, a Muslim to a Christian, and vice-versa for all. Smile when you say that potency. It is Arabic (as are the next three). The nɔal- prefix seems to be some form of *no-good*. Deen very roughly equates to faith, religion, or possibly culture, but the insult had expanded in Asmara from its basic sense to a wider utility.

nɔalaboo - the same uncomplimentary prefix applied to the target's father. Oddly, it is far less potent, roughly equal to *son of a gun*.

nɔaloomock - . . . and applied to the mother. Rarer, and I don't know how potent.

ksoomock - your mother's cunt.

wɔdy (gwal) kalite shinty - half-caste. Literally, son (daughter) of two pisses. Tigrinya may not differentiate between urine and semen; if there is a word for the latter I never learned it.

caffelatte - half-caste. Italian, coffee with milk, descriptive of skin color. Offense was rarely intended, sometimes but not always taken. Those with *three* Italian grandparents were sometimes called *quarterlattes*. Americans would sometimes enter a bar and order a caffelatte on toast. No one ever got the toast.

hɔnfɔts - yet another term for half-caste. Offensive, I have no knowledge of derivation.

agamy - Agame – a sub-group of the Tigree people in an area of Tigrai province, who had somehow acquired a reputation for rustic stupidity. There were not, so far as I know, any "Agame jokes", but otherwise the similarity to *Polack* or *redneck* was inescapable. It could be intensified by a**ga**my wɔdy a**ga**my: Agame, son (of an) Agame.

barya - slave, nigger. The Barya were a Negroid tribe in western Ethiopia and southwestern Eritrea. The Habesha are Caucasian, despite their skin color, and toward Negroid Africans they could be just as racist as any Afrikaner. I think that this prejudice has lessened a great deal over the years.

*k**sha**sha* - trash, garbage. An adjective used particularly in racial denigrations: k**sha**sha Amhara, k**sha**sha Tigree. A noun for garbage, gw**haf**, was used in gw**haf af**ha (-hee) – garbage mouth. Bar girls frequently had occasion to apply this criticism to servicemen, together with the admonition (in English), "Talk nice!"

*lo**mutz*** - no-gooder? Mild noun of disapproval.

*tche**na**wee (-weet)* - stinker.

bitsbits - stinking. These two were often used together, in either order: tche**na**wee bitsbits, bitsbits tche**na**wee.

***tche**n*itadee**ha** (-**ha**ee)* - your mother stinks.

*gjeef **roo**see* - fat head.

gjeef kebty (or kefty) - a little play on words, with the pronunciation likely to be blurred: fat stomach (or cow).

***boo**da* - sorcerer. I would be so labeled when I made faces, rolling my eyes back to show only the whites.

*kot**kot**ee (-eet)* - sorcerer, blacksmith. The two are intertwined in Ethiopian belief; *kotkot* is the sound of the smith's hammer. Often used together: **boo**da kot**kot**ee.

nagram - deriving from the verb for "talk", the perfect translation for this one is *fussbudget*.

fərənjee - American, European, any Caucasian-appearing foreigner. Usually written as Ferenji. It derives from "Frank", perhaps the times of Charlemagne. The word or its cousins are found over the middle east and south asia, at least as far as Thailand, where it appears as Farang.

bəro təhasy - exceptionally difficult of translation. I heard vague explanations that the first word signified a forward thrusting motion, the second a twisting. Stick it in and twist it . . . ? It was not especially potent, so the nearest English relative might be *screw you* or *screw it*. Either word could be used alone, but the combination was more common. A longer, rarer, rhyming phrase was bə**ro** tə**ha**sy kəm (like) Lette Selassie (a proper name) – screw it like Lette Selassie (does?)? Americans were known to substitute Haile for Lette, then pretend to have been misheard.

wah! - an often heard interjection of surprise or disagreement, frequently mingled with reproach.

An occasional feature of conversation was an unexpected and impolite rhyming riposte. I recall only two. The interjection *Gees!* – get out of here, go along with you – could be countered by ə *makworka (-kee)* ə*ntə* **ham**sa la**pees** – up your ass with fifty pencils. *Men?* – who('s there)? – could be answered from the other side of the door with *abooha (-hee) arrigee temen* – your father (is an) old snake.

There was little or no Tigrinyan blasphemy. I heard the phrases *Maryam sharmoota* (Mary whore) and *Yesoo nəalaboo* (Jesus (?)bastard), but I heard them spoken by a resident Italian and Eritreans maintained that *only* an Italian would say such things. The name of Gebre Menfes Kuddus – a medieval Ethiopian saint, literally Servant of the Holy Ghost – was sometimes uttered as a mild expression of astonishment.

"I'm going to kill you, cut your heart out, wrap your body in pigskin, and point you toward Mecca" was reported to me as a Christian-to-

186

Muslim insult. It is suspect, I heard it only from another American, in English.

The Ethiopian version of the unidigital salute was to raise the hand in the peace gesture with the middle finger dangling forward. (I've heard that this is also used in other Middle Eastern countries.) Another hand gesture was to present the clenched fist with the thumb upward and rotating, with or without the verbal accompaniment *nabzee* **kaf**yel *(-yelee)* – sit on this.

The raspberry, or Bronx cheer, flourished in Asmara as nowhere else. The reaction to audible flatulence, whether oral or rectal, could consist of one or (often) more of the following:
– slapping at a neighbor (guilty or innocent);
– flinging the arms wildly;
– rotating the body (if necessary) and delivering the dangled finger toward the sound;
– throwing an object already held, preferably in the general direction of the sound;
– a verbal accompaniment. I have heard torə**wa**, adee**ha**təwa, shə**wa**te, shə**wa**te nəala**boo**, bə**ro** and/or tə**ha**sy, all mentioned earlier, so used. And also:
*gee***dif**! - Stop!
ha*reeha?* - Did you shit?
doo*baharee*! - Shit a melon!
And two words likelier to be used in reproach after the spontaneous reaction had passed:
*tə***ra***tee (-eet)* - farter; one who produces a farting sound, be it anal or oral.
*fə***sa***wee (-eet)* - farter; of a genuine fart, be it audible or silent/ malodorous.

A connection with "evil spirits" was said to underlie all this. I am doubtful. But if not that, what? The literature is silent, the subject being perhaps too scatological for scholars. A possibly related custom was the clapping of two rocks together while squatting; this was said to be done in order to prevent the squatter from overhearing his own

187

bodily noises, in line with the "evil spirits" theory. But I have seen an alternative explanation: that the squatter is merely advertising his presence and preoccupation so that passersby will not encounter him to their mutual embarrassment.

It seemed to me that the phenomenon was more prevalent in Asmara city than in the countryside, and more prevalent in older generations. Not all Eritreans reacted in the manner I've described, but many did, and some of the reactors were virtually Pavlovian. Those most susceptible were termed *twitchy*. We called the practice *blowing farts*. When Authority found an official term necessary (in a notice telling patrons not to harass the waiters in the clubs thus), they used *making obscene noises*. And very recently, I've learned that phonetics has a formal name for it: a *bilabial trill*. The preferred method required a cupped hand to the mouth, thus raising the noise level; producing really good, loud ones took some practice. I was not the loudest at it but I was pretty damn good, near the top.

Many stories were told; most have been forgotten. I heard that an American had been giving some instructions to his Eritrean subordinate on the phone, had said, ". . . now listen carefully," and had blown a loud fart. The line went dead; he later learned that the Eritrean had thrown the phone out the window. I also heard that a gardener had been squatting, watering plants near the driveway of an outlying site, when a fart was blown at him from a distance. Hose in hand, he jerked and, through an open car window, drenched the inward-bound site commander.

X - ISLAND ABOVE THE CLOUDS

The navy barracks and administrative offices were located on Radio Marina, more often known as Tract A. The compound, about twelve acres, also contained some officer housing, warehouses, and three tall, rusty radio towers. The towers, long disused, were a hundred feet (my guess) tall and resembled windmills without the blades. They bore red lights at the tops, presumably to warn off any low-flying aircraft. The lights could be seen from many points around town, and served to guide an occasional drunken sailor back to post. The ladders which ran up the towers had had their bottom 20 feet or so removed to obstruct sailors, drunk or sober, from doing any climbing.

Letters designated the various U.S. tracts. Tract B had no navy presence and I never entered it. Tract C, where I was to work, was the army receiver site; the navy message center occupied one corner of it and also a nearby quonset hut. Tract D was the transmitter site; again the navy occupied a lesser part of it. B, C, and D were a few miles out in the countryside and surrounded by extensive antenna fields. Tract E was Kagnew Station. It was about a mile across town, west from Tract A, newly built and occupied in 1954. It was the "main base", having nearly all army administrative offices and barracks, clubs, a gym and bowling alley, the chow hall, movie theater, commissary, PX, library, dependent school, barber shop, gas station – all of the miscellaneous necessaries and fringes.

Kagnew was said to be a word from the Geez bible, meaning "to bring order out of chaos". We sailors enjoyed remarking that it would have been more fitting if the army had chosen the antonym. It was spoken *con-you* and anyone heard to use the kag-new pronunciation marked himself as a new guy. The word had significance in recent Ethiopian history. At the battle of Adwa a general's horse, named Kagnew, his master having been unhorsed, had charged the enemy riderless and supposedly contributed to Italian fear and disruption. When Haile Selassie sent a part of his imperial bodyguard to aid the U.N. forces in Korea, it was named the Kagnew Battalion. (I have heard it said that the U.S. troops in Korea regarded the South Koreans and their various other allies with considerable disdain, but had high praise for two exceptions – the Turks and the Ethiopians.)

The navy was very much a tenant activity on an army base-complex. I would guess that soldiers outnumbered sailors ten to one. One consequence was that Eritreans had learned to address any American of unknown name as "Sergeant". Sailors were not pleased when thus hailed, but the practice was so entrenched that indignant protests of "I ain't no fucking sergeant!" had little effect.

The 1958 Lebanon crisis had put the Asmara navy into three-section watches for many months. The winding down of the troubles there, along with an increase in manning, had put us back into four sections not long before my arrival; but the watch rotation was 1-1-1-56, the worst I have ever encountered. An evening watch, 8 hours off, a day watch after short sleep, 8 hours off, a midwatch and then 56 hours off. I spent a day sleeping off the mid, had an evening and a full day completely off, then an eve watch the following day. The break was over before I knew it. After some experience of it I began to stay semi-awake all day following the mid, which seemed to increase my time off even if the sleepwalking portion was less than quality time. I thought of requesting a transfer to the transmitter section, just to get away from what I called "this race-horse watch bill". But the chief in charge of the message center (who had refused to consider a better rotation) was transferring soon and it was hoped that his replacement would be more open to change, so I desisted. And said replacement, Wayne

Pendergrass, who turned out to be one of the best chiefs for whom I ever worked, did indeed put us on the familiar 3-3-3-72.

I had been put on a message center watch section and into the job of router, which was more or less number-two on the section, even though two or three experienced RM3s were already there. Every message passed through my central position; I stamped them a time or two and indicated where they went – which might be over the JR or J fleet broadcasts, to our small relay, to the navy admin offices, to another station if something had been missent to us, or any combination of the foregoing. I also drafted service messages and did miscellaneous other jobs, helping out wherever backlogs developed. I was pleased to get a compliment from the RM3 I'd replaced at router; he said he had never seen anyone come in cold and learn the job so quickly.

(I was senior to nearly every third-class anywhere, because my date-of-rate went all the way back to November 1953 when I had made third-class on the *Iowa*.)

We also had an RM2 supervisor, a relay operator, a JR broadcast operator, a circuit controller who twiddled a bewildering array of equipment that I could never quite fathom, a ship-shore CW operator out in the quonset hut, and probably another job or two that I've forgotten. In addition to our Radiomen we also had a duty Electronics Tech, an ET1, attached to the section.

Bill Mote was not quite so well accepted. He went on another section, was tried at a variety of jobs, couldn't do well at any of them, and before long he was transferred to the transmitter site where he could do less harm.

Much of our work was in supporting the Middle East Force ships which copied our broadcasts. There were at least three ships in the force: two destroyers and a small converted seaplane tender which served as COMIDEASTFOR's flagship. Three such tenders rotated on 18-month tours, during which they homeported at Bahrain island in the Persian Gulf and made various show-the-flag port visits. The destroyers rotated in and out from Sixth Fleet, for shorter periods, often making a brief port stop in Massawa. When they, and perhaps a tender also, were rotating we would have five or six ships to serve. And when major portions of the Sixth Fleet entered the eastern end of the Mediterranean they sometimes switched to our broadcasts, our workload soared, and we might go into three-section watches until they went back west.

An identical ex-seaplane tender had been given to Ethiopia; as *HIMS Ethiopia* she served as flagship of the Ethiopian navy, and as Haile Selassie's imperial yacht. HIMS = His *Imperial* Majesty's Ship, imperial highlighting the distinction between emperors and mere kings.

The army had no ships to serve. They were a link in the worldwide network of relay stations, but their major purpose was listening – eavesdropping on the Soviets, middle eastern countries, and in general anything anywhere of intelligence interest. Asmara's elevation and location made it an ideal place for such endeavors.

I was worried about passing the CW performance test so that I could take the August exam for RM2. Don Finch, an affable Texan RM1, heard my concerns and offered to give me the test. I didn't think I did well, but he passed me. Out of charity, maybe.

My car arrived at Massawa. The PN1 (Personnelman) and the YN3 in the admin office wanted me to wait a few days to pick it up, until a navy vehicle went down. They felt the trains and busses were not fit for an American and waggled their heads at the thought. I was impatient, and not concerned by the vague hazards they cited, and took the train in the face of their advice. It was indeed smelly – Eritrean women use *ghee*, a rancid, oily butter, to dress their hair, and they reek of it. It was an unpleasant odor but I got used to it over time; it became part of normal background and I ceased to notice it. Americans sometimes compared the narrow-gauge train to *The Toonerville Trolley* of old comic-strip pages. It was crowded, and the passengers carried a variety of items, mostly edible, including live chickens – feet tied together and carried upside down. But none of this was really any problem, and I was happy I had ignored the admin office advice.

That advice was one of the lesser examples of the racism which pervaded the U.S. military. I've already mentioned (Appendix C) the provision of language-study materials only in Italian rather than any African language. "Nigger" was often heard. Eritreans by and large had no conception of the heavy emotional freight and fighting-word potency of the insult; they shrugged it off with smiles and repartee. (And besides it would have been unthinkable for them to have jeopardized their jobs by making a fuss . . .) There were no U.S. Blacks assigned to Asmara, army or navy. (Later, maybe a year, a couple navy Blacks did arrive, doubtless due to Washington oversight. Although they were allowed to stay, it was said that the OIC – Officer In Charge – reproved Washington by letter and said not to send any more.) The two factors, no U.S. Blacks to overhear and offense not taken by locals, removed all constraints on those disposed to use the word. Sailors intending to go downtown would sometimes jest that they were "going to the colored section", and they sneered at the Habesha classification as Caucasian – a genetically accurate one, skin hue notwithstanding. They would try to provoke reaction by insulting the emperor: Haile Selassie, King of the Coons. Haile Selassie has crabs in his beard. Haile Selassie Eisenhower's houseboy. No one got riled.

Authority had its own problems about what to call the locals, because of the peculiar political situation. *Ethiopians* might not go over well with some Eritreans; *Eritreans* might have displeased the Ethiopian government. The term of choice in officialese thus became *indigenous personnel*. When spoken, it usually bore a touch of condescension at best, of contempt at worst. In less formal dialogue, *these people* was heard and carried the same undertones.

With limited exceptions, servicemen never brought their Eritrean girlfriends to the on-base clubs or movies. The exceptions were a few caffelattes who were employed in the PX or elsewhere on base, and thus known not to be bargirls. There were no written regulations to prevent; it was simply unwritten custom. Remember this was 1959-61 when U.S. domestic racism was worse than today and interracial dating was scandalous.

The three navy barracks were ex-Italian structures with walls of some sort of gray fiberboard. Some 20-30 sailors slept on single cots in an open bay in each one; each also had a couple of small single rooms used for single senior enlisteds and the duty watch. They were unheated, in midwinter they became uncomfortably cold, and Authority was oblivious to our discomfort. Next to the barracks was a small gedunk/branch PX; up the hill at the navy admin offices was another small lounge with pool table and snack bar. The prices were soon to go up slightly, but when I arrived a grilled fried-egg or toasted-cheese sandwich there cost a nickel {34¢} – hamburgers and other items 10-15 cents {67¢-$1}.

In spite of the long distance from barracks to chow hall, we got no comrats. Authority everywhere hated to pay comrats and would provide some sort of theoretical and inadequate transportation to avoid it. The army food was dismal. Third-class petty officers got a break in one respect, we were allowed to eat in the NCO section where waiters brought our food – the army E-4s (corporals) were not! For week after dreary week the dessert was a light-green, toothpaste-like mint sherbet. It was said that this was because of a military gambit called "forced issue" – the commissary had ordered a great lot of the sherbet, very few would buy it and no one more than once. The chow hall was forced to take it from the commissary and for our desserts we singles got what the families would not buy! Many of us ordered the sherbet anyhow and left it to melt untouched, in hopes of getting rid of it faster.

Three houseboys were employed in the barracks. They were a good lot. Each sailor paid a small sum – a dollar or three per month {$7-20} – for their services. It was a bargain. They did all the cleaning and also did a professional job of shining our shoes. Mahari, the head houseboy, was a businessman and something of a wheeler-dealer. He operated a laundry which got all the sailor business, a bar (The Navy Bar) which attracted a lot of navy patronage, and I believe he owned an apartment building and had a few other things going. Asmellesh, his brother, was known as "John" or "Lush" in the barracks. The third houseboy, Russom ("Sam") was also family in some way, brother-in-law I think.

Sam was slim and gangly, soft-spoken and somewhat shy, well-liked in the barracks, and a frequent butt of sailor wit. One day he stood accused of having been seen holding hands with a girl in the Navy Bar, a charge which he denied with unusual vigor and with no success. (What was charged as "handholding" was quite likely nothing more than a prolonged friendly greeting or farewell.) That evening I was drinking in the Navy Bar when malicious inspiration struck. Asmellesh was tending bar; I asked him to show me how to write Sam's name in the Ethiopic characters, and also Tayesh (the girl's name). Returning to the barracks, I found a sheet of scrap paper, drew a crude heart with an arrow through it, copied the names thereon, and tacked it to the door of the houseboys' shack to await their early-morning arrival.

We awoke in the morning to find Mahari and Asmellesh wearing ear-to-ear grins. And Sam . . . it was not in his character to be *really* furious, but he was making his best effort. Asmellesh hadn't ratted on me, and Sam had no idea whom to blame. Before he finally uncovered the real villain he stalked the barracks, the drawing in one hand, confronting first one baffled suspect then another with accusations and a soft-voiced but sincere reproach: "Fucking idiot. You fucking idiot." It was many years later when I learned that Sam had even more reason for embarrassment than I knew. Tayesh, unknown to me, was Mahari's mistress at the time.

I obtained an 11x8" picture of Haile Selassie and his empress from a shop and taped it to the inside of my locker door. I intended it as a sort of a satire on the ubiquity of such pictures downtown; "Everyone who is anyone in this town has a picture of Haile Selassie," I argued. But it fell rather flat, most sailors just stared at it in disbelief and thought me hopelessly eccentric. I've long wondered, after locker inspections were held, what comments the inspecting officers might have made to one another.

Honk – who didn't care for his nickname, arising from a distinctive, sonorous voice – had preceded me at learning a little bit of Habesha, including some of the characters. He gave me some of my first tips at that pursuit. He was strange in some ways. Of German descent, he decided he should therefore be a Nazi and, therefore, anti-Jewish. Bill Mote and I listened with some amusement when he expounded these thoughts. Bill used a white stencil-pencil to draw a Star of David inside Honk's locker door. When it didn't evoke any reaction, we drew his attention to it. It turned out that he didn't even know what a Star of David was.

Bill's transmitter site schedule was different from mine, but occasionally we would both be on a break at the same time and either go downtown or exploring outside town. The first such trip we took was before my car arrived. We took the bus to Dekemhare (Italian spelling Decamere) about 25 miles southeast. There we rented bicycles and set out to explore the old airfield at Gura, just to the south. Almost nothing remained to be seen – the runway itself was still there, and a few crumbling walls of small buildings. We cycled a bit farther south and came to a ruined fort. I was later to see a couple other such forts, all alike. They bore no inscriptions, no clues of any kind as to their history. Years later I heard that they were "Turkish forts", which fits with history and is very likely, but I've never found anything in books to confirm this. They had all been more or less reduced to rubble, piles of red bricks, concrete, and masonry with partially-intact portions. I am also ignorant of, and still curious about, the who-when-why-how of their destruction.

After exploring the fort we started back for Dekemhare and encountered a stiff, steady headwind that slowed our cycling to an exhausting crawl. We dismounted and wheeled the bikes some of the time, and I think our progress was nearly as fast when we pushed them as when we rode bucking that wind. When we were nearly back to town, Bill spotted some women drawing water from a well. We were now so parched that first he, and then I, breached all of Authority's health-precaution preachings and slaked our thirst. The wind delay had caused us to miss the last bus back to Asmara and Bill was in jeopardy of being late for his watch the next morning. I collapsed in a bar's easy chair and began to deplete their stock of Melotti (the Asmara beer) while Bill headed out to look for a missionary he'd met earlier, to plead for a ride home. Bill found him, and we got the requested ride, although my devotion to Melotti drew some looks of disapproval from the churchman.

The well water caused no ill effects, and I began to formulate a personal policy which took shape over coming months and became permanent: when in a foreign land, eat what the locals eat, drink what they drink, suffer the diarrhea or whatever, and build up an immunity. My policy would have shocked medical Authority, but it served me well for many years.

The food mainstays were zigeny and injera. Injera was an unleavened bread made from a local grain called *teff* – millet in English. The batter was cooked into a large pancake-shape, a foot and a half in diameter but seldom more than a quarter-inch thick. The final product was gray to light-brown, spongy, often a bit sourish, and sometimes with some fine grit, which I speculate came from blowing dust. Pancakes of injera were piled up on a large circular tray and the zigeny ladled out on top, in the center. Zigeny was a fiery red stew of *ghee*, shallots, powder, and either chicken (plus hard-boiled eggs), sheep, goat, more rarely beef, or (still more rarely) fish. The "zigeny powder" contained some 15-20 different spices, of which dried, powdered, hot red peppers were the base and the most essential. Garlic, ginger, mint, cinnamon, black pepper, cloves were some of the others – many had no English names. The test for good zigeny was whether it made the back of one's neck sweat. If it didn't, it wasn't hot enough. In such a case the heat deficit could often be cured by raw green peppers (*berbere*) available on the side. They resembled fat jalapeños but were much hotter.

The injera served as knife, fork, spoon, and napkin. Diners would gather around the tray, tear off a piece from the outside of the top injera layer, fold it over whatever tidbit they fancied, or simply soak it in the sauce. Popping a bite thus prepared into a neighbor's mouth was customary, but was not as often done to foreigners, who they knew were strange to the practice.

Pork zigeny was a contradiction in terms. The Habesha shared the Muslim/Jewish aversion to pigs. They also looked aghast at shrimp, lobster, and any seafood except fish.

It was sometimes alleged that in the Ethiopian Cook Book the recipe for chicken zigeny began, "First, steal one chicken . . ."

Once my car arrived, my options for travel expanded. They were hampered by Authority's policy of requiring permission by "special request chit" for any excursions over 25 miles from Asmara. Running such a chit through three or four levels of Authority usually took a day or more. Approval was almost automatically granted; I think the requirement was partly to deter drunken spur-of-the-moment trip ideas, but mostly just so Authority knew where you'd gone in case you went missing. But Authority had left an unintended loophole. I could travel partway down the Massawa road, take a blacktopped cutoff to Dekemhare, and return thence to Asmara. Also, from the road west to Keren, I could take a gravel road that led down the escarpment to the flats and then joined the Massawa road, whence I could return to Asmara. Either of these circular routes, I determined from maps, lay within a 25-mile *radius* of Asmara. Later on, when someone had an accident on the cutoff, Authority awoke and amended the rule to *over 25 **road** miles*.

That gravel road down the escarpment was well-maintained and easy to drive, and the views were, if anything, even more spectacular than those on the main Massawa road. The gravel road was known as the "old" Massawa road, from which one would infer that it preceded the main road, but – another mystery – I have never found any written confirmation. The first time that Bill and I explored it, we went only to the edge of the dropoff where we rambled around on foot. We found some trench-like earthworks and a few cartridge cases that piqued our curiosity. When we returned to the car, I found that my rear window had been smashed to fragments. Bill was something of a photographer and, although he had taken his camera on the walk, he had left some equipment cases on the back seat and they had been taken. A few young boys had materialized at the car, watching developments with interest.

I drove nearby tracks for a short time, hoping to spot a fleeing culprit, but saw no one.

On another day when we drove all the way down, much of the descent was in fog. For much of the year clouds piled up against the escarpment, unable quite to spill over the rim of the plateau, giving rise to the *island above the clouds* description sometimes applied to Asmara. We diverted ourselves by dislodging boulders, some of them huge, from their shaky foundations to disappear, rumbling, into fog below – and perhaps to become an unwelcome monument in some farmer's terraced field.

We hit a break together and decided to go to Massawa. A hazard on the main Massawa road – on any road, for that matter – was the *shiftas*. *Shifta* was not a new word to me; it had been familiar since about age ten, when I was devouring every Tarzan book in the local library. Edgar Rice Burroughs had read of shiftas and had written them into one of his books. The shiftas were bandits.

Within a month after my arrival there was an incident on the Massawa road. A navy vehicle had been returning from Massawa when it and the vehicle ahead were stopped by a shifta roadblock – boulders placed across the road. The SK1 (Storekeeper) in charge of the mail run blasted away with his .45; the driver of the leading vehicle joined in; at least three shiftas were killed and at least one escaped wounded. There were no non-shifta casualties, thanks perhaps to the poor condition of the antique rifles of the shiftas. The accompanying YN3 thought that the SK1 was nuts to have begun firing and lucky that he didn't get them both killed. Authority took over. The SK1 had to leave the country to allay State Department nervousness. The navy could find *no* shore duty for him, U.S. or overseas, and he was sent to a *ship*. A fine reward for doing his duty. They did give him a medal, though (and he retired a Lieutenant Commander).

Such troubles on the roads were the exception, most trips went smoothly and I never encountered shiftas. The road to Massawa ran close to the railroad most of the way, and also to the *Teleferica* – cableway is, I guess, the best translation. It had been mostly for transporting cargo; the rusting towers and cables, and the cargo carriers, about the size and shape of a dump truck bed, were still in place near the highway. It had been built in the late 1930s. When the British drove out the Italians, they didn't find much use for it. It was vulnerable to sabotage, vandalism, and thievery — and not only human thievery. Baboons learned to climb the pylons, enter the slow-moving cars, and help themselves to any edibles they fancied. The British expropriated the motors for use elsewhere and the rest of the system was left to rust.

I experimented once with turning my ignition off at the top of the escarpment to see how far I could coast. Twenty-six miles, and I had to use the brake on some of the hairpin curves.

The slopes of the escarpment – and some of the plateau – were covered with *beles* – a prickly-pear cactus. I wanted to try the fruit. Nearly all those close to the road had already been harvested. I finally spotted an accessible one, but my attempt to clean and open it with a pocketknife drew so many tiny, annoying stickers that I soon gave it up as a bad job. I've read that the cactus is not native but was introduced (by the Italians . . .?) in the 19th century.

Near the bottom of the escarpment was an Italian cemetery, casualties from an Italian 1880s debacle in the lowlands. Some of the graves were decorated with flowers recently placed by contemporary Italians. Soon after the road reaches the flats and becomes more or less horizontal we spotted a fort on a medium-high crag off to the left, stopped, and set off to explore. The fort was in ruins, identical to the one south of Dekemhare. At the base of the crag was a small oasis, green vegetation and a pool of stagnant-looking water. After exploring the fort we came down to the pond. I was walking around on a barren slope beside the pond when I looked at the rocks around me. And looked. And looked again. I was standing in an amphitheater, reminiscent of what you might see in a Greek or Roman ruin, although far cruder. Rough slabs of rock had been dragged into place to create rows of seats and seat backs in the bowl-shaped hillside, hard to differentiate from the natural rocks, but definitely a man-made amphitheater when you looked long enough and hard enough. I never found any mention of it in books and for years I nurtured a belief that I had chanced upon an antiquity that had been overlooked by scholars. But in 1994 I was able to get feedback from an Eritrean archaeologist; they knew about it and believed it to be Roman.

There was an R&R center in Massawa where we could have stayed, but I wanted no part of army rules and regulations. We wound up on dormitory cots in a virtual flophouse, but we slept well and had nothing stolen. Our choice of lodging would have shocked the Asmara admin people. At night we drank Melottis at a seaside bar which had a walkway projecting out over the water to a gazebo with table and chairs. Looking at the bottom, I spied a strange, walking creature which I described as ". . . like some kind of prehistoric monster." This gave Bill quite a chuckle. From the Delaware seaboard, he knew a crab when he saw one.

A U.S. navy commander had supervised salvage operations in Massawa during World War II and had written a book, *Under the Red Sea Sun*, about his experiences. We chortled over his description of the "terrible, scorching desert". Yes, we'd been hot and sweating after our fort-exploration foray, and it was not the very hottest time of year, but we still deemed his words considerably overhyped.

Our explorations of Asmara itself concentrated on the bars, but there was much else to see. Italian businesses and shops carried a lot of Italian (and other) merchandise. One of the odder items I saw was a silencer, openly displayed in the window of a gun shop. There were three large movie houses and some smaller ones; of the large, one carried subtitled English-language movies, the other two Italian. Also popular (with Eritreans, not with me) were interminable four-hour Indian soap-opera movies.

I never heard of the wager being actually offered and accepted, but it was said that money could be taken from a new guy by betting him that Mussolini's name could still be seen on prominent display in a public building. Which indeed it could. The "public building" was the big, red-brown stone Italian cathedral which dominated the main street and the center of the city. At the rear of its principal chamber was a large bronze plaque recognizing the patrons or benefactors who had supported construction of the church. At the top, in foot-high letters, was S.M. (His Majesty) Vittorio Emanuele III, followed in equally-large type by S.E. (His Excellency) Benito Mussolini. Below, in progressively smaller characters, were several lesser fascist dignitaries. I remember none with certainty but assume that they included the minister for colonies, the governor-general of Eritrea, etc.

All along the north side of town, beginning a few blocks north of the main street, was a large area designated *Quartiere Indigeno* – native quarter – on Italian maps. It was a slum, with narrow streets and primitive housing. It was divided into several neighborhoods, the most prominent of which was *Abba Shiaul*. The initial A was lightly pronounced, almost inaudible to western ears. To us, and probably to the British before us, it sounded like *Bashawl* – and from this came "the bosh", which was how all Americans spoke of it. The army had decreed it off limits (navy phrase: out of bounds) after sunset. I thought this ridiculous, that the army had its regulation just for the sake of having one. I would have felt safer in the bosh after dark than in downtown Asmara, where street boys sought to prey on Americans. One boundary of the defined off-limits area ran down a wide, s-curved street with a median – and a bar perched atop that median in one spot. Bill and I sat therein one evening marveling that on *that* side of the bar we would be off limits, while on *this* side we were quite legal.

Two often-seen accessories of city life were zigeny pots and shifta sticks. The former were the Eritrean lunch buckets, metallic, roundish, garishly decorated with red and blue on white patterns, and carried either by a cat's-cradle string attachment or by an intrinsic handle. The shifta sticks were simply staffs – six or seven feet long, commonly carried over one shoulder by rural Eritreans. Other items sometimes carried were fly whisks – long horsehairs attached to a handle – and parasols to keep off the sun. The parasols were especially favored by religious dignitaries and upper-class women.

The bars came in several varieties. Some were Italian-owned with predominantly Italian patronage. Maybe 20 catered chiefly to Americans. The bars with mostly Eritrean clientele ranged from those which were equally-well appointed down to the primitive *myis*-and-*suwa* houses. *Suwa* was a weak, sourish, watery beer, often with floating fragments of the grain from which it was made. I drank it only when necessary to show appreciation for proffered hospitality. *Myis*, altered to "mist" by Americans, was more pleasant. It was a sweetish wine, made from honey, and must be akin to the mead of the old Vikings. It was rumored to contain ingredients which would have been of professional interest to the latter-day DEA. I drank it to excess only once, at a wedding to which the houseboys invited me, and my experience would tend to support those rumors. It was a pleasant drunk of a different sort and the descriptor "high", later to become embedded in the drug culture, fit. But I paid for the pleasure with the worst hangover of a lifetime!

A tin can, painted white, upended and perched on a rooftop stick or tripod, was the sign that a myis-and-suwa house was stocked and open to customers. Bill claimed that he sat down in one on an evening and an Eritrean saw him, said, "Americano! No possible!", pushed away his drink and left – he had had enough and thought he was seeing things!

The Italian brewery's Melotti was an excellent beer, although many Americans disparaged it – perhaps from a conviction that nothing local could have any merit. Italian distilleries produced a great variety of potables, but I was chiefly a beer-drinker and didn't try many of them. Zibib was a popular drink – it is the liquor known in France as anise, in Italian as anice, in Greece as ouzo. Clear, with a licorice flavor which I've never liked, it turned milky if mixed with water. Fiore Alpino (Alpine Flower) was a thick, syrupy liqueur, pale yellow with a faint greenish tinge. It tasted like pine needles smell, and if one touched a match to it, it would burn with a tiny, pale blue flame. Perhaps the oddest bottle that I saw was one labeled absinthe. All I knew about absinthe at the time was "some sort of alcoholic drink", and it was years later until I learned that it had been banned in many countries since the early 1900s and that it contained wormwood, once believed to be a slow poison if drunk regularly. Had I known what I was seeing, I'd surely have ordered a shot just to say that I'd once sampled it. (Absinthe has been re-legalized today in much of Europe, but not in the U.S.)

Nearly all of the Italian-owned bars and quite a few of the other upscale ones contained one or more pool tables. The game played thereon was called "guinea pool" by Americans. I described it as a mix of pool, bowling, and shuffleboard. Five small "pins" resembling chess pawns were placed in the center, a red one surrounded by four white ones in a diamond pattern, about five inches apart. One player had four red balls, the other four white, same size as American pool balls, and there was a slightly smaller light-blue ball. There were no pockets and no cues. The players stood at one end of the table and the first player gently rolled the blue ball to one side of the pins, aiming to get it to come to rest just past the center line. He then rolled one of his balls forcefully into the blue ball. Points were scored for knocking down the pins. A perfect shot, rarely achieved, saw the blue ball rebound from the far cushion, knock down a side pin, rebound from the near cushion to topple all three centerline pins, and finally rebound yet again from the far cushion to dispose of the remaining pin.

After initial experience, I seldom patronized the mostly-American bars. One reason for my avoidance was that they were regularly patrolled by army MPs. That, in itself, would not have been so bad – but the MPs assumed that all male Caucasians were military, even though wearing civvies, and did not bother to inquire. (The appearance of Italians was distinctive, and anyhow they were rarely seen in "American" bars.) And the MP assumptions were exasperatingly correct – tourists, non-military westerners of any sort, were virtually zero. The annoyance level was petty – I don't recall anything worse than someone being told to get his feet off a chair or table – but the principle rankled me greatly. In conversation with Bill I dismissed these bars as "tourist bars".

The flies in Asmara, smaller than average, surpassed all flies of my previous (and subsequent) acquaintance at speed, maneuverability, evasive action, and annoyance factor. My ongoing war with them produced barroom revulsion. Lacking a swatter, I would clap my hands together above a resting fly, hoping that it would flee directly into the impact zone. Or, I would swipe rapidly with cupped hand, hoping to imprison the fly in my fist. I had little success but scored an occasional casualty. I learned early that these actions were upsetting to Eritreans. Getting fly guts on one's skin was disgusting, yucky. Africans had surrendered to the fly eons earlier, hence the carrying of the occasionally-seen fly whisks.

I was much criticized but did not reform. My intolerance for impertinent insects outweighed my regard for local sensibilities. And later I developed a refinement: after a *failed* effort I would examine my empty palm, smile with satisfaction, and simulate popping a corpse into my mouth with relish. If fly innards on the skin were gross, squashed flies as edibles were beyond gross. The reactions mostly beggar description but twice, at least, I sent girls racing, retching, for the rest room.

Urban life had its hazards comparable to the shiftas – less perilous, but more common: street boys and gharry drivers. The gharry (I believe the name is Indian, from the British occupation) was a small, rickshaw-like cart drawn by a small, scrawny horse at the urging of a larcenous driver. It was the local taxi, and could accommodate two or three passengers. I might have ridden in a gharry once or twice early on, but I knew Americans were charged more than locals and so I walked on principle. The drivers could be described as street boys with horses.

The street boys hung out around the gates of Kagnew Station and Tract A, and also outside the bars which Americans mostly patronized. They hoped to be hired as "guides", or as car-watchers (a protection racket), or somehow or other to convince an American to part with money. When refused, they would follow along and annoy, mostly verbally. They had a finely-developed sense of just how far they could go and what they could do without spurring retaliatory violence. After initial experience I developed a policy of ignoring them, making no response to them, unless to repel physical harassment. This did not discourage their attentions in the least, but it gave me the minimal satisfaction of pissing them off as much as they pissed me off.

One rainy winter evening I was suffering from a cough. Fiore Alpino, aforementioned, had little to recommend it as a beverage but it was about as good a cough syrup as any. I walked down to the Navy Bar to treat my cough. I overtreated it.

I did not remember exiting the bar. In the barracks next morning, inventory disclosed missing wallet, shoes, belt, jacket, wrist watch. I had been street-boyed.

I was enraged. A few days later, cough gone, hangover dissipated, I made the rounds of the American bars. In each one I let the girls know that I would pay $50 Ethiopian ($20 U.S.) {$134} to anyone who would identify and point out my thievish escort(s). Somewhat to my surprise, I never got a single response – no one even tried to scam me out of the reward money. It was almost certainly a good thing. Detection and revenge would have been satisfying, but could all too easily have gotten me into a great deal of trouble.

What the reward offer *did* get me, though, was a reputation – a reputation and respect. For the balance of that tour, over a year, no street boy ever followed me again, not even when I sought to attract their company by walking side streets late at night. Indeed I once saw, from the corner of my eye, a young street boy head in my direction, only to be called off and cautioned by an older one.

I did once get the better of a street boy . . . in a small way . . . sort of . . . He was probably not one of the regulars who haunted the Kagnew-Tract A stretch and the American bars. He was standing outside a distant bar in mid-day, in the middle of a short block on a side street. He may have been drunk. As I drove by, he directed a few belligerent remarks at me, asking if I wanted to fight, etc. In keeping with my street-boy policy I made no eye contact and took no notice whatever. As I turned left at the end of the block, he had lost interest in me and was looking elsewhere. I could not resist. I cupped hand to mouth and blew a loud fart in his direction. As I vanished around the corner I was rewarded by the sight of the spin, the upthrust arm, the dangled finger, and the outraged sound of "Adeehatiwa!"

The going price of an all-nighter was $10 Ethiopian ($4 U.S.) {$27}. Many of the girls lacked pubic hair. I thought this was some sort of racial variation, of passing interest but little importance. I was wrong. I didn't learn the truth until many years later. What it was, was a side-effect of female circumcision.

The victims can never know the true pleasure of sex – only whatever vicarious satisfaction they can derive from closeness to a man, from knowing that they have pleased and contented him. They can bear children, and they are normal in all outward respects. They have their jealousies, their gossiping, their flirting, primping, and concern for their appearance, their desire for a husband or boyfriend, all indistinguishable from any unmutilated woman.

The barbarity is cultural rather than religious. Both Muslims and Christians are guilty. It is centered on Ethiopia but extends across a long belt of sub-Saharan Africa to the Atlantic, and into Egypt and parts of the Arabian peninsula and the middle east. It is estimated to afflict 80-90% of the women in Ethiopia, and the estimate about accords with my experience. The supposed social "benefit" is that it reduces temptation to pre-marital sex and also any inclination of a wife to be unfaithful. (I hope the Christian right in the U.S.A. never gets wind of it.)

Most sailors talk about their sexual encounters without restraint and it is odd that I *never* heard any discussion about the pubic-hairlessness or its possible cause. Perhaps I just was not a party to the right bull sessions, but that is improbable. I think the other sailors were as ignorant as I was.

I contracted gonorrhea twice in Asmara. Back while marking time in the Anacostia RecSta I had had a lot of library time to spend, and I had nosed through old copies of *All Hands*, the navy's official magazine. I had learned that, just before World War II, any history of venereal disease disqualified any applicant for warrant officer or limited duty officer. That was no longer true, the navy had long since realized that it could be an incentive for someone to conceal his illness. But, I thought, *was* it no longer true? If my malady was on record, I felt I could not trust Authority not to hold it against me at some future point, without saying so and without even my knowledge.

Mostly for that reason and partly from embarrassment, I said nothing to anyone and took my problem to a downtown Italian doctor. He cured the first occurrence with a couple of shots of penicillin, but when he gave me the first shot for the second case, I had a reaction. I began to feel uneasy, jittery, a blotchy sort of skin discomfort – and I lost consciousness for a microsecond. I was standing at a urinal at the time, went to a squat, but recovered before hitting the floor. The doctor said the one shot would probably be enough. It was.

A couple of months after I arrived in Asmara, we got a new OIC – Officer In Charge. The advent of Lieutenant Commander Lawrence W. Covert in Asmara was not quite as devastating as the arrival of LCDR Queeg on the *USS Caine*, but it bore comparison. After the first personnel inspection he held, he gathered everyone around and announced that the uniform of the day would henceforth be whites or blues, depending on the season. No more dungarees. As my supervisor said, "You could just hear the *plop* when morale went."

Covert was from Maine, a mustang ex-Radioman, and, we heard, a survivor of the World War II "Death March" in the Philippines. He reminded me of Nikita Khrushchev – not so much facially but when seen from the side or rear: the balding head and bulky, pear-shaped body. He had a navy radio put in his bedroom, listened in on our CW broadcast evenings, criticized the way it was handled, and threatened to put us on three-section watches if it didn't improve.

Somebody mishandled and lost an important message. I don't remember if there was actual punishment or merely threats of same. Bill Mote's comment was, "*You *will* be perfect." Don Finch said, "*Only one man was ever perfect and they crucified him." Chief Pendergrass had a relevant observation also: "The gunnery department gets thirty-percent hits and they've done wonderful. They get E's for Efficiency and letters of commendation. Communications handles ten thousand messages, drops one of them, and communications is all fucked up."

Inspired by Mr Murphy, I formulated what I called *Covert's Law*: Anything that can get worse, will.

I passed the August exam and was promoted to RM2 in November. Shortly thereafter I tried to profit from something I had learned while browsing in the BUPERS Manual. Someone who had been reduced in rate could be restored to his former rate, provided that his command so recommended and Washington approved. I had not wanted to try this while I was third-class. I feared Washington might mull it over and perhaps split the difference and approve restoration, but only to second-class – somewhat as they had done when I first sought to reenlist. Better to wait, not to give them that option, to short-circuit the two-year second-to-first gap if possible, rather than the one-year third-to-second, and therefore to hold off until I had *already* made second-class. The command was very much in favor (I had not yet gotten into much trouble) and forwarded my request with a glowing recommendation.

Washington replied: no. I had not been reduced in rate, they said, rather I had been "accepted back into the navy at a lower rate"! Hmmm. It certainly *felt* like my rate had been reduced. I reflected: someone who punched out a superior, who committed almost any kind of grievous offense, could, after good behavior and with a favorable recommendation, obtain restoration. Getting out of the navy to try civilian life – unforgivable.

During that first winter the unheated barracks got so cold that one shivery day I rounded up two or three other off-watch sailors and we drove down the old Massawa road just to get warm. We did get warm in the flats, very much so. We had taken nothing to drink, and when we connected to the main Massawa road and started back up the escarpment, we stopped at the first bar we encountered. Their Melotti was, uncharacteristically, ice-cold – as cold as any beer I have ever quaffed and, in my hot-and-dry condition, as *memorable* as any. Most of the Asmara bars served beer only slightly-chilled and a really cold one was rare.

At about that time, I drifted into living with Yeshu. She rented us a small house not far from Tract A with a small tiled-over courtyard shared by four other households. My major motivation was to escape the barracks; to have a place where I could drink beer peacefully in the evenings. From the neighbors and housegirls I began to pick up a little more Tigrinya. A navy-wide term for a man shacking up was "class B brownbagger"; in Asmara the word sometimes used was "blackbagger".

I spent a lot of time on our house's small front porch, my feet up on the railing, reading. Many a time I witnessed the ritual of coffee preparation. The most common local stove was about a foot square, a foot and a half high. Large holes were in each side to provide draft, and the top was squished downward and perforated with slits. Handles were often attached to the sides. Charcoal was burned in the top, the ash falling downward for later disposal. (Injera was made on top of a much larger and less-portable circular oven.)

Coffee beans were roasted in a long-handled ladle, made from discarded, reworked tinware. They were pulverized by mortar-and-pestle, and the coffee was brewed in a narrow-necked, round-bottomed earthenware flask, stoppered with some fibrous substance that resembled dried weeds and served as a filter when the coffee was poured. As in much of the Mediterranean-middle east, the coffee was exceeding strong and was served in diminutive, handleless cups, heavily sugared. (If you wanted black coffee, you had to say so in time. The default was *sugar*.) Irregular, varicolored lumps of incense were often thrown on the hot charcoal; they might well have been the biblical myrrh or frankincense, perhaps both. Another sometime accompaniment was *meshilla* – a local grain that I described as "miniature popcorn". It is a close relative of millet; the only name I can find for it in English is *guineacorn*. Except for the small size of the popped kernels it was indistinguishable from ordinary popcorn in appearance and taste. Handfuls of meshilla would be tossed on the ground in several directions. When I remonstrated about the waste of quite good food it did not avail, and I never got an answer to my "why . . .".

Once a friend of Yeshu's, from Adwa I believe, came by and brought a present: mushrooms. Great big, foot-long mushrooms. They can't be bought, can't be cultivated, can only be *found* – and he had found them on his journey. Yeshu cooked them up in some zigeny-like sauce and I got to partake. They were superb. Only that once did I ever eat them.

On one of Haile Selassie's Asmara visits I had been downtown, seen him pass, and had returned and was sitting on the porch. Medhin, a neighbor girl, came by and asked where I'd been. The conversation went (it was in my sketchy Habesha; I render it in English here):
"Downtown. I saw the emperor."
"Emperor who?"
"Emperor Haile Selassie." At just this point it occurred to me that the question was obviously not to seek information but to hear me continue to speak Habesha – often a source of entertainment to native-speakers. With a note of scorn I continued:
"Wah! Emperor *who*! How many emperors are there?"
Medhin took the rebuke with amusement and Yeshu's mother, who was visiting from Adwa, was absolutely delighted.

Bill was a frequent visitor at the house and a sometime tenant in the spare room, but his shackups did not endure for long. I had made idle mention of having a dog. Bill bought a pup from a street boy and donated it, but the pup – apathetic and unresponsive from the first – sickened and died in a few days. It turned out that Bill had been sold a jackal pup! But we did acquire a genuine dog soon afterwards.

I continued to make trips from time to time, with Bill, or with Yeshu, often with both. One of our trips was to Keren (which also had an army R&R hotel, which I disdained). It was my only visit thence. Bill and I left Yeshu at our hotel and went exploring farther westward. We wanted to see the World War II battlefield and look for

211

any relics remaining (anything metallic would surely have been long since scavenged, but I didn't realize that yet). But we didn't know just where the fighting had happened, didn't see any wrecked tanks or any such clues. Had we known, we were driving right through the middle of the battlefield, just outside of Keren, but I didn't read the right history books until some years later. We continued on some 70 miles or so to the next town of any size, Agordat, turned around and came back.

Preparing for the drive to Keren, I had taken an anti-shifta precaution: I had stashed nearly all of my money in the driver-side door panel vice my wallet. This was noticed in the patio and must have been commented upon. The intelligence had found its way to the street boys. My broken back window had gone unrepaired for many months, while a local mechanic ordered and – finally – received the replacement. Many a morning I found the door panel unsnapped by a thief hoping to find that I'd made another such deposit!

My first trip to Adwa and Aksum, a little over 100 miles south, was made only with Yeshu. About halfway, we came to a dropoff – nothing like the Asmara-Massawa escarpment, yet quite impressive on its own. It was the valley of the Mareb river, which formed part of the boundary between Eritrea and Tigrai province. Eritrea was then left-hand drive. I read somewhere that when the British entered Asmara in 1941 their first directive, issued before sundown that day, was that traffic would henceforth move on the *left*. At the Mareb bridge it changed to the right-hand which prevailed in the rest of Ethiopia.. I had been driving quite slowly, the better to take in the scenery, and it was beginning to get later in the day. After crossing the Mareb I sped up to 40 mph, the national speed limit throughout Ethiopia.

I had been annoyed previously by the horn-honking of some local drivers, particularly of trucks. It struck me as arrogant, perhaps influenced by Italian driving habits. Perhaps it was, in part, but it had a useful function that I did not yet appreciate: warning the populace that a motor vehicle was approaching. On a flat, straight road I came up behind three ladies walking on the right, in the same direction that I was going. There was plenty of room to pass; I didn't foresee any hazard, didn't honk, didn't slow down, just moved to the left. When the ladies heard the sound of a car on the gravel behind them, they panicked. Two of them scurried off the road to the right, no problem. But the lady on the left ran leftward across the road.

She almost made it. I almost stopped. Almost doesn't count. My left fender bumped her on the rump and knocked her tumbling. We got her in the car and headed onward to find the Adwa hospital, but before coming to Adwa we came to a police post where we stopped to report the matter. (I was following Yeshu's advice in all this.) Instead of expediting getting her to a hospital, the police directed us to drive them back to the accident site so that they could make out a report! *Then*, bureaucracy having been appeased, we took her into Adwa, to a hospital. Her injuries turned out to be not nearly as serious as I feared – a very sore posterior (but no broken bones), plus minor cuts and scrapes from the roadside gravel. I paid her hospital bill voluntarily – I forget how much, but surely minuscule compared to first-world charges. On a future trip Yeshu learned, and told me, that one of the lady's relatives had come to the hospital and prodded her to seek all she could get from the rich foreigner. She refused, saying she had been stupid, the accident was her fault.

About five miles north of Adwa there is a junction of main roads and a little settlement named Adi Aboon (Yeshu's mother lived there). At the junction there was a small, primitive gas station-motel-restaurant where I slept and ate. One of the dishes served me there was one of the strangest I've ever encountered, and one of the tastiest. It consisted of the internal organs of a sheep or goat: lungs, heart, liver, stomach, intestine, diced up smaller than bite-size, and served *raw* with a yellowish sauce (and the usual injera). The principal ingredient in the sauce was the bile from the animal's gall bladder. If you have ever gotten an accidental taste of bile (as I did as a boy on the farm, when chickens were being dismembered) you will know that it is a truly horrible, bitter substance. But they did something to the bile that removed the bitterness, the resulting sauce was delicious, the meal delicious. I never ate that particular dish again. Yeshu said there was some health hazard

213

to it – perhaps the raw-meat factor, perhaps the bile itself – and that it was seldom prepared.

I had left Asmara with less Ethiopian currency than usual. I wasn't concerned – Adwa was a relatively major city (a provincial capital, I mistakenly thought). There would be banks. I should have been concerned. There were no banks, and I had a problem: I would not have enough gas money for the trip home. And no one wanted my American dollars. (The first time I was ever in that situation.) Yeshu made inquiries, and someone put us on the trail of the Adwa pharmacist, Tafari. He made periodic trips to Asmara to replenish his stock, he could dispose of U.S. dollars there, and was quite willing to change enough to meet my needs. We became friends and he visited us in Asmara whenever he came there. He introduced me to some of his friends and to the card game they played. It used at least two, probably three, standard decks and bore a closer relation to rummy than anything else. They were intrigued when I shuffled cards – they had never seen a card-bending shuffle before and knew only hand-to-hand mixing.

We went to Aksum, about 15 miles to the west, to see the famed obelisks and other ruins and relics. Many of the better-preserved pieces, and inscriptions, had been located together in a small park at the entrance to Aksum. Aksum was infested with street boys, and ten years later one of them still remembered me and my refusal to hire his guide services.

The next time we went to Adwa, Bill came along. Adi Aboon is dominated by Amba Soloda, an impressive mountain. It is the first in a jumble of crazily-shaped mountains that run east from Adwa for many miles. The 1896 battle was fought in these mountains, just northeast of Adwa, rather than in the city itself. We wanted to try to climb Soloda. We got going early enough that no street boys were yet on duty and managed to make our climb unescorted. Near the summit it began to get rather steep. We took different paths; Bill didn't make it to the top but I found a way. There was a small ruin of some sort on the summit

– the remains of stone walls. I was told that it had probably been a church.

On one trip to Adwa I was for some reason particularly concerned about thieves. And as I lay in bed half-asleep, half-awake, a white-clad figure raised the window and stealthily climbed in. I played possum until, at an appropriate moment, I threw off the covers and leaped to my feet to grapple with the intruder — and no one was there. The window was still locked from the inside. Dream, hallucination, sleepwalking . . . call it what you will, maybe some of each. I felt befuddled at first, and then quite foolish.

We took another trip to Massawa, this time with Yeshu along. There is a little island quite near the town, no one lives there; one half is covered with scrubby trees/bushes maybe 10-12 feet high, the other half has nothing but grass. It was Green Island to Americans, Isla Verde to Italians, Sheik Said to the locals. We wanted to explore and Yeshu hired us a boat and procured a picnic lunch. On the beaches we found quite a few hard, rubbery, transparent, gelatinous disks, shaped like furniture casters, about three inches across and an inch thick. My knife wouldn't cut them. I never did learn what they were, my best guess is that they were part of the anatomy of ex-jellyfish.

We had seen seabirds at the far end of the scrub half of the island; Bill and I wanted to investigate and set off through the maze of bushes. We didn't quite reach our goal. The open passages were often obstructed by large webs with large spiders in their centers – and Bill had as bad a case of arachnophobia as I have ever seen. We started back, could not find the way we had come in, and Bill was getting increasingly distraught. "Lost" – on a little island that could not have been much more than ten acres! I'm sure we would have found our way out eventually, but we were rescued by Yeshu and the boatmen who came in and guided us back to daylight.

I often ate with Yeshu, sometimes with Bill along, at an Italian restaurant and pizzeria at the edge of Asmara on the Keren road, long-vanished but one of my all-time favorite pizza places. If you ordered pepperoni, they put on so much that you could scarcely see the pizza underneath. (And the slices were distinctly thicker than on today's American fast-food pizza.) We also ordered another topping, the local hot peppers. The restaurant was half indoors, half in a covered outdoors. One busy evening the rains came. Shortly after, the electricity departed. And we heard the elderly proprietor in the midst of his toil at the pizza oven: "Maledetto! Disgraziato! Senza luce! Senza corrente!" (= Damn! Disgraceful! Without light! Without current!) Not especially powerful – there was after all a mixed-company clientele to overhear – but of surpassing sincerity. We laughed about it and the phrases passed into our domestic repartee:

"You maledetto!"

"You disgraziato!"

"You senza luce, senza corrente!"

We watchstanders were pestered by training sessions. "Training" is one of Authority's sacred cows. You don't have to accomplish anything with it, but when visitors arrive to perform an "admin inspection", you do have to have paperwork to show them to prove that you do have a "training program". Personnel turnover happens, and crises (or pseudocrises) occur from time to time and divert everyone's attention from the unnecessary to the urgent. Training programs start up, peter out, start up again, peter out again . . . The instructors are not qualified as such, just senior petty officers who are assigned to the chore. Not knowing what else to do, they "start at the beginning" each time, and thus it came about that three times in Asmara I was re-taught Ohm's law and other such basic electronics – which I already knew both from Teleman school and from Radioman school. (And never used.) Watchstanders are typically ordered to report for an hour or two of this "training" in the afternoon before each evening watch – but *not* if it's Saturday, Sunday, or holiday. It is dandy to train on the watchstanders' free time, but not on the instructors' free time.

There are two kinds of useful training. One is the service schools (e.g. Teleman and Radioman) where one is a full-time student. The other, most valuable of all, is on-the-job, which occurs spontaneously without any planning or effort by Authority. The training programs,

216

which every command is supposed to have, are generally useless and an imposition on those "trained". There are few better practical examples of the old, cynical definition of the military: the unqualified ordering the unwilling to do the unnecessary. (What I have just written applies to communications, with certainty, but I recognize that it may not fully apply to other ratings with different job requirements.)

We got a new operations officer, a mustang, one Charles B. Rockwell. He was about as chubby as Bill Mote. He had a chickenshit side and a more rational side, overall he was not too bad and sometimes the former side was more a source of amusement than annoyance. We called him Rocky. One time when we were in ranks before a personnel inspection, he put us at ease. There was some chatter and Rocky turned around and hectored us indignantly. "I gave the order *at ease*", he said. "I didn't say *rest*!" By the book he was correct. There are three levels of relaxation from the position of attention. At *parade rest* you spread your legs, interlace your hands at the small of your back, and remain in that position. For *at ease* one foot is kept in place, otherwise one may move freely but (technically) may not talk. Only *rest*, otherwise identical to *at ease*, permits talking. But after boot camp *rest* is never used, becomes forgotten, and *at ease* is presumed to permit at least some degree of talking. Only Rocky . . .

One of my friends told me how Rocky had chewed him out. He had from ignorance told Rocky, "Very well, sir . . ." He didn't need to continue, I was already laughing. Of all people to whom to say that . . . ! *Very well* is a phrase used by seniors to juniors, not the reverse.

By January 1960 I was receiving P-1 proficiency pay – always truncated to *pro pay* in conversation. It was an extra $30 {$200} a month. Some time in 1961 I began to receive the P-2 level, $60 {$395}. This was something new, the navy was trying to find a way to increase reenlistment in those ratings for which there was a shortage, which of course were chiefly in technical and electronics fields. It was quite unfair to the non-technical ratings.

In June I began to wear a second hash mark – those two-plus college years that I spent theoretically in the reserves were counted for this purpose. A second-class senior to me, a frequent opponent in verbal duels, had liked to call me a boot – I now began to label him a *one-hashmark boot.*

And it was in June that Bill Mote and I took our most famous (or infamous) trip of all. He and I were off duty on the same day and had the urge to go boondocking. Out by Tract D, the army transmitter site, there was a small waterfall. Bill had been told that this was the source of the Mareb river. (Years later I learned that this was not exactly true, but close – the waterfall stream soon flows into the true Mareb, and does so quite close to the Mareb's true source.) I knew from maps and previous travel that the road south to Adwa/Aksum crossed over the upper Mareb at the little village of Debarwa. The straight-line distance from Tract D south to Debarwa appeared to be no more than 15-20km, around a six-hour hike we guesstimated. And the entire route was within our still-legal 25-mile radius.

So the plan, hastily conceived in mid-morning, was that a non-hiking friend, Gene Rolston, would drop us off at Tract D then take my car and proceed later to Debarwa, to meet us there at about 1700. Gene did his part. When we did not show at 1700 he waited. And waited. And waited. Finally around 2100 he was sufficiently concerned that he returned to Asmara and reported our nonarrival.

Meanwhile Bill and I had set off from Tract D around 1100, making our leisurely way down the bebouldered river bed, which was not totally dry at that season but was about as dry as it ever gets, the water a mere trickle. The hike went as expected in its first stages, interesting, enjoyable. The afternoon wore on. The sun began to lower a bit. There was nothing yet on the horizon ahead that resembled any landmarks around Debarwa. An Eritrean passed by on a trail higher up on the hills a way back from the river. He hailed us, we held a long-distance shouted conversation in garbled and broken Tigrinya/Italian. He asked where we were going. I had a hard time making him understand; I was familiar only with the Italian spelling (Debarua) and mispronounced it badly. Finally I got it across. I asked him "how many kilometers" and his shouted reply caused me my first serious concern that we had better get a move on: "*Troppo! Troppo! Troppo!" (Too much!)

We moved up out of the river bed to walk on the bank, where straighter-line progress was possible and faster. When the sun set we reverted to the river bed to be sure of not losing our way and kept going by moonlight – but the moon, too, went down at about 2100. We saw nothing yet even resembling the faint lights of a village. The night was now too dark, I felt, to risk the possibility of a disabling fall if we kept going. (We had clambered down/over/around too many such potential hazards during daylight.) So we hunkered down to await morning.

We later learned that our "campsite" was about halfway to Debarwa. I hadn't misread the maps, but I had made totally inadequate allowance for the twists and turns and meanders of a river bed – to say nothing of the ups and downs over boulders.

We wore only short-sleeve shirts. It was chilly; an intermittent very light rain or heavy mist added to our discomfort. The leafy branches that I tried to pile around myself were no help. We tried to sleep; Bill had little success, I had none. Around 0200, tossing and turning, I noticed something odd: a star near the horizon was moving around in a peculiar fashion. Stars do not do that. It got my full attention. It continued its strange motions, I realized it had to be a flashlight, and alerted Bill.

When the lights drew abreast of us, I hailed the searchers and there were relieved cries: "There they are!" "There's Bucher!" I said, "*Who's there, and how much trouble are we in for getting you out here?"

The reply came in the unamused voice of Covert: "*Let's put it this way, how much trouble would you be in if we hadn't come out here?" I answered that we were in no trouble, had been stopped only because of the darkness and would have found our way out in the morning.

We walked on downstream with our rescuers, who had come in from the Debarwa end. There was more water in the river here, we often went through ankle- or calf-deep stretches. I began to experience discomfort from sharp gravel that had sloshed into my boot-camp high-top boondocking shoes. Covert was a bit irritated when I requested a stop to empty them. The stop didn't do much good, the gravel was soon as bad as before – and only back at the barracks did I discover that both ancient shoes had become separated from their soles, in crescents all around the heels! No wonder! I had a pair of chewed-up heels and a pair of shredded socks.

Aside from my sore heels, Bill and I emerged at Debarwa in much better shape than most of our rescuers, who were exhausted. Surprisingly, Covert himself was the exception; despite his unathletic appearance he showed no fatigue and outpaced everyone. (Rocky was probably the most worn out.) Back in Asmara the next morning we were sent to see the Kagnew CO, who rerouted us back to Covert, who asked us only about what had happened in the CO's office. Discipline-wise, we escaped unscathed. We escaped even the desk-pounding chewing out we deserved. In the barracks, however, I had to endure all too many jibes and digs about having gotten "lost". I argued then, and still maintain, that we were never "lost" – simply delayed by darkness.

That isn't quite the end of the story . . .

Some weeks before our misadventure Bill had bought a small handgun from a street boy. Highly illegal, and foolish to boot. He had had it along and, when we realized a search party would find us, he did not want to be caught with it. He piled a small cairn of rocks over it and left it there. But it developed that when our nonarrival was reported, questions had been asked as to whether we were armed. Gene had said he thought we had a gun. We were grilled on the matter a day later, and the truth came out. We were ordered back to the Mareb valley to retrieve the gun.

Trekking in from the Debarwa end, Bill and I somehow became slightly separated from the two other sailors who had joined us for the excursion. We were in a spot of high vegetation, head-high and more, when some rocks began to fall around us. We thought it was horseplay by the other sailors. Then I caught momentary sight of the gray-white garment of a rural Eritrean, at just about exactly the same time that his latest rock struck me on top of the head and knocked me briefly to a squat. My instinct was to give chase and retaliate, but I was bleeding somewhat (besides being slightly stunned) and in no immediate condition to do so even if Bill had not forced me to sit back down. We never caught another glimpse of the rock-chucker; I'll never know whether he was angered by trespassers on his land or motivated by general xenophobia. Whichever, he must have been pleased.

Bill yelled angrily at the other sailors to knock off the rocks! They rejoined us and protested innocence, which I confirmed. We got my bleeding stopped with the aid of someone's T-shirt and proceeded onward.

We found the gun. We were surprised to see that someone had found Bill's little cairn and uncovered the gun, but had not taken it, just left it there in the open. (Speculation: the finder may have been a very young shepherd boy who had never touched a gun before and feared to do so.) We returned to Asmara, where my scalp was stitched back together (I still have the scar, almost invisible now), and turned in the gun. The Chief Master-at-Arms demolished it with a sledgehammer. It was, they said, originally a starter's pistol with a completely solid "barrel", designed only to shoot blanks for track meets. The barrel had been bored out to enable it to launch bullets – very dangerous, we were told.

Rocky commented to me on the foolishness of Bill's gun possession, saying that he could have done it legally. (An example of just how far out of touch the married and/or officer community was with single life in the barracks.) I explained that he could not have. Soon after, a regulation was issued allowing barracks singles to check a gun out of the armory for trips to the countryside. Bill once said that between him and me, we had been the cause of four local navy directives being either issued or rewritten. This was one of them; the others must have related either to travel or shacking up.

At around this time I was taken off my watch section and made the station traffic checker. My predecessor at the job was an amiable, but not very adept, first-class with 17 or 18 years in. He had been selected for chief. I had been nettled for months by his work – I felt strongly that my section was easily the most error-free of the four. He seemed prone to "evening out" the gigs, hitting each section roughly equally. He produced a daily "gig sheet" ranging from one or two gigs to half a page of them. When filing traffic I often saw errors by other sections that had gone unnoticed by him, and corrected them if they were worth correcting.

On my first day on the job, I produced a full four pages of gigs. This raised eyebrows. Some perhaps thought that I was "showing off" – and, to a degree, perhaps I was. My own former watch section was supportive, but others, in particular the supervisors of the other three sections, would not have voted for me in any popularity contests. Two or three of the supervisors were first-class, and I was second-class. They felt that they were being "told what to do" by someone junior to them – and besides no one enjoys having his errors or oversights published for all to see. I could understand such feelings but, as I saw it, I had been given a job to do and I was going to do it right. I hung tough in arguments and against criticism, and I must have had some beneficial influence because my four-page gig list dropped rapidly to three and, more slowly, down to one.

I lasted only four or five months in the job. When Chief Pendergrass told me I was going back on a watch section, he said, ". . . I hate to do it, but I just about got to." He gave no further explanation, but I didn't really need one.

At quarters before personnel inspection one day, Chief Pendergrass was required to read something to us. The administration was concerned about balance-of-payments problems, and wanted all servicemen urged to "buy American" whenever/wherever possible. Chief Pendergrass was clearly not in sympathy with this – he read the blurb then waved it down in disgust and added his own opinion, "Hell, it's your money. Spend it wherever you want."

In July I requested a one-year extension of my tour in Asmara. (The tour was 18 months for those without dependents on station, 30 months for those with them. A maximum extension of one year could be requested.) Asmara didn't float, and I was happy and doing fine. Washington, for once, approved something I wanted.

Billy Bob arrived. He was an RM3, Gene Rolston's brother. Gene was a good guy, perhaps a hair below average on the job, but one of my friends. Billy Bob, though, was weird. He drew comment by wearing his working jacket over his uniform in the hot message center when everyone else was working in T-shirts. He seldom spoke to anyone but his brother, and made no other friends. He was assigned to run the JR teletype broadcast. The equipment had three TDs – two were for sending the actual message tapes; at the third a huge tape roll of pre-prepared JR numbers was attached. This TD was geared to put *one* JR number on each message as it was sent. When a thousand numbers had gone out, the roll had to be changed to the next thousand-sequence. That point was getting very near. The supervisor explained carefully to Billy Bob what had to be done, and how to do it. The supervisor then went away to handle other matters. When he next checked on Billy Bob, he found that Billy Bob had not changed the roll. Instead, when he ran out of numbers, he had pulled the old number tape *back* five numbers or so, resulting in a duplication of broadcast numbers. He had done this two or three times, and the resulting mess required retransmissions and a complicated service message to set right.

The next day I overheard the supervisor relating this episode to Don Finch. Don said, "*Did you ask him why he did it?"

The supervisor said, "*No. I was afraid he might have a reason."

Bill's father died, and he was sent back to the U.S. on compassionate leave. He had not extended his tour when I did, and so had only about four months before transfer. Partly because of this and partly because of his escapades with me and his generally low on-the-job reputation, he was not returned to Asmara. He remained one of my best friends over the years. I will recount his history here.

He went to a Norfolk-based destroyer and could not handle the pressure of shipboard communications. I expect he was a butt for sailor ridicule and harassment. He said that at one point he was defying the other Radiomen, backed into a corner, whirling his headphones around by the cord as a threatening weapon. He was given a medical discharge on psychiatric grounds. His mother found him a wife, who was also decidedly overweight. They had one daughter, who grew up to be a druggie, an overweight motorcycle mama, and a thief. Bill worked at McDonalds for a while, then got into the merchant marine as a longshoreman. When I saw him then, he had lost all his baby fat from the hard labor and had an impressive, tapered physique. He said his co-workers called him "Lurch" from a similarly formidable character on *The Addams Family*.

But then he passed some tests and qualified as a merchant marine radio officer. Soft work – he gained back all the lost fat and more. And more and more. By the 1970s he looked, and I do not exaggerate, like a globe with legs. His marriage broke up. He hooked up for eight years with an air force widow who was an alcoholic's alcoholic. Bill was somewhat alcoholic himself by this time, and also required a pharmacy-full of prescription meds. He retired, lived in what sounded like a skid-row section of New Orleans, married a teenager in the Dominican Republic who ditched him as soon as she got her green card, and he needed canes to move his bulk around. But he seemed to stay happy and cheerful through these vicissitudes; I wrote him once that he reminded me of one of those weighted dolls that, when you knocked it down, bounded right back up again. He died in 1996, just short of age 57.

When Yeshu told me she was pregnant, she asked whether she should have the child or abort it. I could not imagine an American woman deferring this choice to the father. I was so floored that I didn't endorse either option. She interpreted my silence as permission to continue the pregnancy.

One day in December I was in the barracks along with a few others who were off watch, when we were told that liberty was cancelled; we were not to go off the base. No further explanation; we were mystified. After an hour or two the Chief Master-at-Arms took pity on our puzzlement and explained: there had been a coup in Addis Abeba. The emperor's son had taken power.

Now it was the houseboys who were perplexed; they could clearly tell that something unusual was happening. In my turn I took pity on them and explained. Mahari was surprised but cautiously non-committal: "Well . . . I'm still houseboy."

Everything that Authority knew about the coup had come in by classified messages. Therefore, those who were not cleared could not be told what was happening. We were put on three-section watches for a week or two and one memory that stands out is relieving the watch and another sailor's query, "*Well, Bucher, is this your first revolution?" It was.

The chief's initial basic explanation was not fully accurate. The emperor had been off on a state visit to Brazil. The principal plotters had been junior and mid-grade military officers, dissatisfied with the slow pace of progress in Ethiopia. The crown prince may or may not have welcomed the coup; after it collapsed, it was given out that he had made his radio address with a rebel gun at his head. According to one account (open to skepticism) the emperor later told him, "I am glad to see you alive. I would have been prouder to see you dead."

The Ethiopian army commander in Asmara (also governor-general of Eritrea) was the emperor's son-in-law and a staunch supporter. Haile Selassie elected to arrive at secure Asmara before going on to Addis Abeba. For impenetrable diplomatic reasons, we were encouraged to go to the airport – in dress blue uniform – for his arrival. Few sailors wanted to bother, but I went and two or three others rode along with me. The police waved us on through the otherwise-deserted airport road.

When the coup failed, the rebels executed about ten hostages, of whom the most prominent was Ras Seyoum Mangasha, grandson of the former Emperor Yohannes IV. Ras Seyoum was a distant relative – very distant, perhaps fourth or fifth cousin – of Yeshu's mother. Ethiopians keep family genealogies and relationships, in their heads, to a degree inconceivable to westerners. Decades later, when Yeshu visited her father's family in Addis Abeba, they told her that she was a sixth-generation descendant of a crown princess. Her father, a young army officer, had died either before her birth or shortly afterwards, but was well-remembered by the Addis Abeba family.

The coup leaders fled to the countryside but were eventually hunted down and hung publicly. During their brief hours in control they had named Ras Imru Haileselassie (mentioned in Appendix B) as prime minister. Many a dark-skinned third-worlder, future VIP, has come to the U.S. for study or training, encountered U.S. racism, and been turned at least somewhat anti-American by the experience. Ras Imru was one such. American-Ethiopian relations might not have been smooth if the coup had succeeded. He was exonerated of complicity in the coup.

A week or two after the coup, I drove by the old, deserted air strip down at Gura. Rows of boulders had been placed across the tarmac to obstruct any landings. I am not sure who feared what might have been done by whom, but the likeliest guess is that the loyalist army in Eritrea was guarding against a possible rebel airlift.

I do not remember exactly when I began considering marriage with Yeshu. There were two obstacles that I had to overcome. One was racism, not my own but the thought of what I would encounter, given the racism of society. Mixed marriages were far more rare then than today. Conversational mention of Sammy Davis Jr and May Britt evoked lame jokes ("What's black and white and has three eyes?") and

226

knowing leers. More than half of the U.S. states still forbade interracial marriages.

The other obstacle was Authority. All the services required permission for any marriage performed outside the U.S. (even if to another American citizen!). None at all was required for a marriage within the U.S. (even if to a *non*-citizen). I'll refrain from a long diatribe here about this disparity. Obtaining military permission was a prolonged, red-tape-filled obstacle course – obviously intended to discourage, delay, and minimize marriages to foreigners, although Authority routinely denied any such motivations and cited the need to ensure that a prospective spouse would meet U.S. visa requirements. I felt strongly that Authority should have no power to restrict such a personal choice. And I also had a gut-feeling distrust of local naval Authority, which was soon to be justified.

Authority thought that it had made unapproved marriages in Asmara not just illegal, but impossible. The Eritrean government would not permit a marriage without the approval of the U.S. Consulate, which would not approve without a military OK.

During my first 18 months two sailors had succeeded in navigating the red tape and marrying local girls – local *Italian* girls. In mid-February 1961 three other sailors who had marriage requests being processed were suddenly given less than 48 hours notice of their transfer to Port Lyautey in French Morocco. Two of these sailors were white, their intended brides were caffelattes. The third was black and his intended was full Eritrean. (The first two did eventually make it back to Asmara to finalize their marriages, at what extra financial and other cost to them I am pained to think.)

The day after the three left, Covert chased everyone away from one corner of the message center and sat down for a teletype exchange with, presumably, Port Lyautey. After he was done he took all tapes and hard copy with him. The belief in the barracks was that he had been roundly chewed out for his action. Be that as it may, Authority was not going to overrule an officer-in-charge, however wrong he had been. The exiles remained in Morocco.

Persons in authority are forbidden to injure their subordinates by tyrannical or capricious conduct, or by abusive language. (Article 1319, Navy Regulations)

(The above is from Navy Regs as they were at that time; I preserved it. There have been a dozen or more different versions of Navy Regs promulgated over the years. Internet search fails to yield even the current version, let alone any historical ones.)

At a personnel inspection shortly afterward, Covert told us that all Asmara Radiomen would soon need to hold clearances for classified information, that marriage to a foreigner would preclude such clearance, and that living with one would have the same effect. He also promised to court-martial the next man caught shacked up. I became more secretive and withdrawn than ever.

Yeshu gave birth to a son in early April. She surprised me again when she passed the choice of a name to me, saying that if I didn't hurry up she was going to give him an Ethiopian name. I settled on Mark – partly because it had equivalents in both Italian (Marco) and Habesha (Markos).

In April I read an article about the American Civil Liberties Union in *True* magazine. I wrote a seven-page letter to the ACLU in May, hoping that they might take some interest in the military restrictions in Asmara. My main subject was obviously the marriage regulations and the treatment of the three sailors who were transferred, but I also detailed a number of other things that might (I hoped) be seen as violations of sailors' civil liberties:
– installation of new lockers in the barracks, for which Authority retained one of the two keys.
– the 25-road-mile restriction on travel.
– we were forbidden to appear in a local court for any reason, even if requested as a witness, without obtaining permission.

– we could not take any employment or establish any business on the local economy.

– we could not exchange U.S. for local currency without signing a record of how much we obtained. (This restriction even forbade such transactions with other American military personnel! There was no justification for it because of black-marketing; the market rate differed from the official rate by only one cent. It was suspected that the records were used to identify "big spenders" who might be shacking up.)

– we could not buy, rent, or even *borrow* a car without obtaining permission.

– we could not make international telephone calls through local facilities, only by going through the military switchboard.

– we could not rent *or occupy* off-post housing without obtaining permission. (It was unthinkable that a single man could receive such permission. It was automatic for marrieds, but they were not allowed to decide for themselves if a given house or apartment was suitable – their choice had to be inspected and approved by three sets of army bureaucrats.)

– sailors could not operate motorcycles, motor scooters, or motorbikes, although soldiers could and did. (History: the former OIC became irritated by several motorcycle accidents in a short space of time and instituted the ban. Covert continued it.)

As a measure of my paranoia, I sent the letter through the Ethiopian mail and requested the ACLU to address any reply to *Yeshu* at our address. No reply ever came. I've wondered ever since whether my letter ever reached the ACLU or whether it might have been intercepted by Ethiopian authorities (and perhaps turned over to U.S. Authority).

There were rumblings that year of an increase in the quarters allowance paid to men with dependents. In May, still aggravated by brownbagger vs. single men inequities, I sent a letter to the *Navy Times* which was printed in their 3 June 1961 issue. It follows:

FPO, NEW YORK. About once a month a letter appears criticizing the disproportionate amount of pro-pay going to the critical ratings. I agree with them – but with qualifications.

Sure it's unfair to give extra pay to critical [ratings] – but it is no more nor less unfair than to give extra pay to brownbaggers. The reasons for both are economic: the Navy can't keep enough critical personnel without the extra money, and the exodus of brownbaggers if their extra pay and privileges were cut off would also be spectacular. And there is not enough money available to extend either type of benefit to everyone. As long as enough single men will serve at their present pay, and as long as enough men in non-critical [ratings] reenlist, neither situation will be rectified. Fairness has nothing to do with it; economics does.

Of the two, pro-pay at least has the merit that it is related, in theory anyhow, to an individual's value to the Navy.

Those non-critical brownbaggers who criticize pro-pay are, I suspect, seeking personal advantage rather than fairness to all. When anyone criticizes the proposed brownbaggers-only raise in quarters allowance with the same vigor that he criticizes pro pay, I can agree with him on both counts. But for those who want pro pay spread out evenly but are perfectly content to receive new benefits which will not go to single men, I can't find any sympathy. You got your racket; I got mine. And yours is still the bigger one.

NAME WITHHELD

The army held periodic "parades", at which the various companies and units lined up as if for inspection, assorted ceremonies and evolutions were held, and an Ethiopian army band marched up and down the field playing both national anthems. The army could not *order* navy participation, but they *invited* it. Failure to accept would have been unthinkable military discourtesy, and in any case acceptance was up to Covert, not up to the sailors dragooned to go stand there. At least it was in place of, and not in addition to, the monthly navy personnel inspection.

At one such parade a new army mess sergeant was called front and center, and a lengthy citation was read, for an award earned at his last post. There were snickers in the navy ranks, and post-parade comments: "That's the army for you. They even give medals to their mess cooks!" But we soon found that our cynicism was misplaced. The food at that army mess hall, formerly far below navy average, improved enormously. In the corner where navy petty officers and senior army NCOs sat, the waiters now took our orders for breakfast omelets.

We moved our receiver-site communications from Tract C to a newly-built navy compound, Tract F. It was in the country off the same road that led to our former facility. Shortly after my arrival NAVCOMMU THREE had been retitled NAVCOMMU ASMARA; it was now upgraded to NAVCOMMSTA (STAtion) ASMARA; Covert became a commanding officer instead of an officer-in-charge and was now addressed as "Captain". Our new workplace was much roomier and state-of-the-art. Much of our work was now done over "covered" (secure, classified) circuits. The building contained one supersecret room known as "SpecComm" – Special Communications. The sailors assigned there were forbidden to talk about what they did within. But from one clue and another it was not hard to deduce that its purpose was communications with the Polaris missile submarine fleet.

("My secrets are more secret than your secrets" is a common ploy of bureaucratic one-upmanship. The NSA and the CIA excel at it.)

The watchstanders, already bedeviled by "training programs" (whenever Authority remembered that it needed one), now also became subject to physical fitness activities. At first these took the form of calisthenics and running (well, trotting); later they consisted primarily of an occasional softball game (which at least was more fun than Ohm's Law). Any actual improvement in anyone's "physical fitness" was marginal at best, more likely negligible. However laudable President Kennedy's initiative was, it just didn't fit into existing habits or – especially – communications work schedules. At other commands, in later years, the requirement took the form of an annual test and then dwindled away into the forgotten.

Covert became upset by the way sailors typically scheduled annual leave. If I wanted to take a string of watches off, I would request a time from the day of the first eve watch until the last day watch. The first day of leave "didn't count", and figuring in the two 72s that preceded and followed, I would get 14 days off for the expenditure of nine of my 30 days of annual leave. Similarly, day workers would request Monday-Friday leaves and get nine days off for the expenditure of four. Covert conceived that such schedulings were "devious practices" – the very words he used in his new regulation which required day workers to start their leaves on a Saturday and end them on a Sunday, and forbade watchstanders to begin on the first day of their watch string, or to end on its last day.

I evaded most of the impact by requesting leaves to begin on the *second* eve watch, and then checked in to return from leave a couple days early. And thus 13 days off out of 14, for the expenditure of eight. Returning early was always, everywhere, legal – perhaps Covert could have prohibited it if he had thought about it, perhaps not. When I first read the new regulation I squawked to Chief Pendergrass, ". . . he calls 'devious practices' what anyone else would call common sense." The chief heard me without comment. I think he agreed.

Covert was required to rotate his junior officers and he moved his favorite, Ted Vroman, another mustang, out to Tract F while Rocky moved in to Tract A as admin officer. Shortly after this I was put back on day working, this time as operations "yeoman". I had a desk in Mr Vroman's office and my duties there were somewhat miscellaneous; I remember only telephone answering, and keeping a log book of incoming messages that required any action by us and checking them off when that action was completed. A month or two before my transfer a real Yeoman was available for the job and I went back on a watch section.

I've mentioned the navy's mania for having everyone on a watch bill or a duty list of some sort or another. The army suffered from the same affliction; in this case it was performing "head count" duties at the chow hall – viewing the chow passes of entrants and keeping a count of how many men from each activity ate. Somehow this must have been very important, but don't ask me just how. The navy was tasked for this on three or four days a month and day-working petty officers were assigned to it.

Covert's pet morale project during this time was starting a *navy* movie theater in a room at Tract F. Day workers were assigned the duty of showing the movies and I was sent for a day or two of army movie-operator school. The small-screen movies were shown free, vs. a quite small charge at the big-screen army theater. Brownbaggers could bring their families. Single men could *not* bring guests. For my morale I'd have preferred winter heat in the barracks.

I still did a fair amount of traveling and exploration. With Bill gone I usually roped in two or three other sailors, whomever I could interest, and packed them into the Anglia. One such trip was to Bizen, a mountain-top monastery about 20 miles down the Massawa road and far above it. It was a steep uphill trail-walk rather than a climb. When we reached the monastery area, one of the monks spoke with us briefly then left us to our own devices.

Looking down one precipice, I noticed a small pile of bare wooden sticks on a rock shelf far below. I looked more closely — and the "sticks" resolved themselves into a human skeleton, on its back, head toward the cliff. Given the great distance, I might have misidentified an ex-baboon, but I thought then and still think that it was human. We speculated that it was probably an executed sinner — had a monk fallen accidentally, they would surely have retrieved his body. But it has since been suggested to me that the monks might leave a body to be picked clean by wildlife, then retrieve the bones for interment. That's quite plausible, and I think the more likely, especially given the apparent posture of the skeleton.

Going back down, still on the flat mountaintop, we saw from a distance several dozen monks working industriously in a field of grain. We got closer and . . . those weren't monks. Baboons, having a feast and a frolic.

(In 1995 I went up Bizen again, on a climb organized by the embassy admin officer. There were about 20 of us, mostly U.S. special forces soldiers there for demining. The sign at the bottom of the trail had been replaced by a newer one, but the words were unchanged: "It is absolutely forbidden for women to visit Bizen." I was told, however, that a woman had done so — one of the female fighters, during the war, presumably absolved by military necessity. The admin officer had procured candles, sugar, tea, and various other goodies for the monastery, and we got a very friendly reception. [*That* was why our reception in 1961 had been so cool. I had had no idea, then, that visitors were not expected to come empty-handed.] We were given cold water and some snacks, taken on a tour of kitchen, *suwa* brewery, church, and given an "audience" with the abbot — who was 87 and had been at Bizen since age 12. I not only could not locate the skeleton I had seen so many years earlier, I could not even locate with any certainty the particular cliff from which I had spotted it.)

Another trip that I took was my second to that particular destination; I had been there before with Bill. South of Gura and the old fort, the road descends into lowland and then forks. As soon as the left-hand fork is taken, a lone mountain looms ahead, dominating the flatland. From the west, approaching it, it resembles the silhouette of an armadillo's back. But it is long and narrow, running north-south, an igneous intrusion. Seen from directly to the south it looks even more forbidding. Imagine an ordinary funnel, upside down, with an inverted ice-cream cone placed over the funnel — that's the closest I can come to a word-picture: gradual slopes at the bottom, turning to much steeper ones. The core of the mountain consists of massive vertical basalt columns, hexagonal, of about five-foot diameter. The road runs close to the base, less than half a mile.

The mountain's name is Amba T'khoyloo — the hardest-to-say Tigrinya word I ever encountered. I was never able to pronounce it satisfactorily enough to be understood without further explanation; "t'khoyloo" is the closest approximation I can make in the English alphabet. I did not think it climbable save by professionals with fancy equipment, but Bill and I decided to have a go at it just to see how far we could get. Unsurprisingly "how far" was "not very". We were wearing only everyday shoes; we soon encountered a stretch of bare rock which was just steep enough and just smooth-slippery enough to frustrate our efforts.

(An Italian website names the mountain as Amba Toqwile – as good an orthographic guess as mine and probably better. It has a great view of the narrow end of the mountain from the south: www.etiopiamagica. it/damassaua.htm.)

When I returned in 1961 it was with three other sailors, tennis shoes, and a stretch of rope. Fortunately one of the others was Jerry Butcher, short, stocky, the point guard on the navy basketball team, and a regular mountain goat. Jerry took a brief look at the smooth, steep stretch, took the rope from me, leaned forward, and strode right up it. Nothing to it. He tossed back one end of the rope and the rest of us made our rope-assisted way up with ease. The rest of the climb was, to my surprise, comparatively easy, nor did we need the rope again.

About three-quarters of the way up we came upon a vulture's nest on a slightly-detached pinnacle. It held one baby bird, featherless, resembling a plucked chicken and about the size of one, too weak and young to sit upright. It wasn't much of a "nest", mostly just the bare, flat rock whitened by guano. The mother soared off at our approach but didn't try to defend her chick; didn't dive-bomb or make strafing runs at us.

The summit was long, narrow, and wind-swept. We found, carved in the rock, names of several Italians who had made the climb in the 1930s. We had nothing with which to chisel, so each of us searched our wallets, dug out something obsolete (I used my army-issued certified-motion-picture-operator ID card), and placed our "calling cards" under a small cairn of rocks. I wonder if they are still there — perhaps with the cards of subsequent climbers added . . . ?

Yeshu told me that the mountain is reputedly inhabited by *"zarti"* (*zar* in the singular) — ghosts or spirits of some sort. We didn't see any.

I thought of a long-shot way in which I might, maybe, be able to end-run Authority's obstacles to marriage. When Tafari, the Adwa pharmacist, next visited Asmara I asked him if it perhaps might be possible to marry in Adwa, outside of Eritrea. He promised to look into it. He did, and the results were favorable. I needed to make a preliminary trip to Adwa – to bring photos, or documents, or something. For some reason Yeshu could not come along so, not wanting to go alone, I convinced "Boats" and Jack to accompany me (without disclosing the true purpose of my trip).

Boats was a former first-class Boatswain's Mate who had gone through Radioman school to convert to RM1. He was my supervisor on a watch section; Jack was an RM3 on the same section. Boats was atypical for a Boatswain's Mate, sunny, jovial, and a real nice guy, from West-by-god-Virginia. He was an alcoholic, but a quite functional one; he never drank at times when it would interfere with his duties or could land him in trouble. Jack was also an accomplished drinker; they were frequent liberty companions. Boats had a very old, decrepit car, which functioned just enough to get them around town. But it wouldn't lock and suffered routine intrusions by street boys looking for anything stealable. The two filled an empty Melotti bottle with urine, carefully bent the bottle cap back on top, and left it in the car to be stolen. It was. They had to imagine the consequences; no feedback came.

I wanted to see some countryside I had not yet explored, and drove the "long way" to Adwa. This consisted of going to Dekemhare and continuing on the main road to Addis Abeba. South of the Tigrai province border a turnoff went west to the Adi Aboon triangle. Boats and Jack had brought whiskey, imbibed in a seamanlike manner, and went to sleep. Nearing Adi Aboon we passed a well-dressed, parasol-carrying Ethiopian lady also bound west. Shortly after that we came to a stream flowing under the road into a fair-sized pool. My revivified passengers, now hot and dusty, saw it and called for a stop. They both went skinny-dipping and had a great time splashing and cavorting in the cold water. While they were so engaged I noticed the Ethiopian lady fording about fifty yards upstream. She must have seen the nudity from a distance and taken a long, semicircular, off-road detour to avoid the berserk foreigners. I expect she had a tale to tell when she reached her destination.

For many months I had been returning to the barracks at bedtime, to sleep there, as a precaution. Covert now came out with yet another regulation, stronger and more threatening than ever. I commented: "Adultery's already illegal. All they need to do now is issue a regulation outlawing masturbation, then they can hold a morning muster and anybody that doesn't have a hard-on is sure to be guilty of *something*." Again Chief Pendergrass heard me without comment. Again, I think he agreed.

(In many a bull session I have heard many a sailor confidently proclaim, "It's against navy regs to beat your meat!" I think over 90% of sailors believed this, it was repeated so often. It wasn't true. Naval Regulations were silent on the subject. Or at least they were at that time. I can't exclude the possibility that some earlier version might have contained such a prohibition.)

One evening when I left the house to return to the barracks I half-noticed lights turn on from a parked car behind me. The lights tailed me all the way to the barracks. I was sure it was army MPs; that evidence for possible prosecution was being sought. I knew a combination of streets where I was pretty sure I could shake off any tail; I looked forward to trying it next time. (After which, I would have gone straight to the barracks.) But next time never came, they didn't lie in wait for me again.

I was so angered by Covert's latest directive that I took Yeshu to the army movie theater on Kagnew Station – an act of symbolic defiance. This was *not done*. I marched in with her, grim-jawed, heard no comments, saw no disapproving looks. But I'm sure there were plenty of both outside of my event horizon.

We were married in Adwa, in early October. It had to be done in an Orthodox (Ethiopian Christian, often called Coptic) church, and I had to list my religion as Orthodox. I did so as a means to the end, having no other option. I remember incense, and a lot of mumbo-jumbo in Geez. No American knew of the marriage.

I was expecting transfer orders any time now. I was eligible for U.S. shore duty but, to get it, I would need two years of service remaining. My four-year enlistment expired in only a year. Authority treats U.S. shore duty as the supreme prize of assignments, not realizing that tastes may be different. I did not want U.S. shore duty. I wanted more overseas shore duty, but – there was a rule against transfers from *one* overseas location to *another* overseas location. So I did not execute any extension agreement. The alternative without one would surely be to a ship. But, on that ship, I could reenlist next September and *then* request overseas shore duty. I already had "Naples" on the brain; Yeshu spoke fair Italian and it would be a perfect place for her to become more westernized.

Jerry Butcher's tour expired at the same time as mine. He told me about having had a dream, in which a message arrived garbled and we couldn't tell whether it was his orders or mine – similar last names. On our next watch I counterfeited just such a garbled message, including every dream-detail he'd mentioned, and arranged for it to be sent over an in-house circuit where he would be first to see it. Sorry to say, it didn't work – didn't fool him a bit.

When my orders did come, they were for *USS Rhodes (DER-384)*, homeported in Newport, Rhode Island. A ship had been inevitable, so I was pleased. It was small and it wasn't in Norfolk.

I had taken the first-class examination in August and was promoted to RM1 in mid-November, just two weeks before leaving Asmara – and three years, two months after reenlisting.

Jerry Butcher left at the same time I did. We flew out of Asmara on Ethiopian Airlines, first-class, to Frankfurt. They brought us our meal and it was quite good, some kind of fish. Then they took the trays away and – that had been just the first course! It was followed with a fine filet mignon, champagne . . . Up until, at least, the 1974 coup, Ethiopian Airlines served the best food of any airline in my experience.

XI - TWO IF BY SEA

I arrived in Newport at the end of December and learned that the *Rhodes* was at sea and would not return for over a month. I was lodged in a transient barracks and had to muster at 0800 every workday but had no other duties. I spent a lot of lazy-time in the base library. I also visited a civilian lawyer who confirmed that my strange-appearing marriage papers were indeed valid under U.S. law, and rented a locker at a locker club in preparation for shipboard life.

The *Rhodes* returned to port, and I reported aboard, on 6 February 1962. She had been on radar picket duty in the GIUK gap (Greenland-Iceland-UK) and had lost one sailor, washed overboard in stormy winter seas.

The destroyer escorts (DEs) were products of World War II, built by the hundreds to counter German submarine warfare. For this purpose they only needed to be fast enough (about 21 knots maximum) to outpace a submarine, and only needed enough firepower (three three-inch guns) to tangle with a sub that had surfaced. As the Cold War took shape and the DEW line (Distant Early Warning) of radar stations was constructed to detect Soviet bombers or missiles, there were gaps in the line. A number of DEs were pulled from the mothball fleet and converted to DERs – destroyer escort, radar – some in the Atlantic, some in the Pacific – to extend the line. *Rhodes* had been recommissioned in her new role in 1955 (and would be deactivated again – permanently – in 1963). The old open-mount three-inch guns were replaced by two later-model three-inch guns in bulbous turrets, one forward and one aft, and extensive radar equipment was installed. The refurbished ships were 306 feet long, had crews of about 150 (including 15 officers), and displaced 1210 tons.

CR division's berthing space was near the stern, a deck below the weather deck. There were some minimal improvements in living conditions. A metal panel semi-separated each man's rack from his neighbor's, but it was only partial and provided no real privacy. Of more value, a small reading lamp was provided at each rack, and there *was* air conditioning. I had a top rack in a tier of three. Our working spaces were in the forward superstructure, one deck down from, and just aft of, the bridge.

For communications, *Rhodes* rated one chief Radioman, one first-class, and about a dozen second-class and below. She had aboard no chief, one other first-class (my orders had been written while I was still second-class) and the proper number of underlings. The first-class already aboard was senior to me, which left me somewhat of a fifth wheel. I was given easy duties as traffic checker and training petty officer, and was assigned to the cryptoboard. (For the first time I learned what the crypto machines looked like and how they worked.)

The communications officer, LT(jg) Charles F. Kohlmeyer, was none too popular in the division. I liked him; his unpopularity was perhaps a product of the division's generally low morale – for which I never understood the cause. He had a noticeable eye twitch and one of the Radiomen had composed an unkind limerick:

A man named CFK
Came to the *Rhodes* one day.
   His eyes, they did blink,
   They were never in synch,
And his mind was a blank, so they say.

The captain, LCDR John Van Tol, was a courtly, austere patrician. I had a feeling that he did not think too highly of me; that perhaps he felt that an enlisted college graduate was not quite in the right order of things, that I ought either to be an officer or a civilian. But I'm attempting to mind-read here and I may be dead wrong. I had no open friction with him, but I certainly disapproved of one instance of his approach to military justice.

It had happened before I came aboard. The captain had gigged a seaman at personnel inspection, for needing a haircut. The seaman felt – quite possibly with justification – that there was nothing wrong with his haircut. He had the ship's barber shave him completely bald.

No rule or regulation was broken, but Authority could not tolerate even a fully legal action, when done as a gesture of angry criticism. The captain restricted the seaman to the ship until his hair grew out to a length of one inch – and restricted the *barber* for the same amount of time! I don't know whether the captain went through the formality of holding a mast in order to impose these punishments. If he did, I wonder what the charges were, what article of the UCMJ was violated?

Rhodes was on short turnaround. Of the eight DERs in CORTRON 16 (esCORT squadRON), two were typically in the North Atlantic (one on station, one in Greenock, Scotland), two at Cuba-Florida (one on station, one in Key West), and the other four either back in Newport undergoing leave periods and upkeep, or in transit to/from one of the stations aforementioned. After maybe three weeks we got underway for Key West.

We sailed right into a North Atlantic storm. The ship bucked and pitched and rolled and moved every unpredictable which way. I've mentioned that I was immune to seasickness on the *Iowa*. My immunity did not carry over to a small ship. After several hours of this I was still functional, but beyond miserable. My stomach, at least, retained its equilibrium and I did not vomit nor come close, but I went to bed very early. We were in calmer seas by morning.

Key West seemed a nice place, but it was not much of a liberty town. The Key West police and also the Key West shore patrol had reputations for toughness, for intolerance of drunken-sailor antics. One of our Yeomen was picked up for strolling the street caroling, *"A Little*

Bitty Queer Let Me Down". He was known for such escapades, but he was safe – he worked in the ship's office, incoming correspondence went through his hands, and whenever a shore patrol report turned up with his name thereon, it went in the burn bag.

After a few days in port we sailed about 150 miles east to "Southern Tip", our assigned picket station, and dropped anchor there off Dog Rocks, a small uninhabited islet belonging to the Bahamas (then still a British colony). Southern Tip's function was to keep a radar eye on Castro's Cuba – his revolution was then only three years old. The water was clear and the bottom was close, we could see a variety of sea and sea-bottom life. I remember particularly the schools of barracuda – maybe 20 or 30 of them in a group. One barracuda had had a chunk bitten from one side, near its tail, in some past battle; it was quite distinctive and I saw it often.

The ship went on "tropical hours" – reveille at 0500, working hours 0700-1200. Fishing and sunbathing were the most popular activities. (Concerns about the long-term effects of sun exposure had not yet arisen or, if they had, were dismissed as fliply as smokers then dismissed warnings about tobacco. A deep suntan was thought to be beneficial, and an enviable sign of good health.)

After (?)three lazy weeks on station we were relieved and went back to Key West for a while, back out to station, again to Key West . . . Eventually we headed back to Newport.

There is a certain military type who achieves power and influence well beyond what normally inheres to one of his pay grade and position. These people are sometimes called *politicians*, sometimes *empire-builders* – the exact term employed is dependent on what aspect of their conduct is under criticism. Their commanding officer sees them as perfection embodied; they can do no wrong in his eyes. They have a following of admirers and hangers-on, some sincere, some motivated by expediency. Most, though, regard them with concealed skepticism – as dangerous to offend, but unpleasant to endure. I was to encounter three such: two E-9s and one E-6. The E-6 was Al Lagerstrom, a first-class Boatswain's

Mate on the *Rhodes*, raucous and outspoken. I believe he wielded more real authority on that ship than anyone but the captain and, maybe, the exec.

One of his jobs was mess-deck Master-at-Arms. We dozen or so first-class petty officers had head-of-the-line privileges at meals. Early on I sat, unknowingly, in "his" seat. He said nothing at first, sat down beside me, and a few bites into the meal he asked me to close the curtain on the porthole. I reached to do so. The curtain was fixed, unmovable. He laughed. It wasn't a joker's friendly, ha-ha, gotcha laugh; it was a nasty laugh – a putting-me-in-my-place laugh. I never sat in "his" seat again; indeed I never sat *close* to it.

His current empire-building project was converting an empty compartment into a berthing space for first-class petty officers. He had obtained approval for this; a lot of volunteer work needed to be done on it, by the first-classes who would live in it. Live in the same space with him? No thank you, I saw quite enough of him at meals. Besides my rack in CR division was satisfactory and, as junior first-class, I would have had last choice of racks in his completed compartment. I did not volunteer.

There was another BM1, a crusty old salt, who wasn't much more pleasant. He didn't oppose Lagerstrom but was not one of his toadies either. One day I was by my rack, getting ready to go on liberty and touching up my shoes with a squeeze-bottle of liquid shoe polish. (That stuff wouldn't give shoes an inspection shine, but it would serve to delete scuff marks for lesser purposes.) The old salt passed by, noticed what I was doing, and harumphed his contempt to anyone who might be listening: "*Modern navy!"

From having two RM1s and no chiefs, we suddenly went to two RM1s and two RMCs. One of the new chiefs was all right, but unfortunately the other – Zesut – was senior. He was a high-strung, fast-talking, aggressive sort. He rubbed me the wrong way by addressing me as "Dad". I stayed out of his way as much as possible. Fortunately neither of the chiefs spent very much time in the communications spaces. Two evaluations will tell the story.

In May, written by Mr Kohlmeyer: BUCHER is an exceptionally thorough worker with a complete understanding of all phases of communications. An extremely valuable man.

In November, written by Zesut: Performs individual duties to a high degree. Prefers to work alone. His leadership duties merit attention and improvement. Fails to voice his opinion and show authority as a first class Petty Officer.

And if I had ever worked under Zesut again, I would have done nothing to change his opinions.

After a time in Newport we sailed again, this time for the GIUK gap picket station. The timing of my ten months on the *Rhodes* was climatically perfect – to northern waters at the peak of summer; to the tropics in late winter and in fall. When we were not out on station we were in port at Greenock, about 20 miles west of Glasgow.

We had a new RM2, Beckwith. He enjoyed needling me and I needled right back. I developed an under-the-skin pimple on the tip of my nose; it turned sore and quite red. Beckwith's comment was, "What happened to your nose, Bucher? Mr Kohlmeyer stop short?"

We were copying a covered broadcast. When the signal deteriorated and we were in danger of losing synch, the gear sounded some beeps from a mini-speaker labeled "audible alarm". The gods of signal propagation frowned on Beckwith and, although a quite competent operator, it seemed that he did more than his share of leaping from his supervisor seat to go twiddle the broadcast. I relabeled the speaker: Beckwith Alarm.

Spanish came up for discussion in one radio-shack session and Beckwith used an almost universally-known bit of Spanish on me:

"*Besame el fundio." (= kiss my ass.) I fired back: "*Chingue tu madre. Chingando cabron."

Our one Hispanic RM3 had been quietly listening. His jaw now dropped and his eyes got big. "Wow . . .where'd you learn that . . . that's really bad . . . where'd you ever learn that?"

I preferred to leave it a mystery. Here I'll confess: I had read the phrases in *Treasure of the Sierra Madre* (when the bandits besiege Dobbs & Co.). I thought I knew the meaning but wasn't certain, and reference sources back then were far too prudish to permit verification. It was another 20 years before I could confirm beyond doubt that the translation was, as I had thought, "Fuck your mother. Fucking cuckold." Anyhow I won the round.

Out on station one evening an immediate encrypted message came over the broadcast for us. (Covered circuits were in their infancy and the old five-letter groups were still sometimes used even when they need not have been.) It was badly garbled, totally trashed, in the earlier one-third of the encrypted text. We serviced for a repetition right away, but I took the garbled copy into the crypto space to play with it.

Such messages carry a group count, so by counting backwards from the end I could note at exactly what point the ungarbled portion began and, therefore, exactly how many garbled groups must have preceded it. I entered a number of Xs corresponding to the garbled part then, at the proper point, I used the ungarbled groups. It worked fine. By luck the garbled part contained information not really essential and I had decrypted the meat of the message.

It sounds simple when explained, and it was simple, but it was something that the junior officers on the cryptoboard would not have thought to try. Mr Kohlmeyer was amazed by what I had done; he took the garbled copy to the bridge along with my decryption, to show the captain and other officers. From dropped comments I gathered that Mr Kohlmeyer had suggested a letter of commendation for me, but that the captain wouldn't hear of it. The captain was right.

The message simply gave the suspected position of a nearby Soviet submarine and directed us to contact and shadow her if we could. We did, and stayed on her tail for a day or two. This was common cold-war practice and Soviet anti-submarine forces did likewise when they detected one of our subs. It was good, live training for both sides. The surface ship won if she forced the sub to surface for air while still in sonar contact. The sub won if she eluded her pursuer without surfacing. I believe we forced this one to surface.

The officers sometimes played a simple word-game on the bridge to relieve the monotony. It involved the guessing of three-letter words. I heard of the game from Mr Kohlmeyer and suggested that he use *nth* – as in "to the nth degree". He did, it baffled the other players, he disclosed his tutor, and the captain chewed me out – less than half-seriously – and held that "nth" was not a word. I said, "*It's in the dictionary, captain." He was not appeased.

There were two variations to our Greenock-to-station-to-Greenock routine. We made a brief port call at Bantry Bay, at the southwest corner of Ireland (it had been an anchorage for U.S. warships in World War I). It seemed a remote place, no town of any size visible from our anchorage. I regret not going ashore – I could have added the Irish Republic to the long list of countries I've visited. But I spent very little time ashore in Greenock or Glasgow either; I was still in newlywed-fidelity mindset and I found little to do in those places.

While anchored in Bantry Bay I had an evening quarterdeck watch when two husky Irishmen came by in a small boat, climbed our ladder, and insisted on speaking to the captain. I had to send my messenger for the duty chief – who found the visitors equally insistent, but he turned them remarkably docile when he began to unholster his .45. They left.

Our other variation was a stop at the Isle of Wight, off England's south coast. I asked for, and received, leave. I wanted to revisit London. It was a disappointing visit. I went looking for the Douglas House and couldn't find it. I hadn't been the first in that predicament – the doorman at Claridges saw my puzzlement and gave me directions to the dog house's new location. I went to the Linguists' Club hoping to see familiar faces. Six years . . . Turnover . . . There was only one familiar face, he had not been a friend, and he didn't remember me.

While at the Isle of Wight we were contacted by a British Radioman on CW, who wanted to pass along the big news of the day (6 August) – the death of Marilyn Monroe.

We headed back for Newport. I had signed an enlistment extension agreement so that I could, having been on the ship six months, request overseas shore duty. It came back rather quickly, giving me my first choice, Naples. I was joyful, but apprehensive.

I had heard rumor, somewhere, of someone who had married illegally. They could not prosecute him for what he had done on a previous enlistment, so the rumor went, but they charged him with having made a false official statement – indicating "single" on his reenlistment papers! The rumor was bum dope – it was possible to court-martial a man for actions on a previous enlistment – but I didn't know that yet. I feared that questions would be asked when I requested "married" on my papers, that the full story would have to emerge. I worried that the orders to Naples might be cancelled in reprisal, and had even drafted a rough letter to my congressman protesting such cancellation.

I need not have worried. When I told the leading Yeoman that the marital status block on my papers needed to be changed from S to M, he simply said O.K., changed it, didn't ask any questions, and didn't tell anyone. It was good that I did this, because the "false official statement" charge otherwise might well have been used against me in Naples – but the full story of those events awaits the next chapter. I began to wear the wedding ring hitherto relegated to my locker.

I reenlisted for six years on 4 September. Since I had received no reenlistment bonus in 1958, I now collected a substantial one – well over $1000 {$6511}.

About this time the leading Yeoman told some of us that the squadron commander was looking for an insignia of some sort to distinguish his squadron, and that the leading candidate seemed to be two yellow lanterns on a blue background. I inquired whether it was to represent the blind leading the blind.

Wrong. It was inspired by Henry Wadsworth Longfellow's poem, *Paul Revere's Ride* – the lanterns hung in the church tower to advise of British movements: "one if by land, and two if by sea". It seemed perfectly appropriate.

When I had a 72 while in Newport, I sometimes visited college friends now in Manhattan. On one such visit they, and consequently me, were invited to a dinner on Long Island. The conversation turned to Ethiopia. Someone said, "There's only one '*the man*' in Ethiopia, and his name's Haile."

The hostess said, "Haile Selassie! Is he still alive?" I assured her that he was. She went on to relate how she remembered his name in the news when she was still a little girl.

We were off again in the fall for Key West and Southern Tip. The lazy days were enlivened a bit when we came across a boatful of Cuban refugees dead in the water. Our corpsman checked to see if anyone needed medical attention, we gave them some water and food and notified the coast guard. It was supposedly the middle and upper classes that were fleeing Castro. These refugees looked much more lower class, however, as someone pointed out to me, several days under tropical sun in an open boat do no good for anyone's appearance.

Monotony was broken again when lookouts thought they saw smoke signals coming from Dog Rocks. A whaleboat was lowered and a landing party sent to investigate. The islet was still deserted; the conclusion was that the lookouts had seen surf-spray pounding up between rocks.

On one of our stays in Key West liberty was abruptly cancelled. Throughout the town the shore patrol was rounding up sailors and ordering them back to their ships. We sailed as soon as everyone was aboard. We didn't know what was going on, but President Kennedy was to speak on the radio that evening, and we all listened with close attention. It was of course the Cuban Missile Crisis. Instead of anchoring off Dog Rocks we spent the week or two of crisis doing whatever we were told, shadowing iron-curtain merchantmen, going here, going there, and listening to all the news that we could pick up.

The crisis abated and in due time we headed back to Newport. I sold my Anglia, now seven years old, to a young gas-station attendant who had coveted it, for $50 {$326}. I said goodbye to the *Rhodes* on 7 December 1962 and headed to the familiar Brooklyn receiving station for transportation to Naples.

XII - CLASS A BROWNBAGGER

I spent only a few days in Brooklyn. Transportation was swiftly arranged on a military flight out of McGuire AFB, New Jersey, to Torrejon AFB in Spain.

I noted a distinct contrast between the navy and the air force on my journey. On arrival at Torrejon I was shown to a two-man room with commodious lockers and mattresses a foot thick – in *transient* quarters! The lowest ranks were lodged in equal opulence. The air force people explained where and when to check for onward flights, told us where the chow hall was, and where to catch a bus to downtown Madrid if we so desired. I was there only a day until I caught a flight to the naval station in Rota, Spain (on the southwest coast of that country, near Cadiz).

Rota was a bit different. As a first-class, I was put in a vacant one-man room, standard thin-mattressed navy rack. Had I been one rate lower I would have slept in an open barracks bay with *three-tier* racks and standard *shipboard* lockers. (Bear in mind that Rota was not a World War II leftover but fairly new, a result of our bases-treaty with Franco Spain in the 1950s. Authority *built* it that way.) Muster at 0730 for assignment to working parties. And the bus downtown? No one could go on liberty until he had attended the chaplain's lecture. It was given once a month.

In 1962 the navy wondered why the air force had far higher reenlistment rates. They were still wondering when I retired in 1977. They are probably still wondering today. Shipboard life was a significant factor, but it was not the only one.

Happily I only overnighted in Rota; a plane for Naples left the next day. On arrival, 16 December, I explained my circumstances (without mentioning the illegality of my marriage) and requested leave to go to Asmara and arrange transportation to Naples for my wife and son. It was readily granted.

In Asmara I took my papers to the army bureaucracy who scratched their heads and decided that they couldn't issue transportation orders, that that would have to be done by the Naples navy. The Asmara navy learned of my presence and activities and Rocky tracked me down. In the course of our talk he asserted that there was a legal way to have done what I'd done. I said, "Yes, sir, and you know what happened to the last three guys who tried to do it legally."

His reply was an embarrassed "Ye-s-s-s." I guess it was as close as he could come to acknowledging that I had a point and apologizing for what he had to do. Covert had retired and there was a new commanding officer. Asmara sent a message to Naples reporting my criminality.

Back in Naples Chief Smith (chief-in-charge of the message center) said, "Did you do what they say you did?" I said, "Yeah, I guess I did." A first-class Yeoman in the barracks was sympathetic and recommended that I see one LCDR Kenneth Bridges in the legal office, a lawyer who had some reputation for assisting the guilty. Mr Bridges advised me to hold off on applying for transportation for the time being, while he sounded out Authority's attitude.

The elongated 1955 "short" title of the command in Naples had been simplified, it was now a handier NAVSUPPACT NAPLES – Naval Support Activity. And things were almost unrecognizably changed. Only the naval hospital was still where it used to be. The navy offices, and the barracks and chow hall, had been consolidated in a group of six tall, slender buildings on what I would once have thought of as the far side of the hospital, still farther west from central Naples. Although they were only eight-story, those hillside buildings seemed so tall, in proportion to their base, that I would not have wanted to be in one during an earthquake.

The buildings overlooked a lower, flat stretch that led still farther west to Bagnoli, a suburb where AFSOUTH (Allied Forces South, a NATO command) was located. Three of the buildings faced a street that negotiated the hillside in hairpin curves; the other three were upslope behind them. The streetside buildings housed the main navy offices; the barracks were in one of the set-back buildings. First-class petty officers lived on the top floor.

The dignitaries streetside included a rear admiral (COMFAIRMED) and a captain commanding NAVSUPPACT. I never encountered either one except at personnel inspections. My horizon reached no farther than the communications officer. She was a Wave commander – the highest rank attainable by a Wave at that time. I was not impressed by her. She seemed to alternate between trying to show what a nice person she was, and trying to prove that she wasn't soft because she was a woman. Below her were about ten LT(jg)s and ensigns, four of them Waves. We had no enlisted Waves.

I was assigned as supervisor of one of the message center watch sections. It was more of what I'd done before, but far busier and more hectic. We had only incoming and outgoing teletype messages to process, no peripherals such as fleet broadcasts or ship-shore CW. I had two other people on my watch, typically an RM3 and an RMSN, supplemented at the busiest times by a peakloader who worked 14-2200 Monday-Friday. (Peakloader = someone assigned to work during the heaviest – *peak* – traffic *load*.) As at earlier duty stations, there was a relay right across a hall with three-four operators to a watch. As traffic piled up in the late afternoon and early evening the three in-baskets (immediate, priority, and routine) at the supervisor's desk filled to overflowing. I could often (not always) keep the afternoons caught up until relieved by the eve watch. And I could often (not always) come on the eve watch and clear the accumulated backlogs by the time the midwatch relieved me. The other three supervisors could rarely match this, but I worked at a frantic pace to do it.

Naples itself had not changed much. There had been one significant change from a sailor's viewpoint though: prostitution was no longer legal. The numbered houses had been shut down but there was little other practical effect. The reformers must have thought they had accomplished something noble. The night clubs continued to operate as in the past (I assume) and there were many more streetwalkers, in more locations. One of these locations was the Mostra d'Oltremare, a waterfront street that led from our offices out toward Bagnoli. The girls there would, in the cold months, cluster around small bonfires while awaiting customers; this led to their designation in sailor-talk as *The Campfire Girls*. (The Campfire Girls were an organization similar to the Girl Scouts, dating back to the early 20th century.)

A remembered sailor-to-sailor conversation:
"What happen, one of the Campfire Girls die?"
"Huh . . . I dunno . . . Why?"
"I notice you wearing your fly at half-mast."

An Italian entrepreneur had had the right idea at the right time. He had opened a bar just down the street from the navy buildings and named it The Hideaway. It got a great deal of navy patronage. One night a young sailor with emotional problems drank himself nearly to death there. He had to be medevaced. His parents were irate; I believe they caused a congressional inquiry. Authority was embarrassed. It had to . . . to . . . to *do something*.

They put The Hideaway out of bounds for a month or two – for serving the sailor when he was intoxicated!

Sometimes the best thing to do is nothing.

I consulted Mr Bridges every two-three weeks and got similar feedback from him each time. The command legal officer, a JAG-corps captain, seemed to encourage my application for dependent transportation but cagily avoided giving Mr Bridges loophole-free assurance that I would not be prosecuted. (They could not court-martial me without my marriage papers, which they would not have until I applied.) Meanwhile I had learned that there was a statute of limitations applicable – they could not charge me after two years from the date of marriage, which point was now only about seven months away. After hearing three or four variations of the same thing from legal through Mr Bridges, I told him that I was disgusted with the cat-and-mouse game they seemed to be playing with me, and that I was inclined to wait out the statute. He enthusiastically approved and said that if I was willing to wait, that was very much my best course of action.

Major changes in communications were in the offing. A Commander John J. Weigel was in Naples to oversee the changes and, shortly, to take command. NAVSUPPACT communications became an independent NAVCOMMU on 28 March. The Wave commander became, briefly, a commanding officer – a status almost never attained by a Wave in those days.

The junior officers in communications were the sorriest group of such that I ever encountered. Among them, the most obnoxious was Stanforth, a pudgy Alabaman. Like Slenker on the *Iowa*, he was another Doctor Fell. Sailors spoke of a theoretical hazard, that he might trip over his lower lip, in reference to the scowl that he often displayed. I recall a conversation when the evening watch supervisor arrived to relieve me from the day watch:
"*Who's the duty officer?"
"*Stanforth."
"*Wish I hadn't asked."

On one watch I needed access to a publication which for no good reason was locked away at night, in order to ascertain the correct charge to levy on a Class Easy (personal telegram) that was being sent. I had to awaken Stanforth (duty officer) to get the pub. He grumbled, "You're a first-class petty officer, Bucher, you should know that."

(To visualize what I "should" have known, think of the mileage chart in a road atlas – dozens of cities down the left of the chart and again across the top. The table I needed was not that extensive – perhaps 25 geographical areas down the side and 15 word-counts across the top – but still far beyond memorization.)

In the barracks one day, someone brought me over a memo. The subject was "Extra Military Instructions". It directed me and another supervisor to make burn runs on specified dates when we were off watch. The memo-bearer told me that an embarrassing non-delivery had occurred, communications was under the gun, and that we two supervisors had initialed the message in question.

I knew I was not infallible and I didn't doubt that I was guilty, especially given the frantic pace of my watches. I was deeply angered by this recurrence of *you **will** be perfect* and I headed for communications to register my dissent thereto. The mishandled message could not be immediately found. The ensign who had signed the memo said, "*See Mr Stanforth." The Wave commander had gone somewhere and Stanforth, unfortunately, was senior among the junior officers.

I told a maliciously-smiling Stanforth that I would prefer to go to mast for dereliction of duty rather than perform the burn-run penance. During our conversation he repeated a phrase at least three times: "*That's your privilege." I left the encounter expecting that the memo was superseded by events and that I would next be given a date for a captain's mast, upon which I would have requested a court-martial. It didn't happen that way.

(The result of such a hypothetical court-martial? Guilty, almost certainly, I came to realize in later years. It had been my duty to handle the message correctly; I had not done so. Period. The workload and hectic conditions which I would have stressed in defense would have been good only for "extenuation and mitigation" if that.)

In the few days before the scheduled date of my burn run, Chief Smith let me know that "they" were not going to send me to mast for dereliction of duty, but (contrary to Stanforth's "*That's your privilege.") were going to charge me with disobeying a lawful order (the burn-run memo). That put a whole new face on the matter. I told Chief Smith that in that case I would perform the burn run.

(While I blame "Stanforth" throughout the narration of this matter, it must be remembered that the Wave commander returned shortly after it began, and must have known of and approved – if not instigated – Authority's subsequent doings.)

It was about time anyhow for a periodic check with legal about the marriage issue. LCDR Bridges had rotated and had passed my case to a newly-arrived Lieutenant. I told him of my new clash with Authority. Apparently my actions had become somewhat notorious within the officer community. He spent some time trying to convince me to perform the burn run without making waves, and I reluctantly yielded. (He cited the submarine *USS Thresher (SSN-593)*, which had just been lost with her entire crew, because, he said, "*someone made a mistake.")

What the new lawyer should have done, and did not do, was to advise me of my right to pursue action under Article 138 of the UCMJ. It begins, "Any member of the armed forces who believes himself wronged by his commanding officer, and who, upon due application to that commanding officer, is refused redress, may complain to any superior commissioned officer . . ." Even if I had appreciated this possibility I would have needed guidance in formulating a request for redress, and then a complaint, and there would have been too little time remaining before the burn run date for the paperwork drill.

(In later years, when I became more UCMJ-knowledgeable, I speculated on this road not taken. Even with the burn run completed, I would have asked for no tangible redress but only that the illegality of my treatment be acknowledged and not repeated.)

Article 138 is seldom used and has been little tested in the judicial system. The lawyer was no doubt reluctant to involve himself in an action which would displease Authority, and at a higher level than I had yet reached. He also probably thought that his advice was in my best interest and, from the 40-plus-years perspective at which I write, it probably was.

An ancient expression of enlisted bull-session wisdom holds, *"They can't **make** you do nothin'. But they suuure can make you wish to hell you had of done it."* In *Catch-22* an old Italian woman gives related advice to Yossarian:

Catch-22 says they have a right to do anything we can't stop them from doing.

Chief Smith spoke to me once more before the burn run day and informed me that, as a first-class petty officer, I was to be in a supervisory capacity over the regularly-assigned seaman, did not need to do any of the dirty work myself, and so need not wear dungarees. Whomever he had ironed out this point with, those ground rules had not penetrated to the officer overseeing the burn run, one LT(jg) Cirincione. Cirincione, while not as bad as Stanforth, could fairly be called a Stanforth-striker. He expressed surprise that I was not in dungarees and yelled at me to do the dirty work along with the seaman. The dirty work (raking the ashes, etc.) was not all that dirty and I didn't soil my uniform significantly. I was so beaten down by this point that I didn't speak to Cirincione of Chief Smith's advice, nor did I even tell Chief Smith how things had gone.

I had never yet seen the message which sparked all the trouble. About a week later, looking for something else in the files, I happened across it. It had been misfiled. I was finally able to reconstruct matters. It had arrived on an earlier watch, and the non-delivery committed then. Later, on my watch, a service message arrived making a correction to the text. My watchstanders made the correction, and I initialed it at that point. It was not my responsibility to recheck the message for proper handling the first time around, but only that the correction had been made. If I had noticed the non-delivery by chance, I would certainly have corrected it, but I did not notice.

I told no one of my discovery. Partly because my crime had long since ceased to be the non-delivery itself, but had become being *uppity*. I would have gained nothing. And partly because the most guilty party of all – the operator who had done the mishandling – had not come to Authority's attention. The junior officers knew so little of the nuts and bolts of actual message processing that they were incompetent to diagnose and identify. That operator was a good guy and a good friend and, even if it had been someone whom I liked less well, I would not have wished to bring Stanforthian discipline upon a yet-undetected wrongdoer.

(Again I speculated on the result of a hypothetical court-martial, armed with this new knowledge. A toss-up, I decided. The matter of responsibility rested on unwritten practice and common sense. I'd have had to request some of the other supervisors as defense witnesses. The respective skills of prosecution and defense could have swung a verdict either way.)

And irony piled upon irony. During the week after I came across the message, I had a slow Sunday day watch. A short, unimportant, misrouted message came in. It was for the Naval Air Facility at Naples' Capodichino airport. In this case, the thing to do was to type a short "misroute pilot" at the beginning and send it on to the correct routing – RBFRF in this case. Simple. But I absent-mindedly typed my *own* routing, RBFRC. The operator across the hall in relay was running on slow-Sunday automatic as much I was, he saw nothing odd about me sending a message to myself, and sent it back to me. Having just seen that same message, I immediately recognized it as a duplicate and filed it!

Ed Torrence, the TE(RM)1 traffic checker, caught it the next day, showed it to me and had a chuckle about it. He told no one higher up. I had committed a genuine and undeniable non-delivery, but this time on a trivial, low-precedence message.

*Disgraceful . . . a professional **insult** **and** a violation of my rights, to be jugged for a stupid crime I **hadn't done** when the crimes I **have** done are so much more **fascinatin'** ~~~~ (Mouse, 7 August 1951 Pogo strip)*

On my next semiannual evaluation, written less than a month thereafter, I got the lowest numerical marks I ever received. They were even lower than those that Zesut had given me on the *Rhodes*. The narrative portion read:

BUCHER does an efficient job as a message center supervisor. A more thorough knowledge of the publications which have to do with his present duties would be of benefit to BUCHER, and improve his contribution to the message center.

I "knew the pubs" better than any Radioman in the command; indeed others in the message center had remarked favorably, and with some surprise, about my knowledge thereof. The second sentence was a flat lie. I could only conclude that Stanforth had recalled, and inflated, my nighttime need for a pub.

After this, considering me suitably squashed, Authority left me unharassed. They had, however, planted one time bomb for the future – but one which, you might say, fizzled.

When the Wave commander's time was up a change-of-command personnel inspection was held. She passed through the ranks beaming – it was *her moment*. CDR Weigel followed in her wake with an expression that bespoke partly resigned boredom, partly begrudging impatience. I heard that after the ceremony he said, "I'm in charge now, let's get to work." (CDR Weigel would turn out to be the best commanding officer for whom I ever worked.)

Until his family joined him in June, CDR Weigel sometimes joined the sailors in The Hideaway for a few evening beers. He was quoted as having said that it's ridiculous to feel that just because a man works for you, you can't drink with him.

On summertime weekends many Neapolitans drove out of the city to various recreational destinations. On Sunday evenings they all drove back – at once. The traffic jams were epic. When stuck in a traffic jam, the Neapolitan knows just what to do about it. He blows his horn. (In another context, Americans sometimes called an automobile horn "the Italian brake".) We heard ample proof of the jams in the barracks – the street by the navy buildings was a major artery for these migrations and the Sunday-evening honking lasted for hours.

I have also driven in Italy, where there is only one traffic law, which is that no driver may ever be behind any other driver. The result being that at all times, all the motorists in the nation, including those in funeral processions, are simultaneously trying to pass. (Dave Barry)

In late June a general message arrived announcing changes to the proficiency-pay program. Radiomen, except for a few technical job-skill codes, were cut off. There was much anger among Radiomen. I reacted with a letter to the editor at *Navy Times*:

Naples, Italy
23 June 1963

Dear Sir:

I have just read NAVACT 12.

During the next few weeks I am sure we can expect to hear many statements from high places, explaining to us just why the new pro-pay regulations are necessary, why they are fair, and why we have absolutely nothing to complain about.

Before we are given the complete Pentagon snow job, there is a point or two I would like to raise.

In the [ratings] which have just been dropped off the pro-pay list, there are many men who have recently reenlisted or agreed to extend, with pro-pay an important factor in their decision. In the case of extensions, pro-pay was very often the main factor. Career appraisal teams have made a big thing of the pro-pay benefits a man's [rating] offered. Now those who listened to the teams find their benefits cut off.

Those of us whose enlistments expire in the near future are fortunate. *Those who, like myself, have over five years left—well, we can only reflect that we've been conned.*

We will doubtless be told that Defense would have *liked* to continue our pro-pay but budget limitations prevented it. Such statements cost nothing—and they don't restore our lost pay. If Defense really desires to be fair to us, two steps should be taken in conjunction with the new program:

(1) Allow anyone who agreed to extend in order to become eligible for pro-pay, and who is now cut off, to cancel the extension.

(2) Allow anyone who reenlisted while receiving pro-pay, and who is now cut off, to refund the unearned portion of his reenlistment bonus and elect an immediate honorable discharge.

These options will, of course, not be offered—because the losses in the [ratings] affected would be enormous if they were. And Defense has no legal obligation to offer us a new choice based on current conditions. I would argue they have a moral obligation—but moral obligations cut no ice in the Pentagon. It seems they consider a $60-a-month pay cut in the same category with adjustments of a few cents in comrats or clothing allowances.

Before the BM's, YN's, etc. revile me for being overpaid to begin with and gloat at my comedown, let me say that I agree with them. Pro-pay was, is, and will be a bad practice—and so are all other forms of pay based on anything except rank and longevity. Sure, I took it and was happy to get it. (Show me the brown-bagger who ever refused his BAQ.) But I would have preferred to see all the non-critical [ratings] brought up to the P-2 level.

A $60-a-month cut in my standard of living is hard to take–whether or not I was ever justified in receiving it.

*Please withhold my name and duty station. Just sign me as:

A Sucker, RM1-P0*

Navy Times sometimes verged on being a bit of a house organ for Authority. They toned me down by editing out the two portions between asterisks and signed me simply as "Name Withheld", but otherwise printed my letter as written. It should surprise no one that the "two steps" I recommended were never implemented. {$60 in 1963 = $391 in 2006.}

Shortly thereafter I had occasion to visit the personnel office for some reason, and in my service record I beheld an unexpected page entry. Stanforth & Co. had withdrawn my recommendation for the next pro-pay examination, saying that I was "no longer considered qualified . . ." Another lie, done for punishment, therefore done illegally, the illegality unprovable. The financial loss, $720 {$4637} over a year, would have been far in excess of any fine imposable by non-judicial punishment or even summary court-martial. They had not informed me of their action. Had it not been for the coincidental personnel office visit, and had not the Pentagon beaten them to it anyhow, I would have showed up, unsuspecting, for the next exam.

Officers and gentlemen, my ass.

I walked into relay on a slow weekend and found the watch busily working in the backs of their refrigerator-sized tape-reception equipment, wiping away excess oil and stray chad accumulations. I asked what was up. The relay supervisor said, "*Commander Weigel don't like dirt."

Most of NAVCOMMU moved down to Bagnoli. Nothing remained "on the hill" except a few people to staff the message center there. I moved with the majority, and was given a new job as watch supervisor in the unclassified relay.

The AFSOUTH compound had a large parklike central plaza, with seven or so buildings clustered around three sides. Our new comm spaces were on a ground floor wing of one of these buildings. They consisted of several offices, a small message center, the unclas relay, circuit control, electronics workshop spaces, and "the box" – a large classified relay, shielded to prevent the escape of any electromagnetic radiation which might be the target of espionage. It could be entered by only one automatic, heavy door which swung slowly open when a footpad was trodden.

Two or three sailors worked under me on the unclas relay watch. It was a rather small space. Along one aisle were the big banks of equipment where tapes came in; along the other a number of TDs where tapes were sent; and between the two a sort of gridwork with slots where incoming tapes, after being logged, were placed to await transmission. It was less hectic than my former job on the hill, but backlogs did develop at the busiest hours. I would have been better described as "senior operator" rather than supervisor. Workers in relay were sometimes called "tape apes".

Zone inspections were held on Friday mornings. This required an extensive "field day" cleanup by the midwatch, including waxing and buffing the deck. It was hard to do this and handle tapes simultaneously, and a time or two the field days in relay were deemed unsatisfactory. Authority decreed: if the midwatch does not have time to hold a proper field day, they will stay late and complete the field day after being relieved by the day watch.

I had no intention of remaining late. I told my watch that at the end of the radio day (0100 local) we would begin the field day and would cease handling traffic until we were done. The problem with this was that "channel checks", a one-line self-addressed service message, were sent to us every hour. When we didn't return them, the other end got agitated. The circuit control supervisor, having been queried on his order wire, came over to inquire. Holding field day, I told him. As 0300 and 0400 passed with no channel checks returned, the agitation – both his and the distant end's – increased. He said, "Hey, Port Lyautey says they're going to log the circuit out!" I shrugged. They could do as they pleased. Around 0430 we completed the field day and turned to communicating. We didn't get every backlog cleared up before morning, but we came close enough that there were no repercussions.

Before I again had a Friday-morning midwatch, Authority had an attack of common sense. They rescheduled the zone inspections to *Monday* mornings. Monday-morning midwatches are the slowest time of all; field days then were easily done.

The legal office captain finally realized that I was determined to wait out the statute of limitations and that he could not decoy nor entrap me into premature action. The new lawyer assured me that I could go ahead and apply for transportation. I made some passing mention of the large retroactive quarters allowance that I would be receiving, and the lawyer said to keep that quiet and not to let the captain hear about it. I gathered that the captain was somewhat frustrated over his inability to prosecute me and would be enraged to hear of a concomitant financial windfall.

In preparation for Yeshu's arrival I house-hunted. I was disinclined toward apartments and, although there was little else available, I did find a quiet little villa a mile or two out in the country – which even had a garage. I also car-hunted. (My dream-car, financially far out of range at $5000 {$32,553} or more, would have been a Jaguar XKE.) Passing by one showroom I gazed with longing at a small, semi-sporty convertible – and found, to my surprise, that it was only $1600 {$10,417}. I was sold immediately. It was a red Triumph Herald.

The villa was not going to be quite ready in time. I rented a temporary room in an apartment building within walking distance of work. Late one evening, already in bed, I heard a knock. It was a sailor from another watch section with an exhausted Yeshu, carrying a sleeping Mark, in tow. She had managed to navigate the airline connections and, somehow, to find her way to the right base. It was 4 August.

Yeshu did not like my villa at all. She felt isolated and friendless out there. She wanted to live in the apartment building, where she had already made friends. An apartment was coming open and I yielded (not without some argument). She also disapproved of my choice of car – with the top down the wind blew her hairdo. The car, we kept.

One of the lessons I learned early about Naples driving was: never make eye contact with another driver. If you do, he knows that you see him – and he can cut you off, and will. Finding a parking place anywhere was as much a challenge as driving. I formed a theory that every *Napolitano* owned *two* cars, one of which he left constantly parked.

While still in the barracks I had bought a large Telefunken radio/record player console at the PX. Ron Columbia, a message center RM2 with a large American car, had given me invaluable help in moving it barracks to villa to apartment. His wife, Maria, was from the island of Malta, and they had three sons near Mark's age. They became good friends and we visited each other often.

Our fifth-floor apartment had a long hall ending in the kitchen, with five other rooms opening off it. It was near enough to the base that I could walk or drive as I chose; another locational advantage was that it was a very short walk from the navy movie theater. One of the earlier films we saw there was *The Victors*, with Lee Marvin as an army sergeant repeatedly belaboring his troops as "Stupid idiots!" Yeshu was delighted with the phrase and I was often on the receiving end of it. (Sometimes on the transmitting end.)

In the fall I was moved to a day-working job, traffic checker, and stayed in it until I left Naples. My work table was in the message center, which I shared with one or two seaman or RM3 watchstanders. This message center handled only the relatively small amount of traffic for NAVCOMMU itself, plus a small ration of classified traffic for the U.S. elements of the NATO command. Actual traffic checking occupied only a part of my time, the remainder spent on miscellaneous and ever-changing odd jobs. We got a new operations officer, a mustang lieutenant, E.O. Christenson. I've ever been distrustful and skeptical of superiors who introduce themselves by implying that they are the toughest, most demanding, son of a bitch for whom you will ever work. But Chris, as we all called him, was one of the exceptions to that rule and it was a pleasure to work under him. Stanforth left; gossip had it that he left early and under a cloud of some sort. If so, it was kept completely hush-hush; our chief Yeoman was the only enlisted man who knew any details, and he wasn't talking. Not only did I never hear a credible rumor, I never heard a rumor of any sort.

Right after his *Ich bin ein Berliner* speech, President Kennedy visited the AFSOUTH compound and spoke on the central plaza. I was still in unclas relay and had a busy day watch that I could not abandon for long. I did step out the front door long enough to get a distant view of JFK, but too far away even to make out facial features. We learned of the assassination when it was announced by the caller at an evening bingo game. A day or two later we watched the Italian news on Signora Fagnani's television (I'll be introducing her shortly). When Oswald was paraded on the screen, she literally spat at the television: *"Ptui! Assassino!"*

With the move from the hill to Bagnoli completed and things fairly well settled down, CDR Weigel decided it was time to hold his first personnel inspection. I offered advice to other sailors: "If this guy holds personnel inspections like he holds zone inspections, you better have your asshole wiped and no ravelings on your skivvies."

In Asmara, someone had given Yeshu an ostrich egg before departure. She had included it in the household-effects shipment, it had arrived intact, and it reposed on end, on a circular base atop a piece of furniture in our living room. As I struggled to fit a fair-sized Christmas tree through the living-room door, a branch brushed the egg and toppled it from its perch. I dropped the tree and dove for a shoestring catch. I missed.

It was beyond doubt a genuine ostrich egg. The mess was just what you would expect an egg that size to make. Luckily the floor was tile with no rugs nearby. I used a dustpan and a pail to scoop up the remains.

On New Year's Eve Neapolitans not only ring out the old, they throw out the old. At midnight all old, broken, or unwanted household items are thrown from apartment windows onto the street. I had not noticed this eight years earlier, living in the hotel-barracks, but I did now. The litter was chiefly glass, dishes, crockery, but also chairs, other defunct furniture, just about anything imaginable. The street-cleaners should have received hazardous-duty pay.

I had a dull ache in my lower back and took it to the naval hospital. After two or three visits with no improvement, they took an upper-GI x-ray. Verdict: "*You've got an ulcer. You'll have to be admitted." But that doctor passed me to another, who chose to treat me as an outpatient. He prescribed a couple medications and put me on a strict diet. I had to carry a bottle of milk to work with me and sip it every half-hour, along with a bit of bread or crackers. No fried foods. No popcorn. No beer. No hot peppers, no spices. No this, no that. I ate a dismal diet featuring boiled meat and salads.

The ache went away with the first pills, but the doctor kept me on the diet for about six months, only gradually relaxing it. There was a welcome side-effect. My weight had been edging up over the last ten years, to 170-180. The diet was so bland that I didn't eat much, and I lost some 25-30 pounds of fat, purely by accident. I was so pleased with my new architecture that I put considerable effort into maintaining it ever after.

It was interesting to read later, in my medical record, that the ulcer was attributed to my worry over the marriage issue and getting my wife to Naples. No mention of workplace stress nor work-related issues. Doctors can be politicians too.

Once I was back on a fully-normal diet, Yeshu did a thorough job of gastronomically spoiling me. Zigeny (she had brought the necessaries), Italian pasta dishes, American food. She was a superb cook.

Sometime in the mid-60s the navy decided to do away with the clumsy TE(RM) and TE(YN) designations and change all those still so-classified into plain RMs and YNs. Back in late 1956 when plans were announced to ax the Teleman rating, the navy had accompanied it with predictable propaganda: no Telemen would be hurt by the change, etc. The navy lied.

It wasn't that *individuals* lied; it was more a case of the right hand not knowing – or not remembering – what the left hand had promised. (Or knowing *but not caring*, I sometimes suspected.) Bottom line: the navy, as an institution, had lied.

On a personal level, the prime injury had been the lowering of the rate I should have been offered upon my 1958 reenlistment. Of more general concern (although it bothered me very little) was the saturation of advancement exams with electronics material. I knew many ex-Telemen (and more than a few long-time Radiomen) who, though deserving of promotion in every way, were simply unable to cope with this electronics blizzard. Navy-wide, there must have been hundreds. People who worked with typewriters and teletypes were tested on vacuum tubes. The Morse code requirement was another hindering factor, although I suspect many ex-Telemen were "passed" by sympathetic shipmates – as I quite possibly had been in Asmara.

There was a Radioman "B" school in Bainbridge, with a *year-long* curriculum, which every Radioman was supposed to be slavering to attend, as Authority saw it. It was said to be almost entirely electronics and equipment. I wanted no part of it, neither the subject matter nor the location, and never listed it as a choice on my "dream sheets". I remembered enough basic electronics from my two "A" schools that I was able to bluff and guess my way through the tests.

There were periodic rumors that Washington would "soon" split the rating in two: one for the technicians and one for the operators. Such action would have received widespread applause, from the operators at least. It never happened.

About this time the navy also decided that the shunting of post-office duties to the Yeoman rating was not working well. They created the Postal Clerk (PC) rating. I decided not to apply for it. YN promotions were scanty; I expected PC to be the same. I would probably not have been selected for it anyhow, having never worked in a navy post office. When the selectee list appeared I recognized many familiar names, ex-Telemen.

Our closest Italian friends were Giovanni and Teresa Fagnani, who had helped us rent the apartment and were one floor away. They were an interesting story. Some 20-30 years earlier, as a young man, Giovanni had proposed, had been turned down, and had gone off to Libya. He had never married, had returned a few years ago, Teresa's husband had died, he tried again and this time was accepted. We were saddened by Giovanni's death while we were there. Yeshu always addressed Teresa simply as "Signora".

Yeshu also made friends in a corner shop run by a husband, wife, and at least three sons (one of whom claimed to be a communist). The shop carried many items but was basically a tobacconists, and Yeshu always addressed the wife as "Signora Tabacchaia" – I don't remember the family's real name and may never have known it. Yeshu often spent time down there chatting and one day she told me of what she had witnessed. The shop had a pay telephone. An Italian driver of a small pickup had apparently had a fender-bender at the corner and was on the telephone to his boss to report same. The boss must have asked him where he was. In his agitation he was saying, "Qua! Qua! Qua!" (Here!) while vigorously motioning toward the floor at each word!

We met Salvatore, owner of a bar around the corner, through the Fagnanis. He took me to a soccer game once – the Naples soccer stadium (named the *Spaghetti Bowl* by Americans) was within easy walking distance from us. It was the first soccer I had ever seen, and I fear Salvatore was disappointed when I failed to show proper enthusiasm at times when the crowd roared.

One day Signora Fagnani invited Yeshu and me to lunch. At the table, I belched. Wifely glare from across the table. "Say 'scuse me'! Stupid idiot!"

I shrugged and said, " 'scuse me, stupid idiot." Yeshu thought it was so funny that she forgot to get mad. Signora Fagnani said, "Como obediente." (=How obedient.)

Yeshu went somewhere one day and left sandwich fixings for Mark and me. As we ate, Mark suddenly became agitated and went for the refrigerator indicating that he wanted milk, urgently. What had happened was that he had eaten a slice of tomato which had been *touching* one of my hot peppers!

There was a duplicate bridge club that met in a room of the American school up on the hill on Monday nights. Ed Torrence was a bridge player and he and I were partners until he transferred. The other 20-30 players were nearly all officers and their wives. For some reason the school could no longer accommodate us, and we switched to playing at the officers' club at Bagnoli, which was otherwise closed on Monday night but was willing to let us use one room. I heard later that there had been indignant opposition by some officers who didn't want enlisted men in their club *even when it was closed*! By faithful attendance and the law of averages, not by skill, I eventually accumulated one whole master point.

When Ed left I found another partner. I once had a game going in our apartment, teaching the game to a couple learners. Yeshu was gone; Mark was playing with toys on the floor and rattling three-year-old babble. Someone bid three hearts. Mark echoed, "*Three hearts, hell." We accused the bidder of overconfidence.

I worked under three different traffic officers, lieutenant(jg)s or lieutenants, while I was traffic checker, got along great with all three and had no problems. The first was Helen Mohorich. She survived a rigorous selection process and was chosen to work for Admiral Hyman Rickover, the navy's untouchable nuclear-propulsion genius, when she left Naples. The later two were Laurin Wilhelm and Don Geffner, both of them amiable and gentlemanly.

It became my habit in late morning, when I'd finished checking the traffic and today's papers had arrived, to walk across the plaza and buy the *Stars and Stripes* and, often, the *International Herald Tribune*, published in Paris. Miss Mohorich knew my routine and asked me if I would pick up the *Stars and Stripes* for her during my paper runs. Sure; no problem. Some others had a problem with it. Two or three people asked me about the arrangement, with disapproval; they seemed to feel that she was using me as – a servant or something. Hell, I'd have done the same for a seaman who asked me.

Another paper that I read regularly was *The Overseas Weekly*, a tabloid published in Frankfurt by ex-GIs. The military hated it; the army hating it most of all. It was often denigrated as a scandal sheet, and as *The Oversexed Weekly* – not only from its coverage of sex crimes and scandals in the American military community in Europe, but also because of the scantily-clad pinups on its front page. Insofar as it could, it printed all the news that the army would rather *not* have seen printed. I had read it on my first Naples tour, and in London, but it was not sold in the Asmara PX during my first tour there. In 1961 *OW* had gained a measure of notoriety in the U.S. press by exposing a major general's ultra-right-wing, John Birch Society troop indoctrination program, resulting in his relief and transfer. (That general, Edwin A. Walker, went on to more press coverage when in Dallas he became the first target of a then-unsuccessful Lee Harvey Oswald.) In 1963 Curtis Daniell, ex-enlisted GI and son of a *New York Times* reporter, became editor of *OW*. He was liberal and anti-authoritarian, and under him the paper became even more of an irritant to the army.

OW once, for April Fools' Day, published a parody of the *Stars and Stripes*, front and back pages only. It looked quite realistic and was titled the *Starts and Stops*. I took it to work and wrapped it around Miss Mohorich's real *Stars and Stripes* when I left it on her desk. It didn't fool her for long.

I wrote occasional letters to *OW*, mostly in 1969-71. Here's one I wrote in 1964, which they headed **Is Barry for the Troops?**:

Reasons for opposing the third senator from Mississippi are many and excellent. Yet, I intend to vote for him—with extreme distaste.

The reason, which unfortunately overrides all other considerations, is: A vote for Goldwater is a vote against McNamara.

We have seen four years of:
– Inadequate, delayed and phony pay raises. (Money taken out of my back pocket and put in my front pocket.)
– Curtailed promotions.
– Erosion of fringe benefits.
– Economizing which all too often has been at the serviceman's expense in the long run.
– Lengthening work hours while civilian unions push for 35-hour weeks and the President himself recommends limitations on overtime to help ease unemployment.

Finally, we have been made the main scapegoat for gold flow problems and have been practically the only segment of the population seriously affected by gold flow measures. In all fairness this started under Ike, but it has been enthusiastically continued by the present Administration.

Clearly this is not a time for the serviceman to consider whom he should vote for but rather whom he should vote against.

A final thought for those who read the polls and conclude that Goldwater doesn't stand a chance. Neither did Cassius Clay.

Angry Sailor
Naples, Italy

Cassius Clay, not yet Muhammad Ali, had just upset Sonny Liston. I wouldn't *really* have voted for Barry, and didn't. But I think historians who examine Robert McNamara's years as defense secretary fail to appreciate the deep resentments he aroused among servicemen, especially the enlisted. When his name was mentioned in bull sessions it was almost always preceded by one or more angry adjectives; the only non-obscene one I remember was *Edsel-pushin'*. When a sailor passed an advancement exam but was not promoted because of quota limitations, a long-standing term for this had been *PNA'd* – Passed, Not Advanced. The new term became McNamara-ed (because McNamara's budget cutting had left less money for promotions). McNamara was also cursed for having put a stop to military travel by first-class on civilian flights. From today's perspective I have to agree that this was justified, but at that time it seemed he was telling us we were second-class citizens.

In 1966, when *OW* was trying to launch a Pacific edition and being refused space on the PX newsstands there, *Newsweek* ran an article about it. Three issues later they printed a letter from a sergeant which contained much truth. In part:

For a typical story, take this: pea-brained company commander, fresh out of ROTC, decrees that bachelor enlisted personnel will divest themselves of all pictures and any personal belongings that cannot be neatly stored inside a shoebox. A cry of protest goes to OW. OW reporter gallops to rescue. Confronts commander's superior with imbecilic order. Order is rescinded. Commander is transferred. The Army momentarily looks more sane than it is. The Army owes OW a debt of gratitude. The Army hates OW because the Army was wrong.

Real sexy, huh? Well, that is what keeps the GI plunking down his 20 cents for The Oversexed Weekly. It is on *our* side for that 20 cents. No other publication in the English language is.

Three Asmara refugees turned up in Naples: one of the three whom Covert had shanghaied to Port Lyautey, with his caffelatte bride; another who had successfully married a local Italian while in Asmara; and "Boats". I welcomed each one to Naples with a blown fart from behind, and we had them all over for zigeny at one time or another. In (?)November someone bet Boats that he could not quit drinking until the new year. He accepted the bet, won it, and spent New Year's Eve in the club with a bottle in front of him waiting for the stroke of midnight. Later in the new year, when the movie *Cat Ballou* reached Naples, Boats often drew comparisons to Kid Shelleen, the drunken gunfighter played by Lee Marvin.

The navy had leased a small stretch of beach to the north of the city and we sometimes went there with the Columbias. The leased-portion sand was kept clean but if you wandered to either side there were many tarry globs from washed-up oil spills.

The St. Louis Cardinals got into the World Series for the first time since 1946. Naples had no local armed forces radio, but I was able to pick up some short-wave broadcasts, although fading in and out and with static. That 1956 bottle of champagne had survived the years and was still awaiting an appropriate occasion. This was it. At the end of the pennant-clinching game I joined the clubhouse celebration, long-distance.

The fabled Moscow Circus came to Naples and we were able to get tickets. Mark stood stock-still throughout the acts and cried at the end because he didn't want it to be over. (He had done this once before, when he saw his first full-length cartoon-movie, *The Sword in the Stone*.)

Navy programs for enlisted men to advance to warrant officer or limited-duty officer seemed to change constantly, Authority unable to keep its mind made up over long periods. It seemed to me that Authority felt that enlisted men should stay enlisted men, that they would rather not have any of these "mustang" programs at all, but that they needed to provide an avenue of some sort to which to point in countering any caste-system criticism. If memory serves, all such programs had been suspended for a year or three while Authority thought things over. The new program introduced in 1964 had no direct-to-LDO provisions; one could only apply for warrant and, perhaps later, be selected for LDO from the warrant ranks. I applied.

(That LDO abbreviation is sometimes said to stand for Loud, Dumb, and Obnoxious.)

The Washington selection board required me to take another upper-GI x-ray because of that ulcer. It was done and sent in; no ulcer showed. I was not on the selectee list when it appeared.

Would I have been selected if not for the recent ulcer? Probably not, but I will never know for sure. When the ulcer was diagnosed, I realized that it had been active at least twice before, the first time in high school! And it was to reappear in future years, more times than I kept track. I never again took it to naval, or other governmental, doctors. As with the VD in Asmara, I feared to have it on my record. Instead

I kept it in check whenever it recurred, with the medicines the Naples doctor had prescribed. I was able to obtain them, or their close cousins, *without a prescription* in many third-world locales.

As far as governmental Authority has ever known, there was just that one ulcer in 1964 that has never reappeared. Had I been open about it and sought on-the-record naval treatment, I believe that the State Department's medicrats would never have greenlighted me for my second career there. Having free medical from one's employer is a fine benefit – *except* that if there is ever a conflict between your best interests and the employer's perceived best interests, you know whose will prevail.

The Defense Communications Agency was created around this time, to "unify" military communications. What it accomplished was mostly to add additional chains of responsibility, additional layers of bureaucracy, additional reporting requirements, and additional complexity. I noticed no effect at all on the traffic-handling level. Ken Kingsnorth, our Master Chief Radioman, told me of an incident related to this consolidation. DCA had decreed a circuit between an army activity and a navy activity, which was up for testing and was satisfactory. From on high, word came down to "secure the circuit". The army put crypto equipment on their end. The navy turned off theirs.

Ken also once stated a dogma: "If, at the expenditure of X millions of dollars, and the utilization of the finest brains available, a communications breakthrough is achieved, increasing the capacity of the circuitry by many orders of magnitude, the inconsequential traffic will immediately expand to fill the gap." I liked this so much that when I quoted it in the future, I credited it as *Kingsnorth's Law*.

I had to park my car on the street near the apartment; there was no garage available. I came down one morning to find – no car! Stolen. But I got it back only two or three days later. The thieves had cut the cloth top to get in and apparently wanted only a joyride. They had parked it nearby in the soccer stadium parking lot, with the windshield wipers lifted to protrude outward and upward – I was sure this was intended to mimic the two-fingered sign for the cuckold!

I had taken the examination for chief in August. When the results came back, I had passed – but not with a high enough score to be promoted. I had been McNamara-ed. It was the first time I had taken an advancement exam and had not been promoted as a result. It was also the first time in a long time that *all* Radiomen (or Telemen, earlier) had not been promoted if they passed the exam. (Qualification: the foregoing sentence is memory and impression; determined research might disprove it in part.)

In December our chief Yeoman came into the message center with a congratulatory hand outstretched and said, "Bucher, ol' buddy, let me be the first." The navy had found a little extra money in its budget, and had promoted a few more chiefs. I was one of the few.

The supplementary promotions were to be effective 16 January 1965, two months late. I thought to keep the news from Yeshu and surprise her in a chief's uniform. It didn't work, one of the other wives let the crow out of the bag.

Promotion to chief came with an initiation ceremony involving copious alcohol, a kangaroo court evaluating numerous charges against the accused, and fines levied by the judge against the guilty and everyone in the courtroom at one time or another; the fines approximately equaling what one would have paid for his drinks. The initiate customarily leaves drunk. I would normally have been taken to this function by Chief Kingsnorth and his accomplice, RMC Skip Rinehart. (Another chief was supposed to have substituted, but neglected his duty.) CDR Weigel would normally have attended an initiation. But all three were gone, on an inspection trip somewhere. Knowing where I was supposed to be, I put on my uniform and went to the CPO club. To another chief at the bar I confessed that I was not one of the guests but one of the victims; he informed the senior chiefs of my status.

No *charges*. I presented a problem. I tried, unsuccessfully, to argue that there were no charges because I had done nothing wrong. Similar goofups must have happened before, because they knew what to do. I was declared a "model chief", seated in a chair at a side of the court. I was given a baby bottle filled with very alcoholic liquid and instructed that whenever a chief passed in front of me, I was to stand, salute, and drink from the bottle. Many chiefs found occasion to pass in front of me, repeatedly.

Three or four others, none known to me, were also being initiated. One of them had tried to thwart the proceedings by getting drunk *before* they started. They took care of him by not allowing him *any* drinks throughout the initiation. There was one Wave chief present; the drunk evoked laughs by addressing her as "Miss Chief".

My baby bottle did not diminish very rapidly, through no fault of my own. This was noticed, I was reproved, and I explained that I could coax very little through that small baby nipple. Some slashes were cut therein to remedy, but the initiation was nearly over by then and, atypically for one initiated, I walked away relatively sober. It was well that I did, because Yeshu had planned a promotion party in our apartment that evening. I survived it also and awoke the next day hangover-free.

The travelers returned late on Sunday and came to work a bit late, about 0900 on Monday morning. When CDR Weigel arrived, instead of going to his office, the first thing he did, without removing overcoat or scarf, was to detour directly into the message center for a congratulatory handshake. Little gestures like that can sometimes mean a lot. This was one that did.

HIMS Ethiopia made a port visit to Naples. I packed Yeshu and Mark in the car and went to the pier to visit. The officer of the deck was somewhat surprised by our appearance and didn't know quite what to do at first, but he turned us over to the petty officers. One of them was Bahata Enghida, a cousin of Yeshu (how distant, I don't know). We had some of them over for a meal, and in future years we would see much more of them in Asmara. The ship's officers gave a fancy reception, but I as a chief could not attend even in full dress uniform. They would have let us sneak in if I posed as a civilian but civilian dress for the affair required a tuxedo and I didn't own one at the time.

Driving Yeshu and some visitor sightseeing in Naples one weekend, I began to sense that an unexpected bout of diarrhea was developing and would soon require treatment. As we neared the apartment, the need became progressively more urgent. We reached home, I parked, abandoned the car for Yeshu to close, and ran. No time to wait for the slow elevator. I took steps two or more at a time – I reached the apartment – I reached the bathroom – I did *not* reach the commode. The bathroom was long and narrow. I left a trail from door to commode (for which I had not a gram left). I cleaned up the mess and told Yeshu to throw out the trousers, but she didn't, she cleaned them.

In the realm of revenge, Montezuma is an amateur compared to Mussolini.

The few Eritreans and Ethiopians then in Italy tended to find each other eventually and remain in at least loose contact. One of the main contact points was Mesfin Haileselassie, who heard about Yeshu and located us. He said that because of his name Italians often inquired whether he was related to the emperor; he encouraged such belief and never denied it. One of his activities was providing bodies when Italian TV or movies needed dark-skinned extras. Yeshu made several such appearances, and was auditioned for a major role as Cleopatra in a TV special. She did not get it; they told her that they did not think her Italian was quite good enough.

Perhaps that was the reason, perhaps they just wanted to let her down kindly. Yeshu had more innate genius for languages than anyone I've ever met. In Asmara she was fluent in both Tigrinya and Amharinya and already knew a good bit of Italian which she built upon in Naples. If you met her today, and did not know her background, it would be half an hour or more into the conversation before a slightly-unusual phrasing or pronunciation led you to wonder if she might be other than native-born American. She tells me that she has learned Spanish just by *listening* to the conversations on Washington DC public transportation, and I can believe it.

Berhe Beyene was another Eritrean whom we saw often in Naples. He was studying law at Naples University. He later became a judge in Asmara, and in the 1970s he was shot. I've never been clear whether he was assassinated by the rebels because of being a government official, or executed by the government for covert assistance to the rebels.

CDR Weigel and several others went to Asmara to perform an admin inspection there; I was disappointed not to be one of the inspection party. When they returned, they told me of what they had seen on a navy bulletin board. Ethiopia had decided to bring Eritrea in line with the rest of the empire by moving traffic to the right-hand side of the road. The notice they had seen gave date and details of the changeover. It seemed quite legitimate and official – until you reached the bottom. The last line read, "In order to give everyone plenty of time to become accustomed to the new traffic flow, for the first 30 days it will be optional."

One of our RM1s made chief, and I was designated his "defense counsel". I asked him if he knew why I had been chosen. He didn't know. "Junior man gets the shit details," I explained. When he faced his court the initial charge was having first ignored a chief's simple question, and then responded with an obscene two-finger gesture. No further details were mentioned in the charge, and the chief concerned was not present. I defended: "Defendant pleads not guilty. The simple question was, 'How much is one and one?' The defendant answered. He didn't answer the first time because he was thinking; no disrespect was intended."

The court found him not guilty on that charge (a rarity) and fined *me* for being such a good sea lawyer.

Our major circuit, the one over which we received and sent most of our traffic, was relocated from Port Lyautey to an air force primary relay at Torrejon AFB. To all its connected stations, that relay sent a 30- or 40-page document every month with many columns of statistical information of very little use to anyone. I had new occasion to envy the air force, for having enough people to measure, compile, and type up such trivia while naval communications seemed chronically understaffed. On their front cover they placed a boast: Number of Station-Accepted Non-Deliveries 1964: 0. 1965: 0.

A tracer action occurred in which they initially placed blame on us. I researched it and rebutted them with reference to appropriate logs and publications. They then had to accept responsibility. We waited to see whether their next monthly cover would show 1965: 1. It did, and you could see in the mimeographing where the former zero had been erased.

"The book" specifically requires that tracers be sent at the lowest precedence, routine. (The damage has already been done; no need for speed in determining cause and guilt.) There was an army general at a base in Turkey who ignored this. (A desk-pounder, no doubt. Quite possibly a screamer.) Tracers from there typically came at immediate precedence with a sentence in the text, GENERAL OFFICER INTEREST. We got one of these and determined that we had forwarded the lost message properly. I conferred with CDR Weigel about the precedence. He asked what the book said; I told him. He said, "We don't work for him. Send it routine." My already-high respect for CDR Weigel went up another notch. I did as directed, with an added remark PRECEDENCE ASSIGNED IAW (publication and paragraph reference). The Turkey station then bypassed us and pleaded with the *next* station down the line to use immediate precedence!

My service messages, tracer or otherwise, sometimes got lengthy and arcane when a matter was complex. This happened often enough that the message center watchstanders gave them a name: *Buchergrams*.

A requirement was laid on all communications activities by Washington, to conduct a complex sampling and survey of messages over each circuit during specified times. Extra logs had to be kept by the relay operators during these times: circuit, precedence, length, destination, time of receipt, time of delivery, etc. One of the operators asked me the purpose of all this. I explained, "They run all the data through a big computer in Washington and they learn that things get busier as the day goes along, busiest in late afternoon and evening, and that traffic gets heaviest on Friday, slows down on Saturday, and dries to a trickle on Sunday." In other words, they would learn what had long been obvious to all working-level communicators.

I described this survey to Mr Geffner as *Caine Mutiny* in reverse: designed by idiots to be done by geniuses. All the data had to be transferred to teletype tape, various functions done just so, and wound up into a large reel which was mailed to Washington. I must have been one of the few who did everything just right for them; we got a letter praising our input.

Vietnam was becoming of increasing interest and concern. The navy put out a call for volunteers to staff the naval activities there. I was nearing the end of my tour and decided that if they needed Radiomen in Vietnam I could handle it as well as most and better than some. I volunteered, but did not get it. Instead my next assignment was to an aircraft carrier, not at all to my liking.

That carrier, *USS Franklin D Roosevelt (CVA-42)*, was currently in the Med and made a port visit to Naples; I seized the opportunity to visit the ship, her people, and her communications spaces.

The navy was facing an overall personnel crunch due to Vietnam, and rumors were in the wind of involuntary three-month enlistment extensions for short-timers. One sailor particularly concerned about this was RM3 Dan Basinski, an operator in classified relay. He was tall, athletic, popular, and outspoken; he often answered to the nickname of "Bruno (the bear)". An extension would disrupt his plans to return to college.

A picture appeared in the *International Herald Tribune*; and surely elsewhere – I have seen it reproduced in at least one history book on the period. It showed Lyndon Johnson, behind his desk, seemingly deep in thought. To his left, at a corner of the desk, was Robert McNamara, who appeared to be speaking and explaining something. I cut out the picture and added a balloon which had McNamara saying, "Let's extend Basinski." I tacked it to the bulletin board in the box. When I next went back there, Bruno roared at me, "Gee, thanks, Chief . . ." The extensions did in fact materialize, and other comedians then added OKs from LBJ.

We got a new exec, who decided that everyone not living in the barracks should have a telephone, and issued an instruction so decreeing. I thought, then and still, that if Authority – or any employer – is going to *require* me to have a telephone, that employer should be willing to bear the cost of it. The Italian phone service was somewhat more expensive than in the U.S., and there was a stiff installation charge. But there was a loophole from which a few benefitted: if you had less than ## days remaining in Naples, you were exempt. Thus I escaped.

I hoped to return to an Asmara assignment soon. Yeshu and Mark returned there in early December, and our household effects were shipped thence. I sold the Triumph Herald to a new arrival.

From the worst group of junior officers of my experience, Naples had evolved to the *best* such group. From being in jeopardy of a bust to RM2, I had advanced to RMC. My years as RM1, the first two at least, were my worst in the navy – and gave me a lasting respect for first-class petty officers, others of whom sometimes did a chief's job but without the pay and privileges.

Pat Ryon was now a Master Chief Postal Clerk, in charge of the navy mail facility at the Capodichino airport. I had Christmas dinner at their house, and caught a plane to the U.S.

XIII - BIRD FARM

In January 1966 I reported aboard *USS Franklin D Roosevelt (CVA-42)* at her home port, Mayport, Florida, about 20 miles east of Jacksonville. Mayport is on the seacoast at the mouth of the St. John's River; Jacksonville is inland on that same river. There was not much in Mayport besides the Naval Station – a handful of bars, locker clubs, and the usual run of sailor-targeting businesses and minor-beach-resort enterprises.

The *Franklin D Roosevelt* was the second aircraft carrier of the *Midway (CVA-41)* class, put in commission just two months after World War II ended. Originally *Coral Sea*, she was renamed between launching and commissioning to honor the late president. The third ship of the class then became *USS Coral Sea (CVA-43)*. Three more sister ships were planned but never begun, it having become obvious that the naval war in the Pacific was largely won.

At 47,000 tons *FDR* was about the same weight as the *Iowa*, and only a little longer, but she appeared far larger – much of a battleship's tonnage is concentrated in her heavy armor plating, while a carrier's cavernous hangar deck is empty air. Even the 27,000-ton *Essex*-class carriers had loomed large when docked across a pier from *Iowa*. The *Midways* were seen as supercarriers when first commissioned, and they were the first U.S. warships that were too wide to transit the Panama Canal, but they were dwarfed in their turn in the 1950s when still-larger carriers began to enter service. *FDR*'s aircraft capacity was 137 when built, but those were World War II planes. By 1966 the planes

287

(Phantoms and Skyhawks) were larger and fewer – about 80 at a guess. She had been built with 18 five-inch guns, staggered on both sides just below flight-deck level, but only two remained. The carriers now depended on their escorting ships for any needed protection. During various alterations she had also been given an enclosed "hurricane" bow and an angled flight deck, standard improvements which were made on all active carriers in the 1950s. The *flat top* descriptor so often applied to carriers in World War II times had largely fallen into disuse, among sailors at least. By 1966 the term of choice was *bird farm*.

The *FDR* was undergoing a period of crew leave and upkeep following her return from her Med cruise. She was due to leave for Vietnam in late spring. No planes were on board. When a carrier returns to port, her planes fly off to a nearby Naval Air Station (NAS Jacksonville in our case) and the air wing personnel debark and spend their in-port time at the NAS.

I was one of three RMCs. We also had one RMCS. The communications officer, LCDR R.L. "Niffy" Smallidge, his assistant Everett Crews (a mustang LT), and the half-dozen junior officers all turned out to be great guys for whom to work. The comm spaces were a deck or two up in the "island" superstructure. We were about to undergo a major communications overhaul – a civilian contracting firm ripped everything out and completely redid the space; we had to do our sending and receiving through the help of nearby ships and the naval station for several weeks while this was in progress. I was put in my typical job, traffic chief.

There were well over a hundred chiefs on the ship, and more than one berthing space. I was lucky and got in the most convenient one – right down a ladder from it was the chiefs' lounge and the chiefs' galley. It had one drawback, though – it was right under the flight deck, about amidships, and near where landing aircraft smacked down. Several thousand pounds of airplane makes one hell of a clang, and right over my head. The catapults, although more distant, made quite enough noise of their own when a plane was shot off. But – like people who live by a railroad – I found that I rapidly got used to it and could sleep right through flight ops, night or day. My rack was in the middle of a tier of three. The chiefs' racks were enclosed by canvas partitions and curtains, and for the first time shipboard I had a reasonable degree of privacy.

That galley – it was fabulous. The chow was the best that I ever ate anywhere in the military, by a large margin. On coming aboard, a chief bought a share in the mess at the current value – $20-something {$124} I think it was – and when transferred he received the then-current value which might be more or less than he had paid in. With these funds, and the funds allotted to the chiefs' mess by the navy, the chiefs who ran that mess did a superb job. I never knew just who they were, never did praise or thank them – I do it here, and I hope one or more of them may happen across these lines. One of the foods I remember was frog legs, a novelty to me.

In the lounge Jim Back, another RMC, taught me the game of acey-deucey, a souped-up variant of backgammon, and I became fairly proficient at it. It is widely played in the navy and the lounge had at least half a dozen boards, along with foot-high wooden towers. One dropped the dice in the top, they rebounded over three felt-covered baffles, and rolled out into a bottom tray, obviating any suspicions of shifty dice-rolling technique.

Chiefs were, like officers, allowed to wear civilian clothing when going on/off the ship. This came as a complete surprise to me – I had read no hint of such liberalization in *Navy Times*. I suspected it was technically illegal, but I certainly was not going to question it.

My last U.S. driver license was long expired and, although I foresaw no need to drive around Jacksonville and remained carless, I thought I had better get a new one. I prevailed on Jim Back to drive me to the road test. And – after surviving Naples traffic for over two years accident-free – I failed it! I suspected that the trooper had an unwritten pass/fail quota and felt that he needed a fail. He didn't offer any reasons and I didn't ask any questions, just turned my back and walked away disgusted. We went back a month later and I passed.

289

One of the CR-division sailors mentioned one day that he wore contact lenses. Mr Wilhelm in Naples had also made such mention. I wondered whether the technology might have improved from what it had been at the time of my unsuccessful London attempt. I asked some questions, the sailor gave me the name of his doctor, I went there and got a pair. They were far thinner (but hard – soft lenses were still in the future) and I wore them successfully for about seven years. (Although removing them at bedtime gave me a sense of relief akin to taking off a pair of stiff shoes at the end of the day.)

We located and talked with Radiomen on other ships who had been on a Vietnam cruise, to absorb whatever useful wisdom they could bestow. One of the things they reported was the very large amount of top-secret messages in the communications traffic. This was worrisome. In the peacetime Atlantic Fleet a ship might receive one or two top secrets in the course of a year. "By the book" each one required extensive extra work: special handling, a cover sheet, signatures obtained from everyone who read one or received a copy, etc. Mr Crews and I talked this over. I advocated ignoring the "book" for the duration of the cruise, treating the top secrets the same as other classified messages – there would be no admin inspections in the combat zone; we could revert to normal handling once we headed back home. He was dubious, but agreed. I was happy that he did; the reports we had heard were not exaggerated.

Admirals, and carrier captains, have a penchant for marshaling white-uniformed sailors on flight decks, spelling out some slogan or sentiment, or making some recognizable iconic pattern, for aerial publicity photographs. (None were taken during my time on the *FDR*, we had more important things to worry about en route to and in the combat zone.) When you see one of these propaganda shots, pause to reflect that all those sailors were *ordered* to be there. Many of them may agree with whatever idea is being expressed, some may well not; almost none would be there if volunteers had been sought. The high-rankers instigate such photos partly to please their own superiors and partly as a display of power – because they *can*. The planning and organization of such evolutions must be good make-work for junior officers.

Our first voyage was a short trip to Boston, the reason forgotten (might have been for Patriots' Day or Memorial Day). Berhe Beyene was there, taking some post-graduate law courses at Harvard. We had stayed in touch by mail and I reconnected with him for a few beers. I remember signs on dormitory doors: Don't Blame Me – I Voted for Goldwater.

We sailed from Mayport on 21 June and made our first stop at Rosey Roads – more formally, Roosevelt Roads – a Naval Station on the east coast of Puerto Rico, where the pilots got in their combat training by bombing and strafing Vieques Island. With no admiral's staff on board, the flag bridge was vacant and convenient to communications; it was a fine place from which to watch flight operations. If you've ever seen the display in the National Air and Space Museum on the Mall in Washington – that's a near-perfect replication of flight ops, and it's just what I saw live so often. On 1 July we sailed south.

I suffered the attentions of King Neptune and his court on the day we crossed the equator. I don't remember the sequence, but these included being ducked in a yard-deep pool of water (liberally laced with garbage), having my face pressed into the fat, greased, sweaty stomach of the chuckling "royal baby", and crawling through a long gauntlet of paddlers equipped with flat, canvas hose lengths. The flight deck's grainy coating wore the knees out of my khaki trousers. The only other damage which was more than fleeting came from the furrows plowed in my scalp by the "royal barber". The rest of the polliwog crew were similarly treated, and nearly all of us chose to have a ship's barber amputate the rest of our hair to match. Consequently we arrived in Rio de Janeiro with hair about a quarter-inch, looking like the first week of boot camp if not worse.

Rio ties with Naples; the two most scenic seaports I have seen. The famed Sugar Loaf mountain was just one of the many prominences in and around the city. For reasons unknown, but which I suspect were diplomatic, chiefs were *not* allowed to wear civvies ashore, the only port in which this happened. I spent my first few hours ashore ambling around downtown, eating and window-shopping, then crossed paths with a couple of young Airmen, one of whom said, "Wow, chief, they got the most beautiful whores you ever saw!"

"Where!?!" I said. Where, for me, was a hill with two whorehouses near the summit. The Airman did not exaggerate. One had to pay an entrance fee to a guard outside the door; prices inside were standard and cheap. I recall with admiration a statuesque mulatta, quiet and dignified, still in memory as one of the most desirable women I ever encountered. I was intrigued by the Portuguese-English slang for sex (which I also remembered vaguely from Lisbon): *fuckyfuck*. On my second night there a couple of middle-aged Brazilians entered, were unhappy to find all the sailors crowding the place, commented audibly and angrily thereupon, and left. We couldn't decipher their Portuguese, of course, but it must have been pretty bad because the girls seemed quite shocked and scandalized.

From Rio we sailed eastward toward the Indian Ocean. As we passed the Cape of Good Hope, two things happened. We hit heavy weather and, during possibly ill-advised flight operations, we lost two planes and their pilots. And we lost communications for most of four days. We were trying to terminate with Asmara but could not get through to them. We developed a large backlog of high-precedence outgoing messages, of which the most urgent were four relating to the deaths of the pilots. On the third day we terminated successfully just long enough to get *one* message out. On the fourth day, the same thing happened. Only on the fifth day did we get a lasting termination.

During the outage I recommended, and we tried, sending "in the clear" – without any encryption of the classified messages, by CW. This is a rare procedure but it is authorized when the need for speed outweighs the need for security, and the chief reason that the messages were classified was so that no word would leak to the next-of-kin before the navy *officially* notified them. We even tried sending "in the blind" – hoping that someone is receiving you, but without knowing. Nothing worked. We were in a communications black hole. After we finally cleared the death messages, I expected that there would be tracers coming to investigate the "excessive delay". These would normally start from the receiving end. I prepared a tracer detailing our difficulties, cleared it with Mr Smallidge and Mr Crews, and sent it to the stations at the distant end. This was unorthodox but it served its purpose; we received no incoming tracers.

The weather improved and the rest of the Indian Ocean transit was serene. Near communications there was a door to a small platform on the outboard side of the "island"; I and others often paused there for a while. It was an excellent place just to unwind and view the Caribbean-blue ocean. At night I took in the view of the Southern Cross and the other unfamiliar southern stars.

We got a surprise one day when general quarters was sounded during the noon meal and everyone rushed to battle stations. This was unusual and we wondered what could be happening. We soon learned that, while moving nuclear weapons from one place to another, one of them had fallen off its cart in the crew's mess decks. It didn't explode. (Obviously!) The GQ was precautionary and soon relaxed.

We arrived at the Naval Base at Subic Bay in the Philippines on 1 August and spent a week replenishing and preparing for the combat zone. Subic is on the west coast of Luzon, at the base of the Bataan peninsula to the south. I did not go ashore on the first night. I had heard the wrong things from the wrong people – that Olongapo (the city outside the base gate) was a dirty and generally undesirable place. I intended to postpone my erogenous foraging until we hit Japan. On the second night the Chief Personnelman and the Chief Postal Clerk invited me to go and have a few beers with them. As soon as I got a look at the beauty of the Filipina women, my game plan evaporated. I spent the next night, and every Subic liberty night thereafter, on the beach enjoying the femininity. The town, or the part of it that was not out of bounds to us, consisted of one long street that eventually petered out in the countryside. It boasted a multitude of bars, and sailors sometimes defined Olongapo (accurately) as "four miles of pussy". The standard time was one hour in a nearby hotel room, the standard price (quoted and paid in U.S. dollars) was $7 {$43}. We did not have overnight liberty. The Filipina method of getting someone's attention was a sibilant *psssst-psssst-psssst*. Sailors had named this sound the Philippine Love Call.

We left for a five-week stint on Yankee Station. The various carriers supporting the land war had two stations. Yankee Station was off the north coast of South Vietnam; from it air strikes were launched on North Vietnam, Laos, and the northern part of South Vietnam. Dixie Station, to the south, was typically handled by smaller *Essex*-class carriers. Communications was on a three-section watch; we three RMCs were each put in charge of a watch section and I was on rotating watches for the first time in three years. There seemed to be a feeling that we chiefs might take exception to this. I had no objections nor do I think the others did. It made sense.

Not only were there many top-secret messages, there were also many flashes – the highest precedence. A flash was seldom seen in peacetime and got everyone's full attention; great care was taken to handle it as fast as possible. In WestPac familiarity bred indifference and a flash became just another high-precedence message.

We copied a multi-channel broadcast; eight channels. I don't remember them all. At least two were primary and secondary fleet broadcast and they ran near-constantly. At least one was for repetitions of transmissions on those first two. I think one was weather which we patched to the Aerographers, and another was super-secret (we couldn't have read it ourselves), patched to the Communications Technicians.

I opined that the way to win the war would be to share with the communists all of our crypto equipment and materials. My theory was that they would need so much manpower to analyze all of those messages that they would have no one left to do any fighting. As it turned out, the communists would gain just about exactly that capability in a couple of years, when John Walker began his spying activities. They won the war anyhow.

Warning: this paragraph is wild speculation from an unqualified speculator. With the ability to read our most-secret secrets throughout the 70s, Moscow would have been able to read our national mind. They might have figured out that we were *not* preparing to attack them after all, that we were as wary of them as they were of us, that we were merely trying to make sure that a Soviet attack could not succeed. This might have influenced the next generation of Soviet leaders, notably Mikhail Gorbachev, and contributed to his policies of *perestroika* and *glasnost*, and ultimately to the end of the cold war. It could be possible that the nefarious Walker, by coincidence and totally unintended consequence, played a significant part in that ending.

I developed a cold with an annoying cough and an *unusually*-raw sore throat, and did something I hadn't done in a long time: I took it to sick bay. I was hoping only to get some sort of cough syrup for it. I needn't have bothered. I got there at 0745 and by 1130 my name still had not been called; I had been standing up for nearly four hours. I gave it up and let the throat cough itself out naturally. My medical record still bears a notation "patient left waiting line". My opinion of shipboard sick bays as worthless except for major illness or trauma was reconfirmed.

When relieved from Yankee Station we did not go to Subic but proceeded directly to the port to which I was looking forward most of all: Yokosuka, Japan. (The pronunciation is more like Yo-**koos**-ka.) The books I'd read, the sea stories I'd heard, the movies, *Sayonara* and others, all prepared me to expect sexual nirvana. I could not have been more wrong. It somewhat resembled going to Oslo after Edinburgh.

The Japanese probably did not invent the "clip joint", but they had refined it to its highest level of efficiency and rapaciousness. "Ladies' drinks" – non-alcoholic – were sold at extortionate prices. This is done, or at least attempted, in other lands – but elsewhere I always countered "Buy me a drink?" with "OK, *beer*." Not in Yokosuka; if you didn't buy her ladies' drinks she sat elsewhere. In an astonishingly short time a grinning, exasperatingly-polite waiter appeared with another drink for her and if you didn't buy it you were both a cheapskate, and abandoned. A man could go through a lot of money in a short time, and I did. The routine could not be countered by getting up and going to a less-piratical bar; every bar was identical. They might as well have all been under the same management. (And perhaps they were. The Yakuza, or Japanese Mafia? But I speculate.) Japan might have been – almost surely was – good liberty in the 1940-50s. I got there too late.

The girls, many of them, were equally unscrupulous, and expert at sizing up a customer and draining him clean. Japan was now prosperous and the girls were choosy; they took you home only if they damn well felt like it, and I struck out repeatedly. They were more likely to favor the sailors on Yokosuka shore duty, for prospective repeat visits and perhaps long-term arrangements. Being in civvies, I tried once to pose as a shore-duty sailor just-arrived. It didn't work at all; the girls were far too sharp to be fooled. One of their tactics was to agree to take a customer home and, when he was sufficiently impoverished, promise to meet him outside – then disappear and leave him standing. It was done to me, once. I didn't try to do anything about it, just walked away – I was sure the system had all contingencies covered. Sailor consensus was that, if given a liberty-port choice of two weeks in Yokosuka or one day in Olongapo, Olongapo won easily. No contest.

At least the beer was good.

Yokosuka was at the mouth of Tokyo Bay, snug up against the better-known and larger Yokohama and only a short train ride from Tokyo. I went to Tokyo once, mostly to say I had been there, but didn't do any sightseeing other than walk the downtown streets. A tailor had a concession to do business on the ship at cheap (relative to the U.S.) prices, and I bought a suit or two and a tuxedo (in case I might ever be invited to a formal affair again). Interesting souvenirs were sold on shore, things that could not have been found in the U.S. Novelty coffee cups with obscene slogans and/or cartoons were one such: Snoopy in congress with Lucy in (how else?) doggy fashion; an obviously-pregnant Lucy reproaching, "Good grief, Charlie Brown!" It was probably illegal on copyright-infringement grounds to take these back to the U.S., but many did.

And I did. The cup that won me was Snoopy, on his back atop his doghouse, saying – or rather thinking – *Fuck It!* It became *my* coffee cup for over 30 years, in offices or at home. (Until it was shattered on a concrete garage floor as we loaded the car to go camping. My wife was so remorseful and distraught that I had to conceal my own grief.)

One morning shortly after we left Yokosuka one of my sailors asked, "*Hey, chief, what're you gonna do if the chaplain sees your coffee cup?"

Cup halfway to mouth, I paused, considered briefly, said, "*Fuck the chaplain," and took my interrupted sip. I don't know which got wider, the sailor's eyes or his grin.

We were not scheduled to visit Yokosuka again. Several sailors reported that the bargirls insisted that we *were* coming again, and persisted in their belief despite repeated sailor denials.

The second day back on Yankee Station a strange vibration was felt. We looked at each other, puzzled, much as people do when a light earthquake tremor occurs. We soon learned that the ship had dropped a screw (propeller). We had to go into drydock to get it fixed, and Subic did not have a drydock big enough for us. We limped back to Yokosuka on three screws and spent another week there.

It had to be coincidence, misinformation circulating throughout the bar district that beat the odds and came true. But those disposed to believe in the supernatural credited the girls with arcane powers of foreknowledge.

My depleted finances were replenished by a lucky hit on the base slot machines, then further augmented when I won hundred-dollar {$618} pools on both the first and third games of the world series. I provoked groans of envious dismay by wondering aloud just how and why I'd gone wrong on that second game.

On my next-to-last liberty night I finally met a girl who consented to take me home with her *and did*. She steered me to a Japanese restaurant where we ate various seafoods while seated on floor cushions around a foot-high table, and she introduced me to hot *sake*, the famous Japanese rice wine. Unfortunately my *last* liberty night was payday. She didn't think the boss would let her leave early on payday night, and he wouldn't. I checked by her bar anyhow, but got only a regretful smile.

A week after we got back on Yankee Station *USS Oriskany (CVA-34)*, which was also on station, suffered a severe hangar deck fire which killed 44 men. We were nearby and could see the stricken, smoking ship. My surprise was not as great as it might have been. On the *Iowa* we had had only two or three real, small fires – a fire alarm on *Iowa* almost surely signaled a drill. I remember none at all on the *Rhodes*. On *FDR*, even pierside in Mayport, fires were frequent, almost routine, although they must have been small and quickly extinguished. The aviation fuel and ordnance on carriers are fire hazards not found on other ship types. *FDR* herself did have one serious fire while at sea, and eight men died. They were working on supplies at the bottom of a shaft deep in the hull. When the fire began they were able to retreat to an adjacent storeroom and were not burned at all – but suffocated when the blaze sucked all the oxygen out of their hideaway. A worse fire was to hit *USS Forrestal (CVA-59)* on Yankee Station in 1967 (134 dead).

Once in a while an offhand, trivial remark or gesture becomes disproportionately meaningful and makes one feel really pleased. CDR Weigel's congratulatory detour when I made chief had been one such. On *FDR* an unusually complex problem arose with one message on a midwatch – I recall no specifics – and when Mr Crews arrived in the morning I showed it to him while explaining what I had done about it. As he read and absorbed the details he said, almost as much to himself as to me, "*I'm glad you had the watch."

Rather than do a lot of rescheduling of a lot of ships, the navy held us to our original schedule, as if we had never missed two-weeks-plus on station, and consequently our post-Yokosuka time was shortened. After only three weeks we headed back for Subic, where we tied up for a week.

Walking between bars in Olongapo I felt a light touch on my lower arm and suddenly I was standing there looking at my watch, which was clutched in my hand instead of on my wrist, and had a broken band. I don't know if the watch was saved by involuntary reflex or the thief's incompetence. He was still visible, slowing up at the bottom of the hill on the side street down which he had run. I have to credit him with good target evaluation; if I had contained one fewer beer I might have given chase. It would have been an unwise move; there were several idlers at the bottom of the hill and if not outrun I would no doubt have been roughed up. I have worn an inflexible strap ever since.

On my last liberty night I met Cely. She was in a bar with a girlfriend. She insisted on a couple dollars more than the usual fee. I normally wouldn't accede to that but, she said take it or leave it, it was getting late, I didn't feel like starting over to chat up another girl in another bar, and acquiesced. She was pretty, but so were a lot of others, and sexy, but so were a lot of others. Somehow there was chemistry there, slow-acting but persistent – working its will on me more than on her, apparently. After the hotel she wanted me to come again on the following night. But I had duty. I said I would, if I could get a standby to take my duty. I didn't try very hard – in truth I didn't try at all. After a week of Olongapo the sexual urgency had diminished. And we would be back. I had every intention of making her my first priority, next time.

Back on station she was much in my thoughts, accompanied by a mental refrain that ran, "Damn, she was nice. *Damn*, she was nice." Next time in Subic I went straight to that same bar. She wasn't there yet. I asked when Cely would be in. No one knew a Cely. Only when she hadn't appeared by 2000 did I seek alternate companionship in other bars. For the rest of that week I continued to frequent the bar where I'd met her, asked around in various bars, found other Celys – the wrong ones. She had told me she was engaged to a first-class on the *Coral Sea*. Her presence the night I met her must have been an irregular, extracurricular fling. I never saw her again. I never met a woman who made such a lasting impression on me *in so short a time*. I still regret not getting that duty standby.

Everything important in life, including love and politics, depends on timing. (Marianne Moore, 25 May 2007 column)

I had submitted a request for my next duty with Asmara first choice, Vietnam second. I got my orders, for transfer to Naval Support Activity Danang in February 1967. The *FDR* made occasional COD flights (Carrier Onboard Delivery) from Yankee Station into Danang. Mr Smallidge was a pilot, although not a combat pilot, and he occasionally piloted the COD propeller flights. I talked to him about hitchhiking along on one in order to reconnoiter my next duty station and he arranged it. I got to do something I'd never expected to do: be *on* a carrier plane at takeoff and landing. The passenger seats faced rearward; the catapult takeoff was quite an acceleration, and the onboard landing, abruptly halted by arrester wires, was quite a jolt.

I visited the comm offices, spoke with my future bosses, and was taken on an EM club liberty by some of the sailors. Their "barracks" was in Danang city, in what had once been a civilian house. Some of them had girlfriends living in the house with them. They carried .45 sidearms. Due to rapid turnover because of the one-year tour of duty in Vietnam, many of the people I met would no longer be there when I arrived. I was introduced to an RM2, one L.D.R. Jones. They explained his initials to me: I forget what the L. was for; the D.R. were for Delano Roosevelt. I said, "*So what do they call you?"
"*Jonesy."
"*I shoulda known. I shoulda known."
I didn't think I drank any more than the others, but the evening ended with them on the front steps of their house in a songfest – *It's a Sin to Tell a Lie* lodges in memory – while I collapsed on the rack they provided for me, too incapacitated to join in.

Our schedule was set for the remainder of the Vietnam cruise, but we did not yet know what our homeward-bound itinerary would be. There was speculation of a final liberty call in Australia or New Zealand, followed by a transit across the southern Pacific and around Cape Horn, thus completing a round-the-world cruise. But when Washington made up its mind, the port chosen was Cape Town, South Africa. I immediately saw the possibilities and set to work: instead of riding the ship back to Mayport I could leave her in Cape Town and fly to Asmara for a month's leave before flying to the U.S. Authority put no obstacles in my way, and it worked out.

But first we had a week in Subic, five days in Hong Kong (our farewell liberty port call in the far east), and another two days in Subic. I remember little of Hong Kong save that, while not as good as Olongapo, it was far superior to Yokosuka. No complaints.

We had no less than four captains during my time on board. None were particularly disliked and morale seemed to me to be much higher than on either of my previous ships. The best-liked was George C. Talley, Jr, who took command in August while we were on Yankee Station. Unfortunately he suffered a heart attack only a few months later; he recovered from it (and reached the rank of vice admiral) but had to be replaced. We had a "temporary" captain for a time until a permanent replacement arrived.

South Africa was still very much in the grip of apartheid, and this had become a political issue, a "cause" in the U.S. Word of a U.S. carrier about to make nice to the pariah country surfaced in the press, and caused a mini-uproar and soul-searching in Washington. It was apparently too late (militarily – or diplomatically?) to cancel the port visit entirely and divert us, although rumor was rife for a few days. The upshot, just before our arrival, was: port visit as scheduled, but no liberty for the crew.

Unsurprisingly, there was much discontent and profanity on *FDR*. My own feelings were mixed – I thought South Africa should never have been chosen for a port visit, but that, since it had, "no liberty" was a rotten thing to do to the crew. The bitching sailors claimed that black sailors were just as angered as they were; whether or not this was true I cannot testify. I was one of the few sailors to get off the ship, on a trip to the U.S. consulate in connection with tickets and travel documents. On returning, I praised the excellence of the whiskey in the consulate's bar and reaped glares and curses from the shipbound.

For my time on *FDR* I received my highest-ranking medal, the Navy Achievement Medal. It was really for nothing more than having done my job right while in a combat zone. And the method of parceling out the medals diminished whatever pride I might have taken in it. Quotas were set by department and division for a certain number of higher awards, a greater number of Navy Achievement Medals, a still greater number of lesser awards. I have to share whatever credit I deserve for it with the sailors who worked for me, especially those who were on my watch section while on Yankee Station.

The *Franklin D Roosevelt* was decommissioned in October 1977. She was not mothballed and was sold for scrap only a few months later, with what almost seemed like indecent haste. Although it happened during the Carter administration, I suspected that conservatives in the higher navy levels might have hurried to get rid of her before any group or city got any ideas about turning her into a museum ship – one bearing the name of a *Democratic* icon.

XIV - TARZAN SCHOOL

At South African airport newsstands I picked up a couple paperbacks by a South African political cartoonist. Much of the content was racist, anti-Black cartoons, lampooning in the crudest way not only their own domestic Blacks but also the black regimes which by now had come to power in much of Africa. My itinerary required airport stops at Johannesburg, Nairobi (overnight), and Addis Abeba (also overnight). On arriving in Asmara, I had a problem: where was Yeshu? To solve it, I had to go to the Navy Bar and consult Asmellesh, who was able to pin it down.

She and Mark were in a ground-floor apartment in a four-apartment building not far from Tract A. The army had told her that, even though still an Ethiopian citizen, as a U.S. dependent she had to navigate their housing office. I was disturbed at that, but what was done was done and anyhow the apartment was quite satisfactory and the rent was fair. In spite of her criticism of my convertible in Naples, she had acquired one – very old, very large, American-made.

Bahata was on leave. I rented a jeep (at surprisingly high cost) and together we made some explorations I'd long wanted to make. Traveling east on the Adi Aboon-Adigrat road we passed a couple of Caucasians walking, and stopped to give them a lift. They were Brits, walking and hitchhiking through distant lands. Conversation proceeded and it was mentioned that Bahata was in the Ethiopian navy. One of the Brits said, "I once met an Ethiopian navy man in [? - forgotten seaport], I wonder, do you know him? His name was Bahata Enghida."

I said to Bahata, "Yes, I know him, do you know him?" Bahata disclosed his identity to mutual astonishment. I've never encountered a more striking example of *it's a small world.*

We visited a ruined temple at Yeha, even older than Aksum but with high walls still standing, and also Debra Damo – a monastery/fortress on top of a flat-topped mountain. It could not be climbed – at the closest point of approach the monks shinnied up 30 feet or so by rope and visitors were hauled up by rope. Just how the *first* human reached the top is unrecorded. The place was one of the rare few to survive Muslim depredations in the middle ages, and consequently the church is one of the oldest in Ethiopia. We saw many marmot-like little animals running around the top and sides; they were hyraxes, also called rock rabbits. Their scientific claim to fame is that they are, biologically, the closest living relative of the elephant.

After several days on the road I was more in need of a shower than usual. The water came from a raised 55-gallon drum, perforated at the bottom, with some gadgetry which allowed the water to be turned on or off by pulling on a cord. It was outdoors, surrounded by a partial strip of metal which obscured only one's chest and waist. The water was cold. The air was cold. But I felt much improved.

The preliminary for naval personnel going to Vietnam was a three-week SERE school – Survival, Evasion, Resistance, and Escape. From what I had read and heard about the school I named it "Tarzan School". It was located on the Naval Amphibious Base in Little Creek, Virginia, right next door to Norfolk.

The first two weeks were classroom time, garnished by light early-morning calisthenics. We were drilled on the disassembly, assembly, and cleaning of .45s and rifles, and I think we spent half a day at a rifle range. Other classes included Vietnamese culture and customs, the Code of Conduct (how to behave in captivity, adopted after the Korean war), survival in the jungle, and the like. We were issued the dull-green combat uniforms and the combat boots that we would wear in Vietnam. Most (all?) of the instructors had completed a tour in Vietnam. One, who wore a Purple Heart, told of how he had earned it: he had been standing, drunk, bracing himself against the concrete wall at a barracks urinal, when a Viet Cong bomb exploded on the other side of the wall.

I would learn later that sailors had condensed navy guidance about respecting the customs/culture of our allies into one simple, short sentence: *Don't fuck wit' da monk.*

For the final week we were trucked to an army post in Virginia and dumped off in the woods to "survive". We were allowed to bring only one pack of cigarets, two packs of gum or Life Savers, and two candy bars. If any excess was detected during a preliminary inspection-search, *all* your tobacco or snacks would be forfeit. I successfully hid more pipe tobacco than I would need inside my clean socks, and one of the others had smuggled a few bouillon cubes. We were provided with various necessities such as sleeping bags, ponchos, canteens, a compass.

We were in seven groups of nine or ten, far enough apart that no group saw the others. I was in charge of my group (senior man). It was April and the woods were cold at night and none too balmy during the day. Given the temperatures in Vietnam, I don't know why they had not located the school in Florida or Panama, some tropical spot, but they had been running classes here all through the winter. Our first priority was to construct a lean-to for shelter. Many such groups had preceded us; we had no need to fell trees or fashion logs, only had to put back together the disassembled logs left by our predecessors and scrounge for a little firewood.

We had no luck trying to catch any small animals. The snareable game, if any, had surely fallen victim to previous classes. Soup from the contraband bouillon cubes was tasty but insubstantial. One day we supplemented it with wild onions that someone found – and shortly thereafter we were all vomiting enthusiastically. The "onions" were the bulbs of some wildflower. The next time our instructor came to check on us he said, "Oh, yeah – I forgot to warn you about those." He gave us a small portion of raw meat, to be smoked into jerky. The food picture was pretty scanty.

One evolution was concealment – digging trenches long enough in which to lie down, placing short sticks over them, then sod and/or leaves over the sticks. Again, there were many readily-found previous trenches. I think I escaped detection in mine. Memory may lie.

On the next-to-last day, the pace picked up. We were given compass courses to follow and, at night, we followed ours so accurately that we came right up behind two instructors who were seated under a tree waiting for us to appear. At daybreak we got an hour's pause during which I let everyone else sleep, then we were directed to follow another course, this time evading "enemy" soldiers. No one was expected to evade capture – but one group, led by a commander, somehow did. And everyone, the successful evaders too, spent that last day in a "POW camp".

During the night trek in the woods a branch had snapped back in my face, knocking one of my contact lenses off center. This was not uncommon; I often misjudged when putting one in and had to manipulate it around until it was where it was supposed to be. But I couldn't manipulate this one; it seemed lodged deep somewhere between eyelid and eyeball. I reported this to the corpsmen who were present. They looked and looked, with a penlight, at every corner of the eye. No lens. The branch had flicked it right out, and without doing any damage to the eye! I don't know what the odds are against that. The doctor had talked me into buying insurance against loss, so I soon got it replaced.

We were harassed in the "POW camp" by "guards", who made themselves as obnoxious as possible. We were put to work placing pebbles to make pathways; the guards would walk by and deliberately kick up our work. The most senior "prisoners" were gradually culled out, forcing others, and I in my turn, to become senior and interact with the head guard – the "sergeant major". Since they could not *really* beat us, ten pushups were declared the simulated equivalent of a beating and frequently awarded. When the various and inventive unpleasantness finally ceased, we were each given a C-ration. We were all famished and I ate everything but the cardboard and metal containers and the toothpick – and I thought about the toothpick.

I never had to eat the much-maligned C-rations day after endless day; if I had, I might have developed the dislike in which they are almost universally held. The few times that I did eat them I thought they were quite toothsome.

What the training lacked was a post-wilderness wrapup, to learn what we had done wrong, or right, while in simulated captivity. There was no such feedback.

The week of involuntary diet had knocked my weight down to 135, its lowest ever, and I was delighted to see that my last sidewall and potbelly fat was extinct. The joy didn't last long; I soon went back to the 140-145 range I inhabit most of the time. My next evening meal was steak at the CPO club. "Boats" (ex-Asmara, ex-Naples) and Ron Columbia (ex-Naples) had both retired and were both working as civil service at the big Norfolk communications station; I invited them to be my guests.

Next it was Norton AFB in California, airport stops in Honolulu and Okinawa, and a night landing at Danang AFB. I was surprised (but probably should not have been) when the first thing we heard on the ground was an order to fall in to *march* to the terminal. It was May 1967.

XV - ALL THAT HEAT AND SAND

There had been change in Danang in the few months since my visit. No Radiomen were now living in Danang city, nor carrying sidearms. Camp Tien Sha had been built, across the river from downtown Danang, and all communicators were now living in the many barracks there. The camp was said to house over 4,000 sailors.

I became Chief in Charge of the Message Center, in the White Elephant building in Danang city. Several other chiefs had held the job over the preceding few months; some couldn't handle it; some could but didn't want its hassles. I stayed in the job for my entire tour and, after a few months to get a handle on things, I found it easy and right in my line. We had a relay site across the river, a receiver site high on "Monkey Mountain", a transmitter site at "Marble Mountain", and communications detachments at four outlying bases: Cua Viet, Dong Ha, Tan My, Chu Lai.

There were about 80 sailors working under me in the message center. A dozen or so were day workers, the rest were on two port-and-starboard watch sections. It was said that this was the busiest message center in the navy at the time, with the most traffic handled, over a thousand messages a day. Authority had decreed that the standard working day was 12 hours, with one day off in ten. But the chow hall hours, and the hours that such things as personnel offices, etc., did business, were geared to a more normal 0800-1700 workday. The standard seemed to be chiefly a device to forestall complaints about long hours from those who did have to work them.

My message-center watchstanders *did* have to work 12-hour watches. About every two weeks each watch worked an 18-hour shift in order to get some rotation from days to nights and vice-versa. I myself, and my day workers, worked only an 08-1700 workday for the most part. Initially I rarely bothered to take my 1-in-10 day off, partly because I wanted to be in the office and keep up with things, partly because there was little to do on a day off anyhow. There was no liberty. That is, there was no *legal* liberty.

To amplify that last sentence I am going to jump ahead to something I wrote six or eight months after arrival (why I wrote it and what I did with it will be told later):

Liberty in Da Nang – and all of I Corps – was cancelled in March 1966. At that time, the pretext was Buddhist demonstrations against the Ky government. Liberty has never been restored. The official explanation now seems to be that it would wreck the local economy.

I am unable to understand how the liberty granted in Saigon and many other towns in the south far smaller than Da Nang is not equally damaging. One currency is in use throughout the country; U.S. spending, if it causes inflation, will surely cause it regardless of where the money is spent.

An American (one of those who resides in Da Nang illegally) told me what he heard from a Vietnamese: The Vietnamese of Da Nang also resent the no-liberty policy. They feel that spending in the south drives up prices everywhere but less spending in the north gives them less money to meet the higher prices. This could be a widespread sentiment or an isolated opinion. I pass it on as I heard it.

There is, of course, speculation among the troops here that economic factors are not the true reasons behind the policy. Guesses range from a fear of VC terrorist activities and a fear of U.S.-Vietnamese incidents to a desire to hold down VD rates and a blue-nosed attitude on the part of officials who could restore liberty. I have also heard that Gen. Walt once stated that if his troops in the field couldn't have liberty the troops in Da Nang couldn't have it either, but this is pure hearsay. The real reason could be any or a combination of the above. Or it could be that economics is the key. If so, I remain unconvinced.

If economic factors are the key, they are not explained adequately to the troops. At a briefing on arrival in-country we are told only that the state of the economy will not permit liberty. That and nothing more. We are not given any details – such as what economic factors would have to improve to permit liberty, whether any progress is being made in this area, whether the policy is ever reviewed or not – or anything of the kind.

Another thing we don't know is just where the policy comes from, and who could change it. Most people think it comes from the commanding general of the III Marine Amphibious Force – now Lt Gen Cushman, formerly Lt Gen Walt. This is the command that wrote the instruction forbidding liberty in I Corps. But there is some speculation that he may not be the villain – or at least not the major villain. Other possibilities are the mayor of Da Nang, Gen Westmoreland himself and U.S. civilian officials in Saigon. No one knows.

Off-limits and curfew violations here invariably run far ahead of other offenses punished at NJP [Non-Judicial Punishment, i.e. mast]. The regulations are widely resented and widely violated. Only two kinds of people never pull illegal liberty here – those who, like myself, are afraid to take even a small chance of getting caught and those who for various reasons would not go on liberty even if it was legal.

Rumors periodically make the rounds that liberty is about to be resumed. Whenever one of these rumors is in circulation, off-limits cases drop for awhile, only to soar again as soon as the predicted date passes with the same old restrictions still in force.

Offenders who are caught are usually punished by heavy fines – and occasionally by a reduction in grade. Heavy as they are, the fines deter few. The average attitude is: I want sex, it is available, my chances of getting caught are small, the regulations against it are unrealistic and unreasonable. I will take the chance. _____ them.

I can make only a wild guess at what the chances of getting caught actually are – well under five percent. An informed estimate could be made only if one had access to the total number of VD cases treated – plus reliable figures on the VD rate among Da Nang prostitutes and semipros and the likelihood of catching VD on a single exposure. The resulting figure would still have to be adjusted downward to consider the number of men who use prophylactics successfully and the men who get away with shacking up.

Despite the combat zone and despite those 12-hour watches my men were working, the communications officer, Commander Ben Coski, had a thing for personnel inspections. Once a month, in the White Elephant courtyard, the off-duty watch was assembled and put through the rigamarole. He was relieved by Commander Lew Denny about halfway through my tour. I hoped to see the personnel inspections forgotten then – and they were.

I had little direct interaction with either commander. My immediate boss was the assistant comm officer, LT Charles Lawrence, initially. He was a dead-ringer look-alike for King-of-Siam Yul Brynner, shaved head and all, perhaps a little huskier. For the most part it was easy to get along with him, but he had one quirk. Many a day, in mid-morning or mid-afternoon or both, someone would come to summon me to his office. In time this became so regular that I began to make sarcastic reference to *the morning crisis* and *the afternoon crisis*. Always he had some complaint to make or some fault to find. Some were legitimate, some were not, some were trivial. I corrected things in the first category; vowed to correct (but ignored) those that fell in the other two.

The White Elephant was a whitewashed, two-story edifice of French colonial construction, on the Danang city (west) side of the Song Han River. It had arcades of various offices on both stories, overlooking a central brick courtyard. Communications spaces were in one corner of the upper level. Right next to us were the admiral's offices – the senior naval officer in I Corps, Paul L. Lacy Jr. initially, relieved by James B. Osborn in February 1968, both rear admirals. Vietnam was divided into four corps areas, I, II, III, and IV, from north to south. The I in I Corps was never spoken as "first" or "one" but always as "eye" corps.

Next to the White Elephant, on the river bank, was a floating barge that served as a ferry landing. The passenger ferry ran every half hour. It was our connection to Camp Tien Sha. About 100 yards from the far-side landing was a main road; navy buses ran but it was nearly always quicker to hitchhike. Many navy vehicles came along and most of them would stop for you. I was exasperated by one pickup that not only never stopped but also bore a hostile sign "No riders – take the bus." It belonged to the public works department – and it was they who ran the buses. It must have seemed to them that hitchhikers reflected upon the bus service and made them look bad.

The CPO barracks were two-story, with double rooms on the upper level, single rooms on the lower. E-8s and E-9s got most of the single rooms. My double room might as well have been a single room; the other occupant was shacking up and I rarely saw him. I had a desk-table with lamp, and an electric fan which kept me cool and comfortable during the worst of the heat. There was a patio between barracks with a beer bar and a ping-pong table, at which I spent a lot of time. We could keep PX liquor in our lockers.

First-class and below had it considerably less luxurious – upper/lower racks in large dormitory spaces in an EM barracks. I believe they had ceiling fans. Camp Tien Sha had a movie theater, library, various clubs. Built on a river delta, it was all sand – which turned to clinging muck during rains. It was surrounded by sandbagged guard towers. It was at the base of jungled Monkey Mountain, and it was said that Viet Cong snipers thereon had sometimes fired into the camp. Nights were sometimes punctuated by small-arms fire from our sentries on the towers, reacting to real or imagined threats.

The galley was at Camp Tien Sha and the food was well above navy average. Given our long ferry-bus-galley-bus-ferry trek to/from noon meals, did Authority give us commuted rations, at least for that noon meal? Of course not. A truck brought meals for the watchstanders. I usually made the chow-hall journey. Many of the day workers went to a city-side EM club, or cobbled together a meal from some of our C-rations and/or local Vietnamese edibles brought in by shacker-uppers, and I sometimes did this.

At first I had two or three other chiefs in day-working slots under me. Five or six day workers shared my office, in a corner of the communications spaces. I was told that one sailor, outside the door of this office, was queried as to his purpose and responded, "I ain't going in there. There's three chiefs in there having a farting contest."

One of the other contestants was Char, a Guamanian. It *was* well to stay upwind of him; I once saw him nauseate others in the back bed of an open pickup doing 35 mph. Other sailors alleged that he got on remarkably well with the Vietnamese because of his resemblance to the Buddha. He exchanged recorded tapes with his wife in lieu of letters. Playing one back, the wife was heard to break her string of Chamorro to say in English, "I don't think you're fat." He was then accused of having elicited her words, in order to rebut sailor criticisms of his weight.

He freely admitted to having "rolled" drunken sailors on Guam as a teenager.

In the galley one day he had some Guamanian hot sauce which he was encouraging other chiefs to sample. Most samplers wowed at the heat. It was about the equal of zigeny but I needled him by calling it mild, and alleged that in Ethiopia they imported that strength of pepper to feed to patients in the ulcer ward.

As the end of his tour neared, Char was expostulating on the virtues of Guam, which he referred to as "God's country". I took a shot in the dark: "Way I heard it, Guam was what God had left over after he'd finished making Saipan."

He bounced off the high stool he had been sitting on and if we hadn't been good friends I believe he might have swung at me. He called me numerous sons-of-a-bitch and wanted to know how I'd known about that. I learned that Guamanians look down upon Saipan, the island, with contempt, and on Saipanese as inferiors.

One morning I came to work and the news of the day was the Middle East. The six-day war had begun and was going full tilt. The news was so grim that J.B. opined that we might be fortunate to be where we were. I agreed: "*I wouldn't want to get sent over there into all that heat and sand."

Heat and sand, be it remembered, were two of the salient qualities of Danang. Another first-class, suffering with a Class-A hangover, was seated on a chair with his head in his hands. The import of what I had said slowly penetrated. He stirred, looked at his watch and grumbled, ". . . eight o'clock in the fucking morning . . ."

J.B. became my leading first-class after others senior to him had left, and he was the best first-class who ever worked for me, in Vietnam or anywhere. He was lean and crew-cut and physically fit; he reminded me of the Mike Nomad character in the Steve Roper comic strip.

We got a five-day R&R trip every three months. The destinations included Tokyo, Bangkok, Manila, Taipei, Jakarta, Kuala Lumpur, Singapore, Hong Kong, and Honolulu. Normally I would have chosen Manila, but I went to Hong Kong for my first one because Merrill Lynch had an office there and I had an account with them.

R&R signified Rest and R(something); the second R was given as either Recreation, Relaxation, or Recuperation. No matter. Servicemen early on retitled it as I&I – Intercourse and Intoxication.

I had a case of plantar (sole of the foot) warts that wouldn't yield to Dr Scholl's and I took it to the White Elephant dispensary. After their stronger medications also failed to burn the warts away after several tries, three medics held my leg immobile while another numbed my foot with shots and then they *cut* away the warts. They sent me off on crutches, which I had to use for about a week. I gained a new empathy for those who must use crutches. The damned things made my armpits sore, offended various muscles, and they were a lot clumsier and more of an inconvenience than I had ever guessed from seeing others use them. Had I known, the cure was worse than the evil.

There was an old, white, mongrel dog that had adopted the courtyard as his turf. He was maybe the scruffiest dog I have ever seen. Most sailors didn't pay much attention to him, but sometimes tossed him scraps from their meals. He would bark at Vietnamese men when one entered the courtyard. And now he barked at me, on my crutches – I walked wrong; I was different. But a worse indignity came when I first entered the office on the crutches. J.B. said, "*Where's your parrot, chief?"

And the warts came back. I kept them far from navy medicine. They went away of their own, came back, went away . . . After some years they absented themselves for good. (I hope.)

A message came through of more than ordinary interest. I reproduce it here:
O 290230Z SEP 67

FM OUTAGAMIE COUNTY
TO RUMHNA/NSA DANANG STATION HOSPITAL
INFO RUMHNA/USS SANCTUARY
RUMHNA/USS REPOSE
BT
UNCLAS E F T O
REQ FOR MEDICAL ASSIST
1.DIAGNOSIS:FOREIGN BODY,EIGHT INCH BOX WRENCH
IN SIGMOID COLON.
2.UNABLE TO REMOVE ABOARD WITH AVAILABLE FORCEPS.
SOAP SUDS ENEMA ADMINISTERED WITH NEG RESULTS.
PATIENT SUFFERING ONLY MILD DISCOMFORT.
3.REQ ONBOARD TREATMENT AND DISPOSITION.
4. ETA DANANG AREA 010745H
BT

The message generated extensive comment and discussion. We concluded that there were two possible scenarios. One of them was that some Boatswain's Mate had finally carried out his threat.

USS Repose (AH-16) and *USS Sanctuary (AH-17)* were the two hospital ships that had been taken out of mothballs and recommissioned for Vietnam service. They posed a communications quandary to Authority. It is well known that the Geneva conventions prohibit any armament on hospital ships. Less well known: also prohibited is any cryptographic equipment. Since all unclassified messages were now UNCLAS E F T O, the two had to pick up their messages when in port, not exactly a form of rapid communications. Truly urgent stuff had the E F T O designator removed and were sent over uncovered circuits to the ships. Different things were tried and found wanting; finally Authority said in effect, *Oh the hell with it*, and allowed UNCLAS E F T O to be sent uncovered, to those two ships only.

I had to stand an utterly useless evening watch at the ferry landing every month or two. I don't even remember what its purpose was or what my duties, if any, were supposed to be. It was another instance of Authority's compulsion to see everyone on a watch bill or rotating duty of some sort. It was terminated about six months after I arrived. One night two drunk (or on drugs?) marines came to the landing and the more dominant one was in full gung-ho, John-Wayne mode. He was going across *now* and tried to browbeat me into sending the ferry early. When I refused, he demanded to know who my commanding officer was. When I told him it was Rear Admiral Lacy he didn't know quite what to say. I sent my messenger to the White Elephant to summon the Shore Patrol, but something diverted the drunks' attention and they wandered off I knew not where.

Bill Mote came by and located me in the White Elephant. He was Radio Officer on a tanker and invited me out to see it. It wasn't one of the monster supertankers that were to come later, but it was impressively large. The only way to board was by rope ladder from the waterline. Memory probably exaggerates, but my mind's eye sees that ladder as a hundred-foot climb. Bill's bulk on the ladder above me was a less-than-reassuring sight.

I never partook of illegal liberty and was never intimate with a Vietnamese woman. You could call that prudence or you could call it cowardice; I wouldn't argue with either description. Consequently my knowledge of the illegal-liberty scene came only from hearsay (of which I heard a plenty). The Shore Patrol (accompanied by Vietnamese police) was charged with catching violators. Violators ran. The resultant episodes were right out of the Keystone Kops. The Vietnamese were protective of the sailors who were contributing to their income; they would hide fugitives, hinder the Shore Patrol, and give early warning of approach. I doubt that either the SPs or their local sidekicks were true believers in the utility and righteousness of their efforts. But they caught a few.

Other than the SP raiders and the stiff fines, there was little effort to deter illegalities. Our officers knew who was shacking up, who frequented the out-of-bounds bars, we all knew. No one would give any willing assistance to Authority in this matter.

Somewhere or other, in my readings about leadership, I've seen the advice that you should never give an order unless you expect that it will be obeyed. The officer responsible for "no-liberty", whoever he was, must never have read about that.

Prohibition is the trigger of crime. (Ian Fleming, *Goldfinger*)

For my second R&R I went to Hong Kong again. This was partly because of the charms of one Lily Ma, but it was mostly because of *The Overseas Weekly.* *OW* had started a Pacific edition and was trying to get it on the shelves at the PXs, the military was resisting bitterly with patently spurious excuses, no space, etc. (*OW* had taken the matter to court. I don't remember whether they ever succeeded or not.) *OW* was available on *Vietnamese* newsstands; but I had a subscription. The Pacific edition was pretty much a one-woman operation with its main office in Hong Kong. I intended to visit that office and, I hoped, to convince the lady that she should visit Danang and do a front-page blast on the liberty situation in I Corps. I prepared a briefing paper (which is what I quoted early in this chapter) for her. But she was out of town, so I left the paper at her office. A few weeks later my paper was printed in *OW* as a letter to the editor. Other than that, and as far as I am aware, neither *OW* nor any other publication ever did an exposé on I Corps no-liberty.

The "letter" did no good. Liberty was not resumed while I was in-country, and I never heard of it being resumed at any future time.

It became time for semi-annual personnel evaluations. CDR Coski kicked them back with vague criticisms. I consulted with Mr Lawrence (who wasn't quite sure about the CDR's problems either), then went over them one by one with my two watch supervisors (who had written the evaluations) and their assistants, asking for more information about each man. I didn't glean much, mostly nods of heads and, "Good man." It is easy to write an evaluation on a sailor who is really top-notch, who stands out among his peers. It is also easy to write one on a real bumbler. The hard one to write is about the average sailor, doing a good job, in any way that will distinguish him from his many fellows, and we had dozens of those. I took the evaluations and tinkered with a little rewriting, but any real difference from the original efforts was minuscule. When Mr Lawrence told me that CDR Coski had okayed the rewrites I shrugged and spread my hands. He didn't repeat the physical gesture, but I thought he shared my mystification.

I came down with some southeast Asian bug and was on my back in the Camp Tien Sha dispensary for four or five days. One part of my head – same shape as an orange segment – was extraordinarily painful; any head movement was excruciating and a sneeze or cough was torture. Mr Lawrence came by to visit the invalid. I was woozy and semiconscious enough that I lost track of a complete day. The navy called it FUO – Fever of Unknown Origin, a standard catchall. When I described the experience to a civilian doctor many years later, he said that it sounded to him like encephalitis.

Having no intention of celebrating New Year's Eve, I stayed in my barracks room. Sleep did not come early and, if it had, I would have been awakened at midnight. The sentries fired their weapons in a spectacular display of indiscipline and ammunition-waste. They kept at it for 15-20 minutes and it was punctuated by yet other noises, grenades and star shells perhaps. It was not as colorful as a Stateside Fourth of July, but every bit as noisy and probably more so. Just as the noise had tailed off and I was looking forward, at last, to sleep, loud voices and the heavy tramp of feet sounded in the corridor. The chief in the cubicle next to mine had arrived with two friends. His stereo came on at high volume and their "party" was clearly going to last for a long time, perhaps until dawn. Remonstrations would have been useless. (I would probably have been invited to have a drink.) After a few minutes I thought of a dirty trick that might work. I unplugged my desk lamp, straightened a paper clip, wound its wire around the base of the plug's prongs, and plugged it back in.

Pop. Smell of ozone. *Skreeek* of a needle on a dying turntable. Darkness. Their voices were now rather muted. They discussed the situation and left for elsewhere. I slept.

On 16 January 1968 I was advanced to RMCS, Senior Chief Radioman, as a result of the test I had taken the previous August. I had made it with the minimum three-year time in rate. The promotion rated me a move to a single room on the lower floor of the barracks.

The navy had been slowly liberalizing in some ways. Chiefs were now allowed, even encouraged, to communicate with the detailers in the Bureau of Personnel rather than just making three choices and then waiting. I wrote the Radioman detailer to say that I wanted to go to Asmara and that, if the chances later would be better than now, I would be willing to extend in Danang. He replied that they would indeed be better, in fact highly likely, so I requested a six-month extension.

Such a request had to be approved by several offices, and one of them was the chaplain's office. I explained my reasons and got his signature but as I was about to go he asked my religion. "None, sir." I had no choice but to listen to his grumpy disapprobation, which was thankfully brief. It included indictment of the Radioman rating in general in addition to me specifically. Other Radiomen had earlier earned his disfavor.

One of those others was one of my RM1s who was engaged to a Vietnamese waitress at one of the navy clubs. He was fighting the battle to gain permission to marry and had to interact with the chaplain for that purpose. His intended was Catholic; I have to wonder how things worked out for them.

Of the waitresses in the clubs it was said that if they had worn their miniskirts any shorter, they would have had two more cheeks to powder and a lot more hair to comb. The shortest waitress at any particular club typically answered to a nickname taken from comic-strip cowboy Red Ryder's Indian-boy sidekick: *Little Beaver*.

On 23 January we listened intently to the morning news about North Korea's seizure of the *USS Pueblo (AGER-2)* and speculated about possible developments and consequences. I am sometimes asked if I am related to Commander Bucher – I am not, to my knowledge. When I first saw his photos I thought there might well be a distant relationship, perhaps third cousin, fourth cousin – his short, chunky build was quite like those of my father and uncles. But then I read his autobiography and learned that he had been adopted into a Bucher family and any resemblance was no way by DNA. He saved his crew and will never be forgiven for it. He *gave up the ship*, and nothing else will ever matter to the jingoistic hard-core.

On 30 January came the Tet offensive. I heard the booms of distant rockets at night, and when we went to work we had to use a bridge farther upstream (south) on the river; the ferry was temporarily secured. At that bridge I saw the stacked bodies of a dozen or so dead Viet Cong and that was as close as I ever came to a "combat experience".

For my third R&R I intended to go to Manila, but our Yeoman in communications hosed up my orders somehow and I was out at the airport with no specific destination. I tried to explain my situation to a disagreeable marine E-8 who was directing traffic and brooked no pleas from anyone. I was sent to Kuala Lumpur.

That was just the first disappointment. On arrival we were told that all the R&R hotels were filled except for the most upscale one – and it was the *only one* that did not allow female guests in rooms! A couple other disgruntled sailors were laying plans to seek another hotel; I joined them and found lodging at a lower-rated hotel not on the approved R&R list.

And the next disappointment: that hotel had a rooftop dance floor with about 25 beauties and almost no men. But only one of the girls spoke English. It was thus collectively decided that I was "hers" – and she was fat. I ignored her, bought her no drinks, responded with grunts, and she still wouldn't leave my table. She was faithful. Whenever I went to that rooftop, the same drill.

The next night I resorted to seeking sex through a taxi driver. After a circuitous drive he found a madam with an available girl, and I brought her to the hotel. The next day when she left I found that she had lightened my stack of cash – by one big bill, $50 {$292} I believe, but I don't recall if that value was in American dollars or Malaysian dollars. I told the R&R office about it, they directed me to the Malaysian police. I had written down the taxi license, so they had no trouble hauling in the girl and the madam. I had also written the serial numbers of my larger bills, but the stolen bill had disappeared somehow. When the police called me back in they were hassling the girl and the madam about it, with no results, and I heard nothing more.

The Malaysian English-language newspaper consistently used a phrase that charmed me – "he outraged her modesty". This apparently covered rape, copping a feel, and everything in between. The paper seemed to have a story or two of this type nearly every day, but with minimal detail beyond the all-purpose phrase.

It was quite my most unsatisfactory R&R.

Jack, another of my day-working RM1s, had among other duties been in charge of collecting and later depositing the moneys received when sailors sent Class E (personal) telegrams. He had a permanent legal wife in the U.S. and a temporary extralegal wife in Danang. After his transfer it was found that he had dipped into his funds to finance the latter, and he was sent back to Danang for court-martial. I think he had plans to repay it by sending money orders to someone in Danang, but the shortage was discovered before he could do so.

I was called as a witness. I don't recall whether his defense wanted me, or whether the court itself wanted to hear from Jack's chief. A legal officer attempted to swear me in, ending with the "so help me God" words. I said, "I'm an Atheist, sir, is there an alternative . . . ?"
"*Do you affirm?" (He didn't miss a beat.)
"*I affirm."
A preliminary inquiry would have been more welcome than an unwarranted assumption, but I think my credibility was enhanced.

They asked me a general question about the quality of Jack's work for me. I testified: "I expected to be asked that, and I've given it some thought. There are nine first-class who have worked for me here. I'd rate Jack seventh. Now, that sounds like faint praise, but it shouldn't be taken that way. I've been lucky, very lucky, here to have the best bunch of first-classes I've ever seen. At any other station, I'd have rated Jack one of the best."

They asked whether I'd want Jack working for me again. I said that I gladly would, with the reservation that I would probably avoid assigning him to duties involving the handling of money.

The court found him guilty, which was foreordained. They sentenced him to a fine and a "suspended bust" – reduction to second-class, but held off for six months and to be forgotten if he stayed out of trouble for that time. But unknown to the court members, a court-martial could not issue a suspended bust – only the authority who convened the court-martial could suspend or reduce a sentence. So the lawyers had to throw out that part of the sentence completely and Jack got only the fine. He smelled like a rose.

One of my watchstanding RM2s had about 14 years in the navy. He had a wife and family, and he was one of those who were more than qualified for promotion, in every way but one – he simply could not do well on those advancement exams. He had, at last, in Danang, finally passed the RM1 exam. While waiting for his promotion, he and another sailor were caught sitting outside the barracks with drinks. At his mast, the promotion was pulled. There was much sympathy for him. He was guilty, but it seemed that his apprehension was based more on suspicion than on evidence; I thought he ought to appeal the punishment and offered to help him with an appeal. He wouldn't do it; he decided to be a good, uncomplaining sailor and accept the workings of fate.

The command was so large, and the disciplinary cases so many, that penalties were handed out in cookie-cutter fashion: if you did X, you got Y. Men weren't considered as individuals. I hope that RM2 passed the RM1 exam again in a future year, but I've never known.

As the work continued to go more and more smoothly, I and those in my office largely had things well under control before noon. Much of our surplus time began to be devoted to practical-jokery. At first it involved thumb tacks on the seats of chairs. After everyone learned to sit with caution, and only after reconnoitering, the locations became more inventive: taped on a typewriter roller where it would be grasped, on desk drawer handles, on the inside band of a hat, on the inside of a book-like message file folder at the point where a finger would be placed to pull it out of its sleeve. (That last one drew blood once.)

Cartridges would be disassembled and their black gunpowder sprinkled in an already-dirty ash tray, scorching the knuckles of the next person to stub out a cigaret therein. The gunpowder was also used in attempts to load cigarets, but match heads were found to be more effective. In its owner's absence, an unguarded package would have a cigaret selected, about a half inch of tobacco carefully removed, a couple paper match heads inserted, and the tobacco painstakingly replaced. The victim would suffer a surprise when his cigaret suddenly flamed and sometimes, if his timing of a puff was just right, he could get a lungful of sulfur. One first-class, looking pasty, said, "Chief, you just about cured me of smoking."

I liked *nuoc mam*, the Vietnamese fish sauce, but many did not and considered its aroma a stench. For them, the method of attack was to dip a straw in the *nuoc mam*, seal the other end with a finger, slip it over the victim's shoulder when his head was turned, and let it run out on his lapel. It was also placed on the bills of caps. One second-class, who disliked the stuff more than anyone else, had his combat boots soaked with it during the night before he was due to catch an early-morning flight to the U.S.; he had no choice but to wear the fragrant boots on the plane.

Vietnamese hot peppers were rubbed on the rims of coffee cups, and on the stem of my pipe. Since I loved hot peppers (although I didn't normally use them in those locations) I just smacked my lips and smiled with pleasure. One day I returned from somewhere to find my Snoopy coffee cup hanging from a hook on the high (12-foot?) ceiling.

The same second-class who suffered the fish-sauced boots had a center drawer in his desk-table which he was always careful to keep locked. But one day he had to go somewhere for a couple hours and forgot to lock it. The contents were removed and safeguarded and, when first attempts leaked, a sealant was found. The drawer was made watertight and filled to the brim. The hope was that he would open it while seated and would get a drenched lap. But he was still standing and the water merely sloshed on his boots.

J.B. had a trick he had pulled successfully several times. When someone was eating a sandwich he would say, "Hey, that looks good. Can I try a bite of it?" When the victim acquiesced, J.B. would take a crocodilian bite, engorging nearly half the sandwich, leaving the owner to stare ruefully at the remains. We prepared an attractive-looking sandwich and covered all but one corner with a liberal amount of hot-pepper powder. (J.B. was known to have no tolerance at all for hot peppers.) A conspirator was to sit near J.B., take a bite from the one safe corner, praise its quality, and await developments. Alas, it didn't work; J.B. didn't try his trick that day. When we gave up and showed him what had been prepared for him, his eyes got big.

One LCDR Marcus Aurelius Arnheiter, a real-life Captain Queeg, was much on the pages of *Navy Times*, and made other media as well, in the late 1960s. He had captained a DER (identical to the *USS Rhodes)* off the coast of Vietnam and had been relieved after only a few months in command. Incredibly, an up-and-coming captain, slated to command the *New Jersey*, sacrificed his own career in a futile attempt to defend Arnheiter. His mindset apparently was that no ship captain could *ever* be seen to be wrong, no matter what he had done. I got some wise-guy mileage out of Arnheiter until he retired in 1971. If I knew that a sailor had received orders to a ship – the *USS Neversail*, say – I would, while glancing over the daily officers-orders in his presence, remark, "Well, I'll be damned – I never thought they'd give that guy another ship." Asked for amplification I would pretend to read, "Arnheiter, Marcus A. From ComTwelve. To CO *USS Neversail*." I never fooled anyone for more than a second or two.

Those daily officers-orders messages were an irritant throughout my career. They were usually long, multi-page, and they violated every standard of necessity for transmission by message rather than by official mail. But RHIP – Rank Has Its Privileges – prevailed.

Admiral Osborn took command in February. He was a hearty, bluff sort, pretty much all right I thought. A story was told that at some early, formal officers' dining function, he noted the presence of the navy nurses by saying, "Well, I see the bushes are all out tonight."

He was, according to the story, overheard, and the head nurse led the nurses out, saying to the admiral's aide, "You can tell the admiral that the 'bushes' . . ." (Full quote forgotten. Sorry.)

About this time CDR Coski was relieved by CDR Denny, and Mr Lawrence was replaced by Tom Perkins, an energetic mustang LT(jg). He upheld the Pacific Fleet, I the Atlantic. On one occasion an erring service message was received from some nearby command and their error involved the definition of a Z-signal. Mr Perkins said, "ZXX means [whatever], doesn't it?"

I rolled my eyes and said, "*It does in the *Atlantic* Fleet, sir." He walked away.

Another time he was harping on practical factors for the watchstanders and said, "My practical factors were never gundecked, chief, and I know yours never were . . ."

I said, "Oh, yes, they were." He went slack-jawed. I continued: "All the way up." I heard no more from him about practical factors.

"Gundecking" is falsification of a document, record, report, etc. The navy could not function without it. Neither could most bureaucracies, governmental or private. Bright-eyed Authority, far removed from the working level, dictates that unnecessary actions be taken, unnecessary records be kept, an infinite variety of unnecessaries. (The earlier-mentioned "training programs" that each command is supposed to have are a prime example of such.) A great deal of gundecking takes place during the construction of Potemkin villages just before an administrative inspection. Nonetheless gundecking is seldom admitted; "the book" is religiously given lip service by those doing the gundecking even while it is in progress.

So much of what we call management consists in making it difficult for people to work. (Peter Drucker)

As for practical factors, they are a long list of actions that a man is, supposedly, required to demonstrate that he can perform before he can be recommended to take a test for promotion. Each man has a sheet in his service record, on which these actions are initialed off as he (theoretically) qualifies for each one. Often demonstration is impossible – for example the cleaning and maintenance of a shipboard antenna, when one is on shore duty. They get initialed anyhow. I once opined that anyone who claimed to be really and truly able to do *all* of the things on his Radioman practical-factor sheet was either SuperRadioman or a great big liar, and that I would be much more likely to believe the latter than the former.

Because of time difference, we heard U.S. prime time in our morning. At the end of March we heard LBJ's renouncement of another term, to our great surprise. I had, thus far, thought LBJ's strategy perfect. As I saw it then, Vietnam was an attempt by international communism to gain by other means what it could not gain by frontal war in Korea, that it should not be tolerated, and that gradual escalation was the right way to stop it while not killing any more of the poor bastards than absolutely necessary. I even hoped to revisit Danang at some future time when peace came. The possibility of *losing* the war was unthinkable and never crossed my mind.

As the years passed, and I saw that a great many of those I admired opposed the war, and a great many of those I despised supported it, my certainty began to suffer. I decided that it was going to take me many years to sort out my views. And I still haven't, not totally. The "domino theory" struck me as valid then; it is generally scoffed today.

But I wonder, if we had not gone into Vietnam, when we did, for as long as we did, would Thailand be a prosperous democracy today? And I have some trouble with John F. Kennedy's words, ". . . pay any price, bear any burden . . ." and reflecting that when we were called upon to do so, we didn't.

My six-month extension carried an extra benefit: a month of free leave, and transportation to the U.S. and back for it. The leave was "free" in the sense that it did not count against the 30 days of leave per year that everyone everywhere earned. Air fare to Asmara would be less than to the U.S. and so would be covered. I went by way of Saigon and had a day or two to wait there. Sitting in a transient barracks lounge, the five-o'clock news came on and I settled to listen. The first words from the announcer were, "*Martin Luther King is dead." The thought that flashed through my mind was *Oh, shit. I hope he hasn't been shot.* I noticed no reaction from the others in the lounge; I may have been one of the last to know the news.

Going through departure procedures at Saigon airport, I had quite a lot of U.S. dollars for leave expenses. I declared what I had and was stopped by a Vietnamese soldier. I either didn't know, or had forgotten, that to take that much out of the country I needed permission-paperwork. I had visions of having to backtrack, even to return to Danang, to sort things out. My next thought was, "I bet he'll look for a bribe. I wonder how much." I would have been willing to part with a substantial sum. But, to my surprise, the soldier just smiled and motioned me to go ahead anyhow!

I had a two- or three-day layover in New Delhi then flew the rest of the way on Ethiopian Airlines. On their south Asia routes they didn't worry about the tender palates of westerners; the food was deliciously *spicy*, and excellent as it always was on Ethiopian.

On my return to the office I bad-mouthed New Delhi: "There must have been 50 guys asked me if I wanted to change money. *Nobody* ever asked if I wanted anything else."

At this point I first began to think about divorce. The marriage had begun to slide downhill from the time Yeshu arrived in Naples, and I had seen no sign of improvement during my two visits to Asmara. Two factors held me back. There was the reluctance to admit, even to myself, that I had made a mistake – a feeling common to everyone. And there was the sure knowledge that every racist who learned of our divorce would say, aloud or silently, some variant of *no surprise – might have known – could have told you so.* (Had it not been for that, I might have begun to think of divorce earlier.) The question came down to: did I want to live the rest of my life like this? Once I began to ponder the possibility my decision became clear in a remarkably short time. I did not.

The walls of the heads in the White Elephant were covered with graffiti. Much, but less than half, expressed ideas objectionable to Authority. I think IHTFP – I Hate This Fucking Place – had its origin in Vietnam. FTN, a nautical parallel of the widely-known FTA or Fuck The Army, was also much seen. *I love the fucking navy and the navy loves fucking me*, ran one lament. Many graffiti referred wittily to cartoon characters, celebrities – *John Wayne wears pantyhose* – or other aspects of popular culture. I was amused by one sequence, apparently inscribed by four different contributors:
Admiral Osborn sleeps with a night light.
I do not.
You do too. – Admiral's Aide
He does not! – Admiral's Mistress

The walls were sometimes called the *Danang Free Press*. Authority, lacking both in humor and in toleration, had the walls scrubbed repeatedly, and wrote ominous missives forbidding the scribblings. Effect: zero. Finally Authority struck with the ultimate in logocide. Every head wall was painted midnight black, all the way up to those high, high ceilings.

I thought of the perfect response. A sharp edge would cut into that black paint and expose the white beneath. I yearned to chisel a large, prominent, white-on-black message FUCK CENSORSHIP (the misspelling deliberate, to deflect any possible suspicion, since I was known to be a near-perfect speller). I never did it. Cowardice triumphed. The heads were often deserted, but one never knew when someone might walk in. And the fury of Authority if a senior chief were found to be the perpetrator was scarcely imaginable.

A fair percentage of the graffiti concerned "shortness" – how many days the writer had remaining before transfer, thus how "short" he was. There were many imaginative descriptions of shortness: *I am so short I could sit on the edge of a piece of paper and my feet wouldn't touch the ground.* I invented one that I think was as good as any: *I am so short I would have to climb a stepladder to kiss a snake's ass.*

"Short-timer's attitude" – a don't-give-a-damn slacking of effort, of conscientiousness, a feeling that the job will be someone else's soon – is a malady that, while it doesn't happen to everyone everywhere, happens often enough to be a condition recognized navy-wide. Once you became the shortest man in a group, you were no longer *short* – you were *next*.

Short-timer checkoff charts of various design were often hung on office walls with numbered areas, each area to be filled in or colored in or scratched off each day as a man's time shortened. These often took female form, traced from *Playboy* centerfolds, with the last 3-2-1 numbers typically being the nipples and the groin. My own simple design consisted only of large, fat letters: FYBIS (Fuck You, Buddy, I'm Short).

Special Services, responsible for athletics among other things, organized a monthly ping-pong tournament. Huge though the command was, fewer than a dozen turned up for them. Most sailors simply could not wangle time off from their duties for such frivolities. I won the first two tournaments then subsided back toward normal. The Special Services civilian made arrangements for an evening event in Danang in which we played against Vietnamese. The Vietnamese were far superior to us; I don't think they even used their best players. I was matched against a girl in singles. I think she won.

I also managed a communications softball team for a few games. It was fast-pitch and we had no real pitcher. We won one game – by forfeit.

The *Stars and Stripes* was flown in daily and passed out in the message center every afternoon, free. It had one good columnist, Ralph McGill of the *Atlanta Constitution*, and a stable of second- and third-raters who covered a narrow political spectrum from just right of center to just left of Barry Goldwater. The political cartoons were more representative, including Herblock and several others of distinction. But not every column, nor every cartoonist, appeared every day – columns or cartoons critical of the war were weeded out and rarely seen.

The inevitable happened, two or three messages were lost, delayed, or mishandled in a short stretch of time. Law of averages at work. Ignorant of that law, Authority reacted: no more reading the papers on watch, when they arrived – they would not be handed out until the watch was relieved. A master chief "ombudsman" had recently been established in an office on Camp Tien Sha, with whom complaints about such doings could be lodged, and I did so. "Childish", he said. A few days later timely reading of the papers was restored. My anger over this incident caused me to begin taking my authorized day off every ten days. I followed the condition reports subsequent to the Robert Kennedy assassination while sunbathing behind the barracks.

During the summer we underwent a complete message center upgrade. Similar to what had been done pre-deployment on the *FDR*, everything was torn out and completely redone. This took two or three months, and during that period nothing remained in the White Elephant except message distribution – the message boxes where messages were slotted for pickup by the various offices we served. All tape cutting, transmission, reception, reproduction were moved across the river to the relay building, whence messages were couriered across to the White Elephant. Only a handful of distribution clerks, officers, and day workers remained there; everyone else, including me, set up temporary shop in the relay building.

Seated there one day, two flies landed on my table top. I slapped my hands together over them; one escaped. A sailor queried, "Did you get him, chief?"

"*I got the pregnant one. Little bastards! Fucking right in front of me when I ain't got no liberty!"

It was in Vietnam that I first heard flies referred to as *the national bird*, but I suspect that the cultural affront is much more ancient.

In a prominent place in the center of Camp Tien Sha a new, eight-sided structure was going up. It proved to be a head. It had four entrances labeled *American Men, American Women, Vietnamese Men, Vietnamese Women*. In 1968. In a land where we were supposed to be "winning hearts and minds". I could not believe it. Was I in the United States Navy or the Confederate States Navy? I hoped that some reporter might pass through, see it and write about it. I thought about taking pictures and sending them to . . . *OW*? *Time* or *Newsweek*? A congressman? But I did not own a camera at the time, and if someone had seen me taking pictures and inquired my purpose . . . I dithered and in the end did nothing.

Bob Hope and his show came to Danang. He had been on the *FDR* the year before, but I had the watch and couldn't go. I saw this one. Prominent among his troupe of entertainers was Anita Bryant. When she did her act, she walked up the aisle-stairs, selected a serviceman, and crooned her love song while embracing him. Did she pick a strapping, handsome specimen of young manhood? No, that was not in the plan. She fastened on a most unlikely, ruddy, round-faced sailor wearing thick-lensed glasses. She chose well; her victim beamed and gave every sign of enjoyment, and the audience roared, but the unspoken sub-text was *look at this poor, silly goof thinking I might really have a yen for him*. This was probably a standard ploy, probably used by other touring sexpots, but it revolted me. I was an Anita Bryant non-fan thereafter, long before she gained notoriety with her anti-gay crusading.

The terms *drifty* and *skater* were much used in this period. A skater was someone who had an easy, undemanding job, one who didn't work much. It was similar to the earlier *goldbrick*. A drifty person was someone mentally lacking, dreamy, or eccentric. Atlantic Fleet sailors spoke of two mythical commands: COMSKATELANT and COMDRIFTPAC. Pacific Fleet sailors claimed that that geography was reversed.

I had received my orders for November transfer to Asmara. A monthly memo was prepared by our Yeoman listing persons due to arrive (and from where), persons due to depart (and next duty station), and similar personnel matters. The Yeoman circulated a preliminary worksheet to be filled in. He already knew of my Asmara orders, and for my next duty station I wrote COMSKATELANT REP MIDDLE EAST on his rough. The Yeoman didn't know any better (or wasn't thinking) and typed the formal memo that way. The commander got a kick out of it.

I had taken a couple of pleasant R&Rs in Manila and intended to go there again for my last one, but the flights thence were already filled and I chose Bangkok from what was available. It was fatal. I met Jamroon. She guided me to elephant log-handling performances, Thai kick-boxing, other tourist sites, and introduced me to her children – all of them. In another month I would be going through Bangkok on the way to Asmara, and I pledged to see her again.

One of the least pleasant parts of R&Rs was the departure, invariably very early morning – 0400, 0500, or thereabouts. The military R&R detachment staffs always semi-apologized for the hour and explained that it was at the insistence of the airlines. On this return I was seated right next to the jumpseats where the stewardesses buckled in for takeoff. They were also grousing about the departure times, which *their* bosses told them were demanded *by the military*! Someone was lying to someone. I never learned who to whom.

If it had not been for family considerations and my wish to return to Asmara, I could have and probably would have continued indefinitely to request six-month Vietnam extensions. The frequent R&Rs alleviated the no-liberty policy enough that I could tolerate it even while resenting it, and there were other benefits: the 30 days of free leave each time, and the tax-free status of my military pay while in the combat zone.

I received a second award of the Navy Achievement Medal for my work in Danang. As on the *FDR*, they were routinely given to those doing good work, more or less on a quota system. This one specifically authorized me to wear the "combat V" – for Valor – atop the ribbon. I hadn't done anything "valorous"; the V authorization was automatic in the combat zone – if you were on land at least. I had thought that the V also went along with the first one and was already wearing it. Possibly not. There would be a big foofaraw about this in 1996 when the then-CNO, Jeremy Boorda, shot himself because shit-stirrers in the media were questioning the combat Vs that he wore. He had earned (or not earned?) them while *on a ship* in the combat zone. Suicide is a drastic action to take over an honest mistake (if it was a mistake?) about a 1/4" piece of metal – I have wondered whether other, unknown, factors were at work in his life.

Looking back, I believe that my best years in the navy – professionally, "how good a job I did" – were those on the *FDR* and in Danang. I thought I had done best of all in Danang; partly because of those smooth, trouble-free, across-the-river and back moves of communications. The respective evaluations I received did not reflect my own assessment. Not that my Danang evaluations were bad; they were quite good. They were fair and, I thought, realistic. They didn't reach the level of the grandiloquent ones Mr Smallidge had written on me, which were of the *he walks on water and farts rose petals* genre. All of which goes to prove the well-understood principle: for whom you work will often carry more weight than what you have actually done.

Authority awoke to the fact that, since the ferry-landing watch had been discontinued, chiefs were not standing any duties. Horrors! Just before my Bangkok R&R, a newly-critical duty was found – a night watch in some distant barracks. The master chief who administered the watch list gave himself one of the earliest watches there ("setting an example"). I was also on the November list – but happily the date fell during my R&R time. I phoned the master chief to inform him of that fact. Watch bills typically have a "supernumerary" or two listed, on call to take a watch if there is some unforeseen glitch; I expected that he would assign a supernumerary in my place. Instead I heard the voice of friendly reason, "Well, now, chief, I'm sure you can get one of the other Radiomen to take it for you . . ." I managed to convince him that I could not do that, and he reluctantly condescended to assign a supernumerary.

I have heard of commands with policies that if you cannot stand your watch, you have to find your *own* standby – even if you are on annual leave, and even if that leave was approved before the watch list was promulgated. This is pure sloth on the part of the administrator of the watch list (and is possibly illegal besides). When I had that same chore in future years I *used* the supernumeraries. That is what they are for. I was not at all surprised to see my name appear for very early December on the next list. I would be gone, permanently. Normally I would have so informed that master chief but, displeased by the runaround he had given me earlier, I did not. I can only imagine what names he called me after no one showed up for that December watch.

All through November I thought about Jamroon. The thought that kept circling through my mind was *Five kids – you gotta be nuts.* I had not contemplated any reentanglement this soon, when I had not yet even broached divorce to Yeshu. Indeed I *was* nuts: I proposed on the second day in Bangkok and she accepted.

Never carried a weapon, never slept outside, never slogged through swamp or jungle, never crawled through a tunnel, never rode a swift boat or a helicopter. If a sniper bullet ever came within 100 yards of me, or a rocket within a mile, I never knew about it. The reader will perhaps understand why I avoid mentioning, in later life, that I am a Vietnam veteran. I don't conceal it if the subject comes up, and it is technically true, but I feel guilty about classifying myself with those who were in combat, or even with those who endured field living conditions.

However I didn't know things would work out the way they did when I volunteered, and I did volunteer.

Which is more than certain prominent politicians can say.

Lest it seem like I am straining my arm to pat myself on the back here, let me clarify that I did not volunteer out of patriotism or any such lofty sentiment. I was likely to be facing shipboard or other unpleasant duty anyhow. The benefits of combat pay and tax-free military pay were attractive. Vietnam might be favorable, and certainly would not be unfavorable, towards future promotions and assignments. Oh, maybe there was a smidgen of patriotism – at the time I believed the war was both right and necessary. But basically I was a mercenary.

XVI - COUNTRY CLUB

I took a month of annual leave in Asmara before checking in for duty in early January 1969. During that month I poked around and talked to people, and I learned some dismaying news: that I was probably going to be assigned to the navy transmitter site at Gura. This had been built, as Tract H, since my previous tour. I had been to the area on 1959-61 excursions; the tract was between the deserted airstrip and the ruined fort. It was about 25 miles from Asmara.

There had been other changes, mostly for the better. The old radio towers on Tract A and the remains of the cableway to Massawa had been dismantled for scrap. The navy barracks was now on Kagnew Station (and had heat!) and the navy admin offices had moved out to a separate building at Tract F, the receiver site. There was now a CPO club on Tract A, dependent housing, and little else. I heard that establishment of the CPO club involved difficult negotiations with the army, who feared a diversion of revenue from their Top 5 Club on Kagnew Station. ("Top 5" referred to the highest enlisted pay grades, E-5 through E-9.) The old restrictions on assigning Blacks to Asmara had been lifted, and both army and navy had a normal percentage of black servicemen. No more did I hear "nigger" spoken. But Kag-new had prevailed and the correct "con-you" pronunciation was no longer heard – Kag-new was used even on Armed Forces Radio and TV, and by our local employees, who would not presume to correct their bosses. And there was still no help for anyone who might want to learn some Tigrinya or Amharinya. Only Italian.

Yeshu's big U.S. convertible was out of whack and immobile. She got around by gharry-cart or with friends. I bought a VW bug for myself, delivered a few months later.

I was indeed assigned to Gura. Worse, a Master Chief Electronics Technician was the leading chief there (a Radioman billet) – and I was assigned to fill an *ET* chief's E-7 billet! This was not in my line and not at all to my liking. The transmitter building had three or four radiating bays with lines of transmitters. I tried to familiarize myself with what I was supposed to be doing, chiefly by cracking the pubs, overseeing the ETs who repaired and maintained the big beasts, and determining what repair parts were needed or should be ordered. A percentage of the transmitters were continually down for repair.

The officer in charge, a mustang LT, his deputy, a warrant officer, and a few of the other senior married people had housing in nearby Dekemhare. They inquired about my intentions perhaps to move there, and it seemed they encouraged such action. I wanted no part of it, even though my workday was lengthened by having to ride a navy bus back and forth from Asmara. There was a barracks for the single sailors, and a club (The Long Branch Saloon).

I delayed through the holidays and the Ethiopian Christmas (6 January) before telling Yeshu I wanted a divorce. No argument; she said OK. We negotiated matters with remarkable amity. She surprised me by wanting to go to the U.S.; she had shown little or no past desire to live there. (Perhaps she had premonitions of the troubles that would beset Eritrea and Ethiopia in a few more years.) I had deplaned in Asmara with visions of a quick divorce and getting Jamroon to Asmara in the very near future.   But I consulted a local lawyer in December and learned that Ethiopian grounds for divorce were narrow and strict. Yeshu's desire to go to the U.S. would also complicate things. I wanted to keep Mark, and she posed no objection. We agreed easily on how much money I would send her, and for how long. She did not seek formal alimony; we each trusted the other. (That was probably a mistake; court-ordered alimony would have been tax-deductible for me.)

As things turned out, Yeshu would file for divorce in the U.S. and Jamroon would not visit Asmara until 24 years later.

It was apparent to all concerned that I was a square peg in a round hole in Gura, and after three months I was replaced there and brought back to Asmara to become a Communications Watch Officer (CWO) on one of the receiver site watch sections. This was a junior-officer billet but depending on personnel available they sometimes dipped as low as E-7 to fill it. I was relieved in Gura by an RMC and after about six months he had *every* transmitter up and running – including even all three of the biggest and most powerful ones, one of which had been drastically cannibalized for parts to keep the other two operating! I commented on his performance: "He's really making himself look good. And making me look bad by comparison – I hope nobody thinks of that."

The watch rotation was new to me, 2-2-2-80: two eves, eight hours off, two days, eight hours off, two midwatches, and then 80 hours off. It was enormously popular, because of how fast the 2-2-2 strings seemed to go and how fast the 80s seemed to recur. Myself, I could have done without the eight-off doublebacks. When the time is split between four sections, you are going to spend 25% of your time on watch, no matter what system is devised. This works out to equal a 42-hour week (which probably ought to be measured as 43, to allow for the overlap time when one watch relieves another and any necessary information is passed along).

The CWO desk was in the message center. Working for me were about eight men in the message center, three or four across the hall in circuit control (including Steve, an RMC, the other chief on the watch), three or four far down the hall in relay, and several more in SpecComm, which was just as secretive as ever. I could not enter their space and, if they had ever made some major blunder, I would not just have been held blameless – I would never even have known about it. There was also a duty ET attached to the section.

Steve had preceded his wife to Asmara; she joined him several months later. During his geographic-bachelor period he had overindulged and overslept downtown, and had gone to captain's mast for it. As Steve told it, it seemed that the captain had strong views on marital fidelity; he got a lecture thereon and an unusually heavy penalty for the offense. He said that he had been punished for telling the truth – if he had concocted a story not involving sex, he felt that he would have gotten off much more lightly.

The navy had, at long last, recognized the dichotomy in the Radioman rating between operators and technicians, and had done something about it. But the change was done half-assed and left things no better than before. They established a new rating, Communications Yeoman – CYN – and set up a short school for it. But no one could rise higher than third-class in that rating! A CYN3 had to choose between trying to advance to RM2 or YN2. It was no improvement at all for those existing Radiomen who were unable to deal with the hellacious overbalance of technical/electronics questions on their advancement exams. Authority's mindset seemed to be: anybody can do clerical work; we need more techs; we'll force people to become techs if they want to be promoted. I had several CYNs on my watch section.

I was thoroughly content with my new job – at first. Several factors would combine to diminish that pleasure. A factor present from the start was the captain, CDR Douglas Smiley, a mustang. And we got a new Operations Officer and a new RMCM, and I got a new RM1 message center supervisor.

One of my tasks when I had a Monday-Friday day watch was to prepare for and present a morning briefing to the captain (plus, usually, the exec, the ops officer, and maybe others). I grease-penciled in various information on three large plexiglass boards, toted them over to his office, and expounded on their contents. The info was largely statistical: how many messages had been handled over each circuit, which circuits were operating, which transmitters in Gura were down, what ships were terminated with us and copying our broadcasts, any problem areas, and the like.

I heard the captain's comments on these and other matters, and I soon sensed major gaps between his mindset and my own. As I've made clear, I strove constantly to reduce the workload and to do things the easy way. While the captain had no objection to efficiency, he wanted to see the workload *increase*, to see those numbers on the boards go higher. An increase in the amount of traffic handled would enhance Asmara's importance, and therefore his, in the overall world of communications.

While none of the work we do is very important, it is important that we do a great deal of it. (General Peckem, to Colonel Scheisskopf, in *Catch-22*)

A more fundamental disconnect, though, concerned chickenshit – particularly the matter of personal appearance and still more particularly haircuts. After my presentation was done, the captain turned to the others with any other matters on his mind, and I got a feeling for his thoughts. He wanted no part of creeping liberalization and was opposed to any easing off on grooming standards to accommodate changing styles in civilian society. After one of these briefings the captain, disturbed by some enlisted behavior or other, said something about not wanting to run a country club.

Yet country club was just what it was. The captain and other higher-ups sometimes spent part of a work day on the golf course. What was important was haircuts, uniforms, personnel inspections, cleanliness. Decidedly secondary to these were such trivial matters as supporting the ships in our broadcast area and handling the message traffic.

The "generation gap" was previously something I'd known of only by reading about it. On the *FDR* and in Danang, Authority had more important things to worry about (and so did the sailors in those places). In Asmara, Authority did not. The generation gap was present in full force – and so was the drug culture. Marijuana – *hasheesh* – was easily available. Over 30 and not trusted, I was not much confided in by sailors; but from half-heard conversations, hints here and there, I was sure that it was widely in use.

(Some weeks later we received a new ensign, tall and handsome, with a long-legged wife for whom miniskirts were invented. When she came out to Tract F it strained one's neck to pretend to look elsewhere. Not long after arrival they were busted for using marijuana in their quarters, and were returned to the U.S.)

I didn't think much of the ops officer, a bearish mustang LT, and was happy to see his relief arrive – a LCDR who seemed more gentlemanly and agreeable. It was not long before I was wishing that the former one was back.

A new RMCM arrived. They had a chiefs meeting at the CPO club soon afterwards. I had the watch and couldn't go, but Steve could be spared from circuit control and he attended. On his return I asked him if they had introduced the new E-9. Steve said, "Well, it was more like he introduced himself."

"Oh, shit," I said. "Just what we need." One of those.

Not much later the RMCM was reported to have said that no one resigned from the CPO club while *he* was leading chief. I was not the only chief disturbed by this. At a meeting of chiefs he was questioned on it, and – but only when finally pinned down – conceded that he could not prevent such an occurrence. During the talk I kept one hand near my pocket, ready to draw out my wallet and throw my membership card on the table if the outcome had been otherwise.

And then I got my new RM1 message center supervisor. He was about average on the job and a nice-enough guy – but he was the farthest-gone alcoholic I've ever observed. To a degree he had reason: he had five children and at least some of them were behavioral and/or educational problems at the dependent school. He often got inter-office notices from the school concerning them. Every now and then he would not show up for a watch; his wife covered up for him by phoning in to say that he was "sick".

It may have been during one of my morning show-and-tells that the captain discoursed on morale and suggested that CWOs might do well to think about organizing off-duty activities for their watch sections (to cut down on sailor-time in the bars, perhaps). I canvassed my section for interest in a possible trip to Aksum and got about half a dozen takers. The RM1 was one of them; he came without any of his family, and it was on the trip that I first observed his glassy-eyed stagger and realized that he had a problem. In Aksum we found that *foreigners* now had to pay to enter the obelisk area. You got a "guide" with your payment, who would probably have expected a further tip. We declined the guide. A couple of Brits were also there, arguing energetically but unsuccessfully about having to pay to walk farther down the street. One pointed to an Ethiopian walking toward the obelisks and demanded, "Does that man have a ticket?!!"

I also organized a dinner at the CPO club for my watch section, and inquired about possible interest in Tigrinya-language classes (I don't think that was exactly the sort of activity that the captain had in mind). With six or eight interested, I lined up a teacher and we met at my apartment for the classes. What struck the sailors as a good idea when I broached it, rapidly fell off due to short attention span and other attractions; after three or four sessions I had to discontinue the classes.

The most popular activity that I initiated for the section was softball-plus-beer games. Everyone had a great time at the first one and demanded another one at the very next 80. The second one was just as great a time. But the third was on a day with heavy rain. I stayed home but they played in the rain! That was the last one, the newness and the enthusiasm had worn off and the section reverted to their usual pursuits. Bahata was visiting and I brought him to one of the games. He did well, considering that we were short of equipment and he was trying to play third base without a glove.

Yeshu departed for the U.S. in July. She went to work for some Washington insurance firm, remained with them for thirty-some years until she retired, and was a valued employee. When she left, Tekebesh moved in, without asking. She was Yeshu's younger half-sister; she shared the room of Abrehet, the maid; she was no problem and I made no objection. Also moving in without asking was Yeshu's half-brother, Alem. I noticed less cash in my wallet than there should have been, and told the girls to tell him to get out. They were both afraid of him and said that I would have to tell him myself. I did. Not long after, Tekebesh told me he had been arrested downtown for stealing a radio.

Abrehet (the feminine of Abreha = Abraham) had been employed by Yeshu before I arrived. She was absolute perfection as a maid; I upped her salary annually without being asked. She did all the non-commissary shopping and paid bills that needed to be paid downtown such as telephone and electricity. Her cooking was scrumptious; Yeshu had taught her (insofar as she needed teaching). One fondly-remembered specialty was the frozen chicken gizzards that I brought home from the commissary; she prepared them in some kind of yellowish local sauce. I also picked up squid at the commissary, from the Red Sea, frozen rock-hard.

No bureaucracy, military, governmental, or civilian has ever found a way to evaluate underlings fairly, consistently, and accurately. They never will; it is a problem without a solution. They never stop trying, though. Earlier that year the navy had cranked in its most recent attempt, a new evaluation form for chiefs. Chiefs were now to be marked on a type of percentile system – in the top 50%, 30%, 10%, 5%, 1%, or in the bottom of those same percentages. The new system was accompanied by unsurprising propaganda: chiefs were collectively outstanding; no one should be dismayed by a ranking in the lower percentages of such a praiseworthy group; the superiors doing the ranking should make every effort to avoid inflating . . .

It did not take long at all for the left hand and the right hand to get out of synch again. Within two years chiefs applying for some program or other needed a paragraph of explanation for any marks "below top

50%"! Had I applied for (whatever), I would have needed such a paragraph. The first such new form caught me in my first floundering month at Gura; I was given five bottom-50s, two top-50s and seven "unobserveds". I did not think the marks were at all unfair under the circumstances. They may or may not have helped me to fail for selection to RMCM in 1969, the first year I was eligible. The "inflation" which had bedeviled earlier evaluation forms predictably migrated to the new ones in a year or two. I would guess that within five years 90% of chiefs were in the top 5%.

The Overseas Weekly carried a short, elegant letter that I liked so much that I not only clipped it out, I carried it in my wallet for a number of years. It was headed **The Noisy Ones**. (SgtMaj Wooldridge had just been selected as Sergeant Major of the Army.)

> Sergeant Major Wooldridge is typical of the men who have been promoted to E8 and E9 the past few years.
> They are the wheeler-dealers, boisterous and overbearing. The army has always looked on this caliber of NCO as aggressive and as a leader.
> A quietly efficient NCO has never had a chance.
> **Name Withheld by Request**

Later in 1969 I wrote *OW* myself, on a different subject. They headed it **Overseas Shaft**. It was rare, almost unprecedented, for a military case to escape the military judicial system and make it to the Supreme Court, but one had.

> The Supreme Court Decision that servicemen could not be court martialed for essentially civilian crimes was a wise and welcome one. But, predictably, the military has interpreted it as narrowly as possible. They will give up as little jurisdiction as they possibly can, it seems, unless and until forced to do so by future court decision. The serviceman overseas has

benefitted not at all. The military has thus far conceded no limitation on its power to try men for *any* offense overseas.

So now we have a situation where a serviceman can forget the Constitution the day he departs Conus. True, hazards have been cited – a man may go unpunished, or be punished by a foreign court in which he does not enjoy Constitutional guarantees.

There is a standard which should be adopted here: a serviceman overseas, off post, off duty and out of uniform, should come under court-martial jurisdiction – but if and only if the act in question would have been a crime under U.S. Federal or host country law if committed by an American tourist!

Additionally, the military court in such a case should be forbidden to impose any penalty that a local or U.S. Federal court could not impose. Finally, the U.S. should not be permitted to request a waiver of jurisdiction from the host country unless the accused concurs in such request.

There would undoubtedly be undesirable side effects if my above daydream were adopted. Tough! The military's insistence on regulating inherently private off-duty conduct in petty detail is insufferable. Let them live with the consequences of a liberalized law.

Should my daydream ever be adopted by a court (or, much more improbably by Congress – and certainly never, voluntarily, by the military), consider three typical benefits:

Foremost: that most flagrant and intolerable invasion of privacy perpetrated by the military – its assumption that it can require a man to obtain its permission to marry overseas – would be eliminated.

Arbitrary military standards for wear of civilian clothing, likewise.

Off-limits orders would be unenforceable.

In all three instances, the military would be free to use persuasion and guidance to achieve its aims, some of which are legitimate. But the final decision would be up to the individual. This, I submit, is the way it should be.

Name Withheld by Request

The Eritrean rebel movement was becoming of more concern to Authority. Tighter restrictions were put on travel. The primary rebel group at this time was the Eritrean Liberation Front, and one of my sailors made spoof "ELF ID cards" for the whole section. The ELF was not exactly either pro- or anti-American, but their shifta tactics could sometimes put Americans at hazard. One of my CWO duties on midwatches became a tour of the Tract F antenna field, by jeep with the duty ET driving, looking at the green-on-black views through what must have been one of the earlier night-vision devices.

Toward the end of every midwatch, we had to compile and send a lengthy end-of-the-radio-day sitrep (situation report) to Port Lyautey, our nominal superior in the communications world, containing mostly statistical information. Our radio day ended at 0500 local. It often happened that our input was not there in time for *their* morning briefing, and we got complaints. This had no effect on any important or operational matters, but our captain, feeling that it made him look bad, made it a top priority.

Well, OK, if statistics and officer politics were going to be more important than operational traffic . . . I took direct charge of the preparation of the sitrep. Well before the end of the radio day 95% of the necessary information was available. I cut a preliminary tape, sat at the teletype awaiting final numbers from relay and circuit control, and as soon as I had them, I ran the tape through to add them. We had each sitrep on its way ten or fifteen minutes after the hour. No other section matched this or even came close. I never heard a word of praise for it.

With the Suez Canal closed, destroyers transiting to/from Middle East Force had to sail by way of the Cape of Good Hope – through the same communications black hole I had encountered on the *FDR*. There were now three directional antennas down at Gura which could be rotated to point directly at such ships. I came back to work after one 80 to find that none of the other three watches had moved the antennas

349

for three days. Meanwhile, the ships *had* moved. I told Gura to reorient the antennas to where the ships now were. Country club.

We came on one midwatch to find that the ops officer had promulgated a new bit of chickenshit: no food outside the lounge (which was by the building entrance, at the opposite end from the message center). My watch was quite upset. I stayed late after the watch ended, to remonstrate with the ops officer. I tried to make the point that the sailors ate at their working positions rather than in the lounge because they had work to do, backlogs to clear. In short, it was because they were conscientious. It was useless; I had wasted my time talking to him. I later learned that the cause of the new edict was an unsatisfactory zone inspection, featuring among other things the discovery of empty pizza boxes on top of some equipment.

On day watches, a noon meal was trucked out from the army chow hall. One of my duties was to write a report on the quality of the chow. I wrote two kinds: bad ones and worse ones. The super-mess-sergeant of 1961 was long gone, and the army chow had reverted to dismal. And army midrats were even worse than navy midrats, no easy accomplishment.

The traffic officer had formerly been one of the other CWOs. He was probably our most intelligent junior officer, but he was punctilious, by-the-book, and nitpicking to a fault. One morning he approached me with a new document. "Now, chief, . . ." he began, and explained that it was an access list giving the names of those authorized to enter the message center, that it would be posted at the entrance, and that no one not on the list was to be permitted entry unless he or a superior approved. This caught me at a moment when I was particularly annoyed with such folderol; I decided to do exactly as ordered and directed my watchstanders accordingly.

Such access lists were standard practice, but their only real value was to make sure that you did not get gigged for *not* having one posted when an admin inspection came along. For practical purposes everyone knew everyone, the chance of a spy sneaking in was zero, and such lists were taped to a door and forgotten until another admin inspection loomed.

The traffic officer then went down to Gura for the rest of the day. After lunch, the techs who had been working on some message center equipment sought to resume and were refused entry. Shortly I got a call from the ops officer, who asked my reasons, then inquired whether his say-so would move me to allow entry. "Certainly, sir." His words were unspoken but I had the definite impression that he thought *me* blameworthy for the traffic officer's chickenshit.

I had long believed, and occasionally preached, that when given an absurd or ill-advised order and respectful persuasion fails, the thing to do is to carry out the order exactly, and let the consequences fall upon the order-giver. This was the time that my recipe failed. True, I had not tried any "respectful persuasion" – but I did not think it would have worked if I had.

Two lines appeared in *OW* that were worth the price of a year's subscription all by themselves. They resonated especially well with sailors because of our disdain for army methods and procedures:

RIDDLE: What's the difference between the Army and the Cub Scouts?
ANSWER: The Cub Scouts have adult leaders.

On one slow midwatch Herbie, a SpecComm RM3, wandered down to circuit control. The Kagnew radio station disk jockey was playing country music and Herbie expressed his distaste therefor. He left, and the others shook their heads and commented on his musical retardation. I said, "Call the radio station, tell them you're Herbie at Tract F, and you'd like to hear Hank Locklin's *The Country Hall of Fame*." Robbie leaped for the phone with a malicious grin almost before I had finished speaking.

The request was duly played and Herbie returned to express his dismay at the misuse of his name, the misrepresentation of his musical tastes, and the particular tune employed to slander him. He received no sympathy.

A new rear admiral, Marmaduke Bayne, took command of Middle East Force. His name evoked a not-really-derisive sailor comment: "With a name like that, he must be one mean son of a bitch!" He was due to visit Asmara as part of a familiarization tour of his new area of responsibility. Flag officer visits to Asmara were rare. Entertaining such a VIP had to include not just a personnel inspection, but a full-dress personnel inspection, with medals instead of ribbons and the officers wearing swords.

The admiral, the captain, and our other senior officers gathered in front of the assembled sailors. The captain motioned for the admiral to precede him, and I had a hard time to suppress my inner laughter at what happened next. RADM Bayne had come to *work*. He wouldn't forbid the ceremonies, but he wanted to get them done. He strode down the rows at what sailors would call "30 knots". This took the captain so unaware that he had to do a stutter-step to increase his own pace and catch up with the admiral.

The friction between sailors and Authority over hair length steadily increased. With seniors roaring "Haircut" and juniors asking "Why", I was caught in the middle. I had no answers to that *why*, nor did I understand it myself. The sailors continually pushed the limit, wearing their hair as long as they thought they could get away with, and longer. Pressures from above reached the point where I convened the watch section and told them they would have to shorten their hair.

I observed that I had wanted a beard myself for several years and could not have one. I said that downtown the length of their hair would be of less importance than the thickness of their wallets. I thought that I had a fairly decent rapport with my section, even considering the age gap. I thought that I was being funny. The sailors stood stony-faced. Not a laugh. Not even a smile.

I reflected on the matter over the coming days and reached some conclusions. What the hell am I doing, letting Authority make me the bad guy over an emotional, but basically insignificant, issue? I mentally resigned from the hair wars and made a silent promise not again to tell anyone to get a haircut. (If push had ever come to shove, I would have had to break that promise out of self-preservation. But it never did.)

Reading at home, I discovered the answer to the mysterious *why*. I pounded my chair arm in delight, startling Mark. It was a short, simple sentence in Desmond Morris' *The Human Zoo*:

Inevitably, dominant animals try to control the behaviour of their subordinates.

The answer that had eluded me for so long was *Because I say so, godammit, that's why!* And I wondered whether Authority ever realized how obviously it displayed its simian affinities. (In many of the places that I have written capital-A *Authority* herein, I could have replaced it with "The Dominant Animal" with no loss of accuracy.)

My alcoholic RM1 was "sick" one time too often. It happened when I had just received an embarrassing memo from another chief concerning his drinking and his absences. I had let it slide for far too long without doing anything about him. I told the watch to call his home and tell him that he had to come in sick or not. He did – and this was the time he truly was sick. He was not at all drunk, but was miserable from a cold and/or flu. I apologized for making him come in when he was in such condition, discussed his drinking with him, ordered him to see a doctor at the army hospital about it, and sent him back home. He saw the doctor, and he went on the wagon for a spell, but it did not last. About six months after I left the section he was sent to a navy drying-out facility in Long Beach, California. I saw his name on a list of retirees a few years later, still RM1. I was pleased that he had stayed dry enough long enough to reach that goal, at least.

For his birthday I gave one of my best watchstanders, a CYN3, the night off. One RM3, an ordinary performer, then decided that he was just as good and should get his birthday off too. When I didn't give it to him, he showed up for the midwatch staggering drunk. I told his supervisor, "Take him back to the barracks and put him on report." The traffic chief pleaded with me to withdraw the report chit. (I do not know his motive.) I resisted, but he approached me again and begged me to allow him to substitute some sort of extra duty in place of a captain's mast. I reluctantly yielded.

On the night the RM3 was supposedly performing his penance, I happened to pass some sports-field bleachers and saw him sitting in the top row. I didn't say anything. I gave up.

The navy had introduced a couple of new wrinkles into the E-8/E-9 promotion processes. Instead of going strictly by test scores, slightly modified by such things as time in rate, medals, etc., there would now be an interview panel at each command and a selection board in Washington would pass the final judgments. After my 1969 miss, I was pessimistic and feared that I might have reached my ceiling at E-8. The other new wrinkle was a list of alternates, to be used if retirement, death, newly-found budget money, or the like opened additional promotion slots.

I was, to my surprise, seventh on the alternate list. They later promoted the first *six*.

One of the flaws in the interview idea was that at a large command few of the candidates would be known to the interviewers, while at a small command like Asmara everyone knew everyone and preconceived judgments could not be kept out of the process. The evaluations by the interviewers were supposed to be confidential, never to be seen by the interviewee. But the Yeomen at Asmara hosed this up and copies of my 1969-70-71 interview sheets found their way into my service record. I had expected the RMCM to give me my worst writeups. I was wrong; his were fair. The worst ones came from the ops officer.

For some time I had been expecting to move up to the operations chief position when the incumbent RMCS ended his tour in mid-1970.

As that time neared, I began to perceive disquieting indications that I might not. Another RMCS was ordered in about that time. I learned that he was junior to me (albeit by only two months), but he had been stationed with the RMCM at some previous duty station and they were friends.

A new traffic officer would be taking over the traffic division at about the same time. He had been CWO on another section, had observed my work, and thought highly of me. He wanted me to be his traffic chief (yet another job that was about to be vacated). I would have liked to do it; I thought there was much I could accomplish in that position. But the increasing possibility of being overlooked for operations chief disturbed me. I told the prospective traffic officer that I would be happy to become traffic chief, temporarily, for about six months, with the understanding that I would thereafter move up to operations chief. He said that he would talk to the ops officer about it.

The answer was no, that if I became traffic chief I would stay there for the rest of my tour. He asked me again if I would take it. I said, "*Not voluntarily, sir."

When you are passed over for a job in favor of someone who is not only junior to you, but also newly arrived, it leaves no doubt about the level of esteem in which you are held. I shortly found myself shitcanned to a nothing-job: education & training chief/career counselor. I had been neatly and surgically marginalized. I remarked to friends that given the circumstances it was probably the best thing that could happen to me; at least it got me out of the operations department. I do not think I even entered the operations building again during the remaining year of my tour. I heard that it had been said of me that I liked my job (true, in spite of frustrations) and did not want to come off my watch section (a lie). I never blamed the new RMCS for any of this; he had nothing to do with it and indeed turned out to be quite a nice guy.

My new location was in a building housing the captain, exec, administration and personnel offices, supply, public works, mailroom, and my office. My duties, such as they were, entailed (1) helping sailors obtain various correspondence courses, both naval and college, and enrolments in the U. of Maryland extension courses taught on Kagnew Station; (2) prodding sailors to become eligible for advancement – practical factors, performance tests, and required courses – and monitoring the exams when given; and of course (3) career counseling, just what the name implies. The admin officer, my new boss, was civil service, an alcoholic old maid who might have been attractive 20 or 30 years earlier. I had no problem getting along with her.

At just about the time of my job-change, I read news in *Navy Times* which was so unexpected that it was nearly impossible to believe. The outgoing Chief of Naval Operations had, shortly before his departure, legalized beards! He may have consulted with his relief, Admiral Elmo Zumwalt, before doing this – and I suspect that ADM Zumwalt may even have been the real initiator. ADM Zumwalt went on to make additional changes that had been heretofore unthinkable, getting rid of much chickenshit and outmoded tradition, and generally improving navy life.

Beards had always been legal, as I mentioned in the *USS Iowa* chapter. The catch was that you had to request permission to grow one. As beards began to be identified with radicalism, drugs, and the 1960s counterculture, such permission became less and less likely, and virtually vanished. Those few commanding officers who might have had no objection to beards themselves, nevertheless feared the wrath of frowning higher-ups. Thus beards had been *de facto* illegal for some years.

I was told that the reluctant captain, in a staff meeting, said, "Well, OK, let 'em have their beards . . ." (As if he had a choice.) Rear-guard actions were fought: you had to submit a special request chit to grow, the navy drill team could not have them, there was talk (unfulfilled) of a ban in the CPO club and in the army clubs. But beards sprouted everywhere. I think more than half of the E-6 and below, and several of the junior officers, sported them. Only four chiefs besides me opted for beards; none of the others kept them for very long.

I filled out a request chit. When the admin officer read it, she looked at me in wonder and said, "*You're joking!"

I snapped a curt reply: "*I'm not." She said never mind the chit, those were for the young sailors.

I patterned my mustache-and-goatee on Vladimir Lenin, partly because I suspected no other role-model would be likelier to displease Authority. A deeper reason perhaps stretched back to childhood and subconscious admiration of comic-book personages – Doctor Doom? Mandrake the Magician? A sailor on my former watch section asked me whether, now that I had the beard I'd wanted, he could have long hair. I encouraged him to hope for the future.

After a later staff meeting, the supply officer paused at the door of my office and told me in a hushed voice, "Hey, chief, the captain really doesn't like your beard." He meant well, and possibly believed that when so informed I would take immediate steps to regain the captain's approval, but I did not care whether the captain liked my beard or not. I cared only that he could not stop me from wearing it. I had to make a slight modification to the beard for four months in 1977, but aside from that it remained unchanged ever after (except for becoming too damn *gray*).

The navy had a ping-pong tournament. I think I finished third. The top player was Bruce Matthews, who had once been junior champion of Ohio. He was one of the best players I've ever faced, and the practice games I played with him were the most enjoyable in my memory. I won maybe 20-25% of the time in practice games but in a tournament game against him I would have had no chance.

In 1961 there had also been a tournament, and I had been selected for a team to play downtown against the locals, mostly Italians. It was a rout; we lost all five matches and I do not think we even won a game. The Italians had been led by Massimo Fenili, champion of Ethiopia. In 1970 I contacted him and arranged a rematch. It took place in the Kagnew gym after a basketball game. I won my match, and Bruce defeated Massimo. Massimo had told me that he was not the Massimo of old. Had a time machine been available and the Massimo of 1961 pitted against the Bruce of 1970 . . . I would not wish to predict the winner.

Bruce was also one of the stars on the navy basketball team, deadly from three-point range (at a time when the three-point rule was not yet invented). The navy in 1959-61 and again in 1969 had had good teams, but chronically finished second to one of the several army teams. Our team in 1970-71 was superb, certainly the equal of small-college and maybe major-college teams. It was said, and I think it was probably true, that the captain had pulled strings in Washington to get good basketballers assigned to Asmara. They outclassed the army so far that when an all-star team was selected the army got only one berth. There was an army-imposed rule against dunking. At the end of each pre-game warmup, the navy center would deliberately sink a dunk. Whistle. Technical foul. The navy could easily spot their opponents a point or two, and did so to register their disapproval of the rule!

The army had a weekly newspaper, the *Kagnew Gazelle*, and the navy had a monthly: *CommSta Commentary*. One day just before lunch hour the latter was being distributed around Tract F when there was panic. Chiefs and officers were seizing and retrieving all the copies they could recover. There is no surer way to arouse curiosity and interest. When the captain returned from lunch and was informed of the cause, he said to go ahead and distribute them. The offending sentence was in a stream-of-consciousness, gossip-type column that poked monthly fun at the foibles of various sailors. It read: *Captain Smiley: your son likes long hair, why don't you?* (The captain's teenage son, with shoulder-length hair, was visiting Asmara.) I gathered that the writer of the column was thoroughly chewed out by several chiefs and was more circumspect thereafter. The captain's green-light raised my opinion of him.

The Overseas Weekly published an editorial inveighing against segregated bars in Germany, whose owners discriminated against black soldiers, and argued that the army should use its off-limits authority against such places. I wrote a letter. They headed it **Freedom**.

I didn't believe it could happen but it did. The law of averages must be responsible. You finally published an editorial opinion I have to disagree with.

It was in your "Serve Me, Serve My Buddy" editorial of July 19. You ask whether the Army has a right to place a segregated bar off limits. You answer yes and refute five possible objections. Four times out of five I agree with you.

But your fifth objection was: "The Army has no right to tell me where I can and can't go off duty." AMEN.

Your answer was: "That's a good point." (AMEN again.) "But (you continue) has the Army a right to put a VD-infested whorehouse, or a crooked car dealer or an unsanitary swimming pool off limits? Then it sure as hell should do the same for segregated bars."

My answer is: The Army has a right, indeed an obligation to *inform* troops of VD hazards, conmen, unsanitary conditions – and segregated establishments. But once this information has been given, the Army has performed its function. It should NOT have the right to enforce its policies, no matter how praiseworthy, by off-limits orders.

I'm 100 percent behind integration; I hate bigots. But I am also 100 percent behind civil liberties and I hate military authoritarians who ignore them. I hope this German bar owner is completely successful in court. But (if he was truly trying to run a segregated bar as charged) I also hope he goes bankrupt.

As long as the military has the authority to place establishments off limits, said authority can be and, doubtless, will be abused. Several years ago there was a bar just across the street from where I worked. It was THE place to go. One night a young serviceman with emotional problems drank himself nearly to death there. He was hospitalized. The command was embarrassed. They had to make embarrassing

359

reports to higher-ups and to the man's parents. They had to "do something"! What did they do? Why of course – they slapped the bar off limits for several weeks. For serving the man when he was intoxicated!

Another objection to off-limits authority is that it opens the road to graft. How easy it would be for an MP or CID type to tell a bar owner: "Your establishment doesn't meet the standards we have set if GIs are to patronize it . . . but maybe it can be overlooked . . . etc." Such shenanigans may never have happened; I have heard only the vaguest rumors. But for those who would dismiss it as fantastic, who would have believed, three years ago, that an NCO conspiracy was milking the clubs dry?

If a court ever does declare off-limits orders illegal, there will be a welcome side effect. A problem you recently complained about in HOTLINE will be solved – that of German bars who display off-limits signs on their own initiative, solely in order to discourage GI patronage.

It comes down to a question of means and ends. When you imply that off-limits orders are all right if used for a good cause, I am reminded of Spiro and his law-and-order lackeys who would attain the desirable goal of crime reduction by curbing Constitutional freedoms and passing repressive laws.

RMCS Larry Bucher
NAVCOMMSTA
APO 09843

I was surprised when a black RM2 came into my office to compliment me on the letter. He had gotten a copy of *OW* before I got mine. I had ended my letter with my customary "Please withhold my name and duty station" but there was a lapse at the linotype in Frankfurt. The RM2 feared that I might have overstepped in disrespect to Spiro Agnew, then vice president. I got no other feedback, pro or con, from anyone in Asmara. I was surprised, and pleased, to receive a letter from Curt

Daniell thanking me for my letter, agreeing with many of my points, and conceding that in some ways I was righter than he was.

Not two weeks after writing me, Daniell was fired. The owner/publisher of *OW* since its inception had died, and *OW* had been purchased by a California businessman, Joseph B. Kroesen. A portion of the *International Herald Tribune* account:

> . . . Mr. Daniell said that under the terms of his resignation agreement, he was not in a position to discuss the issues leading to his departure . . . Mr. Kroesen had objected to Mr. Daniell's policy of exposing racial discrimination at Army posts . . . the editor had "made fun of the generals."

For the next four months *OW* turned into an insipid army lapdog, publishing little or nothing that might upset generals.

One of our ET1s was promoted to chief. At his initiation, the first charge read against him was impersonating an officer. His name was (really) John Paul Jones.

The U.S. Information Service officer in Asmara began a Quiz Bowl program on Kagnew's Armed Forces TV, patterned after U.S. TV's GE College Quiz Bowl. I was on the navy team, which was led by an RM3 who had formerly appeared for his school on the stateside program. In our first appearance we won easily against a team of army officers. The following week we were matched against the army hospital. Our first performance had been so dominating that the USIS MC skewed the questions a bit toward medicine and biology. We lost, but received a later rematch with the hospital which we won. The hospital featured a Dr Levine; he and I were the two 800-pound gorillas of the shows. But neither we nor the hospital finished as champions – the final was between the navy and the U.S. Consulate, which had no outstanding star but had a good and well-balanced team which bested us. The

MC then began a new series; the first show was another navy-hospital rematch – which ended in a tie!

The MC then wanted to do a re-rematch, but I was leaving before it could air and there were other obstacles. I heard that the MC's next post was in Nigeria where he wanted to do a similar show but was prevented by Nigerian policy – no white faces on TV! I regret never crossing paths with Dr Levine again; I've long wished I could face him over a Trivial Pursuit board.

Late 1970 and early 1971 were plagued by two shortages: water and peanut butter. The latter was shorthand for a general shortage of numerous items in the Kagnew commissary. Peanut butter was perhaps the one that had been sold out longest, had become symbolic, and was the item most cited. The army alibied for its shortcomings by pleading Asmara's distant location at the end of a long supply line from U.S. sources. Anent which I commented, "Yeah, and that's only been true for the last fifteen-some years . . ."

The big rains in Asmara start (maybe) in mid-July and dwindle off about mid-September. They can be real cloudbursts at times. I once disoriented some of my watchstanders who were watching a downpour from the doorway by directing, "You three start rounding up all the scrap lumber you can find. The rest of you, start looking for two of every animal." There is also a shorter and smaller rainy season in February-March. If you were looking for the big rains in summer 1970, and if you blinked, you would have missed them. The entire city was affected; at the height of the drought running water was available for only a few hours a day. Drastic conservation measures were recommended: save dishwater to flush toilets, do not flush them for urine only, shower briefly and less often, etc., etc.

I was immune to the water shortage. The four-apartment building wherein Yeshu had located was one of a rare few that had a rooftop storage tank. It was pumped full each time the water was on. If I had never left the apartment, I would not even have known there *was* any water shortage. I kept quiet about my lucky circumstances as I listened

362

to the woes of others; I did not want to flaunt my good fortune in front of those who were undergoing harsh inconvenience.

Armed Forces Radio & TV was looking for suggestions on how they might improve their service and operations. I suggested to the captain that they might consider pronouncing Kagnew correctly. He scoffed at this as nit-picking.

Maybe. I thought, then and still, that, having named our station with a word from the local language, we could have had the minimal courtesy to say it right, over the air at least.

(I suppose the Italians, or maybe the French influence in Addis Abeba, and that *gn* sound could be blamed. If the word had been first transliterated Kanyew, as an English-speaker would have done, the mispronunciation would never have arisen.)

On the very day my divorce became final, someone chanced to ask me if I was married. I had no idea whether finality came at midnight, noon, or the following midnight, nor did I know whether DC time or Asmara time applied. The only honest answer I could give was, "*I don't know."

I had a case of diarrhea, a benevolent one which I wish I could keep on call and reactivate when desired. It lasted for a month, but was not particularly virulent or bothersome. Everything emerged liquid, but I went on no mad dashes for the head. The good part was that I lost ten pounds without even trying. Imagine the riches if someone could isolate that specific bug, patent it, and get it FDA-approved . . .

On an idle day I was nosing through the Awards Manual and noticed a friendly-sounding sentence near its end to the effect that anyone with questions or concerns could write to them. I did so. Two medals had been issued during the Cuban missile crisis: navy expeditionary and armed forces expeditionary. A ship might be eligible for one or both, depending on where it had been and when. From reading the geographical and time-period eligibility criteria in *Navy Times*, and from knowing where the *Rhodes* had been, and when, I knew she should have been eligible for both. But the bureaucracy malfunctioned and she made the eligibility list for only one. I thought this would be rectified sooner or later, but it never had been. Based on the deceptively-inviting sentence in the manual, I informally pointed this out.

They didn't answer *me*. They mailed their form-letter reply to the command, with a snotty box checked: "It is requested that subject member be instructed as to the proper method of submitting official communications to the Bureau." (Translation: I had not gone through the chain of command.) They then went on to tell us what I already knew, that I was eligible for the one medal but not the other. The authors of that response are among those exempted from this book's dedication.

I spotted a new item being displayed by the street peddlers – a tapestry with the heads of John F. Kennedy, Robert Kennedy, and Martin Luther King. I would not deign to haggle with, and be overcharged by, a street boy, so I sent Tekebesh out to purchase it for me. It is a bit faded now, but has hung in a prominent place in my living room ever since.

Mark came down with some illness that was initially diagnosed as tuberculosis. He, and I with him as the only family at post, was medevaced to the army hospital at Landstuhl, Germany, in the Black Forest. It was dismal late-winter, cloudy and rainy. I stayed in a transient facility and visited Mark every day. They never did decide what his malady was, except that it was not tuberculosis. We returned to Asmara after about five weeks. An RMC had been assigned to my job in my absence and since I had only some three months remaining they left him there. I was not given any job; just sat in the office along with him.

I had submitted my preferences for U.S. shore duty a bit before this. When I left Asmara I would have 12 years and two months on continuous sea and/or foreign duty. A few other sailors probably matched or exceeded that at some point in their careers, but not very many. It was sure to give me preference over nearly all others who were competing for openings in the same time-frame. I made an unorthodox and very broad first choice: Anywhere Eighth *or* Ninth Naval District. I wanted to avoid the big bases on the coasts: Norfolk, San Diego, etc. The Eighth was in New Orleans and included Texas and a few other nearby states. The Ninth was in Great Lakes and took in all of the midwest. Shortly after returning from Germany I received my orders: the Naval Air Station in Dallas, Texas. I was delighted. The only thing I did not like about it was Dallas' reputation as right-wing heaven, but I thought I could live with that.

The army had a problem. The school children were bussed the short distance from the school to the club where they ate lunch. Adults were deemed necessary to ride the buses as escorts, zookeepers, or whatever. Volunteers were sought from among the mothers. The number of volunteers became insufficient, despite pleas. The army solved its problem in typical army fashion. The *fathers* were assigned to the bus duty, with the proviso that a wife could substitute for the assigned man – but if she did not, the man *would* perform the duty.

And so I performed that duty, tight-jawed and stony-faced, several times. I steamed, but if Authority could not recognize that some might have different circumstances, I was damned if I was going to beg for special treatment.

In 1970 Congress had passed a new law providing for fiancee visas for prospective foreign brides (or husbands). I had rejoiced when I learned of it; I obtained forms and information from the consulate and set Jamroon to doing what needed to be done in Bangkok. The paperwork was still daunting, but at least no *permission* was required and there was now a dignified and legal alternative to the humiliating military procedure.

And another factor came in to play at just the right time for me. Wives in the U.S. were now organizing charter flights to Bangkok and back, in order to meet husbands on R&R from Vietnam. I corresponded with one of the organizers, inquiring whether one-way passage out of Bangkok might be possible. It often was, some of the wives stayed longer in Bangkok. As my time shortened, things began to fall in place to perfection. A flight was leaving Bangkok at the right time, it would stop in Anchorage, Alaska, and then at two places in the lower 48. The first of those two stops was *Dallas!* I bought six tickets. I had decided that Jamroon's two oldest, in their later teens, were too old for the cultural and linguistic transition and would remain in Bangkok. The others were 12, 10, and 8 – plus a two-year-old that was "ours". Meanwhile I had arranged for Mark to travel separately, with another chief and his wife who were returning to the U.S., and spend some time with his mother in Washington until we got settled in Dallas.

In mid-December *OW* had printed a list of air force terms used on performance reports, and their translations. It follows:

Exceptionally Well Qualified – Has Committed No Major Blunders To Date

Active Socially – Drinks Heavily

Wife Is Active Socially – She Drinks Too

Character and Integrity Above Reproach – Still One Step Ahead Of The Law

Zealous Attitude – Opinionated

Unlimited Potential – Will Retire As Sgt/Major

Quick Thinking – Offers Plausible Excuses For Errors

Exceptional Flying Ability – Has Equal Number of Takeoffs and Landings

Takes Pride In His Work – Conceited

Takes Advantage Of Every Opportunity To Progress – Buys Drinks For Supervisors

Forceful And Aggressive – Argumentative

Outstanding – Frequently in the Rain

Indifferent to Instruction – Knows More Than His Seniors

Tactful In Dealings With Superiors – Knows When To Keep His Mouth Shut

Approaches Difficult Problems With Enthusiasm – Finds Someone Else To Do The Job

A Keen Analyst – Thoroughly Confused

Definitely Not The Desk Type – Did Not Go To College

Expresses Himself Well – Speaks English Fluently
Often Spends Extra Hours On The Job – Miserable Home Life
A True Southern Gentleman – A Hillbilly
Conscientious And Careful – Scared
Meticulous in Attention To Detail – A Nit-Picker
Demonstrates Qualities Of Leadership – Has A Loud Voice
Judgment Is Usually Sound – Lucky
Maintains Professional Attitude – A Snob
Keen Sense Of Humor – Has A Vast Repertoire of Jokes
Strong Adherence To Principles – Stubborn
Career Minded – Hates Reserves
Gets Along Well With Superiors And Subordinates Alike – A Coward
Average NCO/Officer – Not Too Bright
Slightly Below Average – Stupid
A Very Fine NCO/Officer Of Great Value To The Service – Gets To Work On Time

I liked these so well that I wrote a navy version. For the time being, I sat on it. It now follows:

Unseamanlike – A teetotaler and/or undersexed
Gets the most out of his men – A desk-pounder
Dislikes authority – Thinks for himself
Flouts authority – Won't brown-nose
Always acts in the highest traditions of the Navy – A. John Paul Jones Jr. (rare); B. A sacred cow worshiper disguised as A. (common)
Poor supervisor – His men like him
Commands respect of both seniors and juniors – Kisses above; chews below
Needs routine supervision – Smarter than I am
Needs constant supervision – A genius
Impractical – Takes Adm Zumwalt seriously
Helps morale – Takes showers
Contributes to good morale – Drinks
Promotes good morale – Brings the booze
A good shipmate – Bisexual

Potential petty officer – Won't get a BCD before the next exam
Intelligent – Reads *Stars and Stripes*
Very intelligent – Believes *Stars and Stripes*
Highly intelligent – Works the *Stars and Stripes* crossword puzzle
Actively pursuing his education – Reads *Reader's Digest* on midwatches
Cooperative – Doesn't make waves
Impressive military appearance – Shaves
Dedicated to the Navy – Comes back to work in the afternoon
Has devised new programs – An empire-builder
Conscientious – Covers his ass
Excellent attitude – Might re-enlist
Could do better – A short-timer
A misfit – Sane

In mid-January I began to read a new issue of *OW* and thought, "damn, this sounds just like the *old OW*." I looked at the masthead and Curt Daniell's name was back as editor. Then I read his editorial, which confirmed that he had been rehired, praised the new owner, and promised that *OW* would revert to its former self. I assume legions of soldiers had shared my contempt for the Daniell-less *OW* and circulation had plummeted. I sent Daniell a long and delighted welcome-back letter, and enclosed my imitative effort at defining navy terminology, which he printed.

But it was too good to last. In the last issue of *OW* that I ever read (June), Daniell's name had once again disappeared from the masthead. I had been thinking of renewing my subscription, to receive *OW* in the U.S., but had already decided against it. Apparently I had made a good decision, but I saw no news stories and had no knowledge of the second firing and subsequent events, so what follows is largely speculation and guesses.

A book should have been written about *OW* – from its origins on, but especially covering 1970-71 and later. It is a disappointment that neither Daniell nor another ex-*OW* staffer ever wrote that book. There was an army major general surnamed Kroesen in Europe at this time.

Was he related to the new owner? It is not a very common name. I have long wondered whether, following the death of the original owner, the army took an interest in who would succeed her, with the aim of accomplishing a devious, back-door transformation of *OW* into something the army could live with.

Daniell apparently stayed in Europe, took employment on the German economy, and never worked in journalism again. It was a sad waste of talent. He was a great one and would have become greater. The castrated *OW* limped along for a few years; it seems to have ceased publication somewhere around 1975.

In early June I reenlisted for two years. My six-year 1962 enlistment had been followed by three years worth of extensions for various purposes. The two-year hitches were something new, four had long been the minimum. The shorter option was both good and bad – good because you could cash in up to 60 days worth of unused leave at each reenlistment. And bad because you earned 60 days worth in two years. Thus, needing money more than time in those years, I was taking no leave at all in order to collect the cash! Later on, perhaps wising up to this, Authority ended the two-year enlistments.

Mark had sometimes said that he wished he had brothers or sisters. When I showed him a picture of his prospective new family, he wasn't quite so sure about "that many".

I submitted a special request chit for circuitous travel, via not only Bangkok but four or five other cities in the far east. The others were smoke-screen. Except for two or three army guys, friends of Tekebesh who sometimes came to the apartment, no other Americans knew of my marriage plans. If any last-minute complications developed about that fiancee visa, I intended to marry permissionless in Bangkok and let the chips fall. Other chiefs nodded their heads wisely about my itinerary, assuming that I was off for a sex tour. (Under different circumstances, I would have been.)

Kagnew Station was beginning to employ a few female gate guards, in order to search local women who worked on the base. I asked around, talked to some people, and got Tekebesh hired. (A few years later she made it into the U.S., where she met and married a retired sergeant.) I sent Abrehet to English classes and got her a job with a newly-arrived American family. I saw Mark off, and on 7 July with all Asmara loose ends tied up I headed for Bangkok.

XVII - BIG D

The long-awaited reunion with Jamroon was a goal finally attained, but there were still loose visa-ends to be tied and I was worried at times. Everything did sort itself out in time, Jamroon got her oldest daughter married off, and the six of us flew out of Bangkok in late July. I don't remember how long the flight took, but it was *long*, and a grueling one. Unlike current airliners there was a good bit of room under the seats; I was able to stretch out (with legs bent) and get some sleep on the cabin floor, as did some of the others. We went through customs and immigration at Anchorage in the too-cool-for-July nighttime. We were all open-mouthed at the enormous stuffed Kodiak bear, posed standing up on its hind legs in the airport rotunda.

In Dallas we found a motel and recuperated. I was low on cash but had Republic Bank of Dallas money orders with me. That bank had the military money-order concession. The money orders were sold on the base in Asmara; I had used them to send money to Jamroon and to Yeshu and had used them as *de facto* traveler's checks in Asia, where they were accepted without question. I went to a friendly neighborhood bank and tried to cash one. It was my first experience (but would not be my last) with reverse culture shock. The bank was courteous enough but not friendly enough: they wouldn't deign to cash it *unless* I had an account with them. They seemed to think it strange that I expected them to cash it. I could have cashed it at any bank in Bangkok. I needed a refresher course on some U.S. business practices, notably those of banks. The motel owner would have cashed it for me, but it was $200 {$1003} and he didn't have that much on hand.

This happened on a Friday afternoon and we spent a stringent weekend eating the cheapest meal at a nearby restaurant and subsisting on peanut butter and crackers. By Monday I had only coins left, enough to take a bus downtown to the Republic Bank, and cashing was not automatic there. The teller referred me to a dignitary who pondered and decided that since it was *their* money order, they would indeed have to cash it for me. Believing now that any friendly neighborhood bank, wherever we settled, would have been equally unhelpful, I opened a Republic Bank account while I was there.

After getting the necessary blood tests, Jamroon and I were married on 28 July 1971 at the Dallas County Courthouse, overlooking Dealey Plaza of JFK-assassination infamy. By the calendar we had known each other for two years and nine months. Measured by time actually spent in each other's company, it was scarcely four weeks. The marriage lasted for 33 years until I lost her to cancer. Nor was I ever unfaithful.

The next need was to rent a car. More reverse culture shock: the first two companies I called would not do business with me unless I had a credit card! A third would do so on the basis of a military ID card, and did. This soured me on credit cards; I resented *needing* to own one for anything and it was another six years before I yielded.

Checking in at the Naval Air Station, the first thing I heard was an Asmaran fart blown at me. It came from Wally, an RM1 who had been at Gura during my short stint there and who remembered me well. The second thing I heard was congratulations. The promotion lists were out and this time (my third try) I was not on the alternate list, I was on *the* list. I was number seven. Budgetary reasons hosed up the promotion schedule, to my disadvantage. The first *six* RMCMs were to be promoted in September. The next segment was not until February. But I had made it, and did not greatly bemoan the unfortunate timing.

We moved into family transient quarters on the NAS temporarily, while house-hunting. We bought a house in the Oak Cliff district of southwest Dallas, from where the drive to the NAS was a convenient

15-20 minutes. The NAS was not in Dallas but just west thereof, in the suburb of Grand Prairie.

The former owner was a "good ol' boy", ex-Dallas policeman. He was moving to a smaller town in east Texas; I later heard that he had either been fired, or forced to retire, by Dallas due to his racist actions. If what I heard was accurate, he had stomped right across the hood of a black driver who had blocked his way at a crosswalk. We made a gentleman's agreement whereby I paid him a month's rent so that we could move in right away. If closing of the sale took place before the end of that month, he was to refund a proportionate amount. At closure he owed me about $50 {$251}. He never paid it. Good ol' boys are not necessarily gentlemen.

If I sometimes encountered reverse culture shock, Jamroon sometimes ran in to the primary version. On our first shopping trip to the small mall nearby, I had bought a gallon of motor oil. Later that day I could not find it. Jamroon, not knowing what it was, had put it in the refrigerator with other groceries.

The primary activity at the NAS was the training of reserves. This took place on weekends, and consequently the station work week was Wednesday-Sunday. Many of the NAS people were TARs – Training and Administration Reserves. It was a strange status and I never fully understood it. They were reserves – but it was as if they were on permanent, full-time active duty. They did not get sea duty and did not go overseas, but rotated around the States to reserve activities. They were unamused by the riddle that popped into my mind one day:
What's the definition of a substitute prostitute?
A fucking reserve.

The nerve center of NAS was a two-story building just inside the main gate. In addition to communications, it contained the offices of the captain and other senior officers, admin, personnel, switchboard, legal/security, and others. The comm officer and my immediate boss was Jerry Picha, a civilian; we shared a two-desk office. My watchstanders

373

were a mixed bag of sailors and civil service, two to a watch. An RMC and a civil service day worker rounded out the message center.

Jerry was an ideal boss. He had a lot of respect for chiefs, and it was more like I was working with him than working for him. I had a two- or three-month overlap with the incumbent RMCM who was retiring, so I had plenty of break-in time. It was the least-challenging job I had had in quite some time (excluding that last nothing-year in Asmara).

When my VW arrived in the U.S. I had to fly to New Orleans to pick it up and drive it back. One day we were driving somewhere with four or five younger children crowded into the back – some of ours, some of their friends – when someone produced a silent-but-deadly. Accusations, denials, and counter-accusations flew. I said, "*Allll right – whoever did it, laugh."

Dead silence for maybe ten seconds, fifteen. Then one little girl leaked a *teeheehee*. I said, "*Ah-HA!" Her lengthy protestations of innocence, of irrepressible laughter, were to no avail.

I heard that I was likely to have to attend a "CPO Academy" elsewhere in Texas for a week or two. Skeptics described it as "boot camp for chiefs". It was said that one of its impositions was being required to possess, or to buy, a CPO overcoat – some $70-90 {$351-451}, and me in the Texas climate! I would not have done it, unless the consequences of refusing were sure enough and grim enough to force me. Anyhow some factor, probably budgetary, saved me from being sent thereto.

Back in 1956, in London, I had been solicited by one of the chiefs to contribute to a Red Cross drive. I have never liked to be pressured to do something that is – theoretically – voluntary. I declined, but when no one was looking I dropped $10 {$73} in a contribution box in the message center.

When I was on the *Rhodes* I often saw charity-drive messages on the fleet broadcast, coming from various admirals, and preserved some of them. Some excerpts:

> . . . The goal is 100 percent participation by every officer and man. Each commanding officer must personally stimulate and motivate his crew toward this worthy goal. A minimum of $2.00 {$13} per capita will meet this years quota. Maximum effort by all on 15 Oct pay-day will bring the fleet's campaign to a successful conclusion. . . . Now is the time for all of us to let our leadership and community spirit shine. . . .

> . . . Many reports are commendatory, the largest being $7.14 {$46} per person. Others obviously are incomplete, the lowest being $.05 {33¢} per person. With but two paydays remaining in the drive it is necessary that intense command attention generate generous giving if Newport personnel are to pull their weight. . . .

> Commander Cruiser Destroyer Force desires to emphasize the fact that this campaign is endorsed by him wholeheartedly. . . . Contributions given in past years should be surpassed. 100 percent participation through individual solicitation and fair share giving is strongly encouraged.

> . . . although a quota, as such, is neither required nor desired, I do seek 100 percent participation through individual solicitation . . .

Can anyone doubt that commanding officers receiving such exhortations, and reading between the lines, are not tempted to pressure the unwilling into "donating"?

During my short stay at Gura I was assigned – not asked but assigned – to be keyman for a charity drive. The keyman materials were filled with exclamation points. They came very close to ordering me to contribute myself, to set an example. I did not contribute, and I put no pressure on the sailors, just collected money from those who voluntarily chose to donate. One sailor, as he gave me his money, expressed some reluctance about it. I assured him that he did not have to donate. He said, "Yeah, I know they say that, but . . .", and he persisted in donating.

Two years later I listened to a keyman explaining how he had attained the sacred goal of 100%. "X and Y weren't going to give, but I changed their minds. Z still wouldn't give, but Miss Walsh *gave for him*."

What does all of this digression have to do with a chapter on Dallas?

This: the most popular radio talk show in Dallas was hosted by Rob Roddy – he who as *Rod* Roddy went on to national recognition on *The Price Is Right*. Not all talk radio had yet degenerated into right-wing venom. His show was heard in the message center every morning. A United Way campaign in Dallas was underway. One week Roddy talked with numerous callers who were being threatened with loss of job or otherwise pressured to "give". He expressed indignation at the arm-twisting and sympathy with the twistees.

He was fired.

That cemented opinions I had held for years. I regard big charity with the same skepticism with which I regard big business, big government, big labor, big media, big you-name-it. I blame the navy for the tactics which it used (along with the other services, the rest of government, and private businesses). But more than that I blame the charities themselves. They cannot plead ignorance of the methods used to extort "contributions". They innocently accept the money raised and have made themselves almost immune to criticism. Their ability to silence dissent is scary.

Jamroon loved to fish. I did not, but I sometimes ferried her to a park near our house with a small lake. While in Asmara I had bought a cheap mail-order metal detector. (Yeshu had told me of how her mother buried valuables under the fire in her hut – but travel had been so restricted by then that I only tried to use it once and found only a piece of metal scrap.) I took it along to the lake one day, to give me something to do while Jamroon fished. I found a few pennies, a nickel or two, and an abundance of flip-tops and bottle caps. Then later in the day when light was fading, when Jamroon had given up fishing and joined me, I turned up a gleaming silver Mercury dime.

It was from 1945, the last year the Mercuries were coined, and one of the commonest. But I had not seen one for many years. I was hooked. So was Jamroon, and the kids were interested also. Jerry Picha was not only a "coinshooter" (a term for the hobby), he had an out-of-the-pocket dealership with a Dallas company that manufactured detectors. Before long we owned several detectors, better ones, and prowled every park and schoolground within a wide radius of our home. We often turned up silver coins (it was only six years since they were last minted). We found an occasional Indian-head penny, an occasional ring, and many thousands of uninventoried flip-tops and bottle caps.

One of the more unusual items was a flexible sort of metal on which, when cleaned, could be made out the impressed lettering *Three Merry Widows – Agnes, Mabel, Becky.* Interesting, I thought – three young women must have commissioned souvenir trinkets to commemorate their friendship. Jerry thought the same – until he talked with someone older and wiser, who identified my find as a 1930s (or earlier?) three-pack of condoms!

I drove Jamroon regularly to English-language classes. She was past the age of easy language-learning, but made slow, steady improvement. (In later years I was to say that whatever her English lacked in quality, she compensated for with quantity.) The children adapted reasonably well to new language/new school. The youngest girl was almost totally silent in her first weeks there; by year's end she had gotten in trouble for talking when she should not!

Jamroon knew only Thai cuisine and was worried about cooking for me. She need not have been. I loved the Thai food and preferred it even though Jamroon soon enough learned American cooking. A truth known to all men with Asian wives: anyone who marries one had *better* like rice. One problem was that two of my favorites – fried rice and Thai noodles – were also two of the easiest for Jamroon to prepare. She regarded them somewhat as the equivalent of serving hash, or leftovers, and I had to encourage her to fix them oftener. Yeshu, then Abrehet, then Jamroon . . . the magnitude of my culinary pampering cannot be overstated.

I had to stand duty about once a month as OOD (officer of the day), which entailed sleeping in a room at the barracks, taking care of any after-hours problems that might arise (contacting the CDO – command duty officer – if necessary), and not much else. The only specific duty I recall was to eat three meals at the chow hall and write an evaluation on them (they were good). Most such duty nights were uneventful, but on one of them a drunk marine sergeant started a fracas inside the main gate. Among the sailors on duty at the gate was a BM2 Harold Sherman. He apprehended the drunk (who was tall and slender but well-muscled) and held on to him until handcuffs could be brought and applied. By the time I was notified and got there, the drunk was in the brig. (Actually the brig was now the politically-correct "correctional center".)

I read Sherman's report later, in which I was amused to note that he wrote that he "lost control" of himself when repeatedly called "damn nigger" by the marine. The other three men of the gate security force were unanimous in their praise of Sherman, who threw no blows and used only as much force as necessary to restrain the drunk. Sherman *was* deeply shaken by the incident, as I could tell when I arrived.

Later that same evening a report was received that a marine in the marine barracks had taken an overdose of pills and was clutching his rack, refusing to be moved. Again Sherman supplied most of the force necessary to get the recalcitrant restrained and on a stretcher. Again, everything was wrapped up by the time I was notified and arrived.

Relating these happenings in the message center the next day, I sounded off: "I cut down civil service and I don't really mean it. I cut down reserves and I don't really mean it. I cut down airedales and I don't really mean it. I cut down Waves and I don't really mean it. But when I cut down marines, by God, I *mean* it! I don't know whether the marine image attracts psychos, or whether the marines take normal people and turn them into psychos. It's like trying to figure whether the chicken or the egg came first."

I recommended BM2 Sherman for a meritorious mast. He got it, with a letter of commendation.

Having just offended any marine or ex-marine who may happen to read this, let me apologize. Well, partially, anyhow. I recognize and admire the combat record of the marines. If you need a beach assaulted or a hill taken, they are the best there is at it. Unfortunately those qualities which produce battlefield bravery and valor are not always identical to the qualities which one hopes to find in neighbors, friends, colleagues. I apologize (again) to the majority of marines to whom the previous sentence does not apply. But I do believe that, *percentagewise* compared to the other services, the marines attract more than their share of social and/or mental misfits. ("Psychos", which I uttered in the message center while still agitated, was too strong a word.)

I got stuck with heading the committee to plan for and carry out the NAS annual picnic. It went well, and I got a letter of commendation for it. But the credit should have gone to Clare Wynn, wife of another chief, who had been involved with previous picnics and knew much more about what needed doing than I did. A printed schedule was promulgated in advance of each year's picnic, and someone always questioned a schedule omission: "What time will the marines start the fight?" The answer was usually about 1630.

Another duty which I performed was CACO – Casualty Assistance Calls Officer. This involved notifying north-Texas-area next of kin when a sailor died, and helping them with funeral arrangements, application for any relevant benefits, etc. Vietnam was winding down and there were not nearly as many combat-related deaths as in earlier years, but accidents and other causes still happened. Two lists were kept – officers performed the duty for officer casualties, chiefs for enlisted. After you were assigned a case, your name went to the bottom of the list and worked its way back up.

I handled two cases. The first involved an NAS sailor in his mid-thirties who dropped to a heart attack while temporarily in San Diego; his early-twenties wife was as sweet as they make them and well-known around the NAS. Duty took me to a small rural funeral home some miles away from Dallas; Jamroon rode along. There were two or three bodies in open caskets there. Only back in the car did Jamroon tell me how surprised and scared she had been – the dead are not thus displayed in Thailand. (She was also extremely superstitious about cemeteries.)

The other case was that of a young sailor at a smaller NAS in south Texas. He had just started to drive to visit his parents in Fort Worth, and was killed in an auto accident right outside the gate of his duty station. The parents already knew something was wrong; they had tried to phone the other NAS to check on their son and had gotten evasive answers. The navy manual forbade any information being given out until the next of kin had been *officially* notified by the CACO. In my wrapup report I strongly recommended a little more common-sense flexibility in the regulations for cases such as this one. I don't know if any such change was ever made.

I was lucky in the cases that fell my way. Both the young wife and the parents thought highly of me and were appreciative of my efforts on their behalf. The parents even wrote me a thank-you letter. Not all CACOs were so fortunate. From other chiefs, I heard of avaricious spouses who grieved scarcely at all and were interested primarily in how much money they would be collecting. And I heard of next of kin who succumbed to "hate the messenger" in their grief and were difficult for the CACO to handle.

CACO is a job for which I would never volunteer. Barging in on strangers to inform them of the death of a loved one is not pleasant. But in the aftermaths I had feelings of satisfaction, of having done good.

Approaching Dallas from the flat countryside, the tall skyscrapers in the center of downtown were an arresting sight. In outer parts of the city, even moderately-tall buildings were few, and from afar it seemed that those central towers sprouted right up out of the landscape. The same was doubtless true of other prairie metropolises. I haven't seen them all, but of those I have seen none could match Dallas in impressiveness from a distance. I could well understand how the *Big D* nickname came to be applied to the city.

The *Dallas Morning News* of that time was about as far-right as a paper could get. Every week or two they printed, as an editorial, details of some alleged welfare fraud or related misbehavior, and made it a point to describe the fraudster as black. I nevertheless subscribed to it, in preference to the less-hysterical afternoon paper, because I wanted my news on the doorstep in the *morning.*

Dallas came in for a lot of criticism after the Kennedy assassination because of children rejoicing in their classrooms at the news. It was a bum rap. Not for being false; I am confident that it happened. But I remembered my Republican schoolmates in Illinois, equally jubilant at the news of FDR's death. Children, mimicking their parents' politics, are the same everywhere.

The NAS had a ping-pong tournament. In the 3-of-5 match that would have given me the championship I won the first two games and had a 20-15 lead in the third. I managed to lose that game, and the next two. It was double-elimination and that put me in the losers' bracket, where I lost my only match and finished third. They gave trophies only to first and second. So it goes sometimes.

Because of the Wednesday-Sunday work week I sometimes watched the weekday daytime TV at home, and particularly one quiz show, *Tic-Tac-Dough*. I measured my answers against those of the contestants, and realized that I could do better than most of them. I gambled $90 {$433} on a ticket to New York City to take their test for aspiring contestants. It was harder than I had expected and I knew I had missed at least 13 of the 50 questions. But the written test (I later realized) was a superfluous gimmick.

They took front and side pictures of me and at some point the woman running things let slip the telltale words, ". . . if you'd be right for the show." Back home, hoping for a summons that never came, I figured things out. They didn't give a damn about ability or knowledge as long as a low minimum standard was met. They were looking for the "telegenic". Telegenic I am not and never was. The test was primarily a device which could be used to stonewall inquiries from the persistent. The experience disillusioned me concerning *all* quiz and game shows. I expect that legions of the charisma-challenged have been similarly enticed and then ignored.

I had an RM3 in the message center who was continually in debt; letters from various creditors came to the NAS. He had borrowed from Navy Relief also, and ignored summonses from the chaplain about it. I physically marched him down to the chaplain's office once myself to make sure that he *did* see the chaplain. He always had some plausible excuse. Previously not planning to reenlist, he changed his mind and submitted a special request chit to do so. I had considerable doubt about that, but his continuing alibis swayed me and conned me, and I approved it. I should not have; it was one of my major mistakes. A few years later, when he had gone to a ship, I chanced to meet and chat with his division officer. The RM3 had not changed a bit – the division officer was fielding a stream of complaining-creditor letters.

I remembered the political lapel buttons which were such a fixture of campaigns from childhood through my mid-50s college years. I did not realize that they had gone out of style, replaced by bumper stickers. Reverse culture shock again. My search for a McGovern button led me to a local Democratic headquarters, where they *sold* me two for a $25 {$120} campaign contribution. They were four times as large, but the little ones of my memory had been passed out free.

The NAS had a rather small, basic commissary. From time to time we drove to Carswell AFB in Fort Worth, where there was a full-sized commissary. An airman gate guard there admired my beard and lamented that he could not have one in the air force. I advised him to hope for future leadership as enlightened as ADM Zumwalt. Some of ADM Zumwalt's reforms were, in the light of my past experience, nearly unbelievable. Wearing of civvies on/off ships was extended to all pay grades. There was a *beer machine* in the NAS enlisted barracks. Sailors were allowed to patronize PX, commissary, and the like in dungarees, and arbitrary dress codes for *dependents* at such facilities were abolished. The traditional white hats, jumpers, and 13-button blues were being phased out in favor of more modern uniforms with jackets and visored caps.

I met a civilian who worked for H. Ross Perot's corporation. He also envied my beard and mentioned that Perot would not allow beards on his employees. Perot lost my vote years before he thought of running for office.

I was happier with, more contented with, the navy during those Dallas years than at any time before or after. The NAS was perhaps the *least* chickenshit environment I ever encountered. I even did something I would formerly have scorned to do: I affixed a *Go Navy* bumper sticker to my VW. For too short a time I was proud of my profession, proud when wearing the uniform. It was not to last. Authority was merely hunkered down and dormant.

In late 1972 we learned that another RMCM was ordered to Dallas. It was for his "twilight cruise" – the last two years of a full 30-year career. One who reached that point could virtually write his own ticket, within reason, for his last assignment. There would be nearly a six-month overlap (in the event it was a year) before I transferred. Rather than sit with him on my lap or vice-versa, I volunteered to work elsewhere – wherever the command thought I might be of use. In January I began to work in the legal and security office.

My new desk, on the second floor, was backed by circular windows overlooking the main gate. In the other direction, my view was of the backs of a YN2 and a shapely civilian secretary. Jolene was one of the best typists I have ever seen; not only fast and accurate but also with the ability to proofread and correct on the fly without slowing down, without even the need to pause to consult a dictionary. I have known only one other typist who could do that: myself. The YN2, a good athlete, was later transferred to special services and replaced by a second shapely secretary. Miniskirts were then at their zenith. That was one scenic office.

My new boss, LCDR Ed Jones, occupied an adjacent office. In addition to security and the main gate, the correctional center – ex-brig – and CACO matters came under us. Whenever the switchboard got an incoming phone call and did not know where else to send it, they transferred it to legal. We called these "Dear Abby" calls, dreaded them, and snickered when one of the others had the bad luck to pick up the phone to field one. A wife's complaint about a distant husband's failure to support her, or a pregnant girlfriend's charge of breach of promise were typical. I was stuck with one call from a man who spoke at length of what he thought the navy ought to know about the flying saucers he had seen.

Jack Howell, the new RMCM, was of the Will Rogers school, as friendly and agreeable a man as I've ever met. Tall and slender, he had made chief – E-7 – about the same time I was getting out of boot camp. I dropped down to the message center at least once a day – not to offer my advice, which was unnecessary, but just to keep posted on communications matters and to visit. Jack collected coins, specializing in wheat pennies; thus there was considerable overlap of interest with my own and Jerry's coinshooting.

We also got a new TAR YNCM who became leading chief. He was as much bad news as Jack was good news. He took over the personnel office, and there I noticed the friendly Bill and Edie turn extremely formal and begin to speak of each other by the book – as "Mrs Gilland" and "Petty Officer Ousley". Than that, you cannot get much more chickenshit. I heard that the YNCM chewed out an E-7 chief for *jokingly* referring to the Master Chief Petty Officer of the Navy as an "E-10". He also launched a – Chief Petty Officers' Association, I believe he called it. I viewed it dimly and declined to attend one of its first functions. He probed for my reasons; I would not give him any. I shortly found myself removed from a couple of boards or committees and replaced by his sycophants – marginalized, somewhat as I had been in Asmara, but this time it didn't bother me. The removals were trivial and there was not much else he could do to me. My job remained unaffected and I liked it.

When the YNCM retired he went to work as personnel officer for the mall at Six Flags Over Texas, the amusement park. When I revisited Dallas some 10-12 years later, hearsay claimed that he had somehow gotten himself into bad, potentially fatal, trouble with the Dallas Mafia.

The navy was broke – its typical condition during the post-Vietnam budget cutbacks. This brought me short-term good news and long-term bad news. The good news was that all tours were extended by six months to save money on transfer costs. Those on shore duty applauded, those on ships did not. Instead of looking at a July transfer, I would now be leaving in January 1974.

The bad news was that personnel with more than three dependents would no longer be ordered to overseas shore duty. Over the past year or two Authority had been making noises about reducing family separation – and here was a new policy that was bound to do the opposite. Another left-hand/right-hand discontinuity. I thought of writing *Navy Times* to point this out, but never did get to the typewriter. I now faced certain sea duty with no chance of overseas.

In March I reenlisted, for two years again. The navy had revised, yet again, its warrant officer and LDO programs. I applied, unsuccessfully, for warrant in 1972 and 1973. I would probably not have accepted warrant if I had been selected; the pay, initially at least, would have been lower than that for master chief and it would have been several years before I could have caught up, even if promoted rapidly. Mostly I just wanted to see whether I could make it or not. I also applied in these years for conversion to the new rating of Legalman, and for the personnel exchange program, whereby a few of our sailors spent a year or two in friendly foreign navies and the foreigners served in ours. I had no success with either.

An evaluation written on me at this time contained the sentence, "He supports whole-heartedly equal opportunity and the other changes in today's navy out of conviction and not expediency." I was doubly flattered at this, because the wording was exactly what *I* had written when evaluating the message center RMC about a year earlier! Whether the writer recalled my words consciously or subconsciously I do not know.

The NAS held an open house one weekend and many civilians attended. A visitor from Fort Worth had some damage done to his expensive car in our parking lot. He gave the legal officer a great deal of grief about it. I never observed him myself, but apparently he was pushy, aggressive, and generally disagreeable – a VIP in his own mind. At one point Mr Jones directed me to prepare a preliminary rough of a formal investigation of the incident.

A naval investigation report contains three sections: findings of fact, opinions, and recommendations. Each section has numbered paragraphs beginning with "That . . ." In my rough, under opinions, I began with: "1. That [name forgotten] is an arrogant son of a bitch." Mr Jones concurred and chuckled, but it turned out that no formal investigation became necessary.

A full-dress personnel inspection was held and as the ranks were dismissed, two or three officers approached and questioned the cuffs on my trousers. I looked around in surprise – no one else had cuffs on their trousers. I could not have said, before looking, whether uniform trousers were supposed to be cuffed or not – nor could I have said whether my own were cuffed or uncuffed. I had simply bought from the Naples PX uniform shop when I made chief and worn what they sold me.

The quandary was solved when I came home. Jamroon, a habitual garage-sale shopper, had bought me a pair of blue trousers that, by chance, perfectly matched the shade of my blue uniform. Somehow they had migrated to the uniform's clothes hanger and displaced the incumbent. I do not think any other sailor can boast that he wore civilian trousers to a full-dress inspection and got away with it! (Maybe I can't really claim I "got away with it" because they didn't go undetected, but the officers who challenged them were more amused than anything.)

I talked with the Radioman detailer on a navy phone line, and the upshot was that I was assigned to COMCRUDESGRU TWO (Commander Cruiser-Destroyer Group) in Newport, a rear admiral's staff. Said rear admiral was none other than my one-time division officer on the *Iowa*, Sam Gravely. Unlike the other east-coast CRUDESGRUs, Group Two made no Med cruises – only occasional two- or three-week stints aboard various ships for training exercises. I would be at sea for only short periods. The assignment was as good as I could have hoped for, but there turned out to be an inconvenient wrinkle: Group Two was moving from Newport to Charleston in June. The navy would pay for movement of my dependents and household goods to Newport *or* to Charleston – it would *not* pay for Dallas to Newport and then to Charleston.

I talked things over with Jack and Jerry. The obvious thing for me to do was to go to Newport alone, then move the family from Dallas to Charleston in June. Jack and Jerry promised to look after Jamroon and give her whatever support and help might be necessary.

I would reach the magic 19-and-6 number in March – 19 years and 6 months of service, at which point one can retire as if it were 20 years. I would be pleased to reach it, and to know that at any time thereafter, if displeased with anything, I could retire on six months notice. But

I had vaguely planned, as long as things went well, to continue on to 30 years.

(A sailor in Naples once expressed surprise at my intention to pursue a 30-year vice 20-year career, and was amused by my reply: "*Why fuck around?")

I had heard others describe continuing past 19-and-6 as "working for half pay". They were right, but I did not yet realize it. The 75% 30-year retirement vice the 50% at 20 years attracted me. I had not yet done any serious thought or planning for post-retirement. I could have requested retirement in March and never gone to Newport, and by hindsight that is what I should have done.

The Yom Kippur War and the resultant gas-price shock hit in October. I took note of my first-ever five-dollar-plus {$23+} tank of gas. Nixon spoke and requested the nation to observe a voluntary 50-mph speed limit. The *Dallas Morning News* and most Caucasian Texans worshiped Nixon. Out for a Sunday drive on a major four-lane 70-mph highway, I decided to test compliance and drove at 50. I was an obstacle to traffic, the only driver doing so.

I had tried to teach Jamroon to drive shortly after arriving in Dallas. Driving around the deserted perimeter road of the local elementary school, she promptly steered into a metal traffic guard and did unwelcome things to the front end of the VW. I gave it up as a hopeless project. But one day, as my transfer neared, she flabbergasted me by showing me her new drivers' license! Without telling me, she had located a driving school and taken their lessons. She had felt that it was a necessity in my absence. A used car was located for her with Jack's help.

I left Dallas by VW on the last day of January for a three-day drive to Newport. It went well until I entered an evening blizzard halfway across Connecticut. I arrived at the naval station without accident, and with a feeling of relief at having done so.

XVIII - GROUP TWO

Admiral Gravely said that he remembered me from the *Iowa*. I don't think he really did; I think he just said what I wanted to hear. Our overlap on the *Iowa* had been a mere month or two. I had only minimal conversation or interaction with either RADM Gravely or his two successors.

Again I had plenty of break-in time, my predecessor RMCM had a month or two left before transfer. The staff was on shore, in a building on the naval base. It had, at a guess, 12 officers and 20-30 enlisted. The comm officer, LCDR Jack Borho, was a live-wire mustang submariner. Four RMs, ranging from RM1 to RMSN, stood a rotating one-man watch, cutting tapes on outgoings and performing distribution; traffic was delivered to and picked up from the base comm center. I lived in a single room in a bachelor CPO barracks.

The week after I arrived I was sent to a one-week COMSEC Material Custodian school on the base. This was so that I would be able to perform COMSEC (Communications Security) inspections on the ships of Group Two. Each ship and communication activity had a Custodian responsible for crypto material, usually a junior officer, and the 10-15 others in the class were all junior officers. The instructors liked to single out the tallest student and remark that Portsmouth would be pleased to have him on their basketball team. Portsmouth (Maine) was then the naval prison, and the implication was that any custodian who lost, or could not account for, any of his materials would become an inmate. There were a couple of coast guard officers in the class, and the naval officers liked to serenade them with what was alleged to be the coast guard equivalent of *Anchors Aweigh*, namely *Harbor Lights*.

Group Two was preparing to go to sea for a training exercise. Mr Borho and the RMCM were engrossed in preparing the "frequency plan", which would be an annex to the OpOrd – Operation Order, the master document governing the exercise. Their debates over what frequency would be best for such-and-such a circuit went largely over my head. I had no background for this. I was as much a misfit as I had been at the transmitter site at Gura. This time I had no excuse. This was an RMCM job, I was an RMCM, I *was* supposed to know it.

Over the next month or two I became so despondent over this inadequacy that I considered asking to refund the money that had been spent to transfer me, and to retire immediately. I never voiced this thought and it turned out to be unnecessary. Mr Borho was more than capable of writing frequency plans unassisted, and he did. So, also, did his eventual relief. Frequency plans were not the only part of the job, and I made myself useful in whatever other ways I could, chiefly message handling.

Soon after the COMSEC school ended I was sent to another requisite function: a three-day Racial Awareness Seminar. The navy had been plagued by race riots recently; those on the aircraft carriers got the most notice and publicity. Partly as a response to this – perhaps it would have been done anyhow – ADM Zumwalt was requiring everyone in the navy to attend one of these seminars. I overheard one sailor tell another, regarding the seminar, "If you're not prejudiced when you go in, you will be when you come out." I think he was overly cynical.

At the seminar about 20 participants and three "facilitators" sat in a circle. One of the first things said was that everybody participates in the discussions, right? Of course everyone nodded their heads or mumbled agreement. I should not have. I should have said something like, "No. If and when I have something to say, I will say it. When I do not, I will not." Too late. I found myself receiving all too many prodding questions, usually after having seen a movie or a slide show – How do you feel about that? What do you think about whatever? I felt sandbagged; I was making inane remarks about things that I was still considering, about which I had not yet formed intelligent opinions.

In the aftermath of the seminar I had one disagreement and one worry. I could not agree with the facilitators' several assertions that all ethnic jokes are always bad. Many are. But there is a vast difference between vicious anti-Black jokes and those that poke friendly fun at, say, the Italians' propensity to talk with their hands. Moreover, I foresaw where this could lead. "Politically correct" was yet to become a catch-phrase, but I envisioned a time when I could be censured for telling a joke about a gay, a Wave, a marine, a fat lady, an old man . . . I think I discerned the future.

My worry concerned a film that had been shown on Cesar Chavez and his labor movement, which was then seen by many as far-left, verging on radical. I recalled the 1961 cashiering of MGEN Edwin Walker for force-feeding his soldiers John Birch Society materials. Here I feared the reverse might happen; what if congressional right-wingers learned that the navy was indoctrinating sailors on Cesar Chavez? Apparently they never got wind of it.

The seminars, imperfect as they were, were better than doing nothing about racial frictions. ADM Zumwalt had accomplished one other long-overdue and praiseworthy racial reform: he had integrated the Steward rating – the officers' servants. From very early days it had been populated entirely by Blacks and Filipinos. Until Harry Truman integrated the armed forces, Blacks could serve *only* in this rating – and even after integration no whites could enter it. The ratings slide-show I had seen in boot camp showed the Steward with a shaded face. Sometime in the late 50s or the 60s the navy announced under pressure that white "volunteers" would now be accepted in the rating. Unsurprisingly there was a dearth of volunteers. ADM Zumwalt finally integrated the rating by eliminating it – by merging it with the largely-white Commissaryman (cook) rating.

In late February we went to sea for 10-14 days for a NATO exercise, aboard the *USS Biddle (DLG-34)*, a relatively-modern destroyer type. Think of one of those plastic or metal puzzles with 16 spaces and 15 movable, numbered squares – the puzzle being to get them lined up in 1-2-3 order. In the *Biddle's* radio space I felt like one of the pieces in such a puzzle. It was overcrowded, both with equipment and with people, and in order to move from one place to another, several others would have had to move to let me by. I was less like a fifth wheel; more like the 19th wheel on an 18-wheeler. I did not feel that I had contributed anything while on the ship except to get in the way. I was happy to get back to Newport.

For most future deployments only the officers and a handful of enlisted, not including Radiomen, accompanied the admiral to a ship. This was fine with me. As it turned out, only once more would I go to sea.

On weekends in Newport I often indulged my metal-detector mania, even in bitterly cold weather when I had to pry into frozen ground. One little park beside Narragansett Bay was the most productive I had yet found, yielding coins from early in the century and a watch fob portraying "Our next president - William Howard Taft".

Just as I arrived in Newport, there came unwelcome news. Without any warning, Congress had suddenly abolished USAFI. In addition to my 1950s studies I had taken a year of college-level accounting from USAFI while in Dallas, partly to have something to do, partly with an eye toward post-retirement life. The incumbent RMCM had also used USAFI and was as angered as I was. Had we known, this was one of the first harbingers of the mid-1970s cutbacks and tinkerings that would soon become known, profanely, as the "erosion of benefits".

In April I heard that the *Saturday Evening Post* carried a picture of RADM Gravely. I saw the picture over someone's shoulder and promptly procured my own copy. The picture was handsome. The article in which it was embedded appalled me. It lashed out at nearly every reform that ADM Zumwalt had initiated and argued that the navy was in terrible shape as a result. It was written by Hanson W. Baldwin, military editor of the *New York Times*. Baldwin was a 1924 Annapolis graduate and had served three years as an officer. He had been a Pulitzer-prize winner, and he hobnobbed with admirals.

One of the fundamental basics of military life, one of the most sacred of all cows, is this: before a matter is decided, before an order is given, debate and discussion are allowed and even encouraged. But once the decision is made, the order given, debate and discussion are at an end. Everyone is required to support and implement the order, no matter what doubts they may have about its wisdom, no matter what feelings they may have about it; and they may no longer criticize it. For many years this time-encrusted principle worked to Authority's benefit, serving to stifle dissenters and malcontents. During the Zumwalt years it gave Authority fits. Viscerally opposed to nearly every Zumwalt-initiated reform but hamstrung by its own commandments, Authority seethed and fumed – yet could never be seen to do so.

In Baldwin, Authority had found the perfect mouthpiece to say what it could not say publicly. I re-read his article many times, brooded over it, underlined, and covered the margins with angry comments. But doing anything more would have to await getting settled in Charleston.

Jamroon had had her misadventures while I was gone. Her first car had been a repair-prone disaster but Jack had found her a small Toyota wagon as replacement. She had gotten lost while trying to return from a trip to the Fort Worth commissary, but eventually found her way. She had, while fishing and barefoot, stepped on a large, rusty fishhook and impaled it deeply in her heel. Somehow she managed to drive in pain to the NAS dispensary where they removed it and took care of her.

I took a month's leave, drove the VW to Charleston, then flew to Dallas. When I went to the NAS to touch base, I learned that Jamroon had put a minor dent in her front fender. When I returned home I went to take a look. Jamroon saw what I was looking for and her laughing outburst was, "*God damn Jack! God damn Jerry! Big mouths!"

She never matched me in seamanlike language, but her Thai-English amalgamations were equally serviceable.

We sold the house for a small loss. I had bought for $18,500 {$92,790}, put in a $1000 {$4809}central air conditioner, and sold for only $19,000 {$83,287}. The area was perceived to be in the path of future black expansion and prices had stagnated.

Half the family flew from Dallas to Charleston. I and the two older boys went by Toyota. I have been in 48 of the 50 states (missing only New Hampshire and Maine) but my claim to having been "in" Mississippi depends on definitions. In 1974 Mississippi was the hard-core, last-ditch bastion of segregationists. I made a point of gassing up just before the Mississippi line, and did not set my feet on the ground again until I was in Alabama. I would not do that today – not that I believe Mississippi has become a model of racial harmony, but I believe it has at least mellowed to the point that it may no longer be the worst of the worst.

The 55-mph speed limit was now law. I did not believe Nixon was going to recompense me for the extra day the drive would take at that speed, and ignored it. That went well until shortly after I entered South Carolina and heard the siren. I'm not sure whether the cost of the ticket exceeded the cost of an extra day on the road or not.

We lodged in temporary navy family quarters and house-hunted. The children having become older, I wanted a five-bedroom. Almost none were listed, and none in my price range. We bought one that was advertised as five-bedroom but was really only three – a large closet was a "bedroom", and the garage had been enclosed for another! The mortgage payments were $100 {$438} a month more than we had had in Dallas. During rush hour the 20-minute drive was a 30-40 minute commute from the naval base – the longest commute I had yet encountered. We were across the street from an elementary school and not far from the middle school that most of the children now attended.

The staff was now on the *USS Sierra (AD-18)*, a destroyer tender. She was a good-sized ship of 14,000 tons. It was nearly like working in an office building ashore, because the *Sierra* rarely moved from pierside – and never did while the staff was aboard. When, later, she made a cruise to Norfolk and back, it was said that the cruise was scheduled so that the coffee grounds could be dredged from under her hull.

Shortly after getting settled in Charleston I typed a lengthy rebuttal (much of which I had already composed mentally) to the Baldwin *Saturday Evening Post* article. I mailed it to *Navy Times*. My cover letter ended, "please do not identify it as coming from Charleston (it is relevant to the whole Navy, and it is not my intention to place local commands or individuals on report–despite my obvious distaste for the Chief of Staff here). And please do not use my name or rating. I would appreciate being identified as a master chief, but not as a radioman. (If you should print the enclosed, everyone present at the meeting I describe on the last two pages will recognize it. It is likely to cause a witch hunt for the writer. I am willing to risk this, but I certainly don't want to give them any help!)"

Navy Times printed nearly all of my input in the 17 July 1974 issue. They headlined it **Chief Takes Up Gauntlet In Defense of Zumwalt, By "MASTER CHIEF"**. It follows:

THE MAY 1974 issue of the Saturday Evening Post carried an article titled "Troubled Waters in the Navy," subsequently condensed in the Readers' Digest.

The article is, in my opinion, filled with innuendos, distortions, half-truths and opinion presented as fact. It can fairly be interpreted as a hatchet job on Adm. Zumwalt's policies. I fear that its appearance, at a time of widespread speculation as to the course the new CNO will take, is a calculated effort to pressure Adm. Holloway to turn back the clock.

The article was written by a very distinguished naval writer, Mr. Hanson Baldwin. It saddens me that such a well-known naval expert should ally himself with the anti-Zumwalt faction.

The article cries for rebuttal from those who disagree. Since I have seen no one else attempt such a rebuttal, my inadequate effort follows. I have italicized the direct quotes from the Post article.

"The Kitty Hawk violence was a frightening manifestation of the winds of change sweeping through the Navy's rigging today, symptoms of a sickness afloat, a widespread malaise never before experienced by the American fleet."

Sickness? Widespread malaise? Even if we accept these scare words as true for the sake of argument, is all of the blame Adm. Zumwalt's? Indeed, should any of the blame be his? Hasn't he been running several lengths ahead of most of the Navy in his awareness of and attempts to deal with racial problems?

* * *

Mr. Baldwin quotes in part from the Hicks subcommittee's report:
"An environment of leniency, appeasement and permissiveness has led to lowered Navy morale and a deterioration in appearance and performance."

There are a few of us around who might argue that Adm. Zumwalt has raised morale. Those who claim appearance has deteriorated are those who equate crew-cuts with "good" appearance; contemporary grooming styles with degeneracy. As for deterioration of performance: prove it.

* * *

Mr. Baldwin tries to present Zumwalt's Navy as popular only with the lower ranks, both enlisted and officer. As a generalization this is likely true; there is doubtless more relative support for the Zumwalt innovations in the younger age groups. But it is inaccurate and misleading to suggest, as Mr. Baldwin does at every opportunity, that a large majority of CPOs and senior officers are unhappy with Zumwalt's policies. It has not been proven that even a bare majority are unhappy. Adm. Zumwalt has, with only a few exceptions, righted the wrongs I bitched fruitlessly about on my first hitch.

"The Z-grams have at times been so vague and imprecise that they have required a bewildering stream of follow-up clarification."

The only Z-grams I can think of that might merit this comment are those on personal appearance. And those would not really have needed any clarification if the authoritarians had grasped and followed their intent, rather than continuing to harass their subordinates over petty details.

* * *

"At many naval stations men in dirty or frayed dungarees quickly became a common sight."

Dirty and frayed dungarees have always been a common sight. Those who work get dirty. They even "fray" their clothing. Adm. Zumwalt allows our manual workers to patronize clubs, exchanges and commissaries on base without having to first make a trip of sometimes miles to their barracks to change clothes. Mr. Baldwin's article is the thanks he gets. Mr. Baldwin is not a manual worker.

Mr. Baldwin quotes a *"chief in the Sixth Fleet: 'It's nonsense the amount of time we have to spend on a simple thing like haircuts.'"*

Right on! Grown men should have more important matters to occupy their time. If all the man-hours that have been expended on hair in the last four years had instead been directed toward a real problem – race relations – would those shipboard riots have happened?

"The net result of the Z-grams on grooming and personal appearance has been, most naval personnel agree, a marked deterioration in the look of the men, 'slovenly' appearance as the Hicks subcommittee put it."

Most?

*   *   *

Mr. Baldwin criticizes such programs as minority affairs officers and human relations councils for bypassing the chain of command and diluting the authority of middle management. He writes:

"Especially rankling is the fact that many of the Z-grams . . . involve petty administrative details that have previously been exercised by commanding officers."

Exercised? Yes, and exercised fairly by many. But ignored by far too many and exercised arbitrarily by many more. Hence the need for the Z-grams.

*   *   *

"In ships with a small number of blacks there is usually little trouble, but in larger ships with several hundred black sailors, polarization inevitably occurs . . ."

The only ships large enough to have "several hundred" black sailors are the carriers. Our racial incidents have not been limited to carriers. I am not convinced that polarization is inevitable on any size ship. Fortunately Mr. Baldwin does not try to blame Adm. Zumwalt directly for "polarization."

*   *   *

"The appellation 'racist' is easily applied but hard to outgrow in the service today . . ."

At my last command I was called upon to write the rough evaluation for an E-7. I had heard him express relatively mild racism in whites-only conversations. I felt that the kindest thing I could say of him was that he "gives adequate support to equal opportunity programs." (Which he did, on the surface.) My mild comment didn't even survive the next level up the chain; it was improved to "actively supports." Suppose I ever felt compelled to write of an otherwise outstanding petty officer: "X is an outspoken bigot and should not be placed in charge of minority personnel"? How far would it get? Easily applied, eh?

*   *   *

"Blacks who are disciplined . . . seek relief from just punishment by writing to their congressman, or organizations such as the American Civil Liberties Union."

Mr. Baldwin would have his readers believe that military punishment is always just. I differ. I also, and very specifically, resent his implication that the ACLU is some kind of unsavory organization. I belong to it. My interest in it was initially sparked by the military injustice I have witnessed in my career.

"The inevitable result is a 'rocket' from Washington which requires answer, even if the disciplinarian is not reversed."

This is as it should be. (And I've helped draft one or two of those answers myself.) Incidentally, it was true long before Zumwalt. The disciplinarian has nothing to fear if he has in fact observed the law and been just. I have long felt that those who deplore letters to congressmen are on the wrong side in the cold war. There are no letters to congressmen behind the iron curtain. There aren't even any letters to the editor. All you need to do is defect and you will never be troubled by such phenomena again.

*   *   *

"The CO who tries to keep his justice evenhanded – black or white – may not be supported in his efforts."

I don't believe it.

"The naval training stations reflect much of the same permissiveness as the rest of the Navy. They are rarely tough and hard. Many CPOs refer to them scornfully as "charm schools." Some of the recruits themselves have complained about the looseness of the boot camps."

I haven't been near a boot camp since 1952 and can't deny this from experience, but I doubt it. Oh, do I doubt it. In any event I have never heard recruit training described as "Charm school." Charm school, as Mr. Baldwin should know, is a nickname of long standing for OCS.

*   *   *

"The Navy is having a tough time keeping men aboard once they have served a single tour."
Three sentences later:

"The retention rate of first-term enlistees – only 10.3 percent in 1970 – has risen . . . to a respectable 23 percent in fiscal 1973."

Case closed.

*   *   *

"Many of those who chose to stay in the Navy were not nearly as qualified as many of those who got out."

This is nothing new. It has always been true. My own impression is that we're doing better than ever in this respect lately.

"Many who leave the Navy are influenced in their decisions by the red tape and delay and the judicial leniency now prevalent in military disciplinary procedures."

I thought I'd heard just about every reason men give for leaving. I never heard that one before.

*   *   *

"In one Sixth Fleet ship a brig annex, three times the size of the original brig, has been created to house offenders."

Great! One of the key points of Zumwalt's approach is that the many should not be penalized for the sins of the few. I am glad to hear that the few are being punished.

And at my last duty station, a major Southwest city, we had a small transient brig to house awols who were apprehended in the area. The Marine population of that brig consistently outnumbered the sailors by 3 and 4 to 1. Those who persist in holding the Marines up as an example of "being on the right track" might do well to ponder this ratio. (Bearing in mind that the Corps is less than half the size of the Navy.)

A substantial portion of Mr. Baldwin's article is devoted to "The erosion of military justice." I need only quote some of the terms he uses. (The first two he quotes from a retired Marine colonel, the rest are his own.)

"radical lawyers"
"libertarian civilian courts"
"a shocking judgment" (by the Supreme Court)
"the bizarre judgments of civilian courts"
"aberrant court decisions."

* * *

"Theft, almost nonexistent in the old Navy when military law permitted the immediate bad-conduct discharge of a proven thief, is now a fairly general problem both afloat and ashore . . . the kids can't leave anything lying on their bunks."

So, neither could I. In 1954 I had my locker jimmied open and $200 stolen. Again this is nothing new.

* * *

"To win public support and to restore that sense of excellence which is the key to all morale, the Navy must clean its own house. It must restore the high-spirited, wise leadership it has usually had in the past, leadership dedicated to holding the line against unwise congressional and bureaucratic, political and sociological pressures; leadership that puts first things first: a disciplined, dependable and effective fleet."

I read the above as a direct insult to Adm. Zumwalt himself rather than criticism of his policies. For four years we have had exactly the kind of leadership at the top that Mr. Baldwin advocates. It is a pity that he cannot recognize it.

* * *

402

A few months ago, temporarily quartered in a CPO barracks, I heard a chief stomp down the passageway one evening shouting: "God damn that (obscenity) Zumwalt and his (obscenity) long hair and his (obscenity) beards and his (inaudible). The sooner we get rid of that (obscenity) the better off we'll be."

I don't know what set that chief off, but his tirade typifies those who cannot seem to wait for the door to slam. The only difference between that chief and Mr. Baldwin is that Mr. Baldwin expresses himself more genteelly.

And while writing this, I attended a meeting of all area E-9s, chaired by the Chief of Staff of the Naval Base. It lasted an hour. At least 50 minutes were devoted to various aspects of personal appearance. Some of the happenings:

– Several chiefs advocated abolition of the shipboard civilian clothing privilege.

– The Chief of Staff declared that he disliked beards and hoped to see them banned again after Zumwalt's departure.

– A shore patrolman told of advising two CPOs in an off-base bar that they were required to wear ribbons with their tropical khaki after 1800. The chiefs returned to their car, took off their shirts, and returned to the bar in legal T-shirts. It would seem they gloated. Chief of Staff: "You should have taken off your shirt and punched them out." Laughter and applause.

– Monthly personnel inspections were suggested.

– It was reported that a certain Vice Admiral is thinking of requiring more ships to anchor out. Not because of any lack of pier space; solely to make it more difficult to go on liberty.

– It was suggested that uniforms be made mandatory for conducting business at dispensaries, personnel offices, disbursing, etc. No one spoke up for the watchstander who has no choice but to visit such facilities on his off time.

– Race relations were not mentioned once, not even peripherally.

– The Chief of Staff stated several times that he supported Admiral Zumwalt.

I didn't say a word in that session; after the first ten minutes I felt like an atheist at a revival meeting.

The Navy that awaits us if the authoritarians prevail is a frightening one. I'm one of the lucky few; I can put in my papers at the first sign of reaction. Adm. Holloway: Please let me do 30.

Navy Times deleted the portion between the lines, probably because of what I'd said in my cover letter. If I had known they would do that, I would have left out that part of the cover letter, or at least revised it. The chief of staff's "support" of ADM Zumwalt was particularly cogent.

Four weeks later *Navy Times* began printing a number of letters commenting on my article. The best one came from a recently-retired master chief journalist who understood things better than I did. In part:

... With more career-oriented defenders . . . Adm. Zumwalt might have been more successful in his plans to reform military practice. However, there weren't and he wasn't. . . . From the very beginning, Adm. Zumwalt never had a chance.

Early in Adm. Z's administration, I heard a chief say, "Zumwalt wants them to let their hair grow? Okay! We'll let it happen and show him how wrong he is."

So some of the enlisted men became sloppy. There was no control exercised. Nevertheless, CNO usurped no leader's authority; most of the leaders abdicated their responsibilities.

. . . In a thousand nit-picking ways "Operation Enough Rope" was informally devised. There was no conspiracy, to be sure, because none was necessary. If great minds travel in the same channel, mediocre minds frequent the same rut.

"Operation Enough Rope" didn't hang Adm. Zumwalt. It wasn't necessary. It just tied his hands.

. . . Another admiral is CNO now. Whether he is just "another admiral" remains to be judged. He has pledged to support some of the Zumwalt policies. If he does and how he does remain, for now, unknown factors.

Now that the window to intelligence, compassion and understanding has been opened to give a brief glimpse of what the Navy could be like, my one hope is that anyone – be he admiral, mustang, chief or superannuated PO2 – trying to slam it shut will find himself attempting an impossible task.

Navy Times printed only one letter that disagreed with me. (I had no way of knowing how many letters, critical or supportive, might not have seen print.) The critic was a marine lieutenant colonel. His letter follows in large part:

. . . "Master Chief" entered mined waters . . . in his novel contention that a greater percentage of awol Marines indicates the Corps is not "on the right track."

I would remind the Chief that Marines train continuously for combat, and obviously we have a number who occasionally find the pressure unbearable.

Marines are not, after all, enjoined to enlist "to have more fun," but combat generally has been less than entertaining for those Marines participating. It must be prepared for arduously.

Navy Times negated part of the Chief's defense by running the photograph of the Midway protesters (a group of awol black sailors at a press conference) in the same issue.

Because of this I won't mention the percentage of blacks in the Navy compared with a Corps "less than half the size of the Navy."

"Master Chief" appears to equate discipline with authoritarians. Any young NCO could enlighten him.

Do your 30, Chief – but don't give Marines advice. Our drummer beats a different march.

I seemed to have struck a nerve, but he did make some good points. *Sailors Have More Fun* was a popular and much-seen bumper sticker at the time. I gave a lot of thought to the "equate discipline with authoritarians" charge. There was likely some truth to that. At the same time, I would have been greatly surprised if the colonel were not equally guilty of equating discipline with chickenshit. Anyhow, I had had no intention of giving advice to marines. Such an effort would have resembled an attempt at dialogue between a blind man and a deaf-mute.

There was some feeling that bigotry accounted for much of the opposition to ADM Zumwalt. I never thought so; I saw it as a factor, but a minor one. I believed that a much greater stimulus came simply from the resentment of dominant animals at any limitations on their dominance.

I like to think that my effort served to delay the reimposition of chickenshit. I will never know. Beards, the most visible and symbolic of the Zumwalt reforms, and perhaps the one most hated by Authority, were not totally banned for another ten years – at which time the then-CNO accompanied the ban with an asinine statement to the effect that there was a time when beards were right for the navy, but that time had passed! The courtesies of never publicly criticizing another high-ranking officer, never implying that a predecessor could have done wrong, had to be preserved no matter what.

There was an "underground" monthly newspaper when I arrived in Charleston, passed out by hippie-looking types as cars departed the naval base. It was of some value in reporting on chickenshit and hair/beard nonsense, but overall I didn't think much of it. It used much more space on socialistic, far-left causes. I no longer saw it after mid-1975.

It did not take me long to decide that I did not like Charleston. The *Low Country*, as the coastal belt was called, was *too* low, too flat, too swampy, too humid, too much mildew. I acquired a permanent distaste for the eastern time zone. I take eight hours of sleep a night and even in retirement my bedtime is 2200; too many TV programs ran beyond that, notably the Monday night football which I had watched regularly in Dallas. The one newspaper was conservative (no surprise) and focused on old-line Charleston civilian society. It nearly ignored naval affairs; when major naval news transpired we had to wait for the arrival of *Navy Times* to read about it. But Charleston attracted the Patton-strikers. Several admirals whose deeds and policies I remembered unfavorably were living there in retirement, and the active-duty admirals during my time there were largely knuckle-draggers. The only thing I found to like about Charleston was the Spanish moss and those big, ancient trees it covered.

I learned what an earwig was. A little black-and-yellow insect with a crescent-moon tail, inoffensive but with no manners at all about taking up in-house residence.

There may have been a deeper, more subliminal, reason for my dislike of the city: Charleston was where we happened to live when the worst of inflation did its worst to us. We lived payday-to-payday and lurched from one financial crisis to another. I would not go into debt; there was one week when I had to default on the kids' allowances and one year when Christmas would have been effectively cancelled if not for Jamroon's providential win of a bingo jackpot at just the right time. When our two cats could *not* be kept from getting pregnant, I took first one and then the other to the pound with their latest litter. I suspected

407

that free spaying might be available somewhere for those who could not afford the cost – but I was *sure* that I made too much money to be eligible for such a service if it existed. As I told another sailor at work one day, I had never made as much money in my life – and had never been broker. When the TV died I could afford neither a new one nor repair; I discontinued the cable service and for the last year-plus we had no TV in the house.

In December my father died. Airlines all booked in the holiday season. Jamroon and I headed for Illinois in the Toyota. Outside Cincinnati the Toyota broke down. The garage to which it was towed would not take my check for repair. A saying sometimes heard is that, "the navy takes care of its own." It did. I called the recruiting office in Cincinnati for help. They sent a car for me, a master chief endorsed a check for me, we got the repair done and got to the funeral on time (I wore my uniform to it). We arrived back in Charleston late on Christmas night to expectant kids and a delayed present-opening. I sent a letter of praise and gratitude to the recruiters' next superior up the chain. That was one time the navy really came through for me when I needed it.

In February I went on what would be my last cruise, ten days on the *USS Saratoga (CVA-60)*; it was a NATO exercise with the entire staff embarked. I remembered those gourmet meals on the *Franklin D Roosevelt* and was looking forward to eating in an aircraft carrier's CPO mess again. I was disappointed. *Saratoga's* CPO mess served humdrum fare, indistinguishable from an average crew's galley. It was only then that I fully appreciated how unique *FDR's* mess had been and how lucky I had been to experience it.

We found a little suburban park near the ocean that produced finds even older than those of Newport, including a "half-dime" – a little silver five-cent piece, literally half the size of a dime. They were minted in the 1850s. I tossed dozens of civil war minie balls into the bushes as junk, not realizing what they were until I saw some for sale in a souvenir shop.

I spent a lot of time these years on another hobby: wargaming. (Not shooting paint at people in the woods, but pushing cardboard counters around on game boards.) I had bought my first game in Asmara, and added many more in future years. When a woman hears the word *wargaming*, it evokes just about the same mental reaction and degree of interest as does the word *knitting* when heard by a man. Jamroon tolerated but deplored. I often had a game laid out on the bedroom floor, tucked just under the bed. Once I awoke to use the bathroom in the nighttime. Instead of returning to bed I reclined on the floor beside the current game in my normal playing posture (the room was in bright moonlight). The following dialog ensued:

"What you do?"

"I play game."

"No, no, come bed!"

I did, with a gesture of disgust. I had but the vaguest memory of it in the morning and recalled annoyance at the interference. I told Jamroon that if I ever did it again, not to say anything. I would still like to know whether my "moves" on the game board while asleep would have been inspired or disastrous.

Several changes occurred in mid-1975. The staff moved off the *Sierra*, into offices in a building on the naval base. Mr Borho retired, and RADM Gravely was relieved by RADM Bruce Keener III. Mr Borho's replacement was LCDR Dick Meade, a sharp naval academy graduate; I enjoyed working under him. Keener was another matter.

In Keener's earliest days, while we were still on the *Sierra*, he had grabbed a startled, liberty-bound sailor on the pier for some trifling uniform or civilian-clothing violation and chewed him out. This occasioned sarcastic remarks about the "two-star pier sentry". His philosophy, as reported by other staff officers, was that the trouble with the country, in general, and the navy, in particular, was that *nobody wants to be a prick*. At a social event, he was said to have commented on the *pickaninnies* present. He exchanged messages with Bruce IV, his ensign son on a far east destroyer. He only did this two or three times. It was a flagrant misuse of official communications – but who was going to tell him that?

It was becoming obvious that chickenshit was returning. I had been favorably impressed by Holloway, the new CNO, at first, especially by his espousing the need for productivity, imagination, "doing more with less". I thought much could have been done along those lines. But it turned out that productivity only meant that the first day of annual leave no longer counted as "free", and you did not get off on the day after Thanksgiving unless you took leave that day. Productivity = erosion of benefits.

Chickenshit was reimposed not openly, but by stealth – and slowly, gradually. No directives came from the new CNO. Instead the deeds were done on hundreds of local levels, and now there was no one in Washington who would say, "Knock that shit off." I am confident that this was planned, calculated, passed by word of mouth. My first-class came to work a half-hour late one morning and explained. He had driven to work in civvies (still legal) and would change to dungarees on the ship before beginning the work day. He had stopped by the dispensary to refill a prescription and was turned away. New policy. Uniform of the day only. He had to return home to change and start over again. Productivity. I phoned the leading chief at the dispensary to remonstrate; he heard me out but didn't hold out much hope for change. I had not expected that there would be. There was none.

Moving into a building on shore should have allowed us to receive comrats? It should have but it didn't, despite the prolonged and eloquent efforts of our personnel officer and chief of staff. I forget the details of the pertinent legalities. Sailors working in other offices in the *same building* received comrats; Group Two did not. I began to eat both breakfast and lunch regularly in the chow hall, which was right across the street from our offices.

A change that raised a lot of hackles was our reclassification from sea duty to neutral duty. This meant that our tour counted as neither sea duty nor shore duty. The practical impact was that for someone coming from shore duty to Group Two, as I had, when his tour was over it would be as if he were just coming off shore duty – and he would expect sea duty. A man coming from sea duty to Group Two would accumulate no additional sea duty while in Group Two and would be no nearer to shore duty than when his tour began. Neutral duty was a new idea and it was, actually, a good one, a good concept (with one caveat) – but I felt strongly, as did we all, that those already at a command should have been grandfathered rather than having the rules changed in the middle of a tour. Rubbing salt in our wound, the *Sierra* had been changed from sea to neutral at the same time we had, and those aboard her *were* grandfathered. The reason, we were told after protesting the disparate treatment, was that *Sierra* had a crew of some 900 and it would have been too much work for Washington to change all those records!

The one caveat: neutral duty made perfect sense *for married men*. For singles, who would have *shipboard* living conditions while on neutral duty, it was far less fair.

The erosion of benefits was in full swing by now. I wish I could go into more detail about it, but neither my papers, my memory, nor internet searches are very productive. Most of it came from Congress whether directly, or indirectly because of budget cuts. Vietnam was over, we had lost, and the military was held somewhat in contempt by too many congressmen. There was a rash of either price increases, or fees imposed on what was formerly free, for such things as the base movie, the base swimming pool, etc. The military was due approximately a 7% pay increase; Gerald Ford sought to hold it to 5%; I forget whether he succeeded. I thought of a letter, but never sat down at the typewriter to produce it. If I had written it, it would have been something like this:

I've read that during the Kennedy years Republicans had a lapel pin, or a bumper sticker, that read:

I MISS IKE

Hell, I even miss Harry

I once looked forward to the arrival of *Navy Times* every week. In these times when I now dread its arrival, fearing what *new* bad news it may contain, the serviceman needs a bumper sticker of that pattern. In hope that some firm may see fit to produce it, herewith:

I MISS MENDEL RIVERS

Hell, I even miss McNamara

L. Mendel Rivers, a Representative from South Carolina, had died at the end of 1970. He was a drunk, a racist ex-Dixiecrat, and an arch-conservative. But, as chairman of the House Armed Services Committee, he looked out for the enlisted man and had done much to protect us from ill-intentioned economies. If not for him, the erosion of benefits might well have started earlier and been more fierce. If he had lived, it might not have happened, or at least been less injurious. His successor in the chair, Hebert of Louisiana, was no friend of the military.

Some anonymous congressional or Pentagon wordsmith birthed a weasel-word suffix which was thereafter appended in anything emanating from official Washington. The phrase we now saw was, "erosion of benefits, *real or perceived*".

The PTA of our local school had a membership drive going and there was some sort of competition between various PTAs over which one could achieve 100% membership first or come the closest. I received a phone call at home from one of the PTA officers urging me to join. I told him that I had been a member during my first year in Charleston, and earlier in Dallas, but that I was not going to join again because of the prayer with which they began PTA meetings. This was a response for which he was clearly not prepared. He hemmed, hawed, made some oblique reference to prayer in the schools, and said that he was sure that the majority did want an opening prayer. I told him that I was equally sure of that, that it was their privilege, and that it was my privilege to refrain from membership if I felt otherwise.

Jamroon became an American citizen in November, on her second try. I had coached her extensively on U.S. history, the Constitution, etc.; and she did well on everything except the writing. The examiner, a pleasant sort, failed her the first time (salving his bureaucratic conscience) and passed her the second time (recognizing reality) even though she did no better. It sounds eminently reasonable to say that an aspiring citizen should be able to read and write English – when it is said on the floor of Congress. When applied to a 42-year-old housewife who has been out of school for a long time, it is a good deal less reasonable. The examiner, incidentally, was not just a clerical employee but a full-fledged *attorney* – surely receiving a salary well in excess of what I would have thought appropriate for such tasks.

Early in 1976, angered by I-forget-just-what instance of the chickenshit revival, I ripped my *Go Navy* bumper sticker off the VW in disgust. I was climbing the walls at work over chickenshit, then returning home to climb the walls at our latest financial crisis. By spring I had decided to retire and be done with it, and began to consider the timing. The end of the 1976-77 school year seemed best. I began resume-writing and contacted government agencies and a couple civilian firms that had done communications work for the navy. The very week *after* I had sent a letter of inquiry to the State Department, a classified ad from them appeared in *Navy Times*, seeking communicators! That seemed promising. If nothing bore fruit, I intended to load up the family and drive west looking for work.

There was speculation about a military union in these years, in *Navy Times* and various other media. One day the head honcho of the biggest government employee union mused out loud about the possibility of organizing the military.

You would have thought he had advocated the legalization of cannibalism. Congressmen tripped over each other (well, OK, not literally) in their haste to run down the aisle and drop bills in the hopper forbidding any such thing.

. . . *the master group always fears its slaves more than any foreign enemy; at the least stirring of the helots, the ruling caste is subject to terrible imaginings.* (Bergen Evans, *The Spoor of Spooks*)

413

A new rear admiral, Graham Tahler, took over as COMSIX. He was invited to speak at the CPO club. He announced his topic as "Leadership" and I thought oh-shit, I'm in for half an hour of how all our troubles will vanish if we just tell enough people to get haircuts often enough. To my surprise he actually did speak about *leadership*, a good speech that gave just a bare passing mention to haircuts. But my initial good impression rapidly reversed. It became one of my unpleasant duties to attend a monthly meeting with him and three other master chiefs – his way of "keeping in touch" with enlisted men. He was death on drugs, and cited the *Reader's Digest* as his authority on the subject. One day the subject was grass, sailors walking upon. It seemed they trod dirt pathways in Tahler's greenery when taking the shortest route from point A to point B. Various solutions were batted around: post signs, post sentries, build barriers . . . No decision was reached. I thought about saying, "Why not build the sidewalks where the paths are?" I bit my tongue.

A few months after I retired, Tahler was reported in *Navy Times* and elsewhere as having gone too far in his exhortations to courts-martial to impose stiff sentences on drug users. This was "command influence", and prohibited. In a phrase popular at the time, he had stepped on his crank. He was relieved and retired.

I was tasked with writing a Message Drafting Guide – a how-to-do-it with tips, rules, and requirements. It was only ten pages, but was made a good deal bulkier by appendices. It was issued to all of our officers, and courtesy copies were sent to a number of our ships and to other places, as a possible model if they wanted to do something similar. I got chewed out over one line in my draft. In an appendix of common abbreviations, I had included WTF – widely understood as What The Fuck – and had defined it as Request Clarification. The chief of staff, Captain Frank Conlon, had lined it out. But it had first gotten past Mr Meade and Commander Rumney (the operations officer). That made them look bad, the captain catching something they had both overlooked. My chewing-out, by Mr Meade at CDR Rumney's direction, was perfunctory and *pro forma* – they were amused but wanted to be sure I didn't do something like that again. If it had escaped CAPT Conlon and had been printed and circulated as it was, I don't know how much trouble might have come my way.

I was at a meeting about various aspects of the enlisted duty watch bill. One of the items that arose was a recent finding of crabs in the duty watchstander's rack. There was some joking about it and I mentioned the boot-camp-learned remedy, whiskey and sand. The one officer and several enlisted men present were all young. They were mystified and I had to explain: the crabs all get drunk and throw rocks at one another.

This led me to a theory: that when a particularly good joke, or apt phrase, is told or used so widely that "everyone has heard it", it thenceforward falls into disuse and is no longer heard – perhaps to be resurrected in some future decade, perhaps not. My theory was supported by another instance, which follows.

On *Playboy's* joke page, I read a "new" one that delighted me and at work the next day I targeted an RM1: "Do you know how to keep an asshole in suspense?"

He was suspicious and hesitated. Mr Meade was at his desk listening and asked, "How?"

I had to answer. "I might tell you tomorrow." Mr Meade knew I hadn't intended any disrespect and took no offense. Instead he picked up the phone to inflict it on another officer. It spread rapidly throughout the building. Decades later I acquired a book that was a reprint of a collection of "dirty jokes" that had circulated clandestinely in the *1930s*. There it was.

I had been letting my hair grow somewhat longer and bushier, and going longer between haircuts. Now that chickenshit was returning and the standards were being enforced ever more strictly, I was probably in violation. CAPT Conlon called a meeting of all chiefs and officers about hair length and emphasized that his concern included "khaki shirts". I sat there trying not to look too smug because, with accidental but perfect timing, Jamroon had cut my hair the very night before. I was sure I was one of his intended targets, probably the principal one, and I thought I saw him eying me with sidelong glances as he spoke.

With the exception of the Newport interim, Jamroon cut my hair from the time we were married until her last illness. It was the only shop I ever found where I could kiss the barber and get away with it.

During Jimmy Carter's presidential campaign I sent a letter to his campaign headquarters, suggesting that he might garner a few military votes by a campaign promise to let all servicemen grow their hair as long as that of their commander in chief. It was no doubt filed in the nut file; I got no reply and he made no such promise.

I often talked politics with one RM2 when he had the day watch. I was skeptical of Carter for other reasons and inclined toward the obviously-doomed independent run of Eugene McCarthy. The RM2 argued that getting rid of Ford was the priority and therefore I should vote for Carter. He had a point, but I still dithered. Then Carter made up my mind for me during the third Ford-Carter debate. He allowed that it had been a mistake for him to do his famous interview in the pages of *Playboy* earlier that year. That did it. He had caved in to the bluenoses who disapproved of *Playboy*. I voted for McCarthy while hoping that Carter would prevail on election night – or, more accurately, hoping that Ford would not.

The more modern enlisted uniforms which ADM Zumwalt had introduced were now to be phased out again. Back to the white hats (sometimes sneered at as "dixie cups"), 13-button blues, and neckerchiefs. Authority brandished polls showing that the great majority of young sailors wanted the traditional uniform back.

Strange. ADM Zumwalt had had a poll done in 1970, and 80% had favored change to a modern uniform at *that* time. I can conceive of only two possibilities. One is the natural cussedness of enlisted men: what we have is terrible; we want something different. The phrase *enlisted men always bitch* is far too often used as an alibi for inaction, for ignoring legitimate complaints, but there is a good bit of truth in it.

The alternative is that Authority used techniques well-known to pollsters – question-phrasing, sample selection, etc. – to get the answers that it wanted to get. I will not attempt to guess which explanation is the more valid.

A job with the State Department came to seem more and more probable. In early November I submitted my request to BUPERS for a 6 June 1977 retirement date.

They replied, approving a date of 6 *September*. They said that this date would put me over 25 years of service for pay purposes and that this would give me higher retirement pay. I did not think so. I had done the math and moreover, in the process of eroding benefits Congress had again rejiggered the retirement laws. Before, a man who retired was guaranteed to receive retirement pay as great as any previous retiree of the same pay grade and length of service was receiving. Now, the deal was that a retiree would receive as much as *he, personally,* could have received by retiring earlier. What with inflation boosting the pay of the already-retired and pay caps holding down the pay of actives, this was much to my disadvantage. In effect I spent my Group Two years working for free, with respect to retirement pay. If I had retired in 1974 after Dallas, I would have received the same retirement pay that I would now be receiving from a 1977 retirement!

There were "fogies" – longevity pay increases – at 22 years and at 26 years. There was none at 25 years. I wrote the Bureau again in December to tell them that I had consulted my personnel office, as well as the career counselors at my own and two other commands, and that no one could explain how I would benefit financially from a September date as opposed to June. I asked to be advised of the amount of pay by which I would benefit.

Their reply was a masterwork of bureaucratic issue-dodging and ass-coverage. It made no reference to the monetary factors; it simply

417

authorized my retirement in June, *provided that I signed a service record entry that I desired the June date.*

The chairwarmers had unknowingly, and certainly unintentionally, done me a big favor. I was already getting my first whiffs of State Department sluggishness and was beginning to fear that I might not begin employment until well after June. I asked our Yeoman if he was in any hurry for me to sign that service record entry. He was not. In effect I now had a June *or* September option. As it turned out it would be September – and by the ultimate in lucky timing I began to receive State pay on 8 September with only one day of unemployment preceding!

We had a new admiral, RADM Paul Gibbons. He was the best I saw while in Charleston; he spent minimal to zero time on chickenshit and he took a dim view of Tahler – which was, in itself, enough to earn my esteem.

I had not washed my Snoopy coffee cup in years. It was covered with brown ex-coffee and had become a conversation piece. When asked why I didn't wash it, I would reply with a puzzled, "*What for?*" I maintained (without basis) that it improved the flavor. Brad Veek, one of the commanders on the staff, as his last act before transferring, washed it in the evening after I had left. I came to work and found it gleaming white.

A 5x8" stiff-paper document survives in my files. I believe it dates from 1977, but might be from a year or two earlier. I am not sure how I came by it, but it might have been given to one of my family at PX or commissary. It reads:

IMPORTANT NOTICE - PLEASE READ CAREFULLY

COMNAVBASE CHARLESTON promulgated regulations for appropriate civilian and military attire while aboard Naval Base Charleston. Current styles are authorized; however, the following items are not appropriate nor authorized: Tank top shirts, shorts above mid-thigh *(hot pants and short shorts)*, halters which display a bare midriff, white undershirts as outer garments, cut-off shorts, dungarees with ownership markings, uncovered hair rollers, dirty/mutilated clothing and see-through attire. Shower shoes, wooden clacks and go-aheads are not appropriate footwear.

You have been refused entrance/service to our facility for a clothing discrepancy. Future embarrasment [sic] can be avoided by compliance with COMNAVBASE directives.

At the end of March Authority (in Washington) promulgated new restrictions on facial hair. It could not "bulk" more than ½" from the skin, and the maximum length of an individual hair was set at 3/4". (Was this a regulation for *beards*, or for looking like one needed a shave?) The part that affected me was a pointless, imbecilic requirement that beards and mustaches, if both worn, must be connected. I continued to shave the corners of my mouth right up to 1 May, the date the new strictures became effective. The tip of my goatee might have been a tad too "bulky" between trimmings, but I was never called on it.

I once said that if maximum beard length had been set at 36", there would have been sailors trying to attain 37" – and captains equipping their Master-at-Arms forces with yardsticks to ensure that no one did.

It had become definite that State was going to hire me. When they sent a security officer around to do the requisite background checks on me, he came to my door, introduced himself, and told me what he was doing. I thought this was a nice contrast with the navy way, which you knew about only from whatever feedback you may hear from friends who are interviewed. My destination was established: Islamabad, Pakistan. I knew little about it and began to bone up. It was an Asian version of Brasilia, a new capital built from scratch – in Pakistan's case, not quite in the middle of nowhere, but next to the ancient town of Rawalpindi. Family size was apparently a major factor; Islamabad had spacious housing.

The entire staff was to deploy on a ship, for the first time in a long time. When I mentioned to State that I would be at sea and out of telephone-touch for a couple weeks, the lady oohed and said "Oh, we might have to delay your training until the next class!" I reported this to my superiors and was excused from going to sea. I felt badly about this, as though I were shirking (although a part of me rejoiced, and my presence at sea would have been of little or no value). I felt even guiltier when the staff returned; I had had no phone calls from State and could just as well have gone. I was to learn: this was typical for State.

I was sometimes asked why I was retiring and I had a standard answer: "*Admirals trying to put the navy back in the 50s and congressmen trying to put the military standard of living back in the 30s, about 50-percent each." I gathered that I was quoted around the naval base. A captain commanding a destroyer squadron asked me in to talk about it. He didn't address the congressmen part, and was diplomatic about the admirals, saying, "I think there's no question that we went too far in some respects, but I don't think we need to go all the way back to the 50s."

I was asked what I would like to have for a retirement ceremony. A personnel inspection was suggested. It should surprise no one that that was the last thing I wanted. I suggested a softball game. I did not expect to get it (we had had one only two or three months ago) and I didn't. Jamroon came; RADM Gibbons presided at a soft-drinks-and-cake function in a room in the building; I was given praise and handshakes, a couple of plaques, and a decorative coffee mug. I was then "piped over the side" – out the door, in this case – and given the boatswain's pipe as an additional memento.

Upon returning home, the first thing I did was to grasp my hat by the visor and sail it frisbee-like up on the roof. The second thing I did was to shave the hair off the corners of my mouth where Authority had forced me to cultivate unwanted mustache-beard connectors for the last four months.

The rest of my life in one paragraph: Islamabad (1 year), Washington DC (2 ½), Tegucigalpa, Honduras (3), Lahore, Pakistan (4), Vientiane, Laos (4), Asmara – again! – (2). After all that *voluntary* time in hardship posts, State next tried to make me go to another one – Vilnius, Lithuania. I gave them impolite disposition instructions for Vilnius and re-retired instead. Compared to the navy, State was unbelievably generous and supportive in some ways, unbelievably petty, obstructive, and stingy in other ways. At least there were no personnel inspections or hair/beard hassles. After spending my navy years trying to maximize my overseas shore duty, the Foreign Service had nothing else (except for DC). When I retired to the Black Hills in 1995 I was running away from two things: state income taxes and the population explosion. (I thought "sun belt" for many years, but too many others thought of it first.) I could write another book about the Foreign Service and, if I did, State management would not like it one bit better than navy Authority will like this one. But I probably will not. Married, middle-aged, in a different institutional culture, I didn't encounter nearly as much sea-story material. The reader will probably have noticed that *this* book became more staid and less entertaining as the chapters wore on. I certainly have.

I have enjoyed every sensation that human flesh is heir to, except childbirth and the consolations of religion. (H.E. Teschemacher, old time Wyoming livestock man, quoted by John Gunther in *Inside U.S.A.*)

XIX - MOHAMMED

This chapter has no relation to the rest of the book.

Mohammed ate pork with his left hand. He died of AIDS, contracted from his pet pig. Piss be upon him.

Salman Rushdie. Taslima Nasreen. The Danish cartoonists. Theo van Gogh. Few things have disturbed me more in the past couple decades than the weak, namby-pamby Western responses to outrageous Muslim crimes against free speech: we must be "tolerant", we must be "sensitive", we must not give offense. We must not "hurt their feelings" (a phrase often used in the Muslim press). The Muslims did bad to assassinate and riot and kill but Rushdie, Nasreen, van Gogh, and the cartoonists did (not-quite-so) bad first. So goes the politically-correct line from the orchidically-challenged.

Horse shit.

Let's review: in much of the world, and in nearly all of the West, there is a right to free speech (may it ever be so) – including speech that criticizes, lampoons, or otherwise offends religions and the beliefs of the religious. There is no right, anywhere, not to have one's feelings hurt. There is no right not to be offended.

I believe the West – authors, writers, publishers, media (but not governments) – should react to the despicable Muslim assaults on free speech with intransigent more-of-the-same. I believe the imams and the ayatollahs and the assassins should be furnished with so many worthy targets that they cannot possibly keep up. Having now become an author, it would be dishonorable for me not to act on my convictions. And that is why I have written this chapter and, particularly, its second paragraph.

(Governments? They should respond to Muslim protests with some variant of, "Sorry you feel that way, but *we* have free speech. Can't do a thing about it.")

This book is almost surely fated to languish in vanity-press obscurity. But in the remote event that it gains notoriety and comes to the attention of the *fatwa*-spouters, I have one request to make of them. If you send an assassin after me, make it fair. Send one that is approximately my age (74 in 2007) and weight (140). Send him unarmed. (I've never owned a gun.) Surely he will succeed in his mission – Allah will see to that, will he not? Or do you lack faith?

Somehow I don't expect that request to be honored. But when it happens, if it happens, I could ask for no more honorable death than at the hands of a fanatical Muslim. (Preferably with my finger raised.)

And in the event – unimaginably more remote – that Islam ever evolves and civilizes to the point that it can counter critics with words instead of bloodshed, violence, and riots, I will not insult Mohammed again.

I won't need to.

. . . you can't conquer a free man; the most you can do is kill him. (Robert A. Heinlein, *Revolt in 2100*)

About the Author

Larry Bucher grew up in small-farm-town Illinois and was miseducated at the University of Wisconsin. He spent 23 years hating the navy and 18 more hating the State Department Foreign Service, and is now a comfortably retired hermit in the Black Hills. He was a communicator – one, that is, who worked with transmitters, receivers, and (most of all) with teletypes – a communicator in the original sense, before the job title was pirated by professional bullshitters. He refuses to respond to the term "telecommunicator".

Made in the USA